INU-YASHA

犬夜叉

ANI-MANGA™

Vol. 3

CREATED BY
RUMIKO TAKAHASHI

Inuyasha Ani-Manga™

Vol. 3

Created by
Rumiko Takahashi

Translation based on the VIZ anime TV series
Translation Assistance/Katy Bridges
Lettering/John Clark
Cover Design & Graphics/Hidemi Sahara
Editor/Frances E. Wall

Managing Editor/Annette Roman
Editor-in-Chief/Alvin Lu
Production Manager/Noboru Watanabe
Sr. Director of Licensing & Acquisitions/Rika Inouye
Vice President of Marketing/Liza Coppola
Executive Vice President/Hyoe Narita
Publisher/Seiji Horibuchi

Printed in U.S.A.

Published by VIZ, LLC
P.O. Box 77010
San Francisco, CA 94107

10 9 8 7 6 5 4 3 2 1
First printing, May 2004

www.viz.com

store.viz.com

Story thus far

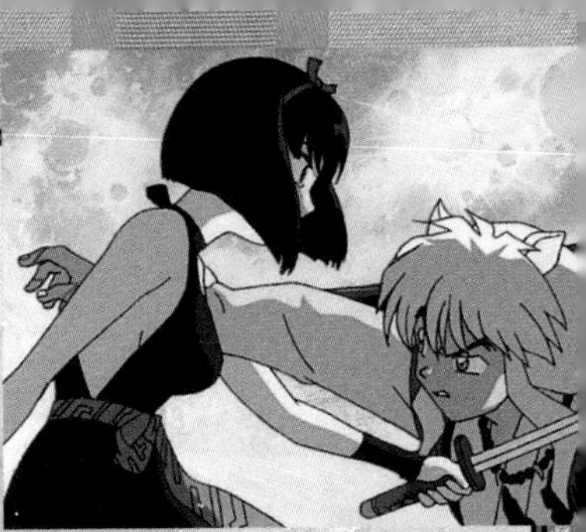

Kagome, a typical high school girl, has been transported into a mythical version of Japan's medieval past, a place filled with incredible magic and ter[illegible] demons. Who would have gu[illegible]at the stories and legends Kagome's superstitious grandfather told her could really be true!?

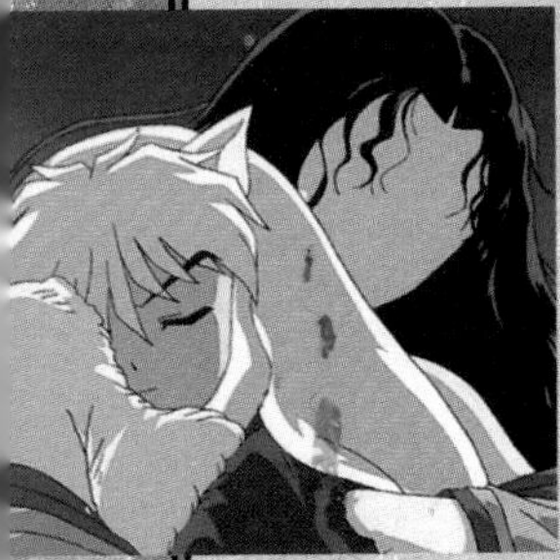

It turns out that Kagome is the reincarnation of Lady Kikyo, a great warrior and the defender of the Shikon Jewel, or the Jewel of the Four Souls. In fact, the sacred jewel mysteriously emerges from Kagome's body during a battle with a horrible centipede-like monster. In her desperation to defeat the monster, Kagome frees Inuyasha, a dog-like half-demon who lusts for the power imparted by the jewel, and unwittingly releases him from the binding spell that was placed fifty years earlier by Lady Kikyo. To prevent Inuyasha from stealing the jewel, Kikyo's sister, Lady Kaede, puts a magical necklace around Inuyasha's neck that allows Kagome to make him "sit" on command.

In another skirmish for possession of the jewel, it accidentally shatters and is strewn across the land. Only Kagome has the power to find the jewel shards, and only Inuyasha has the strength to defeat the demons who now hold them, so the two unlikely partners are bound together in the quest to reclaim all the pieces of the Shikon Jewel.

Now, Inuyasha's demon half-brother, Sesshomaru, has stolen their father's tomb from its resting place in Inuyasha's eye, and lured Kagome and Inuyasha through a portal that leads to the graveyard of the father's bones. Here, Sesshomaru and Inuyasha vie for possession of their father's sacred sword, Tetsusaiga. But the enchanted sword is firmly embedded in the graveyard, and though Inuyasha and Sesshomaru try to draw it out, the only one who is able to pull it free is... Kagome!?

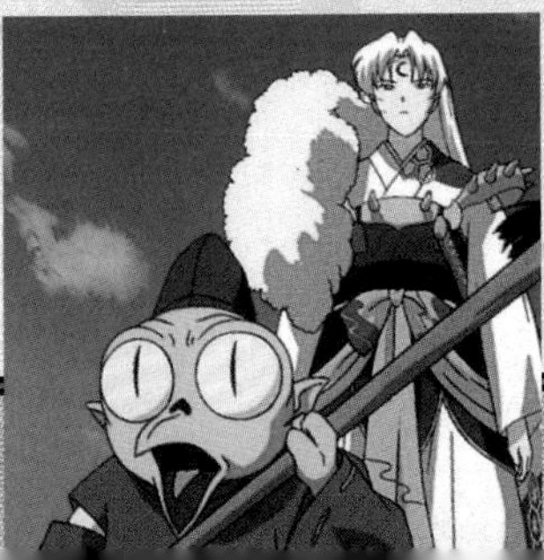

INUYASHA

ANI-MANGA Vol. 3

Contents

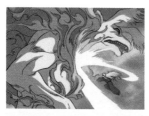

7
Showdown! Inuyasha vs. Sesshomaru

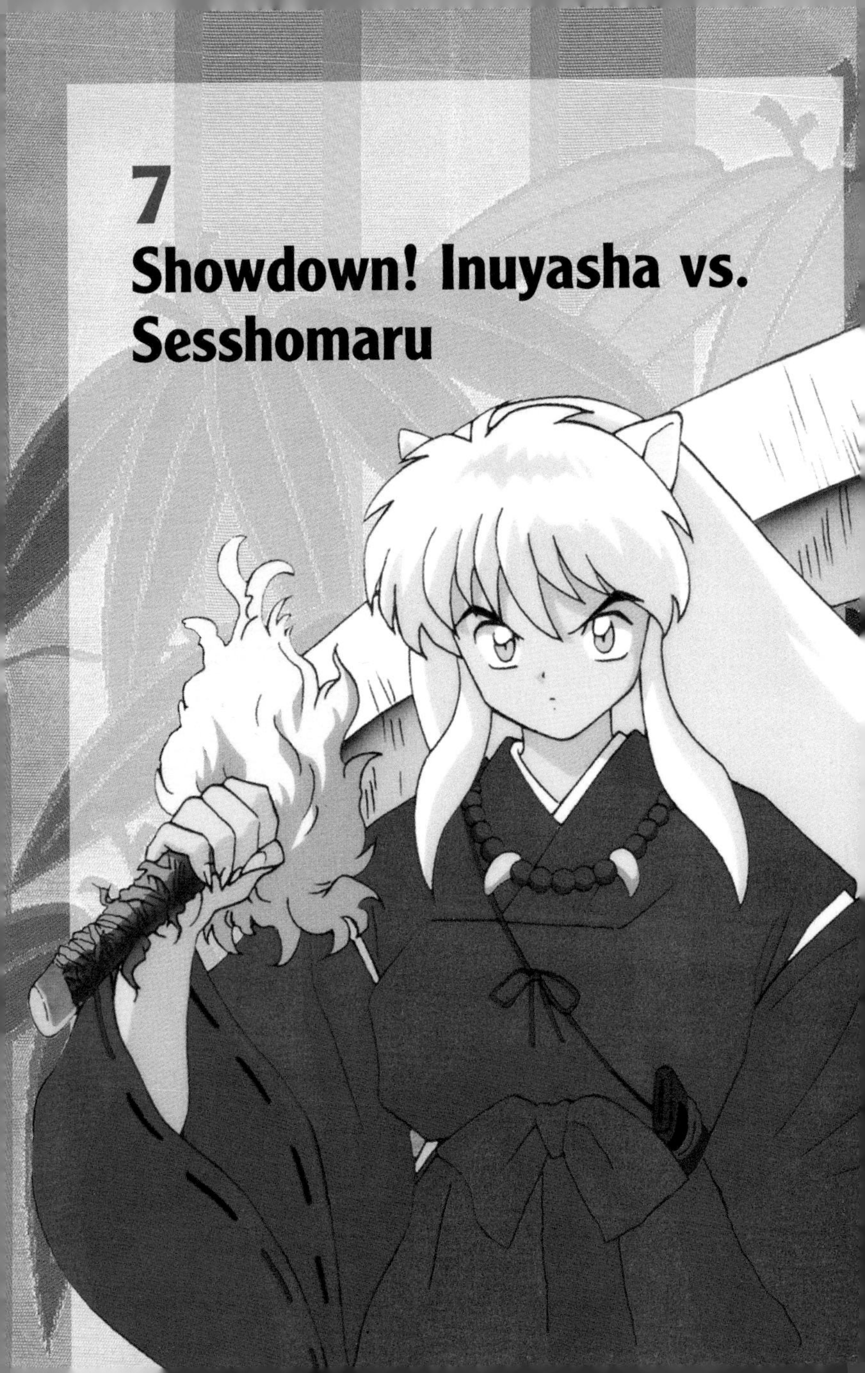

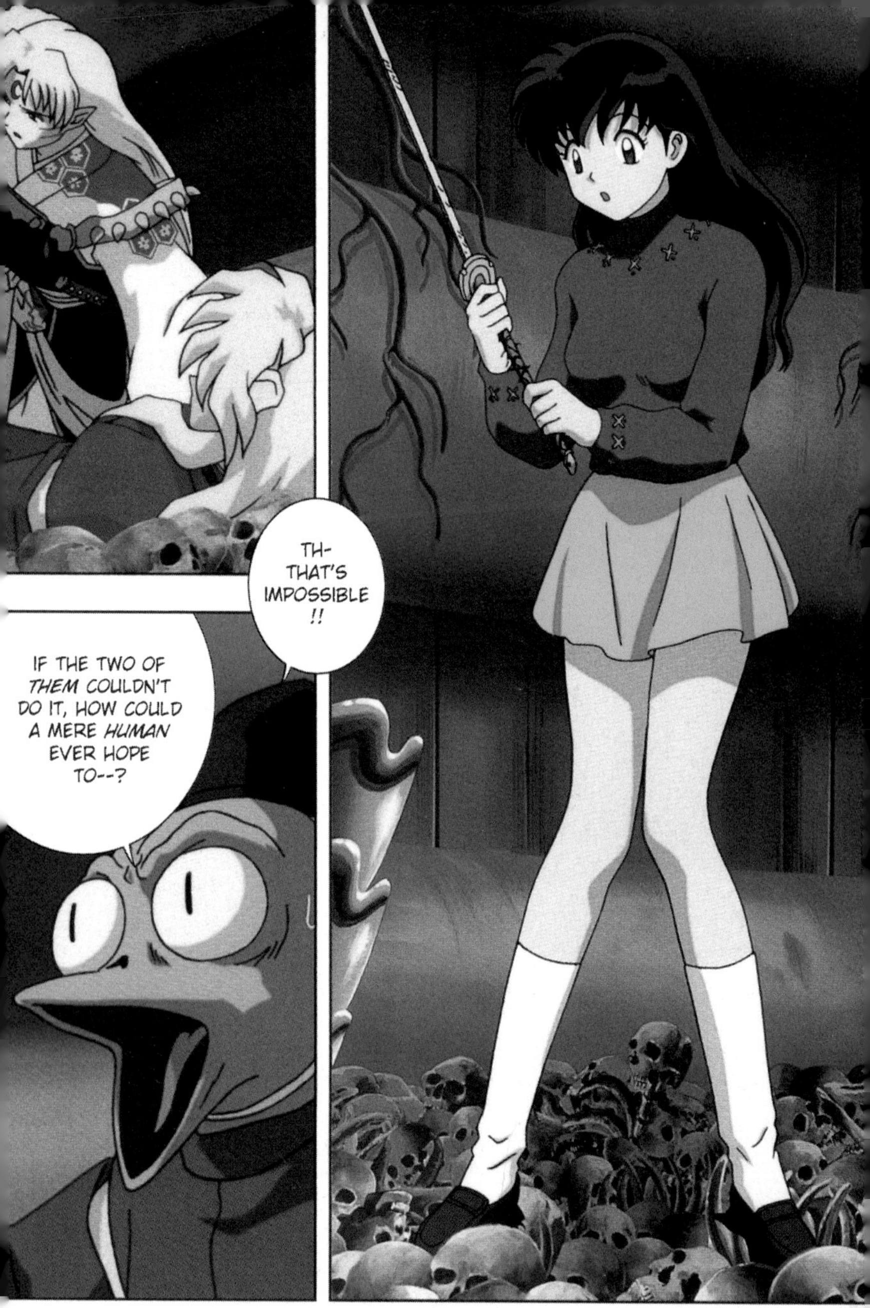
TH- THAT'S IMPOSSIBLE !!
IF THE TWO OF *THEM* COULDN'T DO IT, HOW COULD A MERE *HUMAN* EVER HOPE TO--?

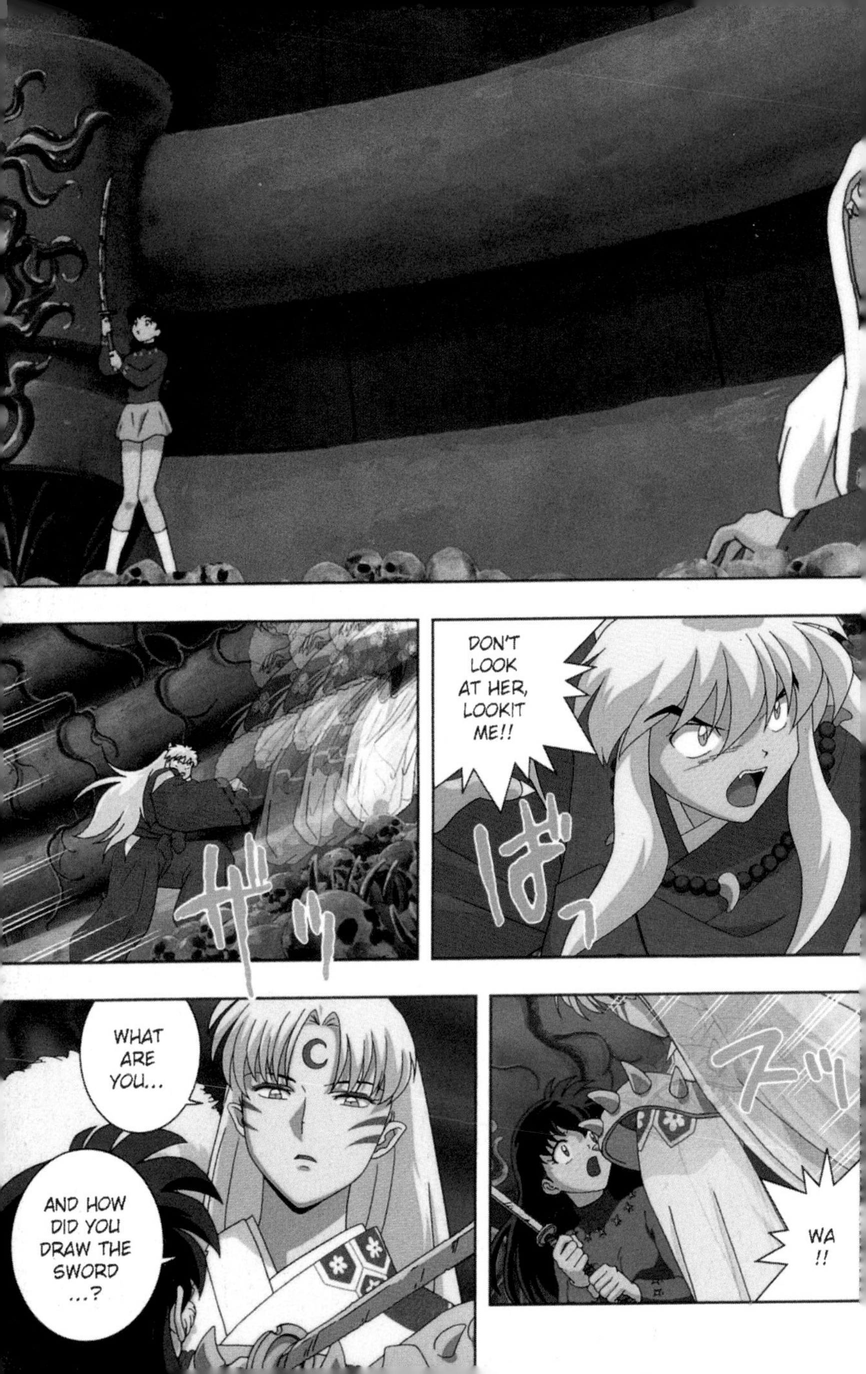
DON'T LOOK AT HER, LOOKIT ME!!
ぼっ
ザッ
スッ
WA!!
WHAT ARE YOU...
AND HOW DID YOU DRAW THE SWORD ...?

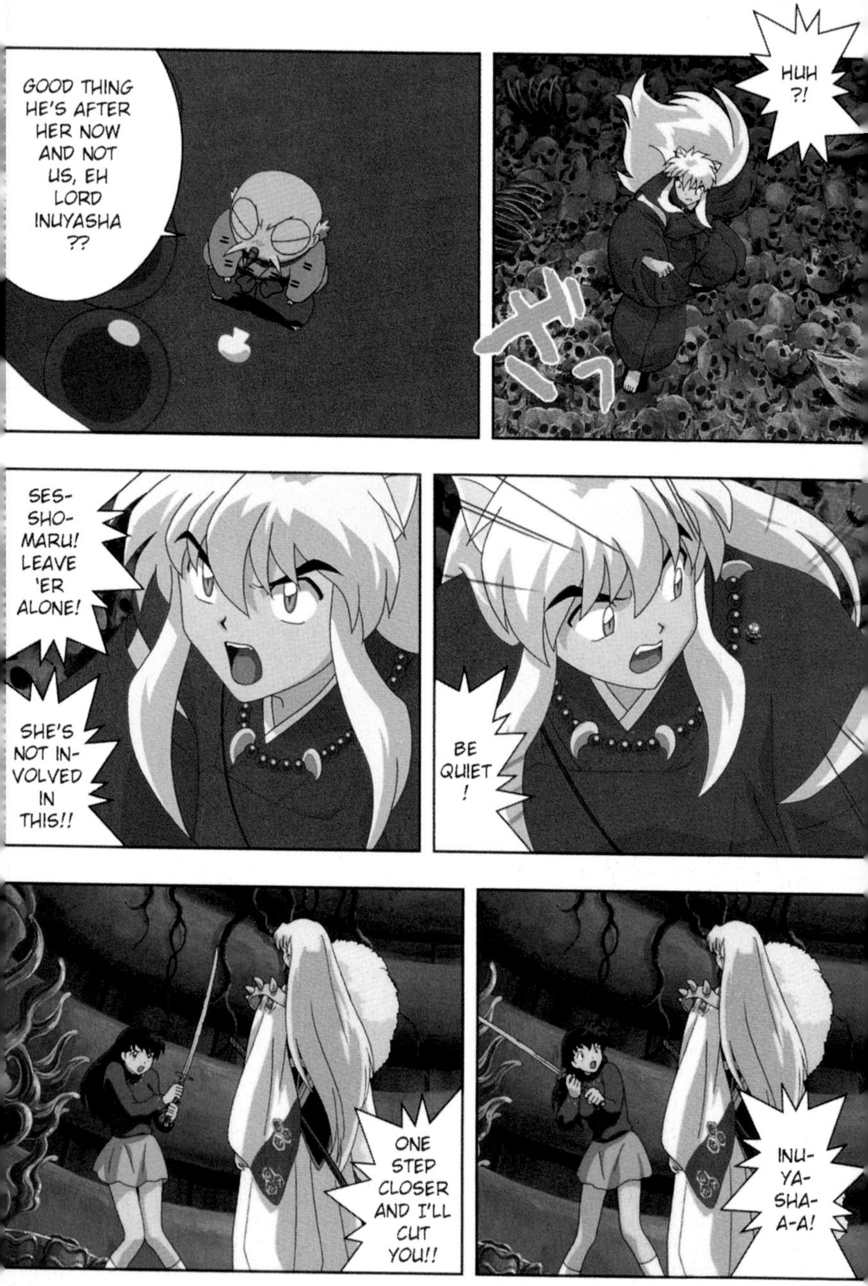
HUH ?!
GOOD THING HE'S AFTER HER NOW AND NOT US, EH LORD INUYASHA ??
BE QUIET !
SES-SHO-MARU! LEAVE 'ER ALONE!
SHE'S NOT IN-VOLVED IN THIS!!
INU-YA-SHA-A-A!
ONE STEP CLOSER AND I'LL CUT YOU!!

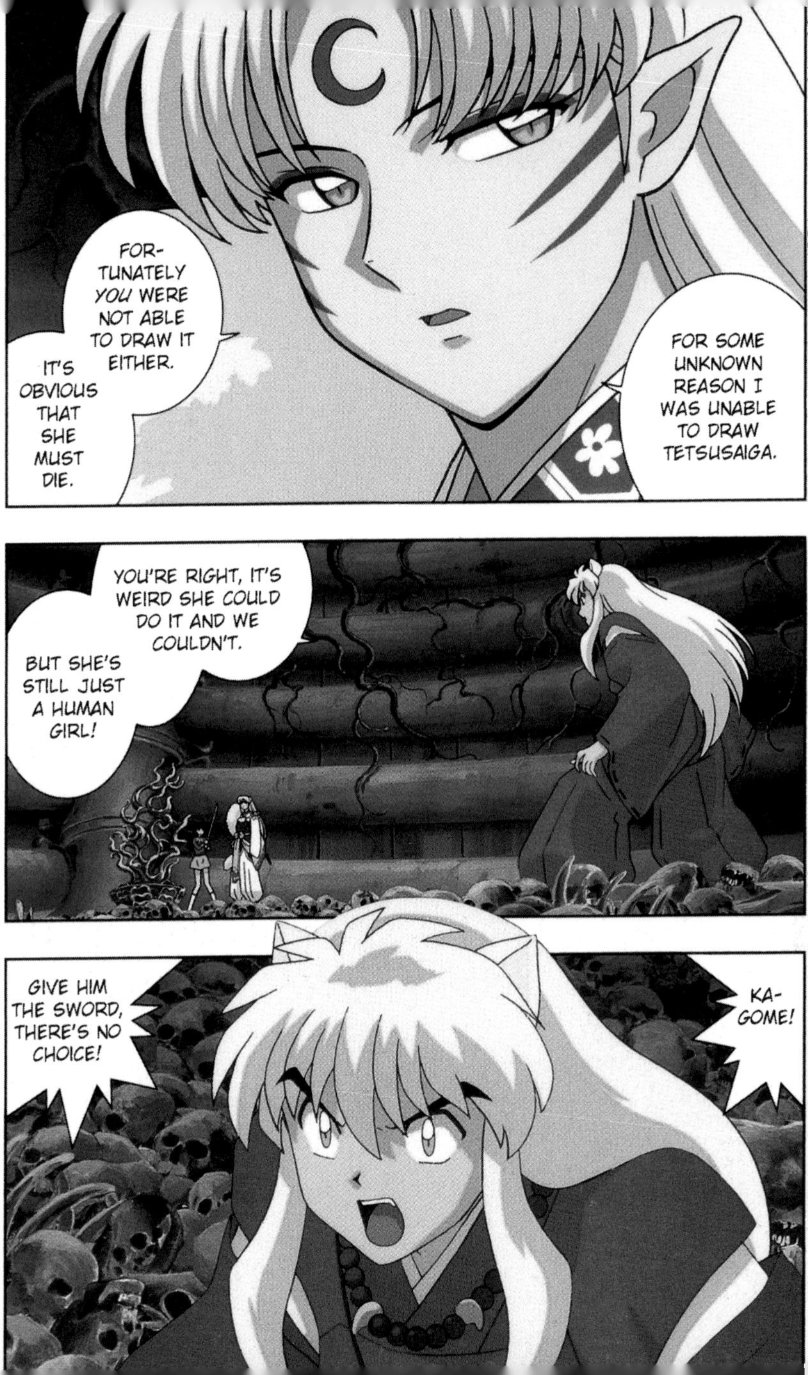
FOR SOME UNKNOWN REASON I WAS UNABLE TO DRAW TETSUSAIGA.
FOR-TUNATELY *YOU* WERE NOT ABLE TO DRAW IT EITHER.
IT'S OBVIOUS THAT SHE MUST DIE.
YOU'RE RIGHT, IT'S WEIRD SHE COULD DO IT AND WE COULDN'T.
BUT SHE'S STILL JUST A HUMAN GIRL!
KA-GOME!
GIVE HIM THE SWORD, THERE'S NO CHOICE!

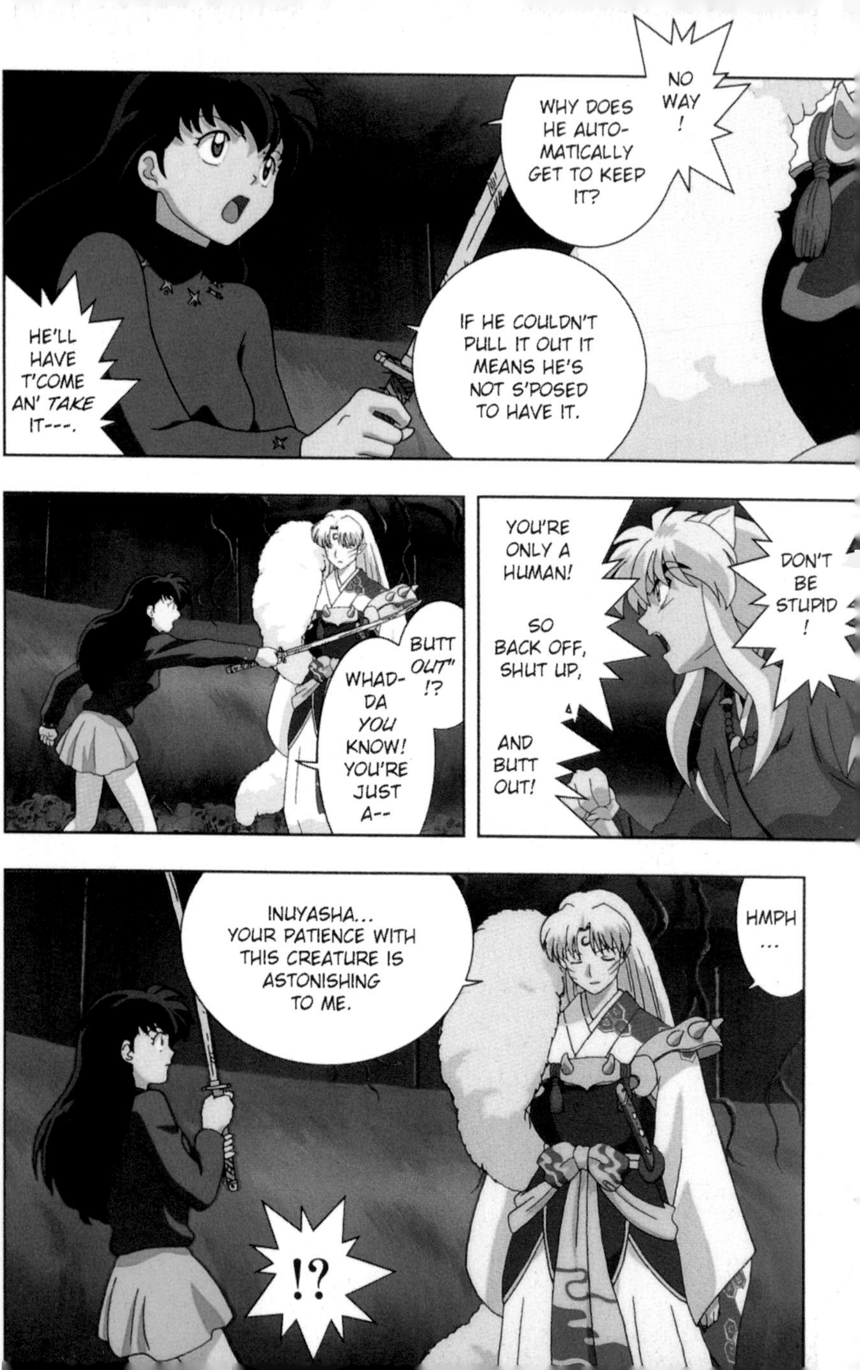
NO WAY!
WHY DOES HE AUTO-MATICALLY GET TO KEEP IT?
IF HE COULDN'T PULL IT OUT IT MEANS HE'S NOT S'POSED TO HAVE IT.
HE'LL HAVE T'COME AN' *TAKE* IT---.
DON'T BE STUPID!
YOU'RE ONLY A HUMAN!
SO BACK OFF, SHUT UP,
AND BUTT OUT!
"BUTT *OUT*"!?
WHAD-DA *YOU* KNOW! YOU'RE JUST A--
HMPH...
INUYASHA... YOUR PATIENCE WITH THIS CREATURE IS ASTONISHING TO ME.
!?

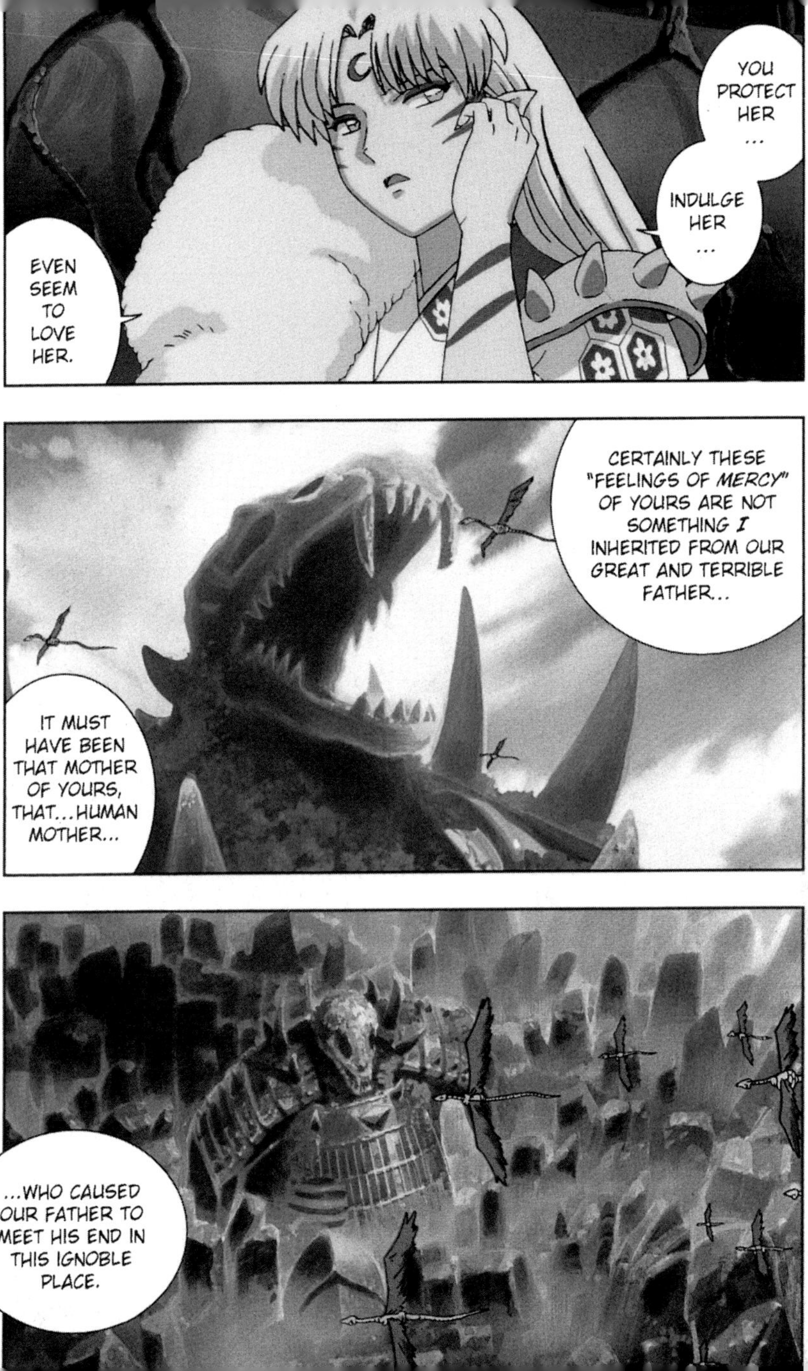
YOU PROTECT HER ...
INDULGE HER ...
EVEN SEEM TO LOVE HER.
CERTAINLY THESE "FEELINGS OF *MERCY*" OF YOURS ARE NOT SOMETHING *I* INHERITED FROM OUR GREAT AND TERRIBLE FATHER...
IT MUST HAVE BEEN THAT MOTHER OF YOURS, THAT...HUMAN MOTHER...
...WHO CAUSED OUR FATHER TO MEET HIS END IN THIS IGNOBLE PLACE.

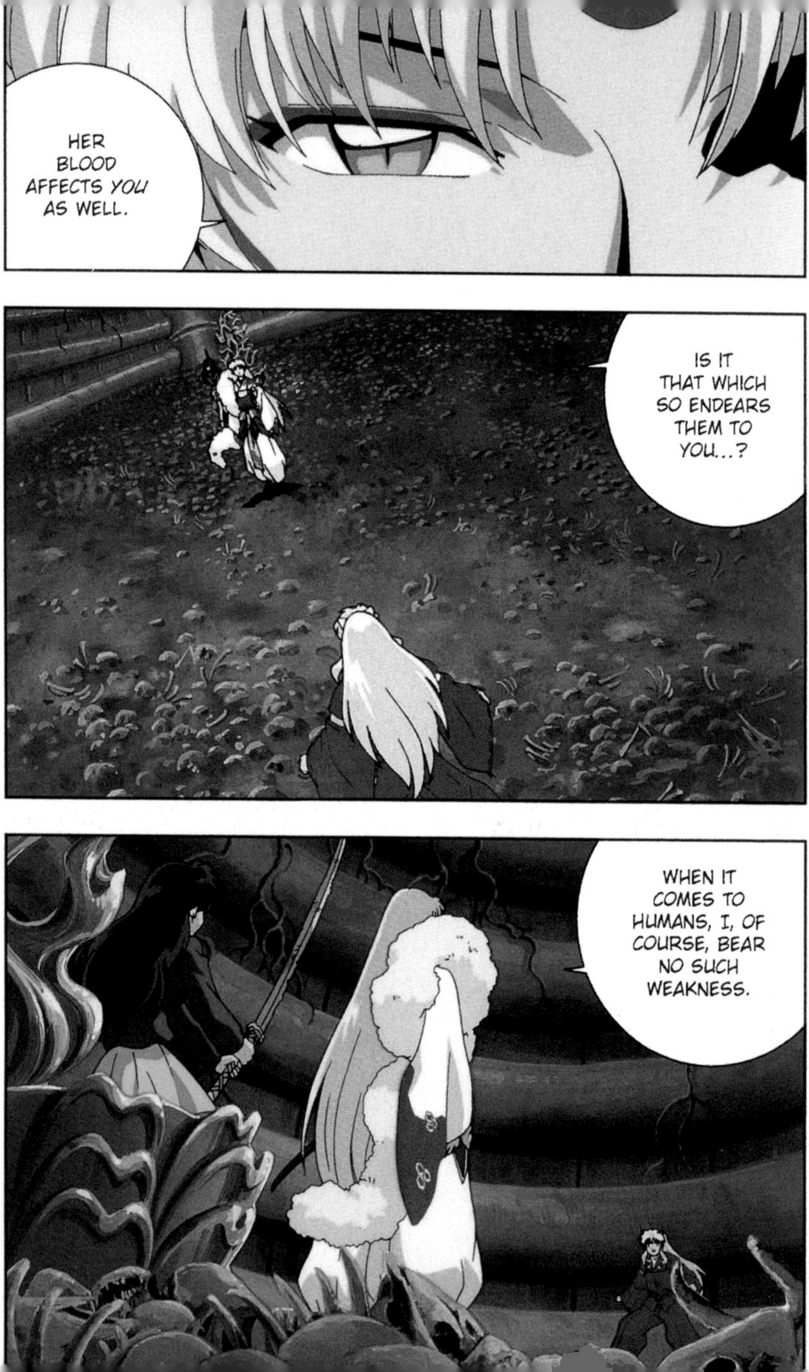
HER BLOOD AFFECTS *YOU* AS WELL.
IS IT THAT WHICH SO ENDEARS THEM TO YOU...?
WHEN IT COMES TO HUMANS, I, OF COURSE, BEAR NO SUCH WEAKNESS.

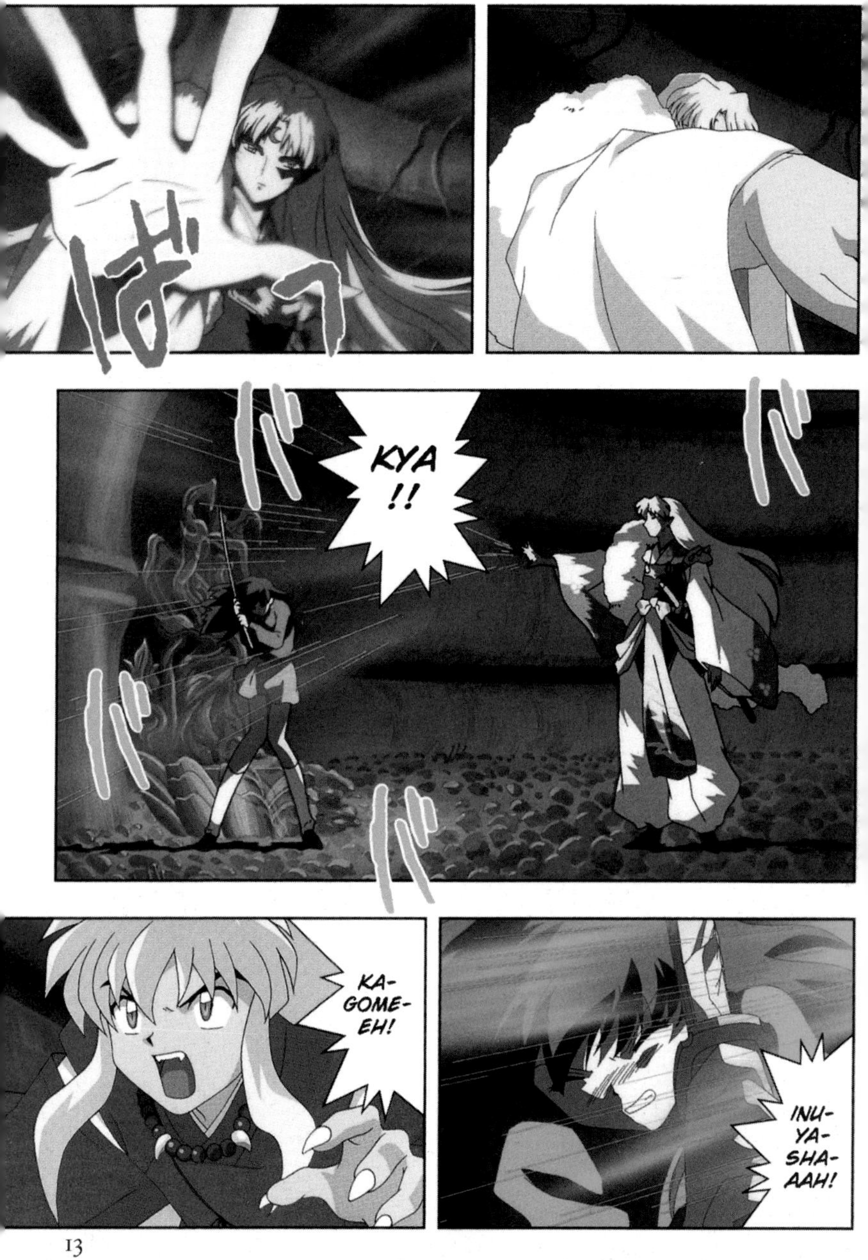
ぱっ
KYA !!
バ
バ
バ
バ
INU-YA-SHA-AAH!
KA-GOME-EH!

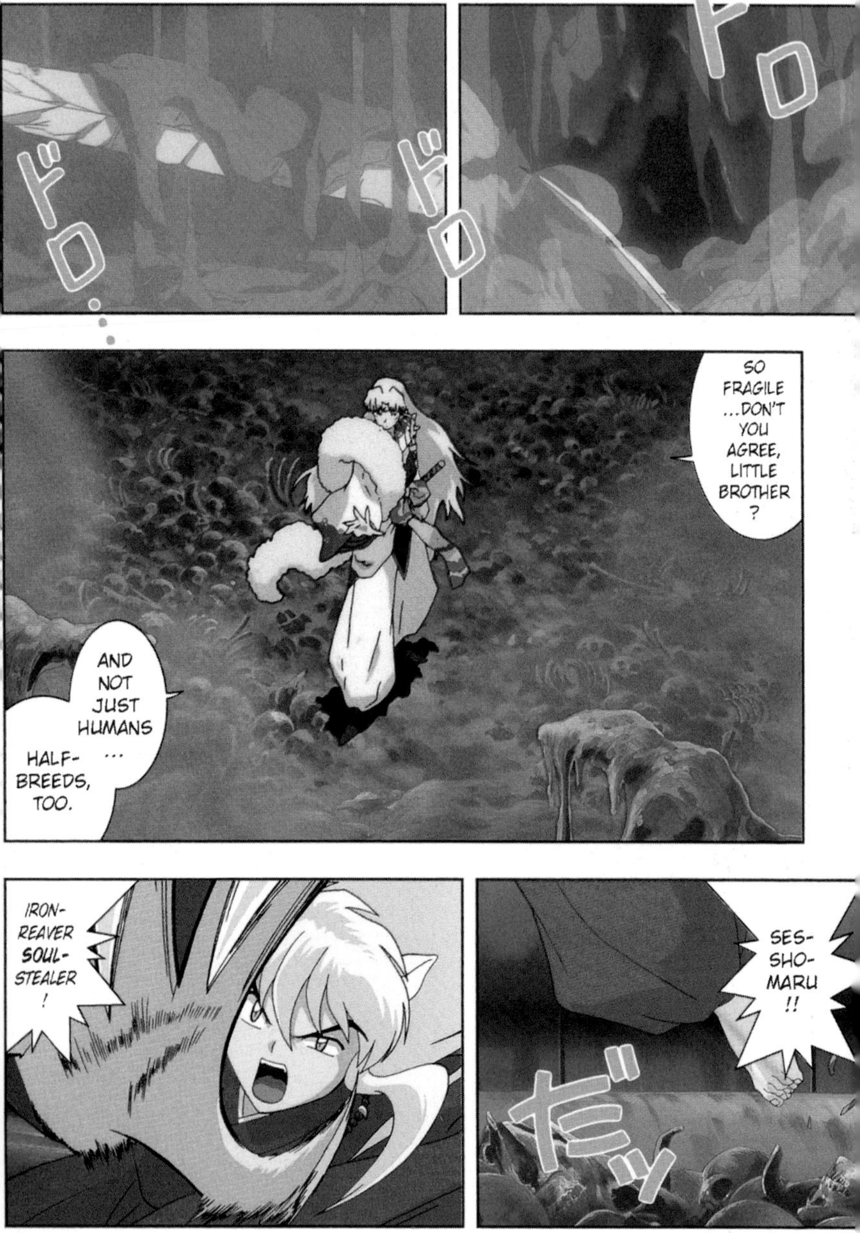
ドロ
ドロ
ドロ…
SO FRAGILE …DON'T YOU AGREE, LITTLE BROTHER ?
AND NOT JUST HUMANS …
HALF-BREEDS, TOO.
SES-SHO-MARU !!
ダッ
IRON-REAVER SOUL-STEALER !

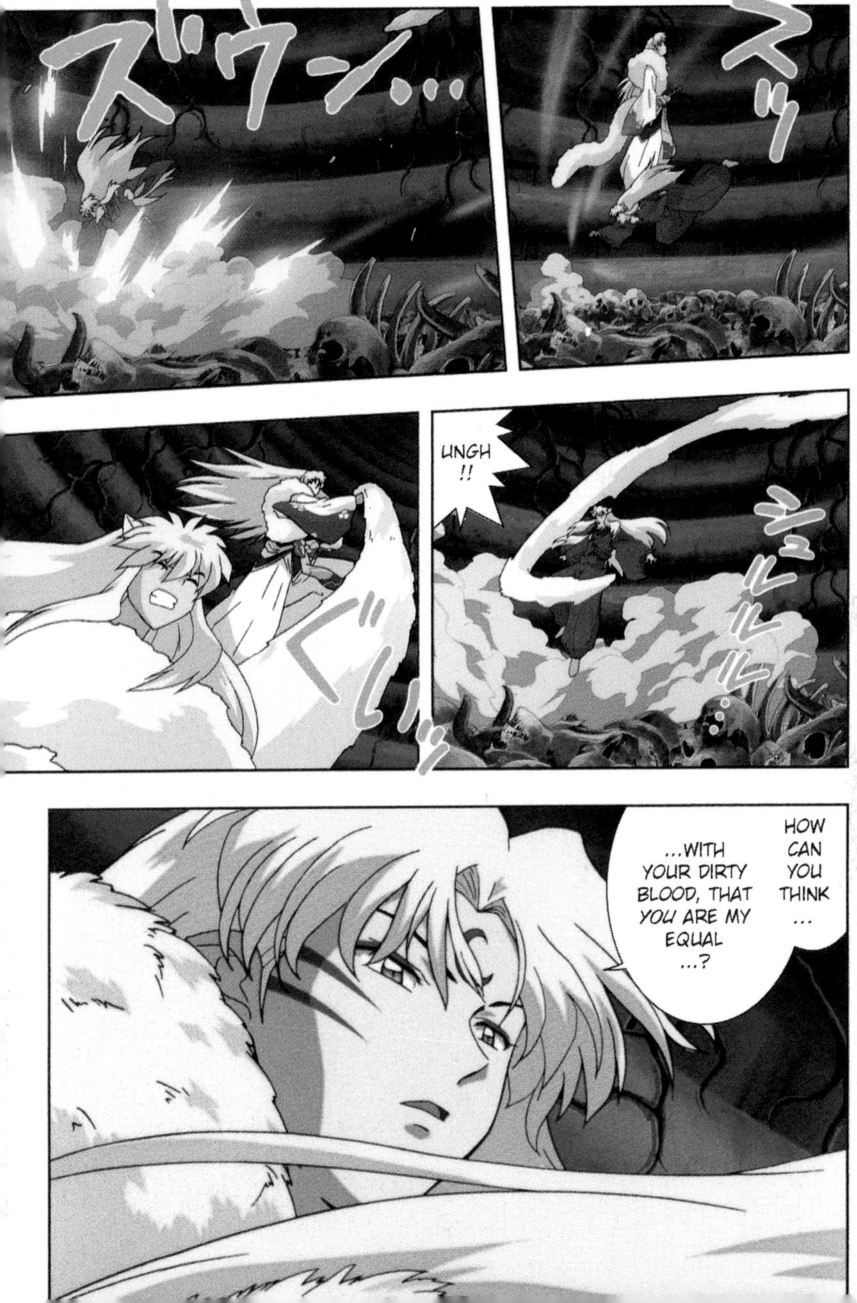
スッ
ズゥーン…
UNGH !!
シュルルル…
ぐいっ
HOW CAN YOU THINK …
…WITH YOUR DIRTY BLOOD, THAT *YOU* ARE MY EQUAL …?

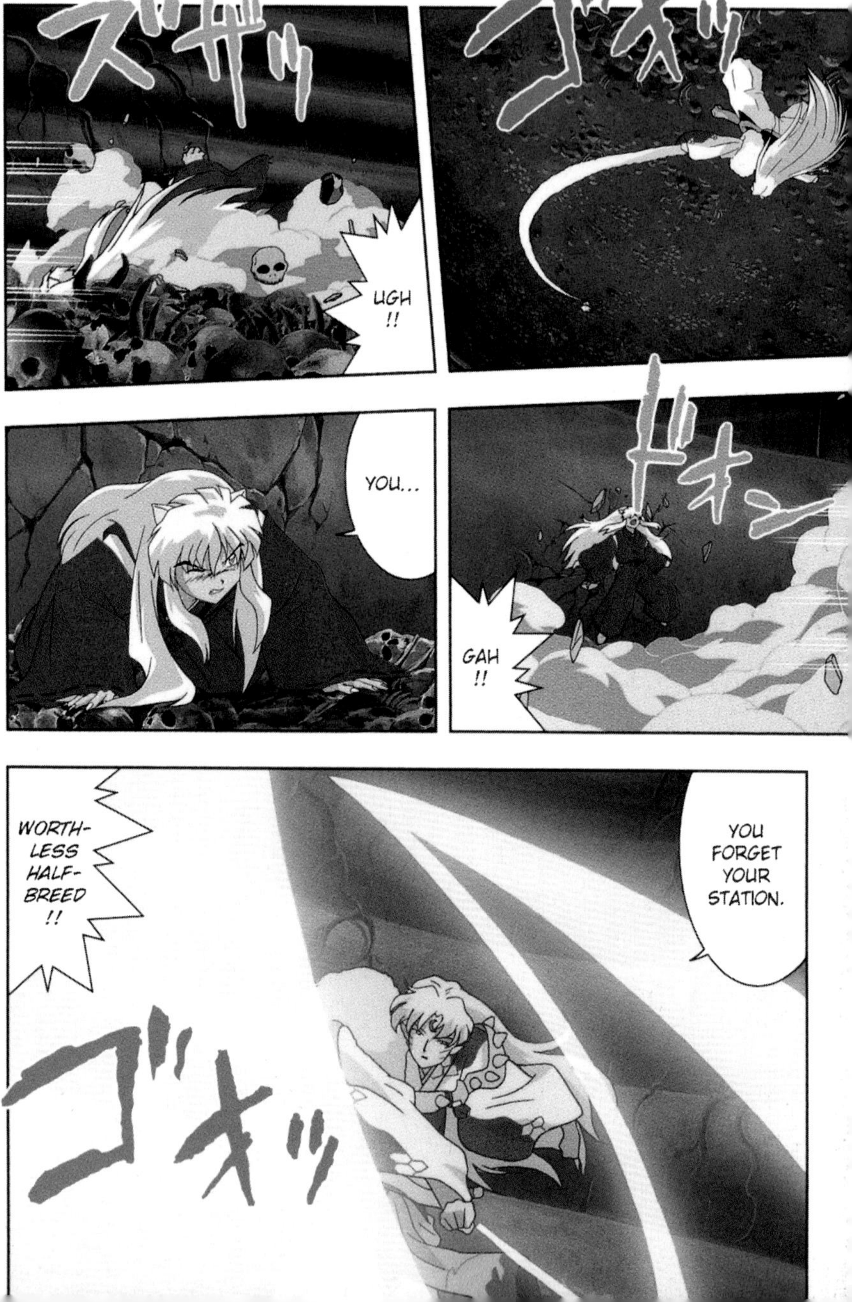
ゴオッ
ズザッ
UGH !!
ドオン
GAH !!
YOU...
YOU FORGET YOUR STATION.
WORTH-LESS HALF-BREED !!
ゴオッ

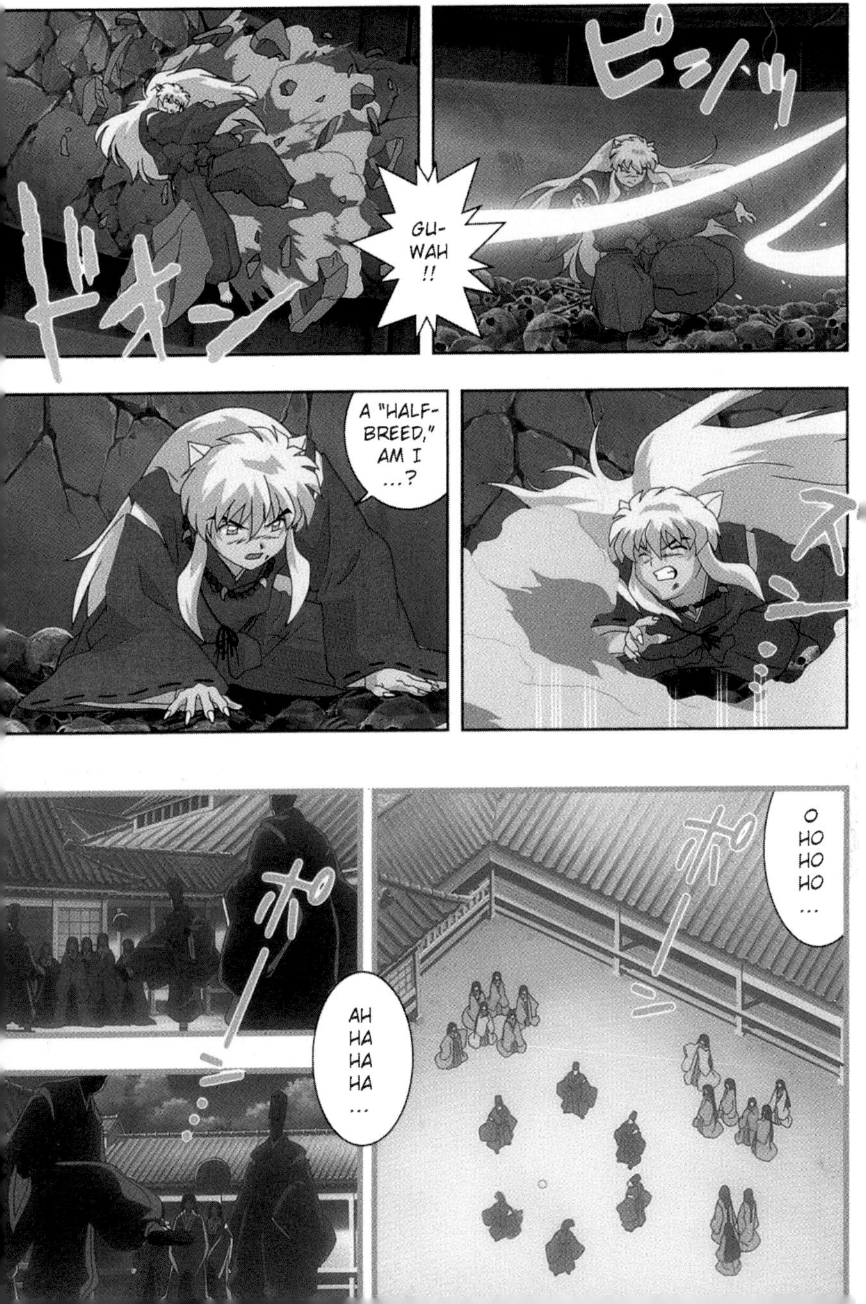
ピシッ
GU-WAH !!
ドォーン
スッ
A "HALF-BREED," AM I ...?
O HO HO HO ...
ポーン
ポーン
AH HA HA HA ...

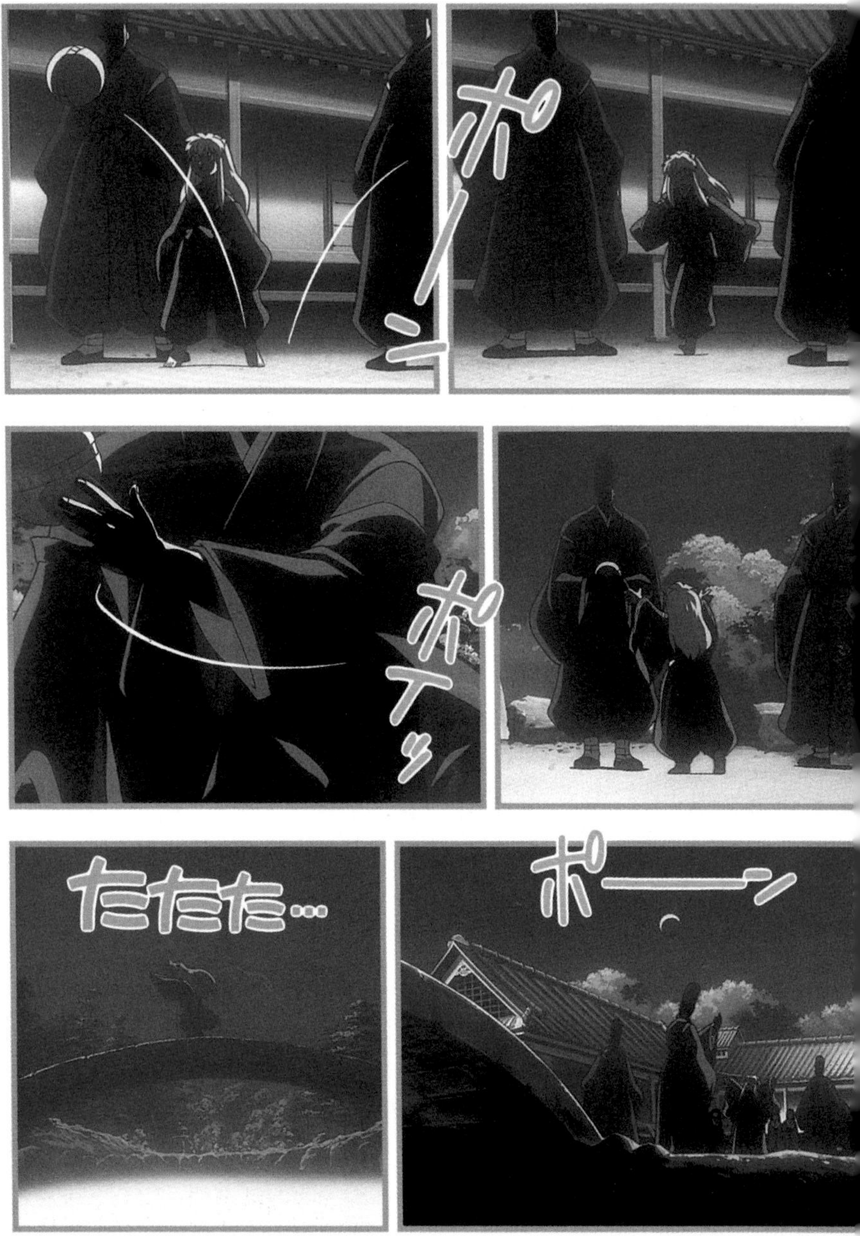
ポーン
ポフッ
ポーーン
たたた…

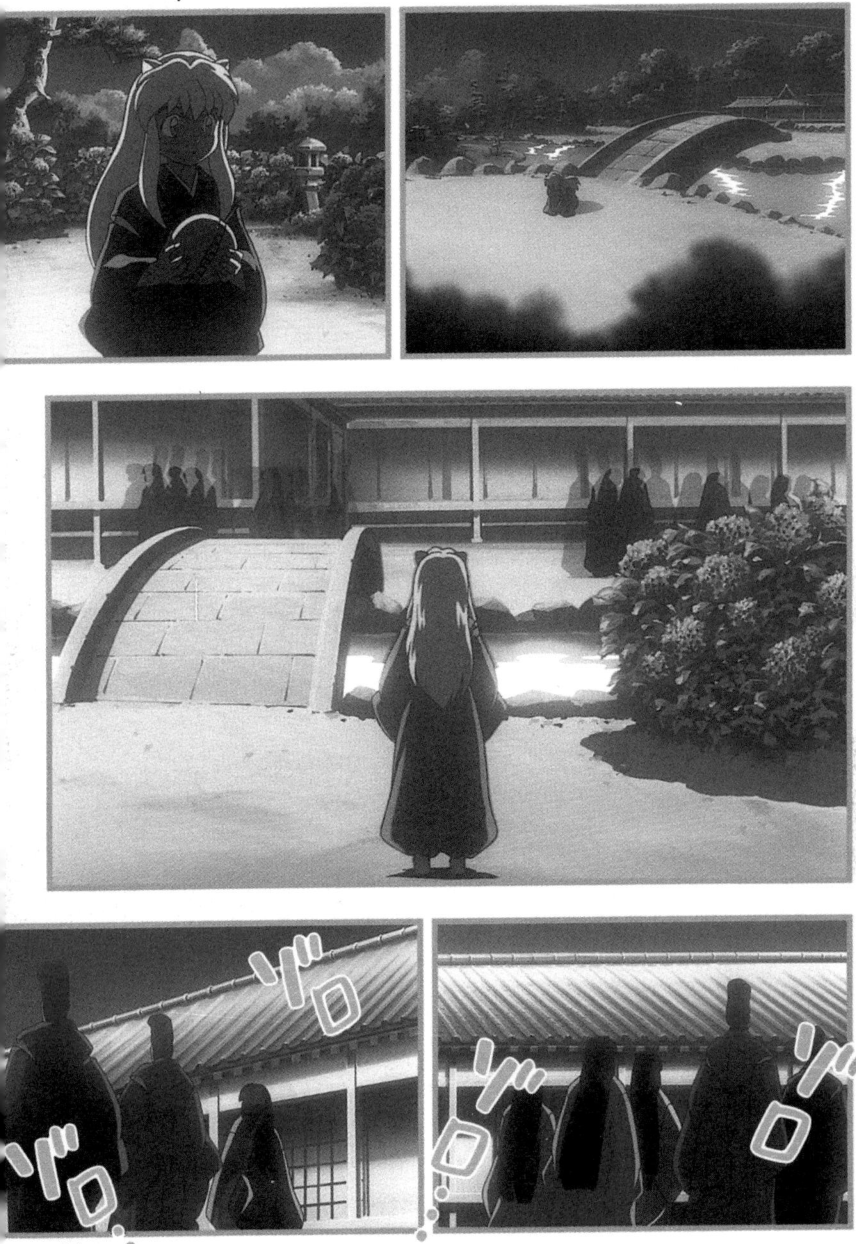
ゾロ
ゾロ
ゾロ
ゾロ

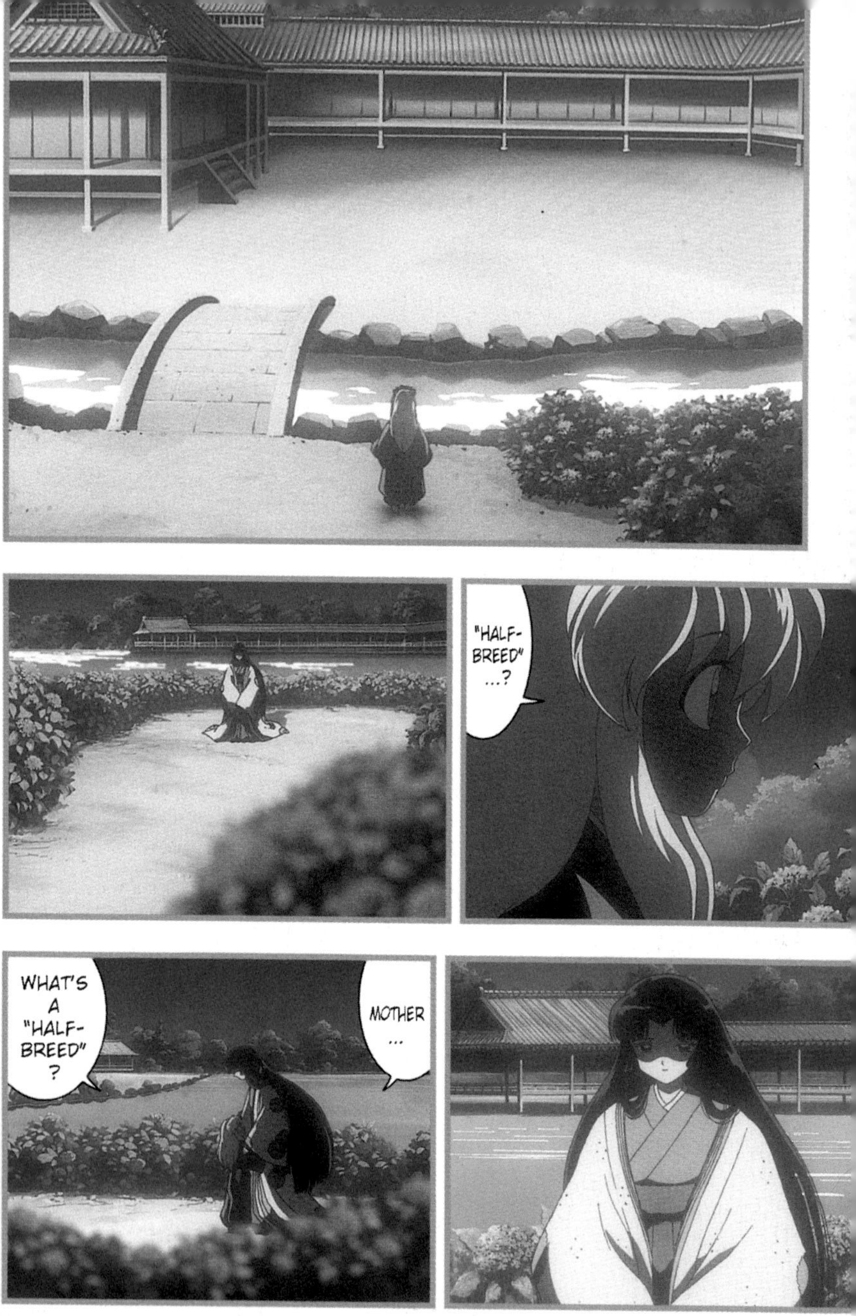
"HALF-BREED" ...?
MOTHER ...
WHAT'S A "HALF-BREED"?

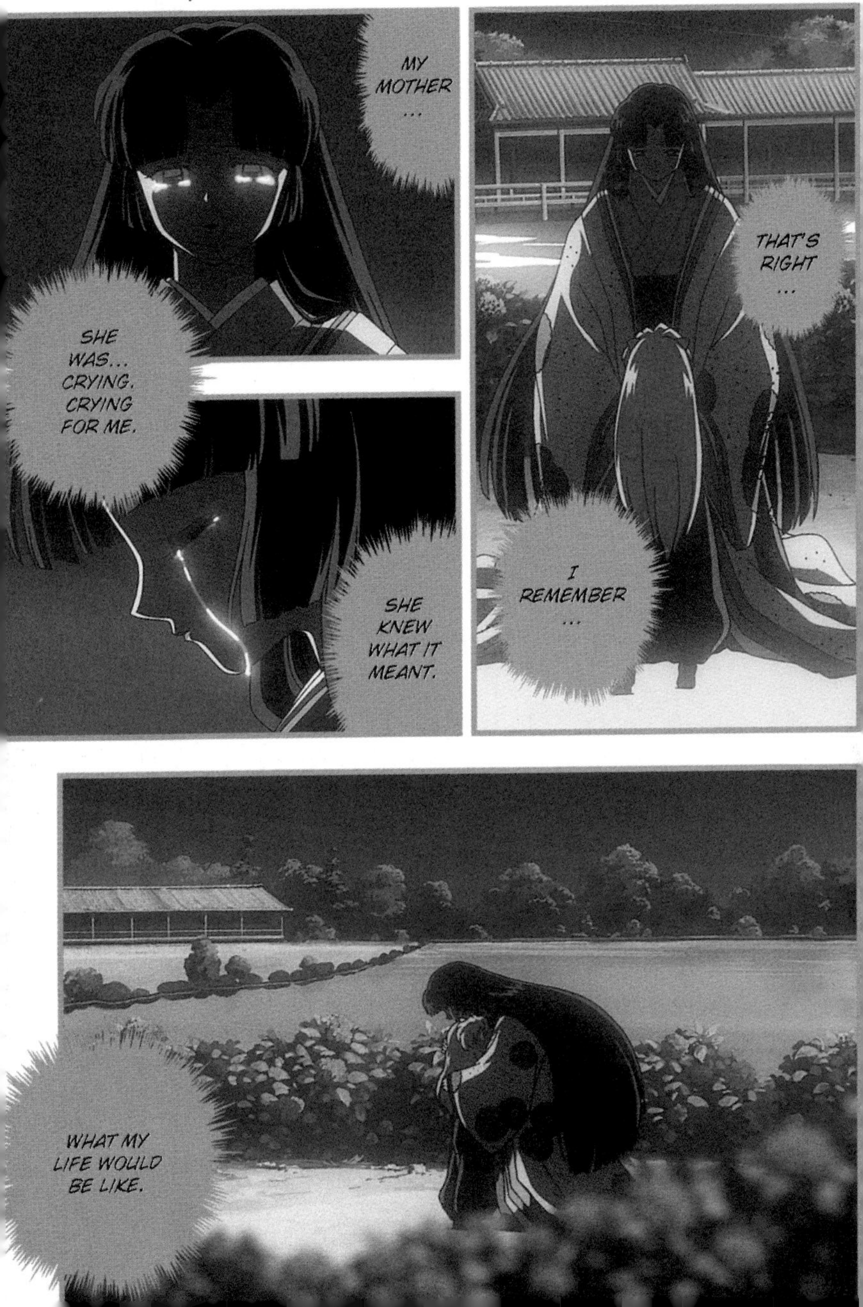
THAT'S RIGHT ...
I REMEMBER ...
MY MOTHER ...
SHE WAS... CRYING. CRYING FOR ME.
SHE KNEW WHAT IT MEANT.
WHAT MY LIFE WOULD BE LIKE.

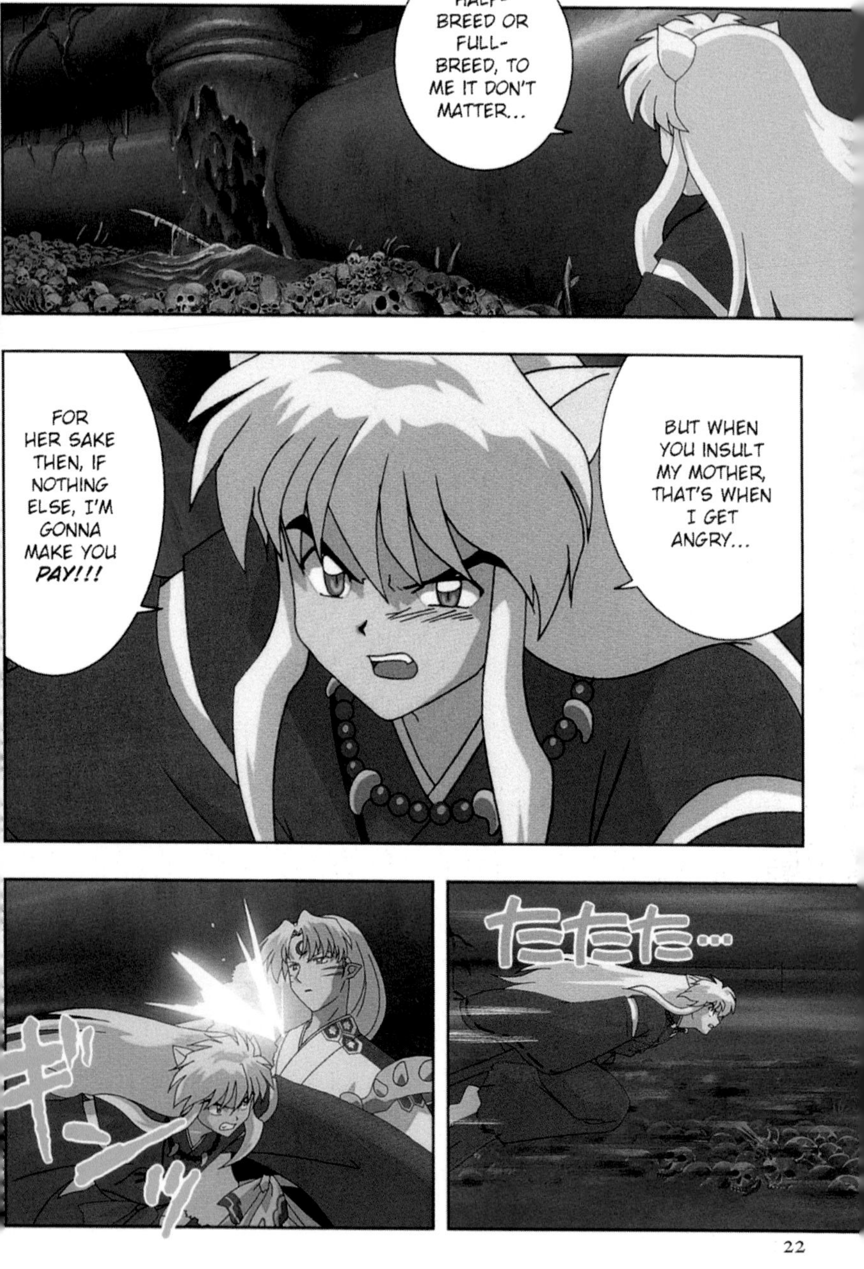
HALF-BREED OR FULL-BREED, TO ME IT DON'T MATTER...
BUT WHEN YOU INSULT MY MOTHER, THAT'S WHEN I GET ANGRY...
FOR HER SAKE THEN, IF NOTHING ELSE, I'M GONNA MAKE YOU *PAY!!!*
たたた…
ギンッ

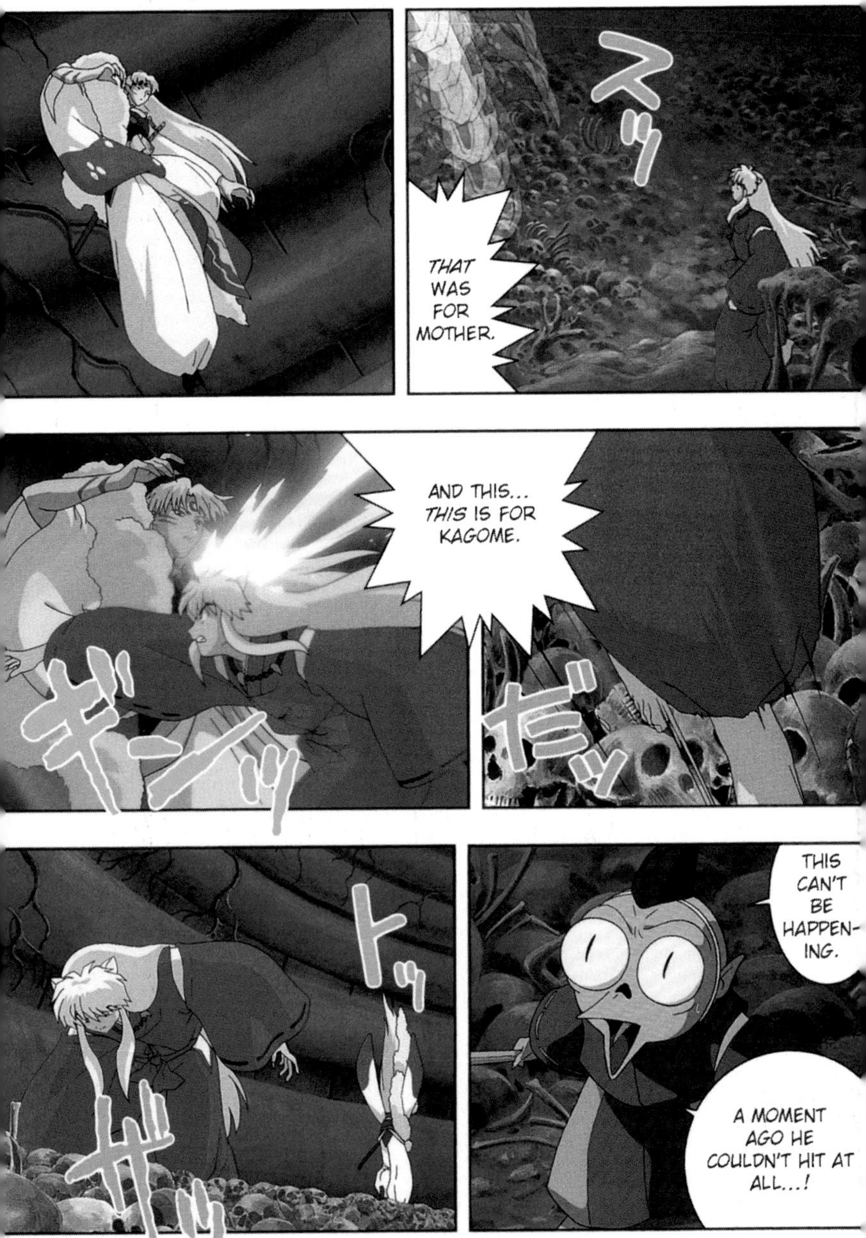
スッ
THAT WAS FOR MOTHER.
ダッ
AND THIS... *THIS* IS FOR KAGOME.
ギーンッ
THIS CAN'T BE HAPPENING.
A MOMENT AGO HE COULDN'T HIT AT ALL...!
トッ
ザッ

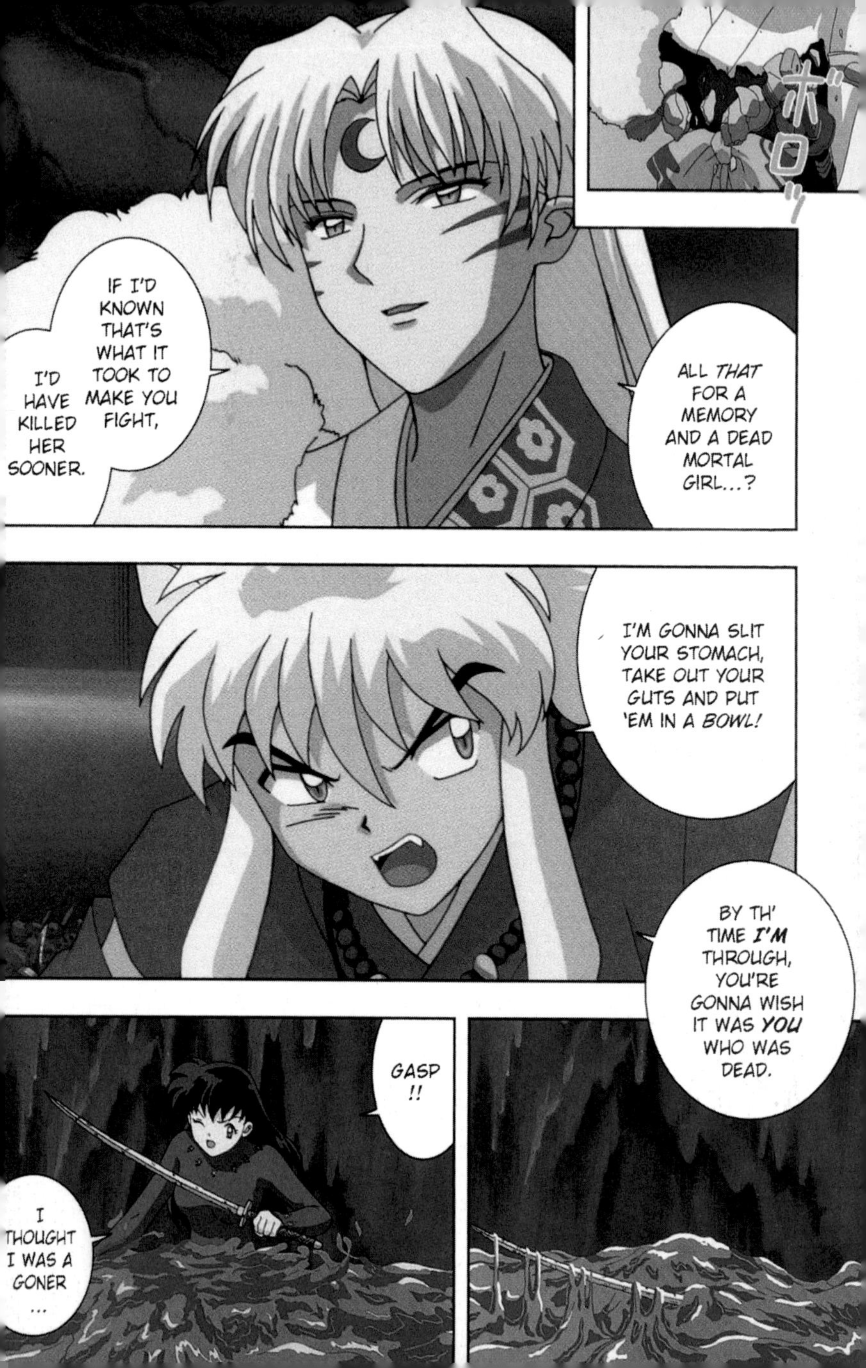
ボロッ
ALL *THAT* FOR A MEMORY AND A DEAD MORTAL GIRL...?
IF I'D KNOWN THAT'S WHAT IT TOOK TO MAKE YOU FIGHT, I'D HAVE KILLED HER SOONER.
I'M GONNA SLIT YOUR STOMACH, TAKE OUT YOUR GUTS AND PUT 'EM IN A *BOWL!*
BY TH' TIME ***I'M*** THROUGH, YOU'RE GONNA WISH IT WAS ***YOU*** WHO WAS DEAD.
GASP !!
I THOUGHT I WAS A GONER ...

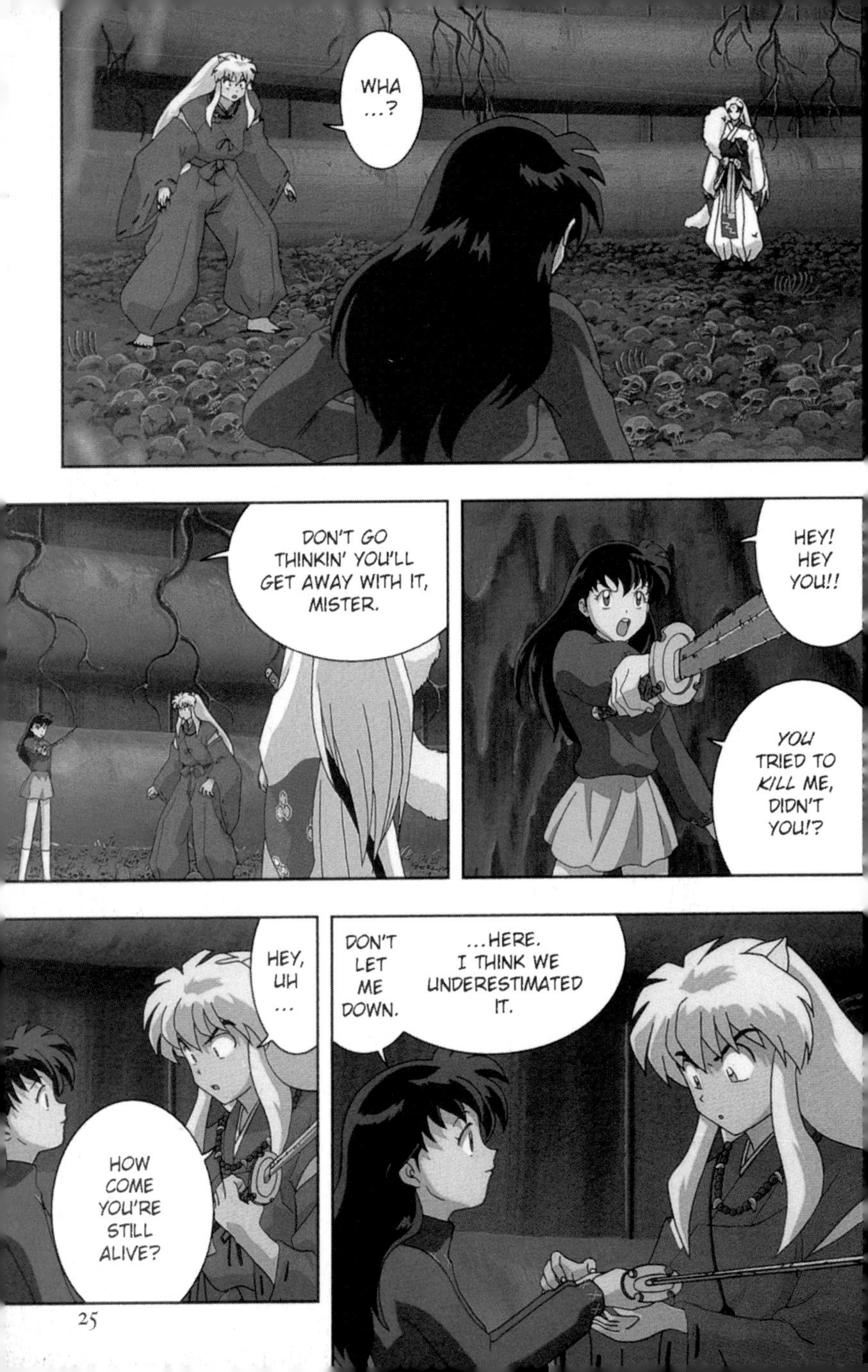
WHA ...?
HEY! HEY YOU!!
YOU TRIED TO *KILL* ME, DIDN'T YOU!?
DON'T GO THINKIN' YOU'LL GET AWAY WITH IT, MISTER.
...HERE. I THINK WE UNDERESTIMATED IT.
DON'T LET ME DOWN.
HEY, UH ...
HOW COME YOU'RE STILL ALIVE?

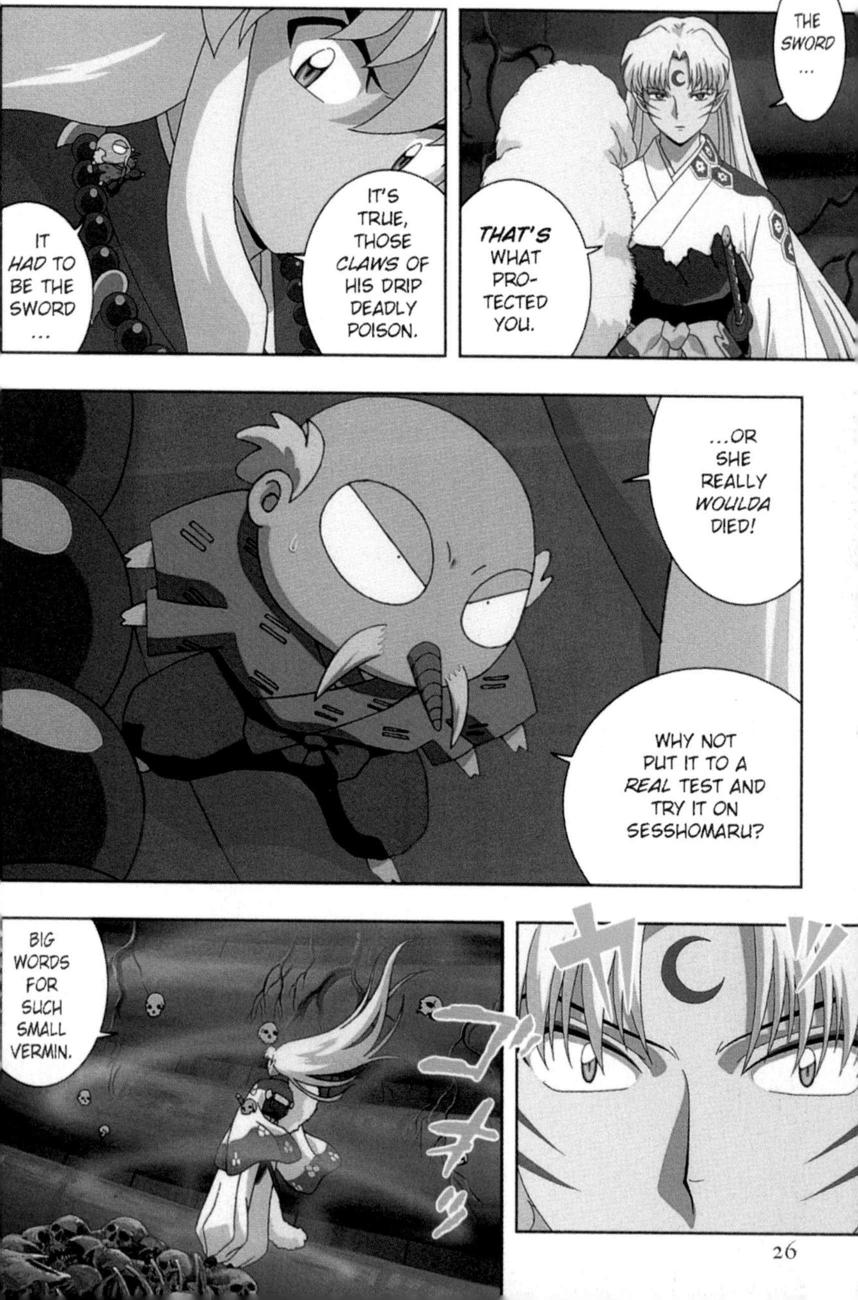
THE *SWORD* ...
THAT'S WHAT PROTECTED YOU.
IT'S TRUE, THOSE *CLAWS* OF HIS DRIP DEADLY POISON.
IT *HAD TO* BE THE SWORD ...
...OR SHE REALLY *WOULDA* DIED!
WHY NOT PUT IT TO A *REAL* TEST AND TRY IT ON SESSHOMARU?
BIG WORDS FOR SUCH SMALL VERMIN.

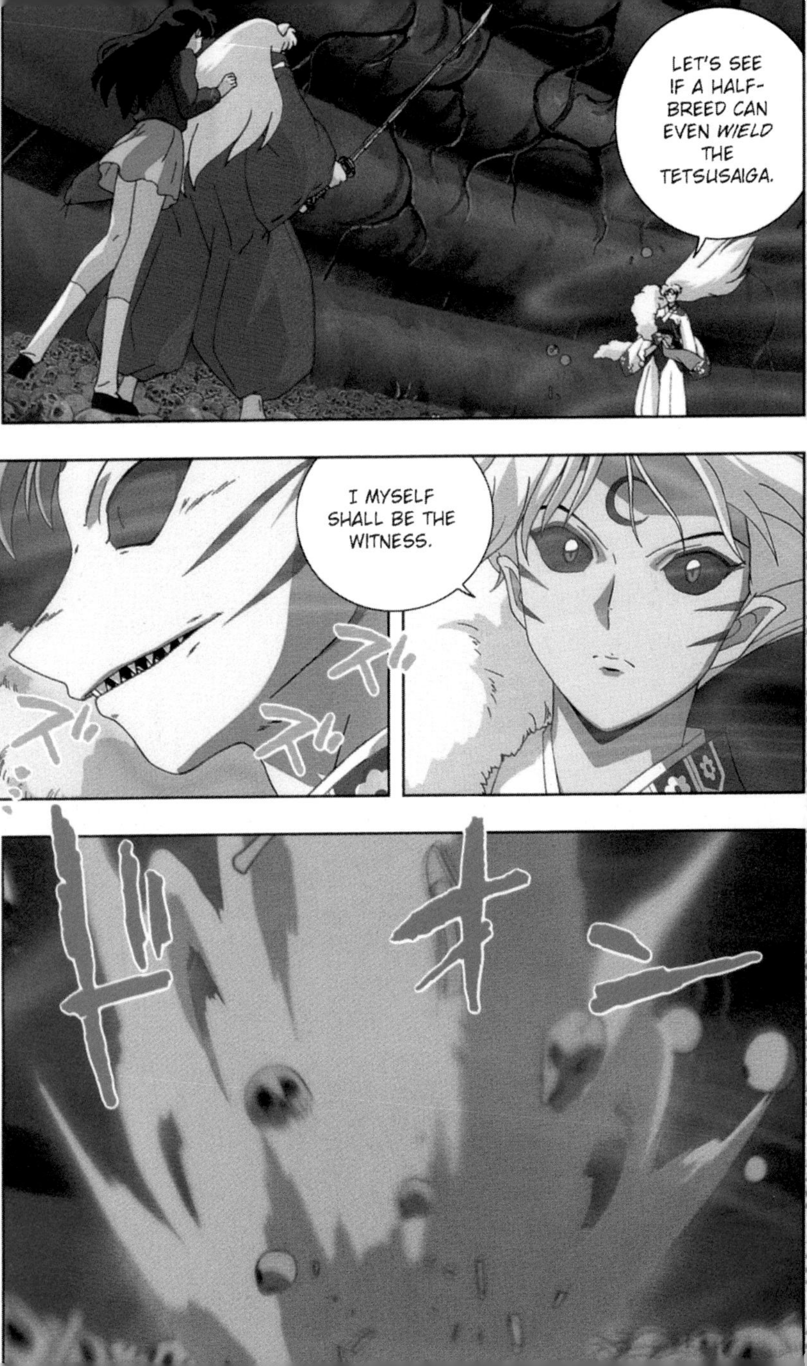
LET'S SEE IF A HALF-BREED CAN EVEN *WIELD* THE TETSUSAIGA.
I MYSELF SHALL BE THE WITNESS.
ズ ズ ズ
ドオン

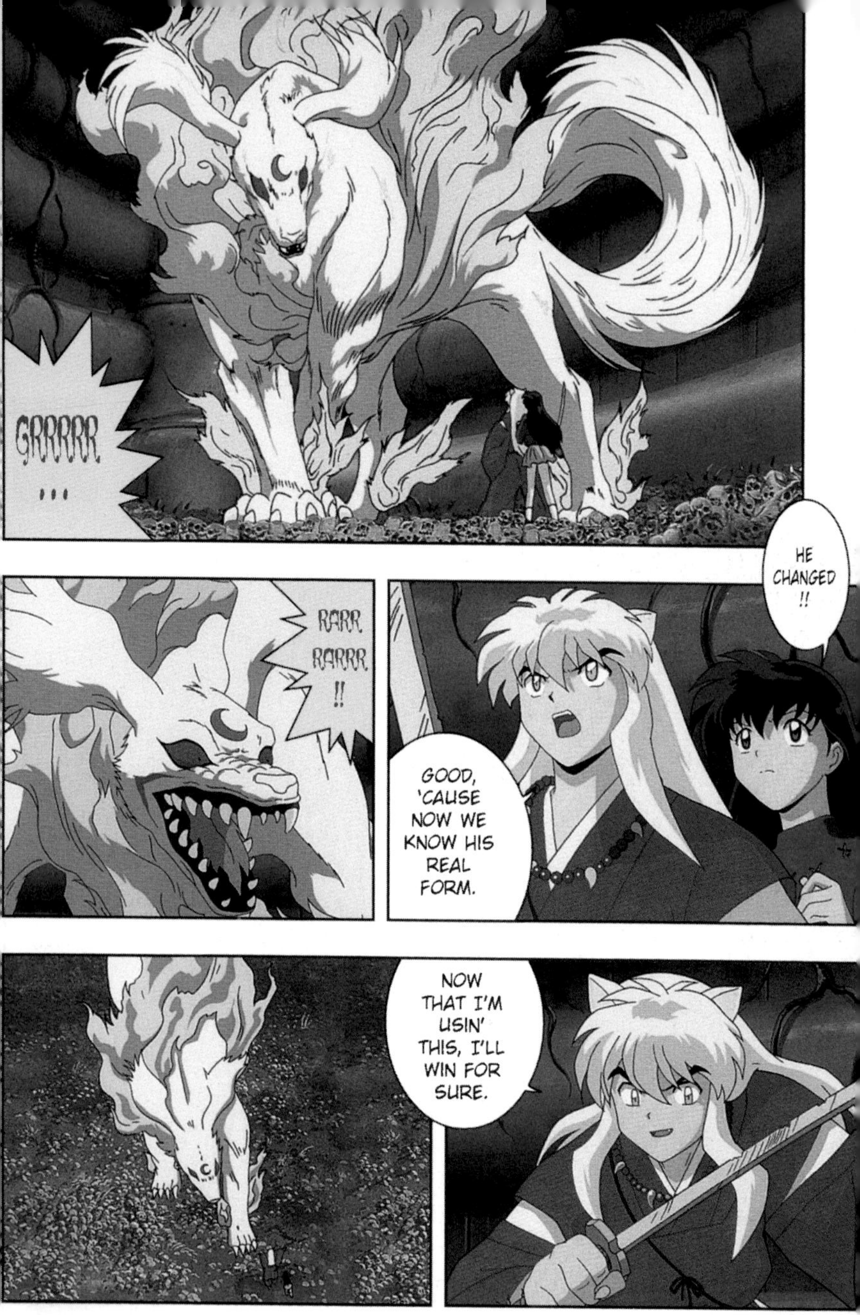
GRRRRR...
HE CHANGED!!
GOOD, 'CAUSE NOW WE KNOW HIS REAL FORM.
RARR. RARRR. !!
NOW THAT I'M USIN' THIS, I'LL WIN FOR SURE.

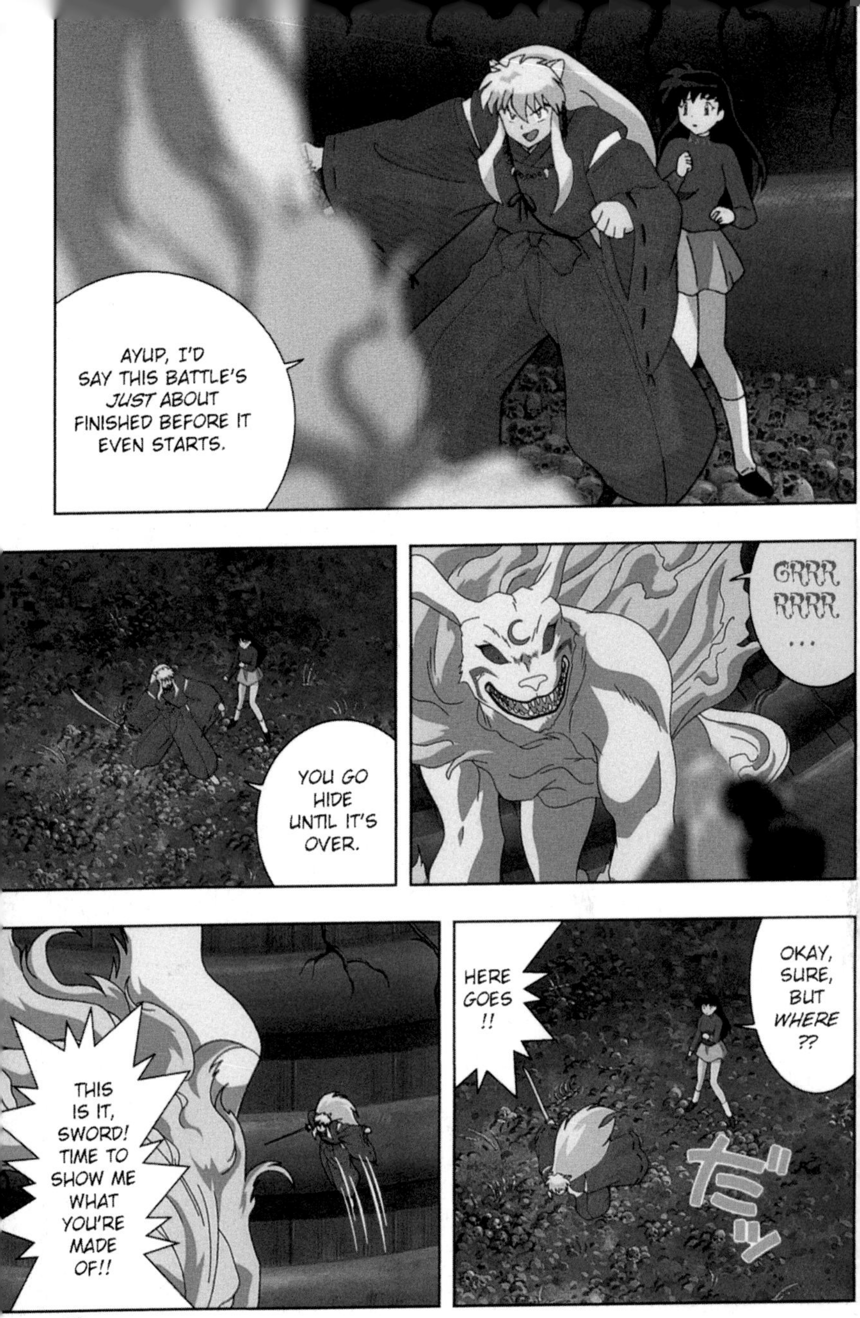
AYUP, I'D SAY THIS BATTLE'S *JUST* ABOUT FINISHED BEFORE IT EVEN STARTS.
GRRR RRRR ...
YOU GO HIDE UNTIL IT'S OVER.
OKAY, SURE, BUT *WHERE* ??
HERE GOES !!
ダッ
THIS IS IT, SWORD! TIME TO SHOW ME WHAT YOU'RE MADE OF!!

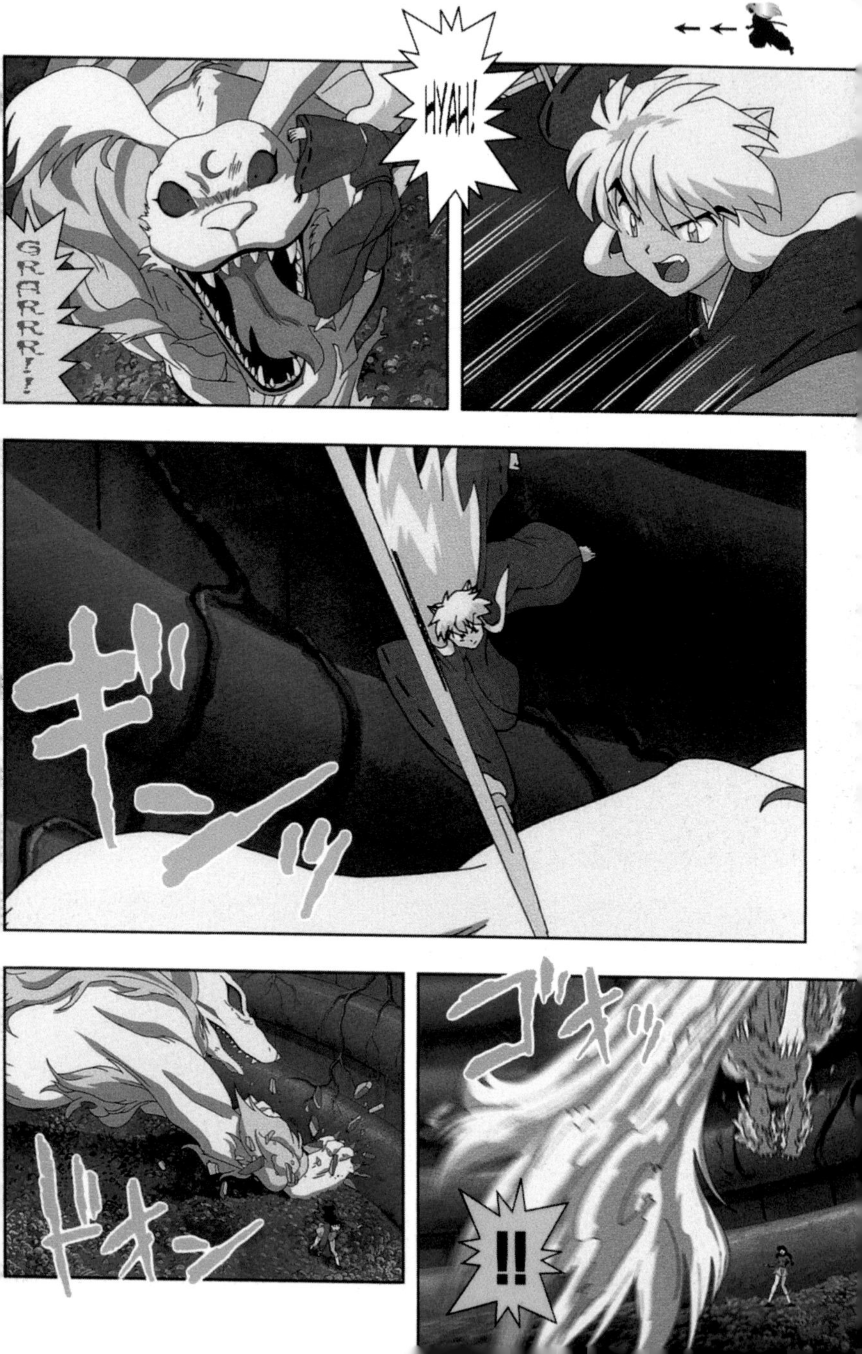
HYAH!
GRARRR!!
ギーンッ
ゴキッ
!!
ドオン

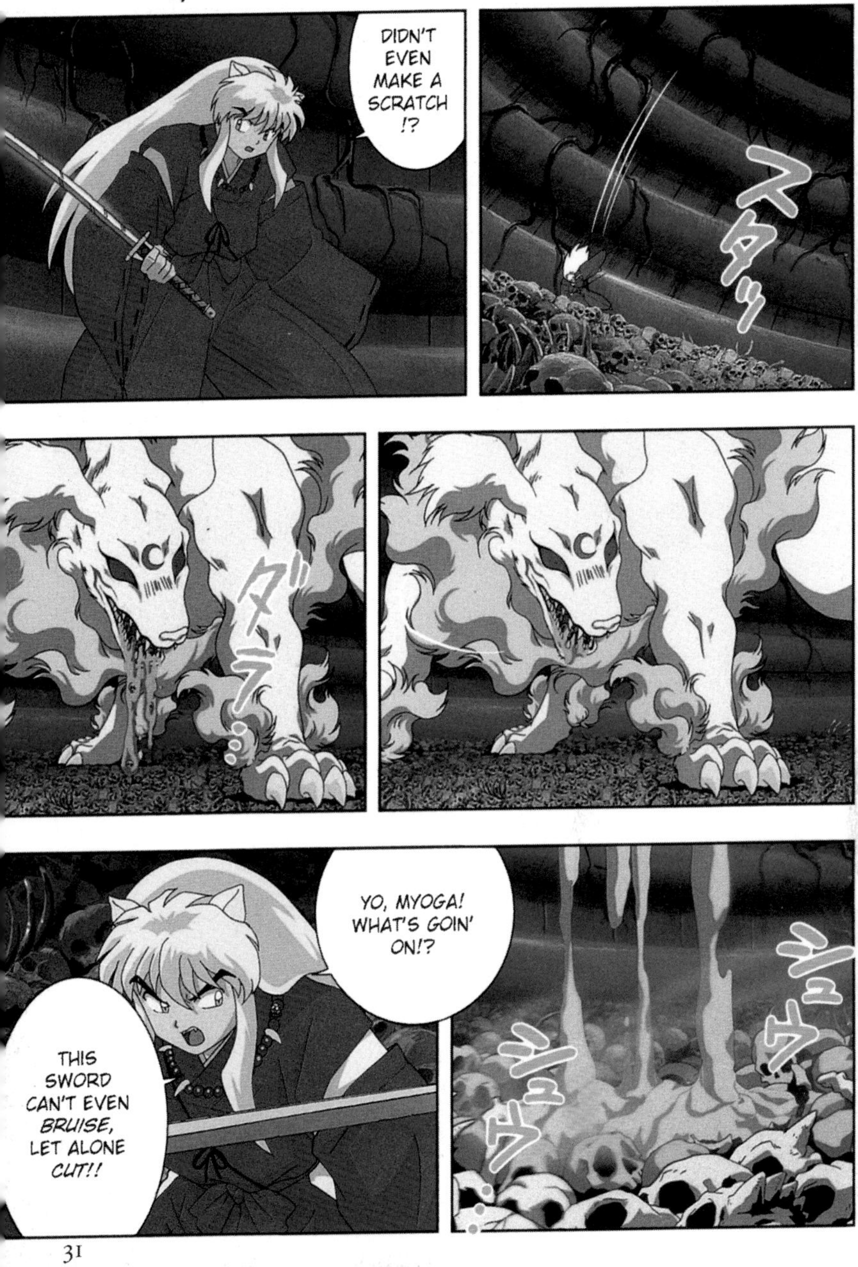

スタッ
DIDN'T EVEN MAKE A SCRATCH !?
ダラ…
シュウ
シュウ
YO, MYOGA! WHAT'S GOIN' ON!?
THIS SWORD CAN'T EVEN *BRUISE*, LET ALONE *CUT*!!

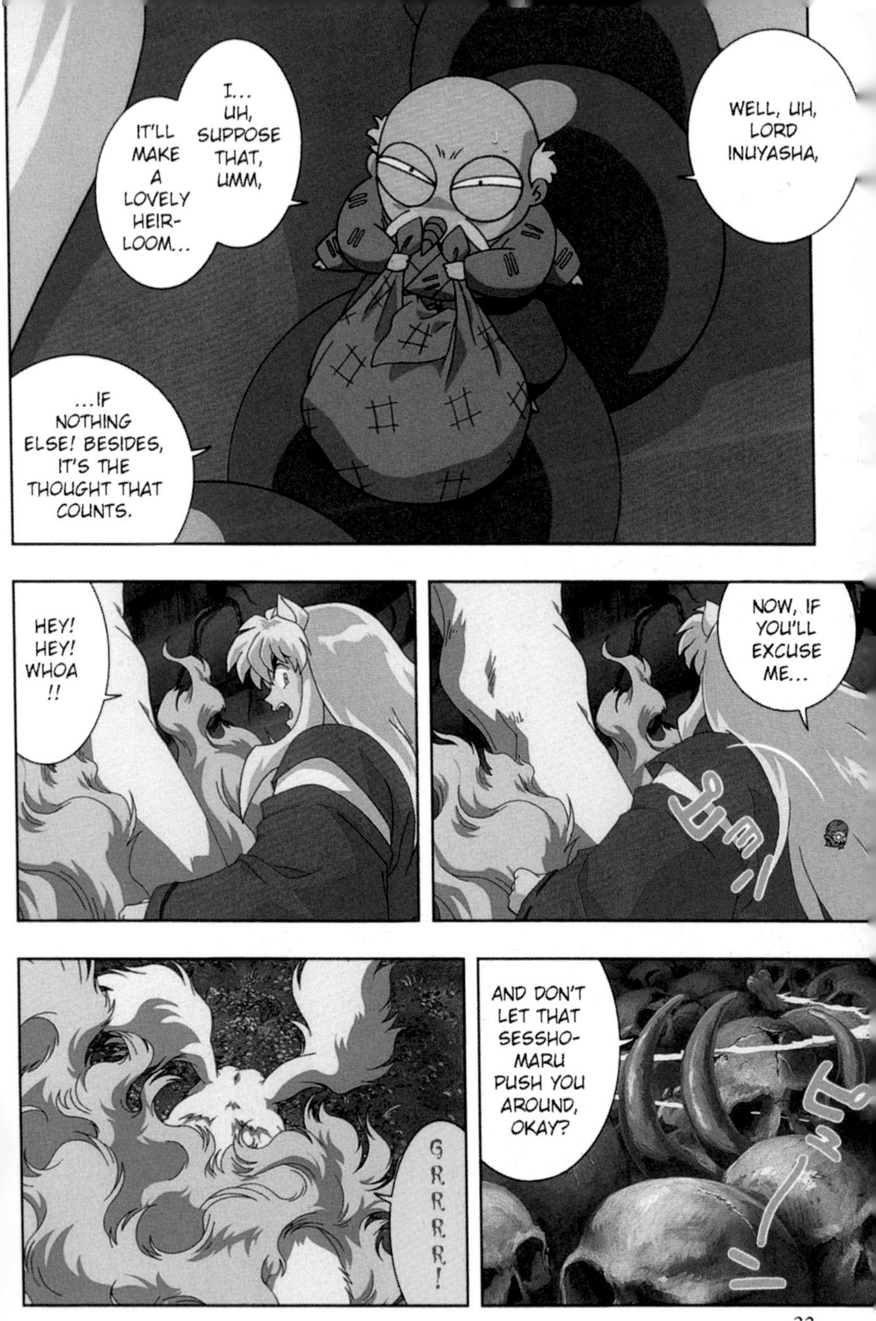
WELL, UH, LORD INUYASHA,
I... UH, SUPPOSE THAT, UMM,
IT'LL MAKE A LOVELY HEIR-LOOM...
...IF NOTHING ELSE! BESIDES, IT'S THE THOUGHT THAT COUNTS.
NOW, IF YOU'LL EXCUSE ME...
HEY! HEY! WHOA!!
AND DON'T LET THAT SESSHO-MARU PUSH YOU AROUND, OKAY?
GRRRR!

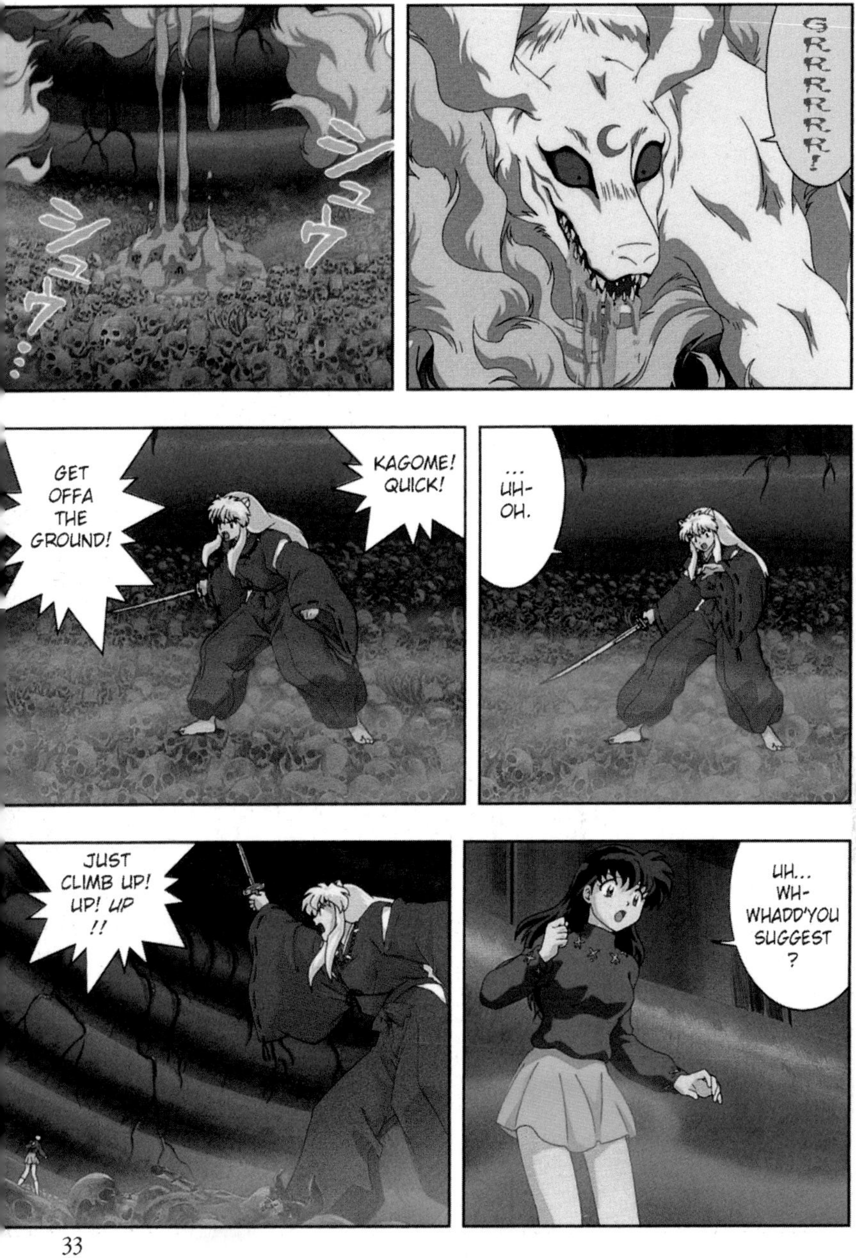
GRRRRRR!
シュウ
シュウ…
…UH-OH.
KAGOME! QUICK!
GET OFFA THE GROUND!
UH… WH-WHADD'YOU SUGGEST ?
JUST CLIMB UP! UP! UP !!

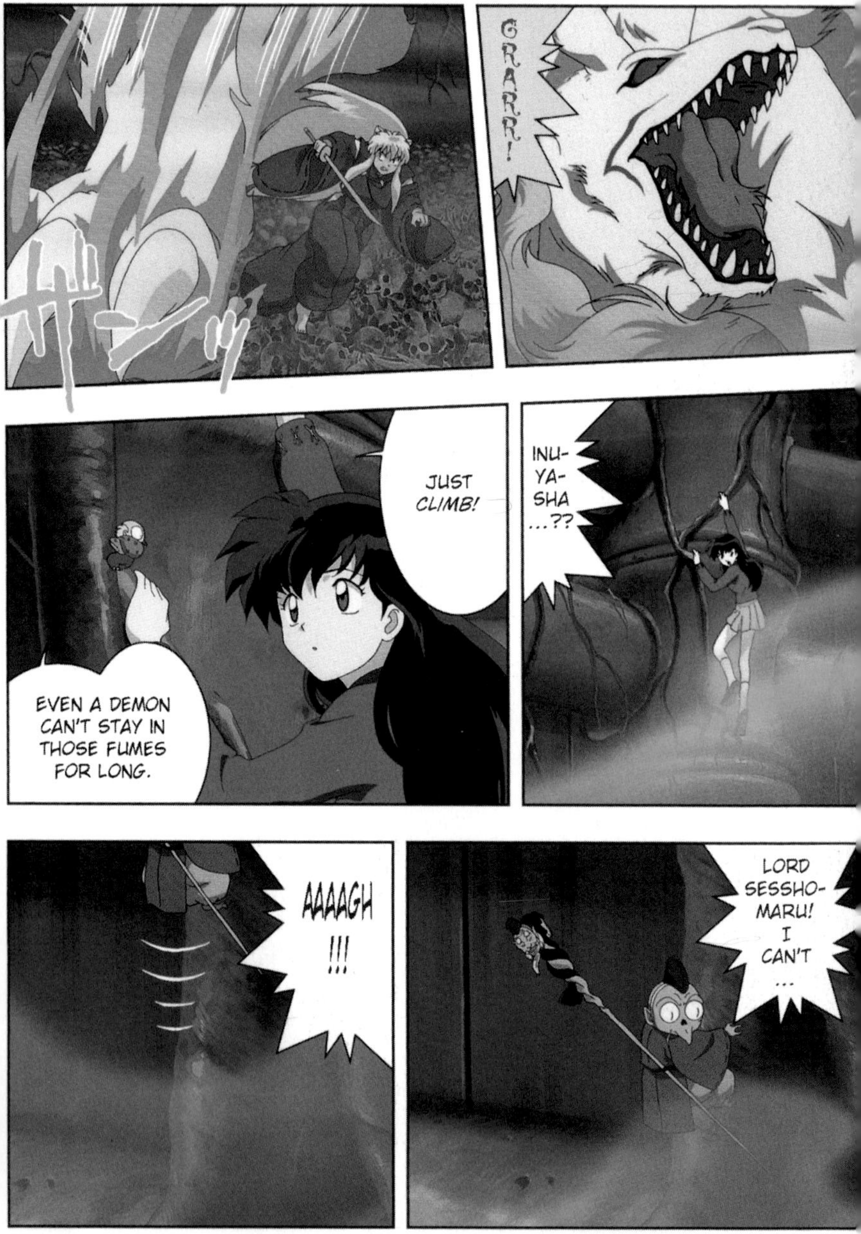
GRARRR!
INU-YASHA...??
JUST CLIMB!
EVEN A DEMON CAN'T STAY IN THOSE FUMES FOR LONG.
LORD SESSHOMARU! I CAN'T ...
AAAAGH!!!

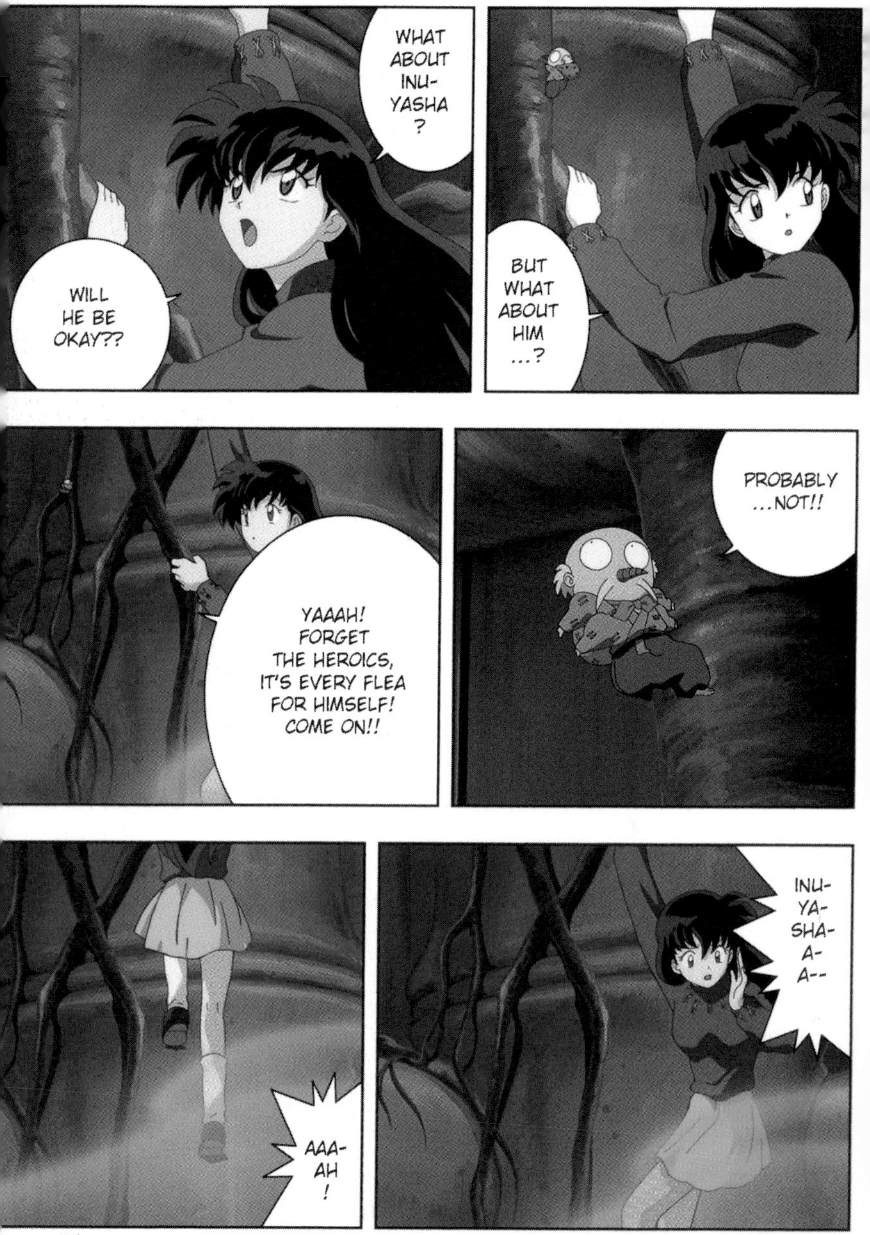
BUT WHAT ABOUT HIM ...?
WHAT ABOUT INU-YASHA ?
WILL HE BE OKAY??
PROBABLY ...NOT!!
YAAAH! FORGET THE HEROICS, IT'S EVERY FLEA FOR HIMSELF! COME ON!!
INU-YA-SHA-A-A--
AAAA-AH !

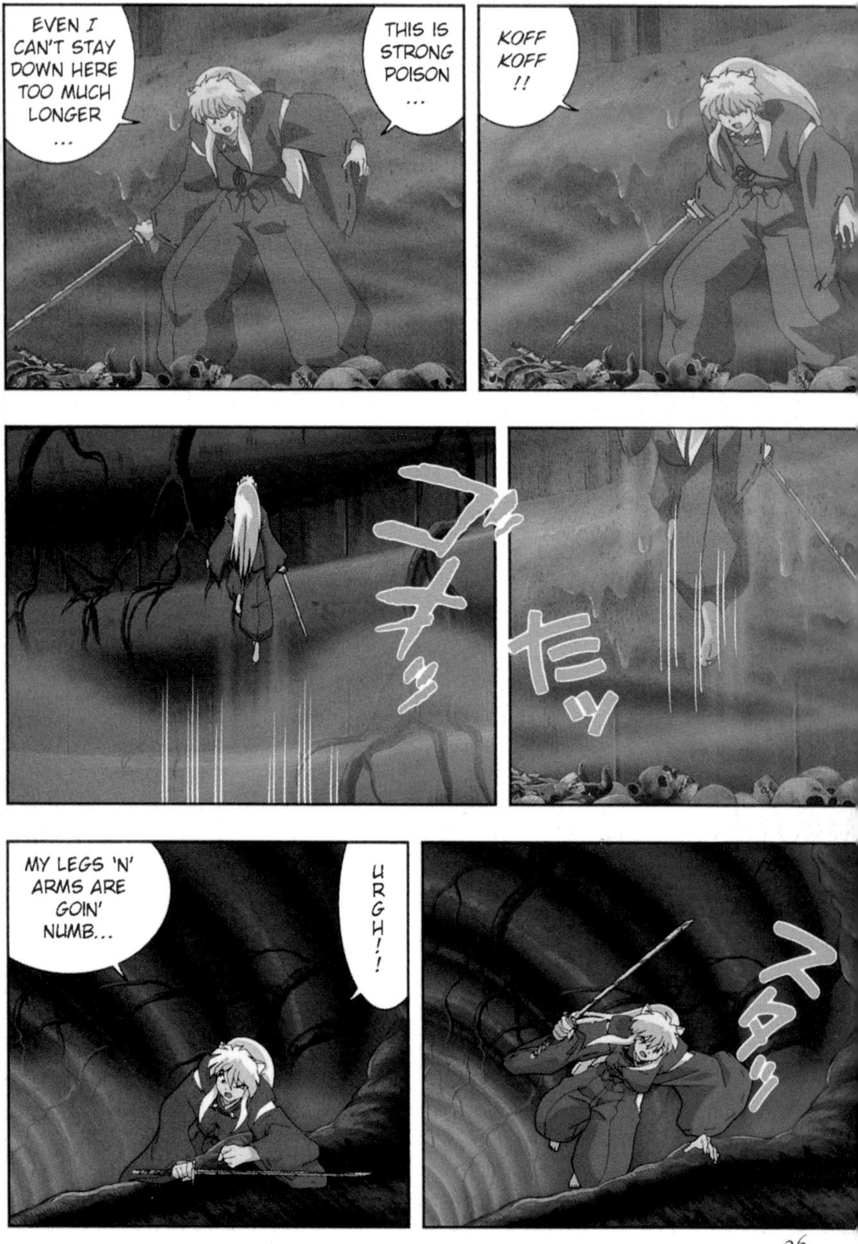
KOFF KOFF !!
THIS IS STRONG POISON ...
EVEN I CAN'T STAY DOWN HERE TOO MUCH LONGER ...
スタッ
URGH!!
MY LEGS 'N' ARMS ARE GOIN' NUMB...

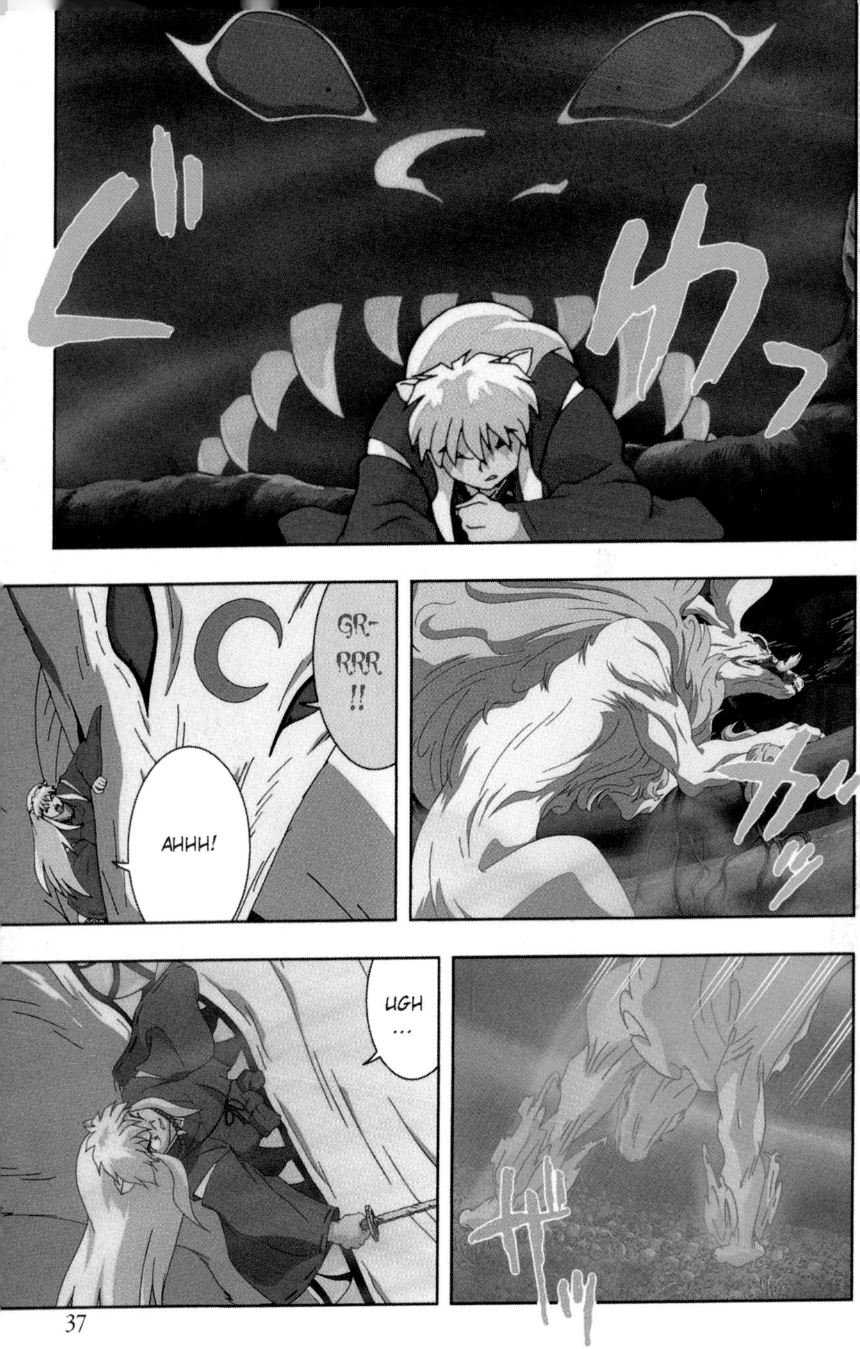
GR-RRR!!
AHHH!
UGH ...

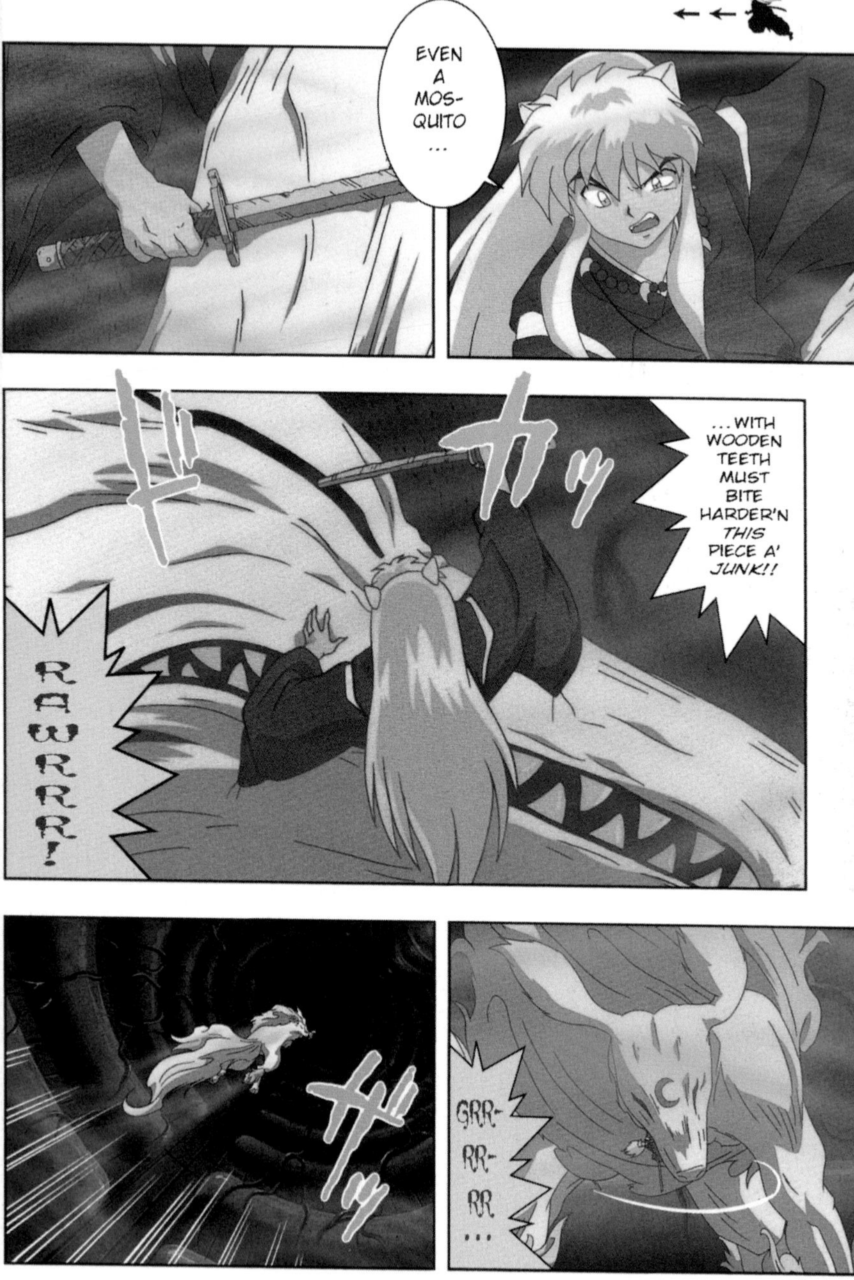

EVEN A MOS-QUITO ...
...WITH WOODEN TEETH MUST BITE HARDER'N THIS PIECE A' JUNK!!
カッ
ド
RAWRRRR!
GRR-RR-RR ...
ザッ

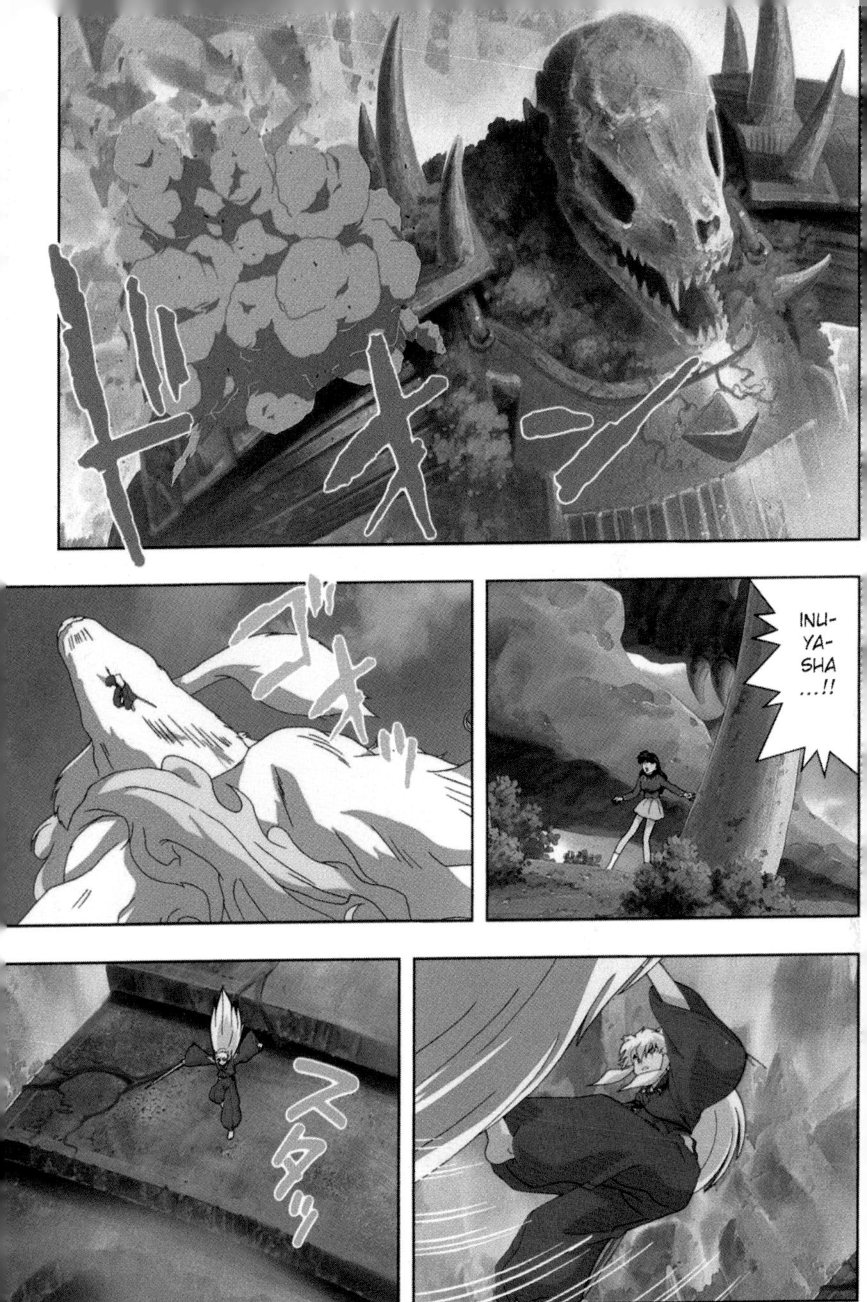
ドオーン
INU-YA-SHA ...!!
スタッ

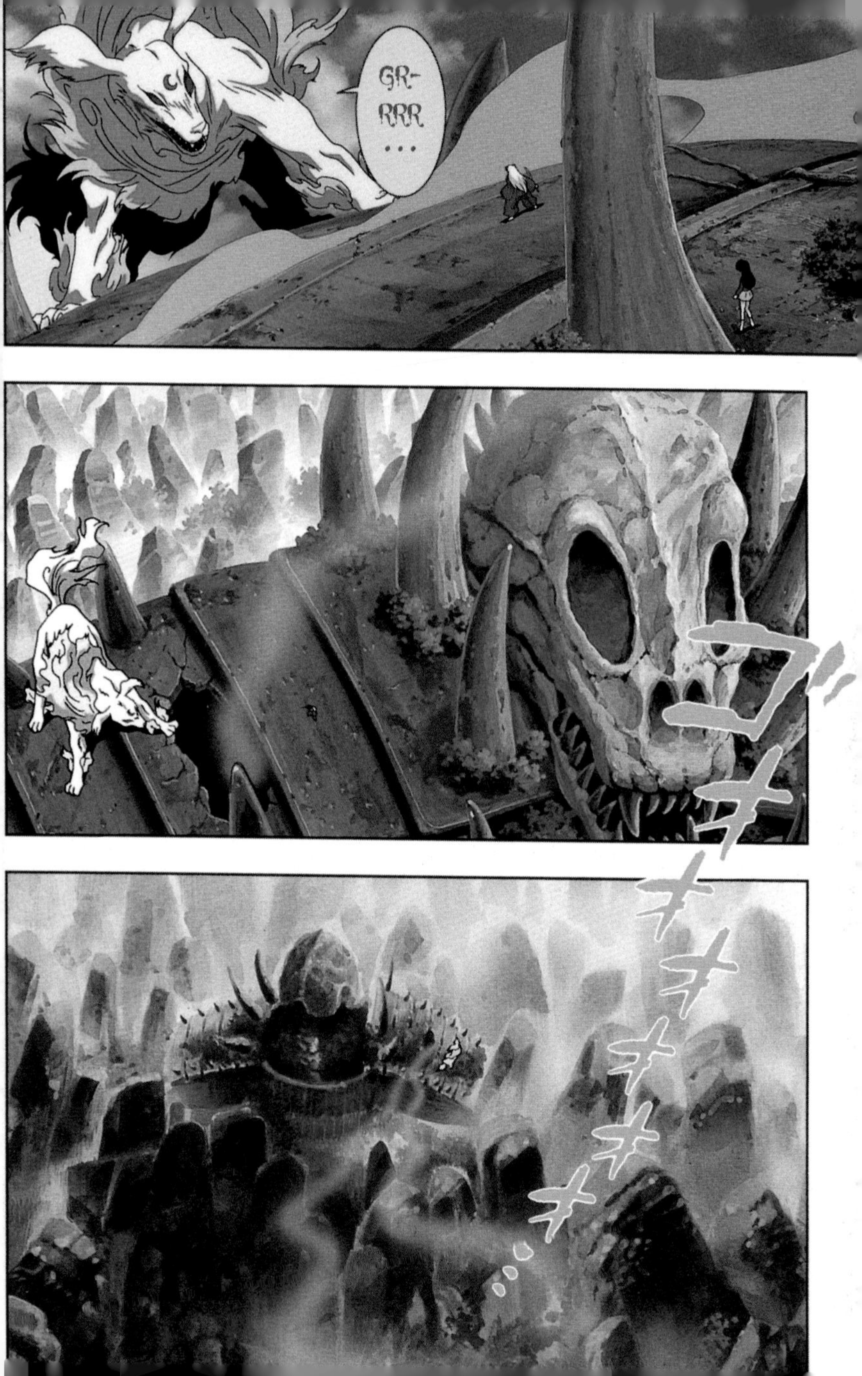
GR-RRR...

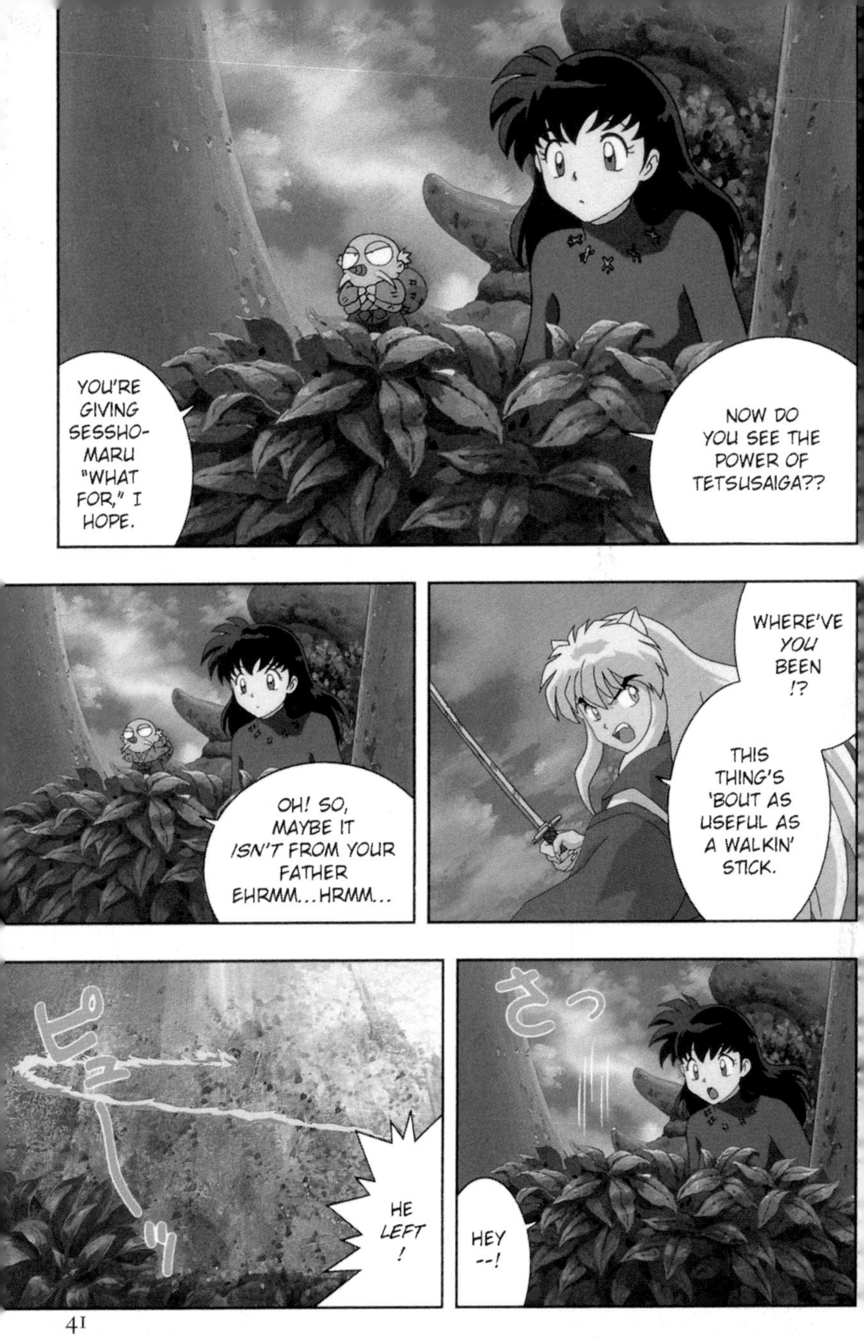
NOW DO YOU SEE THE POWER OF TETSUSAIGA??
YOU'RE GIVING SESSHO-MARU "WHAT FOR," I HOPE.
WHERE'VE *YOU* BEEN !?
THIS THING'S 'BOUT AS USEFUL AS A WALKIN' STICK.
OH! SO, MAYBE IT *ISN'T* FROM YOUR FATHER EHRMM...HRMM...
さっ
HEY --!
ピューッ
HE *LEFT* !

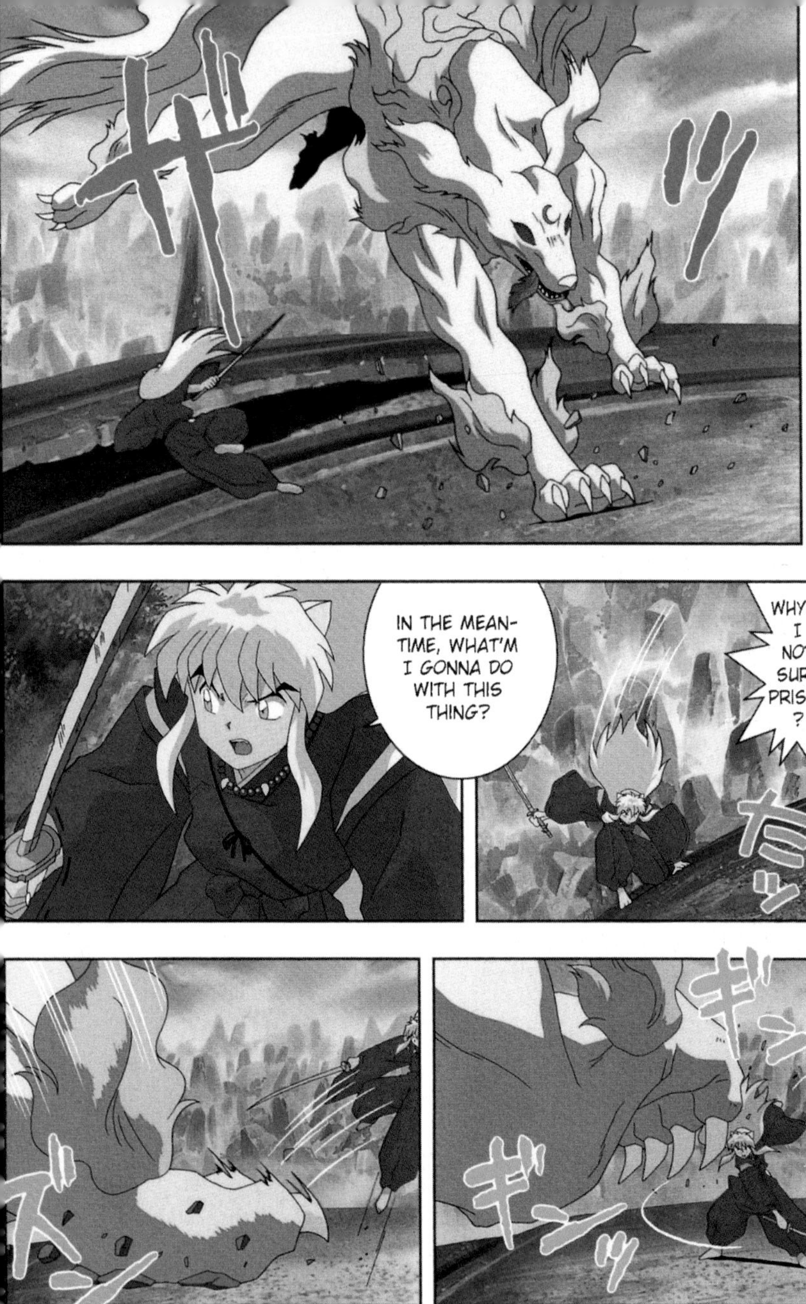
WHY'M I NOT SUR-PRISED?
IN THE MEAN-TIME, WHAT'M I GONNA DO WITH THIS THING?

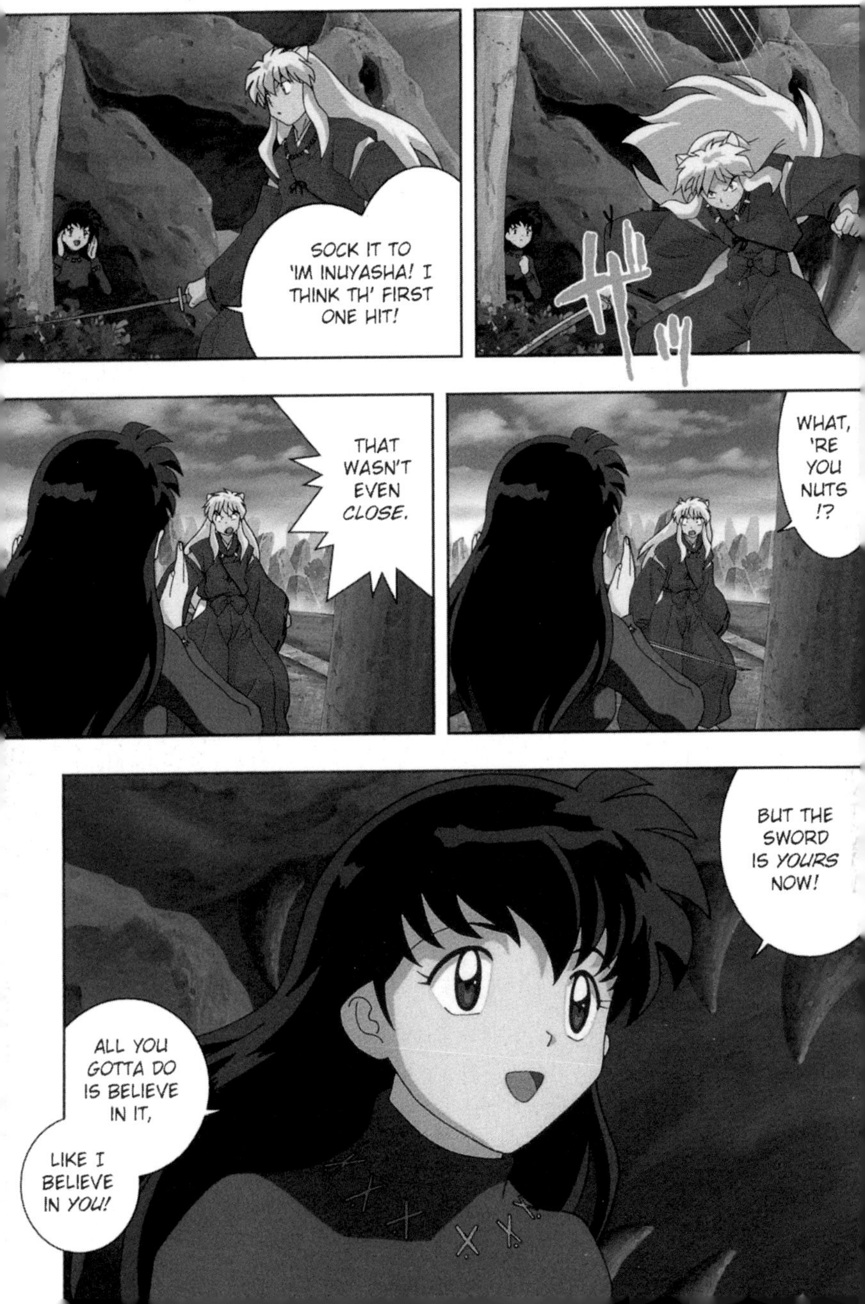
SOCK IT TO 'IM INUYASHA! I THINK TH' FIRST ONE HIT!
WHAT, 'RE YOU NUTS !?
THAT WASN'T EVEN CLOSE.
BUT THE SWORD IS *YOURS* NOW!
ALL YOU GOTTA DO IS BELIEVE IN IT,
LIKE I BELIEVE IN *YOU!*

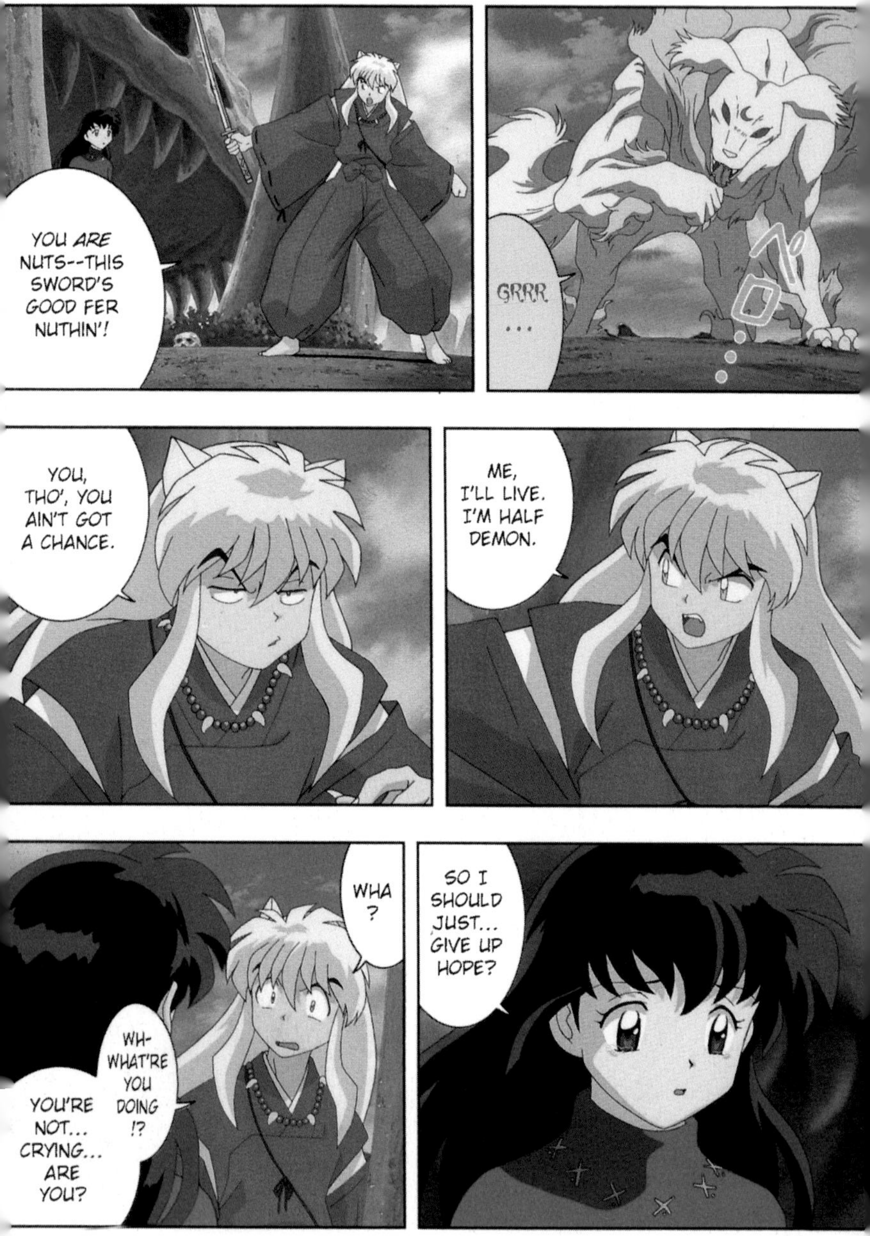
GRRR ...
YOU *ARE* NUTS--THIS SWORD'S GOOD FER NUTHIN'!
ME, I'LL LIVE. I'M HALF DEMON.
YOU, THO', YOU AIN'T GOT A CHANCE.
SO I SHOULD JUST... GIVE UP HOPE?
WHA ?
WH- WHAT'RE YOU DOING !?
YOU'RE NOT... CRYING... ARE YOU?

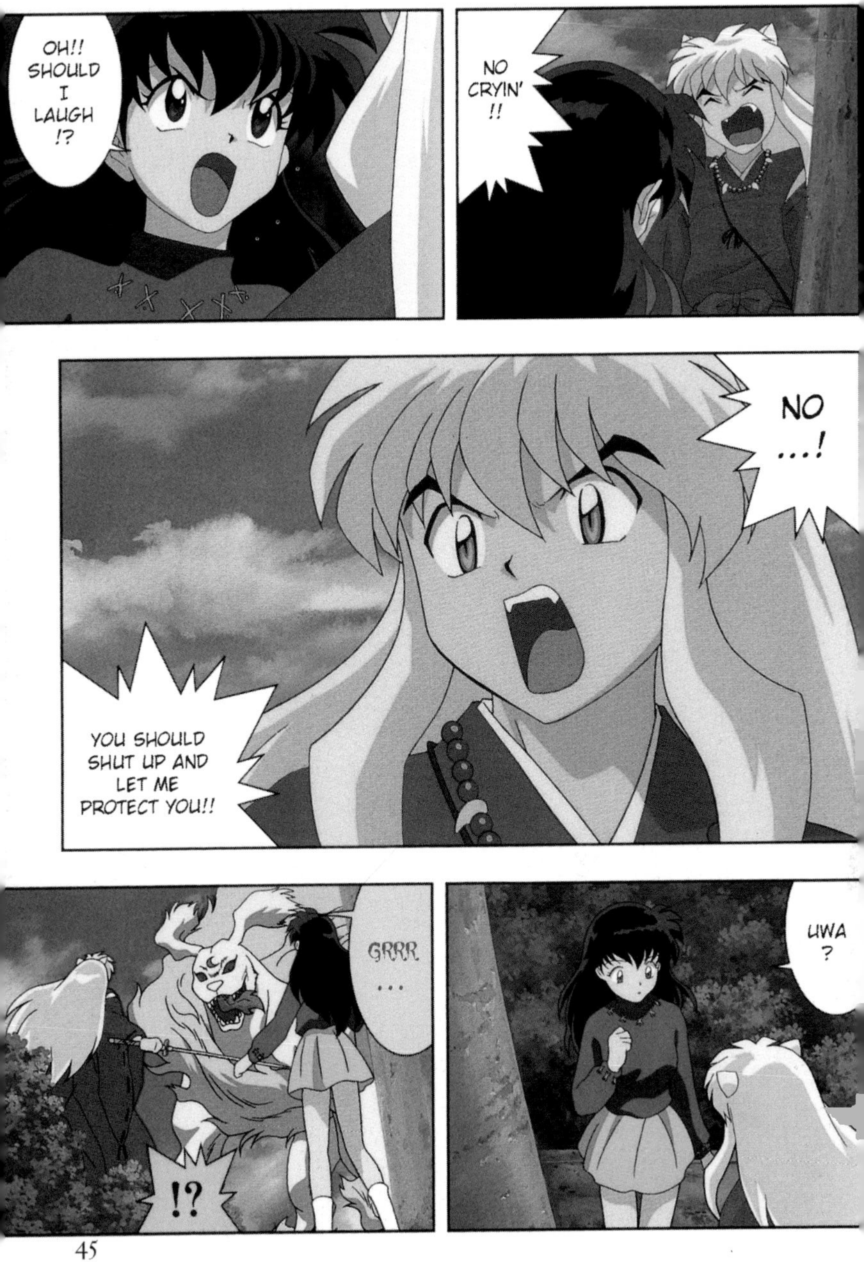
NO CRYIN'!!
OH!! SHOULD I LAUGH!?
NO...!
YOU SHOULD SHUT UP AND LET ME PROTECT YOU!!
UWA?
GRRR...
!?

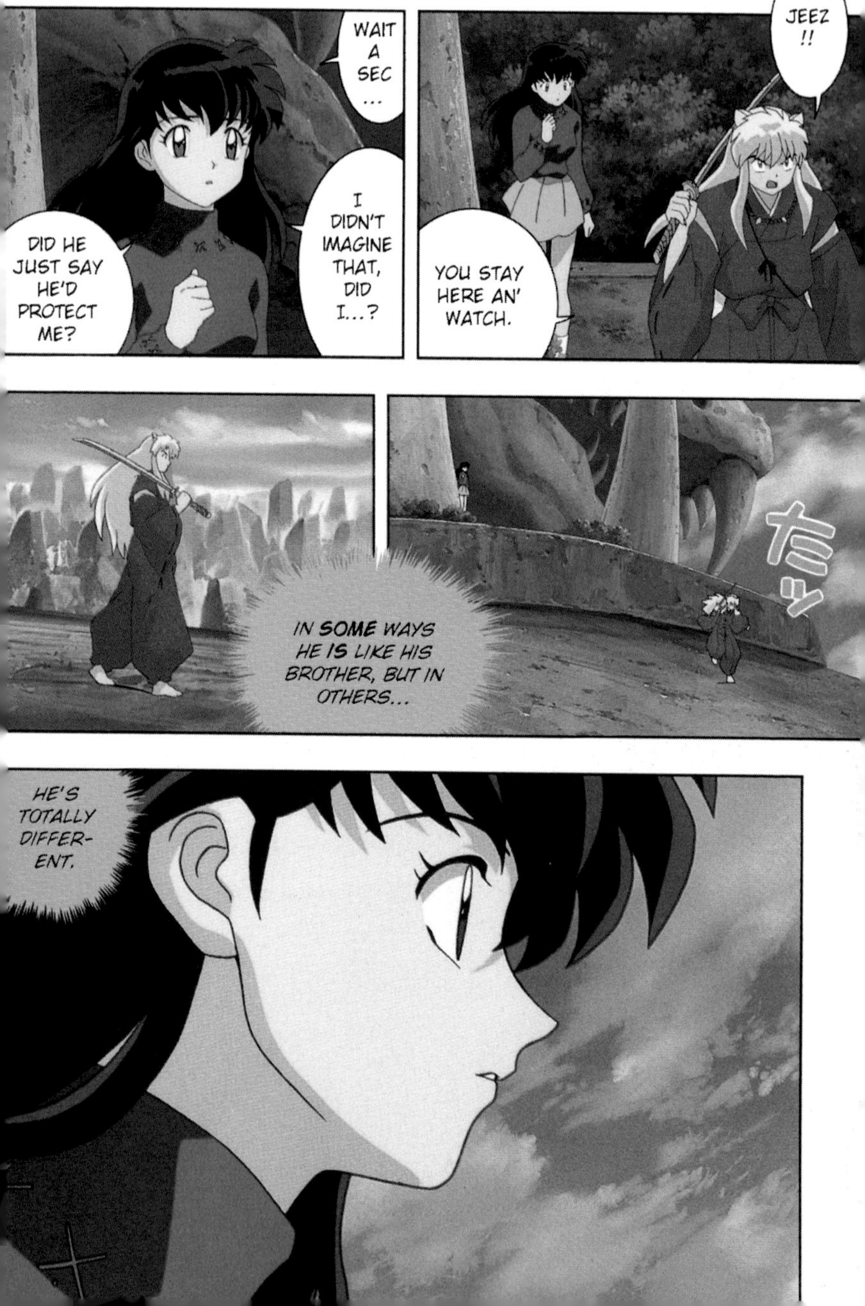
JEEZ !!
YOU STAY HERE AN' WATCH.
WAIT A SEC ...
I DIDN'T IMAGINE THAT, DID I...?
DID HE JUST SAY HE'D PROTECT ME?
たッ
IN SOME WAYS HE IS LIKE HIS BROTHER, BUT IN OTHERS...
HE'S TOTALLY DIFFER-ENT.

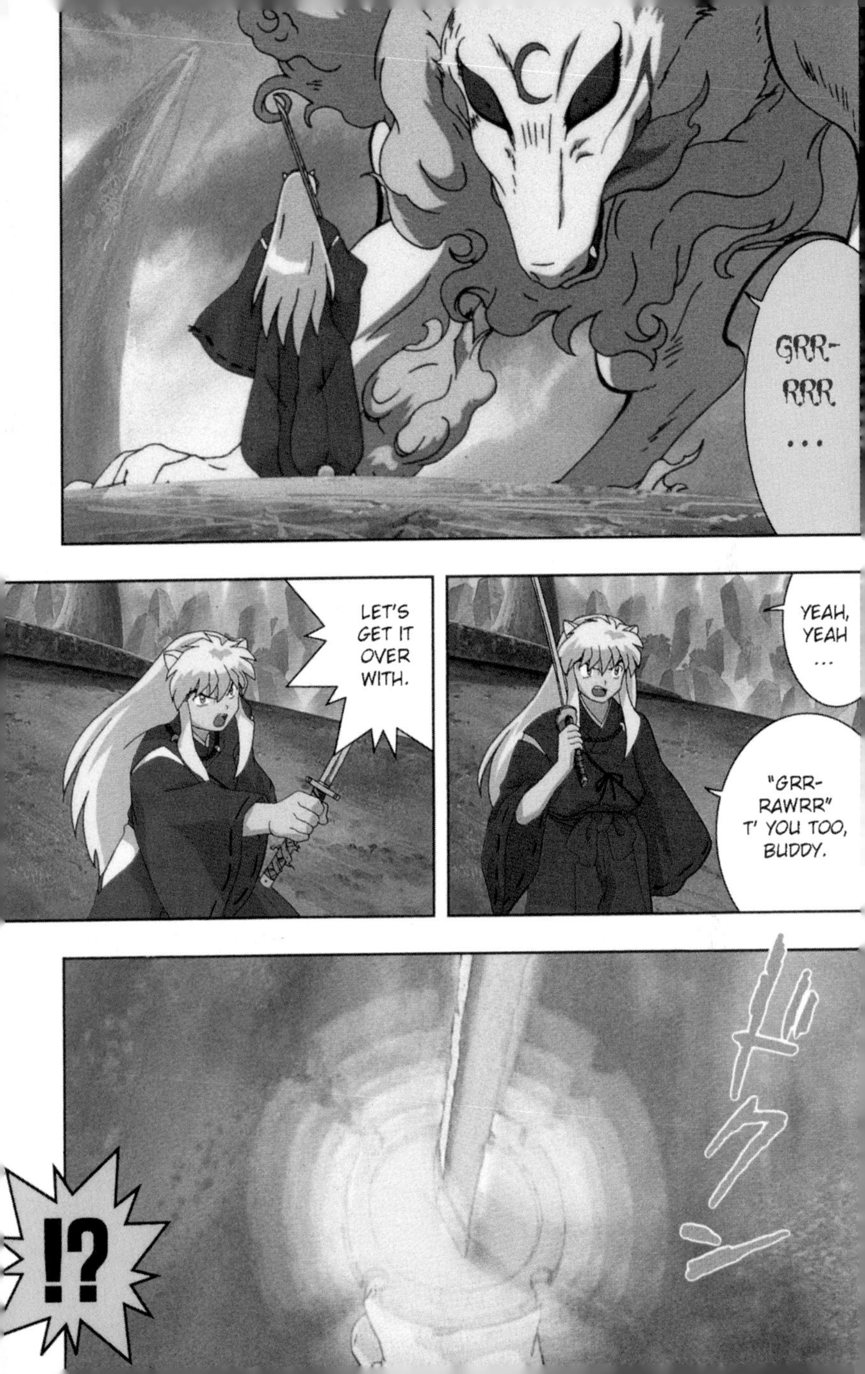
GRR-RRR...
YEAH, YEAH...
"GRR-RAWRR" T' YOU TOO, BUDDY.
LET'S GET IT OVER WITH.
!?

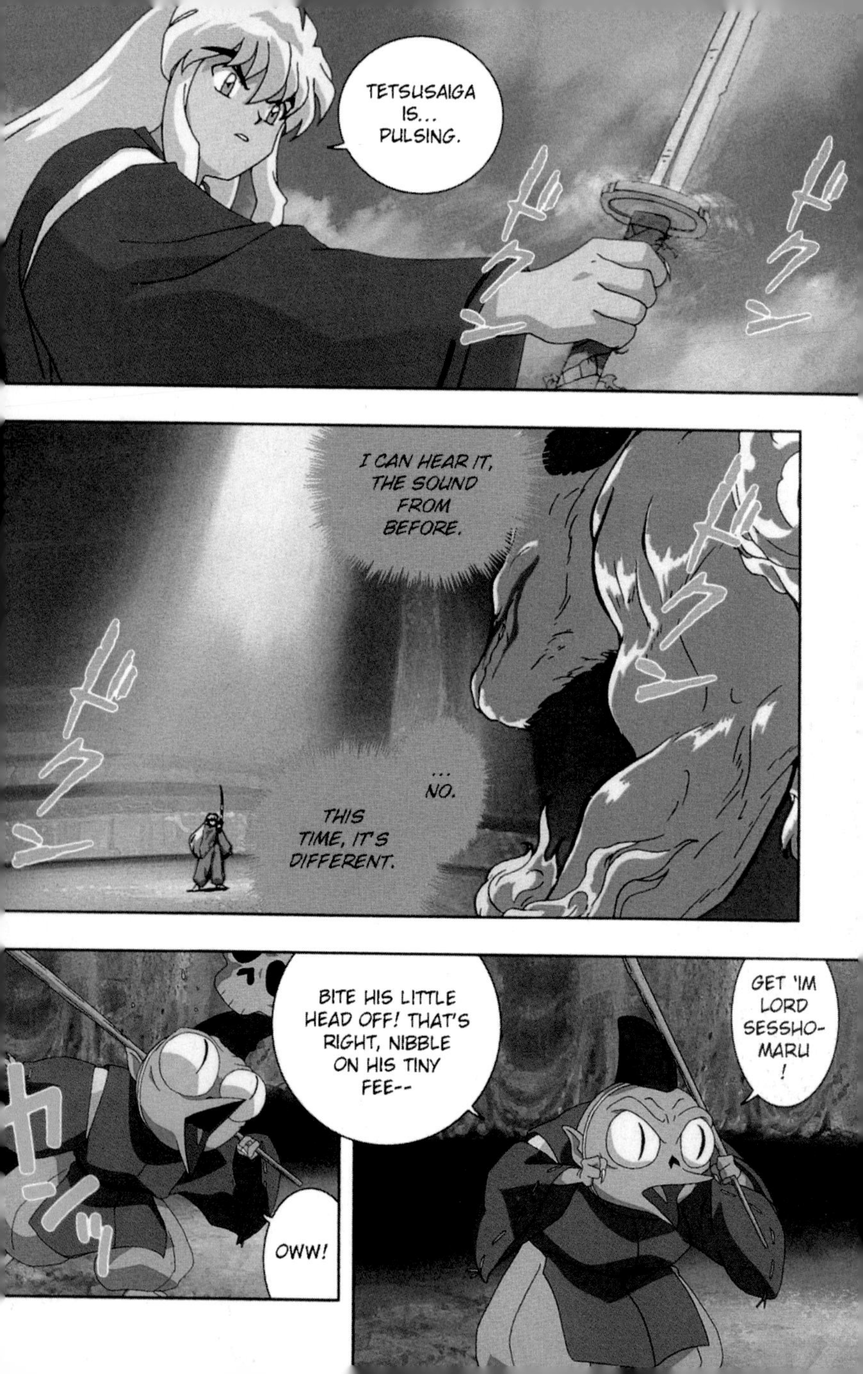

TETSUSAIGA IS... PULSING.
I CAN HEAR IT, THE SOUND FROM BEFORE.
... NO.
THIS TIME, IT'S DIFFERENT.
GET 'IM LORD SESSHO-MARU!
BITE HIS LITTLE HEAD OFF! THAT'S RIGHT, NIBBLE ON HIS TINY FEE--
OWW!

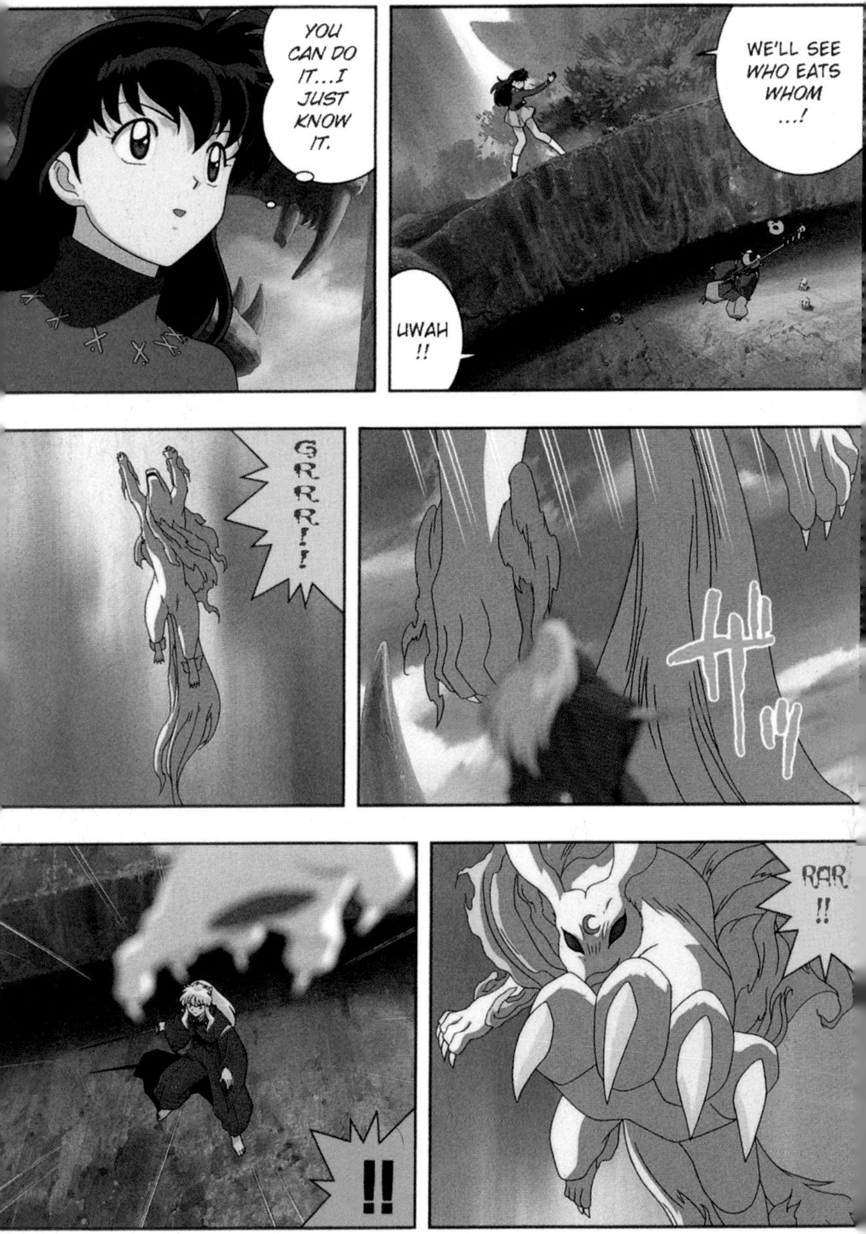

WE'LL SEE WHO EATS WHOM ...!
UWAH !!
YOU CAN DO IT...I JUST KNOW IT.
GRRR!!!
RAR !!
!!

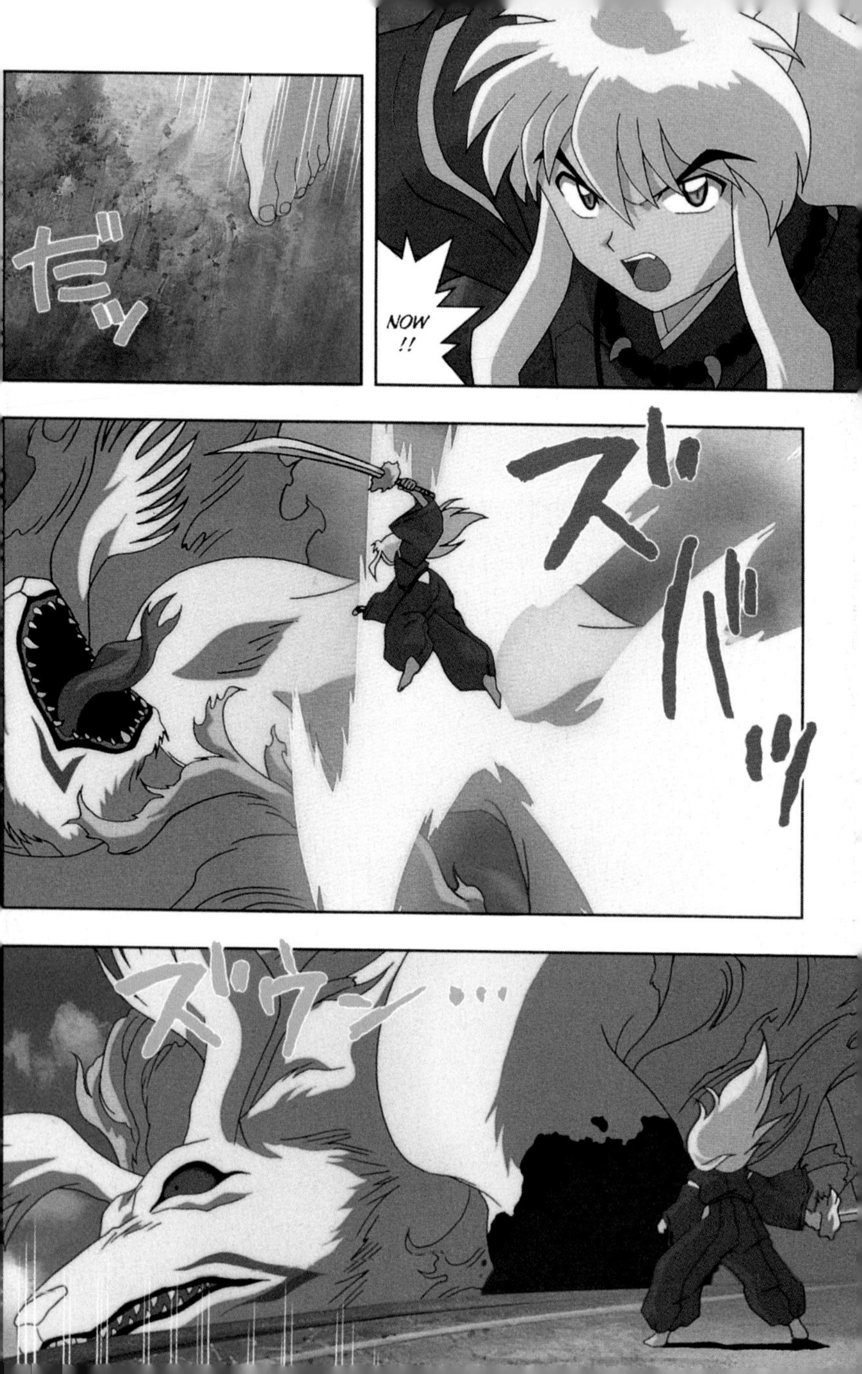
NOW !!
だッ
ズバッ
ズウーン…

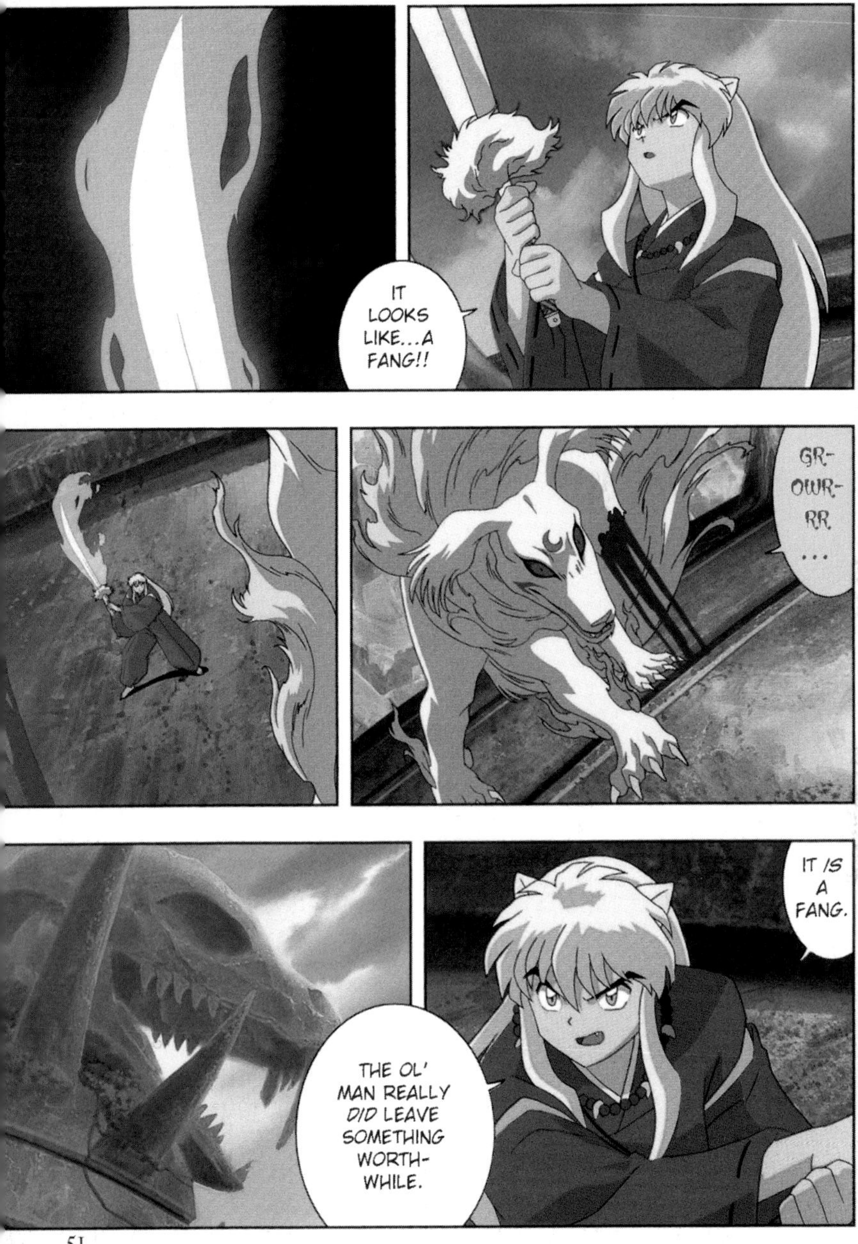
IT LOOKS LIKE...A FANG!!
GR-OWR-RR. . . .
IT *IS* A FANG.
THE OL' MAN REALLY *DID* LEAVE SOMETHING WORTH-WHILE.

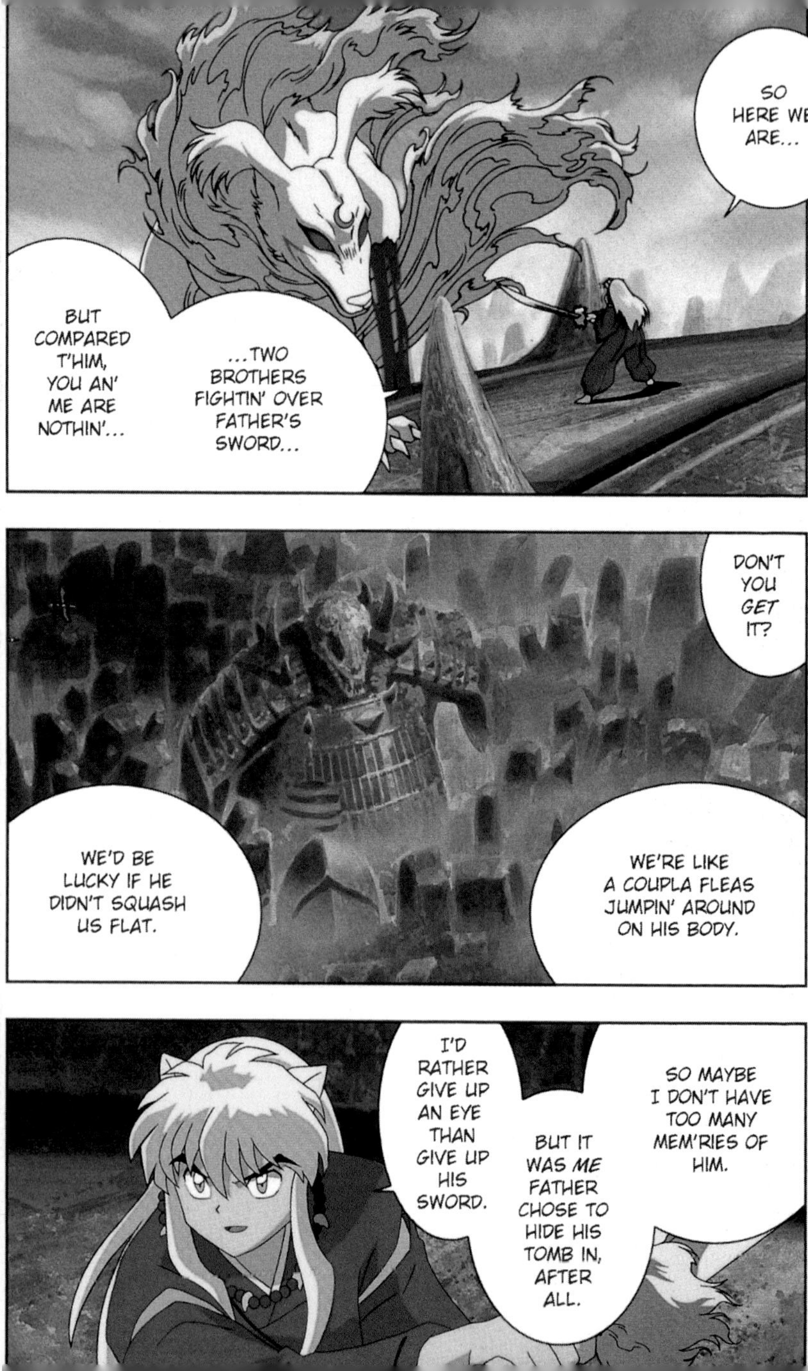
SO HERE WE ARE...
...TWO BROTHERS FIGHTIN' OVER FATHER'S SWORD...
BUT COMPARED T'HIM, YOU AN' ME ARE NOTHIN'...
DON'T YOU *GET* IT?
WE'RE LIKE A COUPLA FLEAS JUMPIN' AROUND ON HIS BODY.
WE'D BE LUCKY IF HE DIDN'T SQUASH US FLAT.
SO MAYBE I DON'T HAVE TOO MANY MEM'RIES OF HIM.
BUT IT WAS *ME* FATHER CHOSE TO HIDE HIS TOMB IN, AFTER ALL.
I'D RATHER GIVE UP AN EYE THAN GIVE UP HIS SWORD.

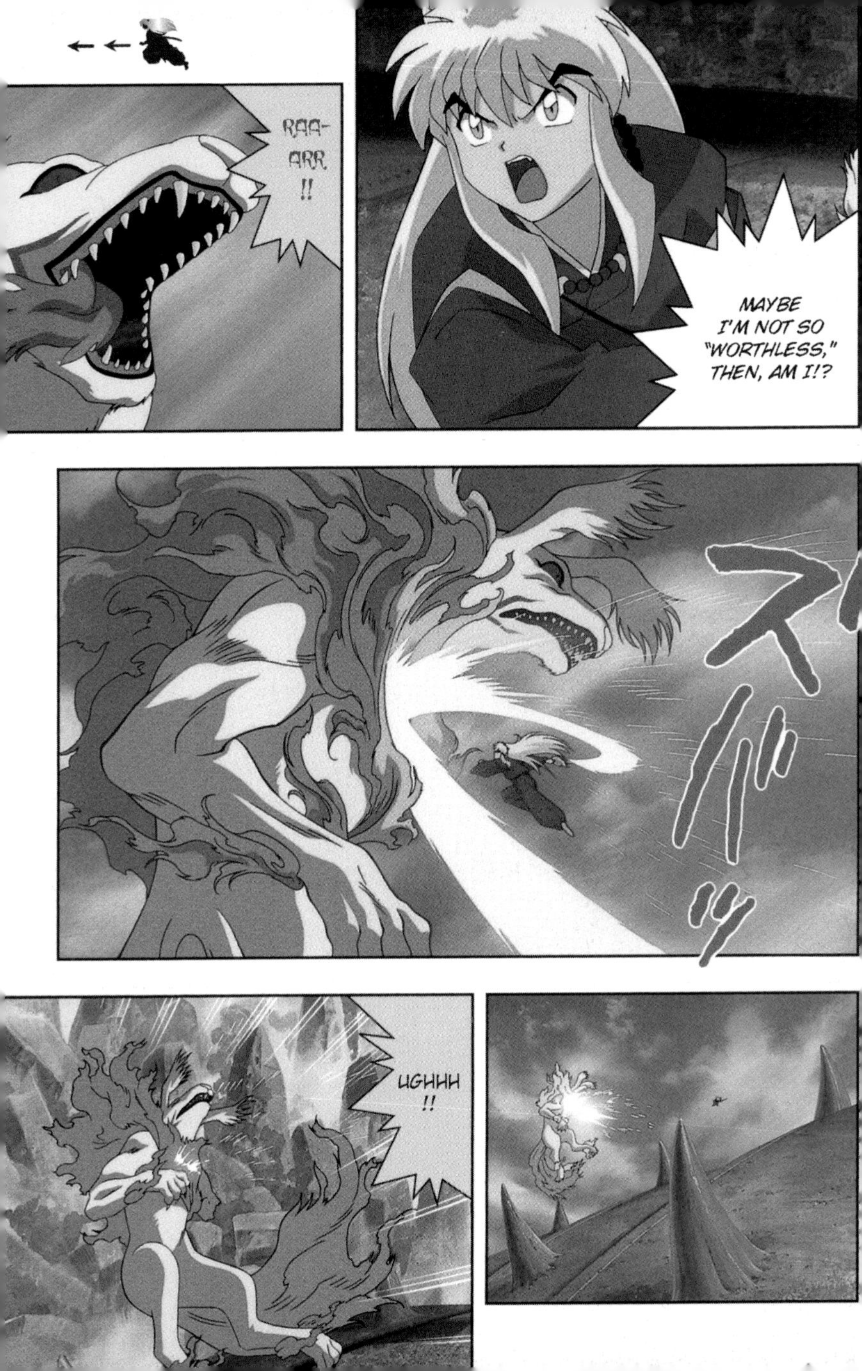
MAYBE I'M NOT SO "WORTHLESS," THEN, AM I!?
RAA-ARR !!
ズバッ
UGHHH !!

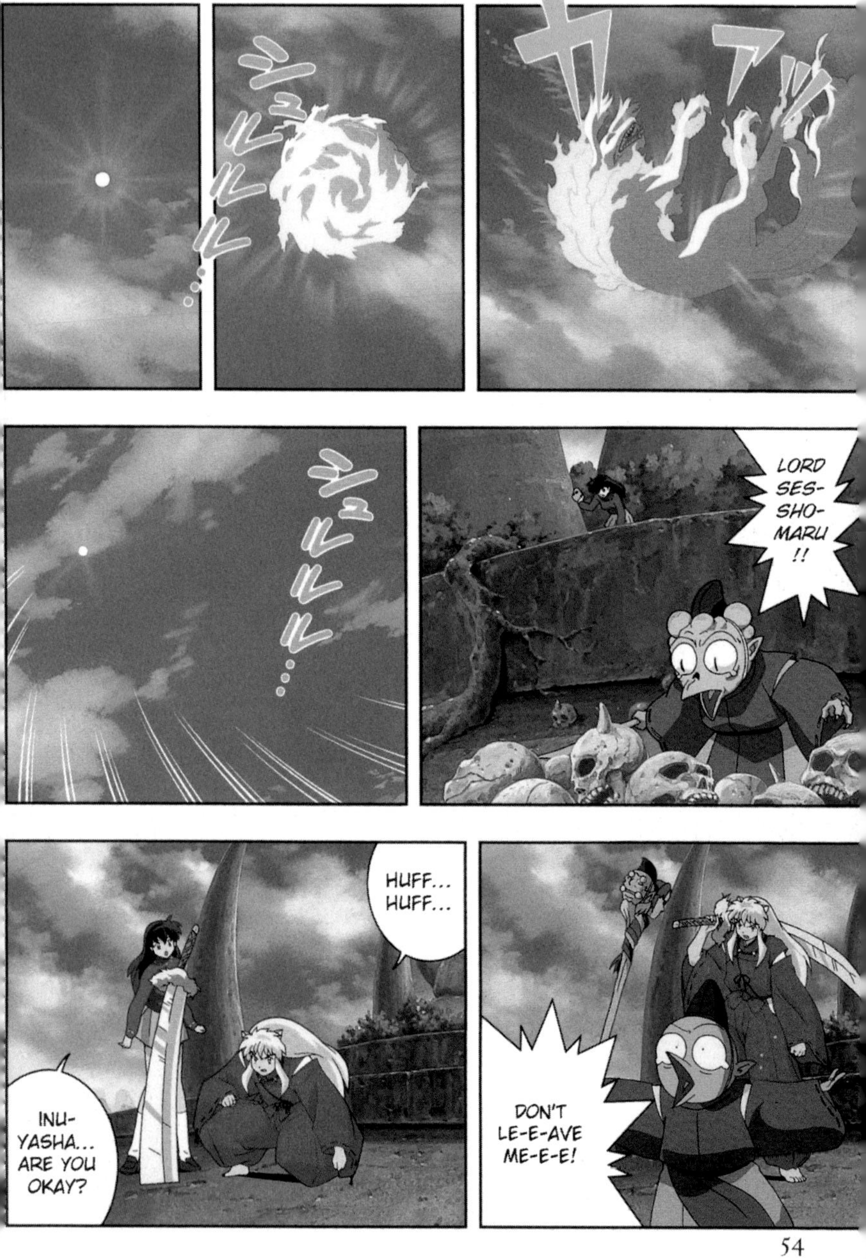
カァッ!!
シュルルルル…
LORD SES-SHO-MARU!!
シュルルルル…
DON'T LE-E-AVE ME-E-E!
HUFF... HUFF...
INU-YASHA... ARE YOU OKAY?

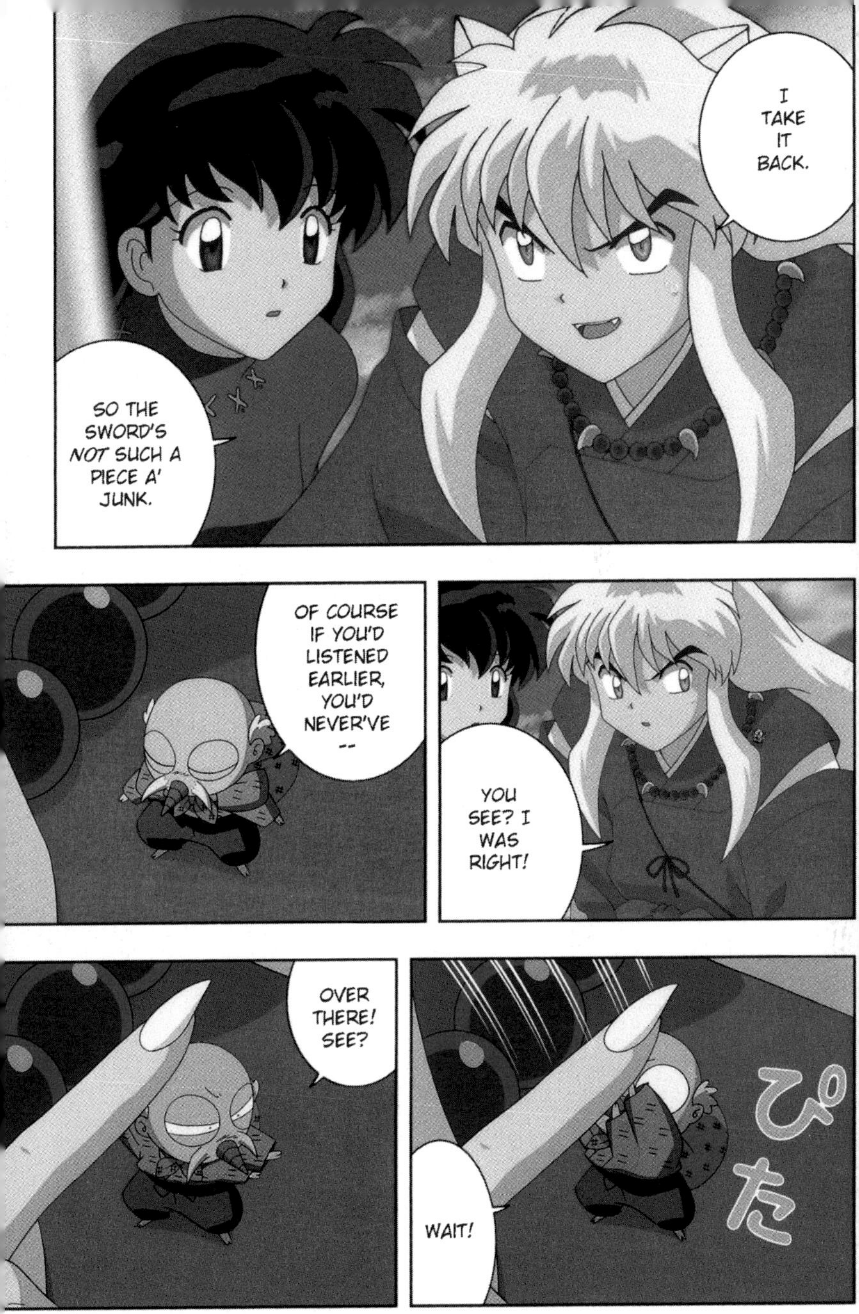

I TAKE IT BACK.
SO THE SWORD'S NOT SUCH A PIECE A' JUNK.
YOU SEE? I WAS RIGHT!
OF COURSE IF YOU'D LISTENED EARLIER, YOU'D NEVER'VE --
ぴた
WAIT!
OVER THERE! SEE?

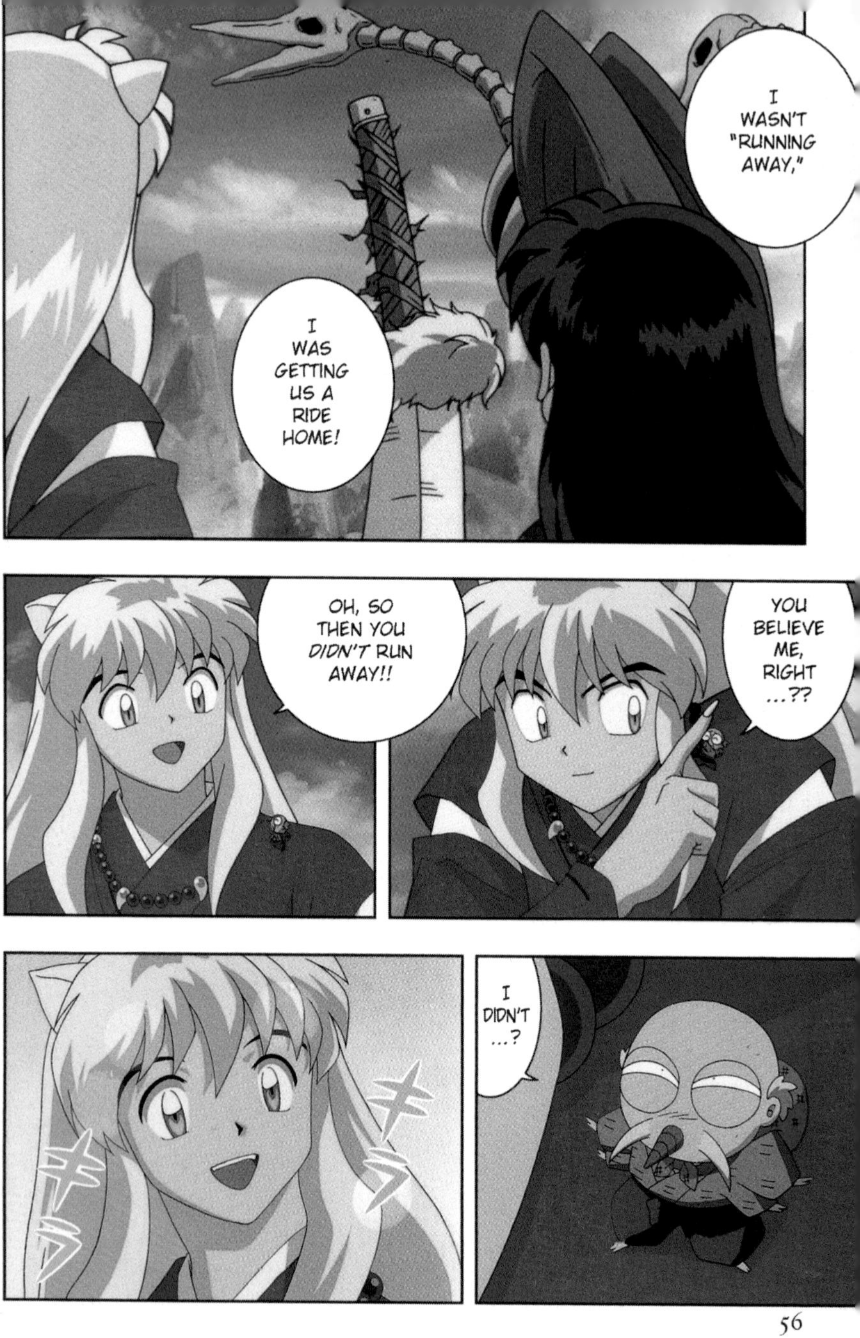
I WASN'T "RUNNING AWAY,"
I WAS GETTING US A RIDE HOME!
YOU BELIEVE ME, RIGHT ...??
OH, SO THEN YOU *DIDN'T* RUN AWAY!!
I DIDN'T ...?

OKAY, I ADMIT IT, I RAN AWAY.

...UH...

BUT YOU HAVE TO BELIEVE ME! IF I HAD KNOWN YOU'D MAKE A COMEBACK, I WOULD NEVER HAVE LEFT YOU!!

I'M ASHAMED OF MYSELF.

I OUGHT TO HAVE MORE FAITH. PLEASE, FORGIVE ME... IF ONLY I COULD MAKE IT UP TO YOU--

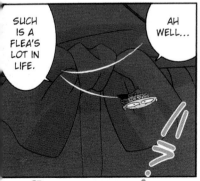

SUCH IS A FLEA'S LOT IN LIFE.

AH WELL...

ARGH!!

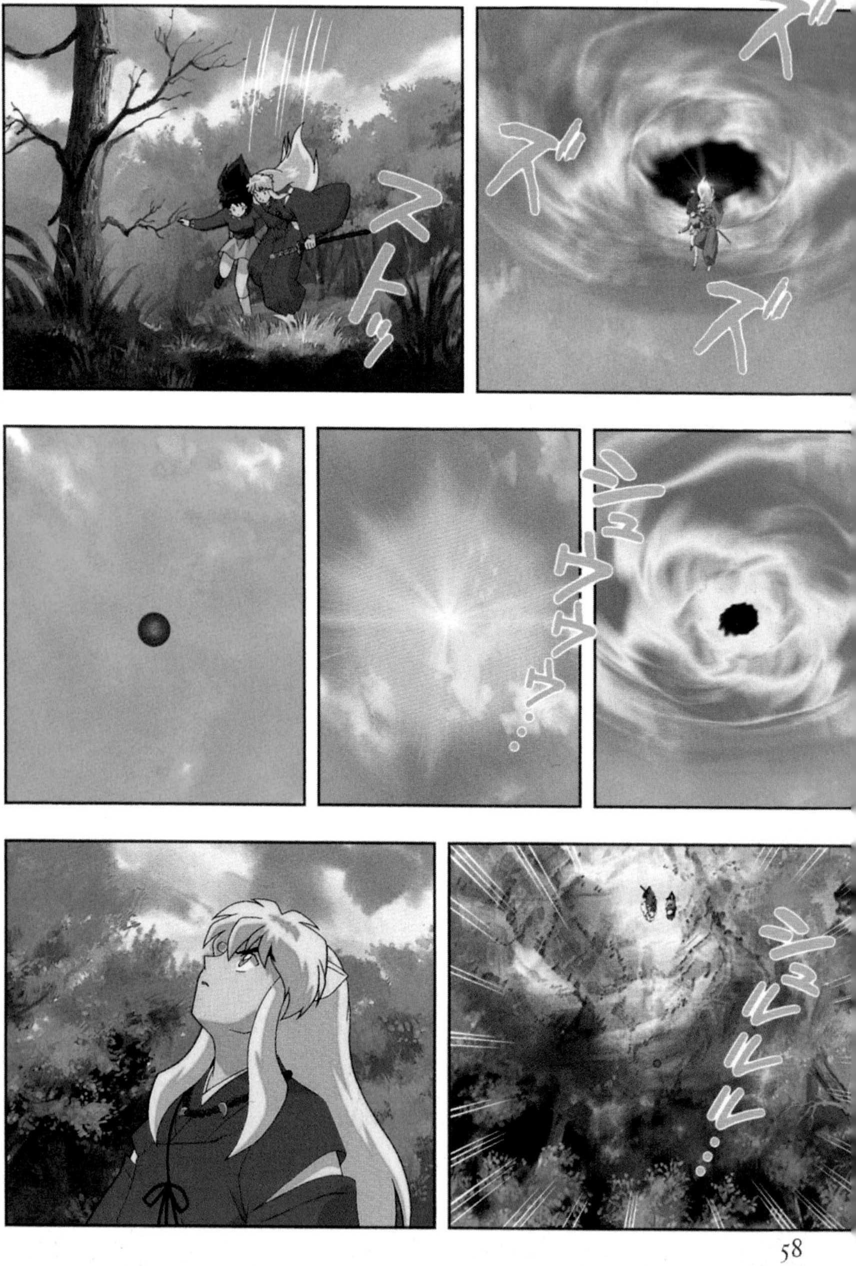
ズ
ズ
ズ
ストッ
シュヴヴヴ…
シュルルル…

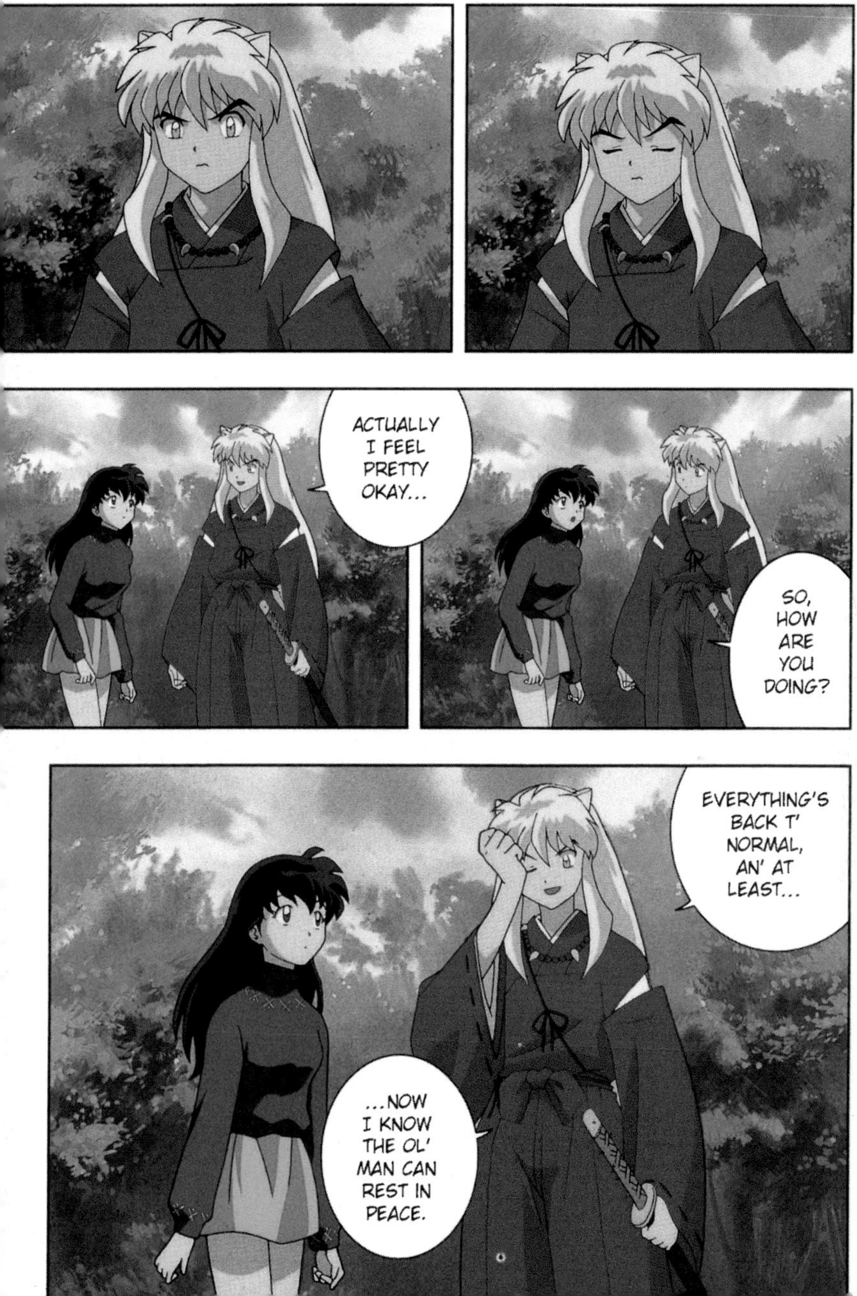
SO, HOW ARE YOU DOING?
ACTUALLY I FEEL PRETTY OKAY...
EVERYTHING'S BACK T' NORMAL, AN' AT LEAST...
...NOW I KNOW THE OL' MAN CAN REST IN PEACE.

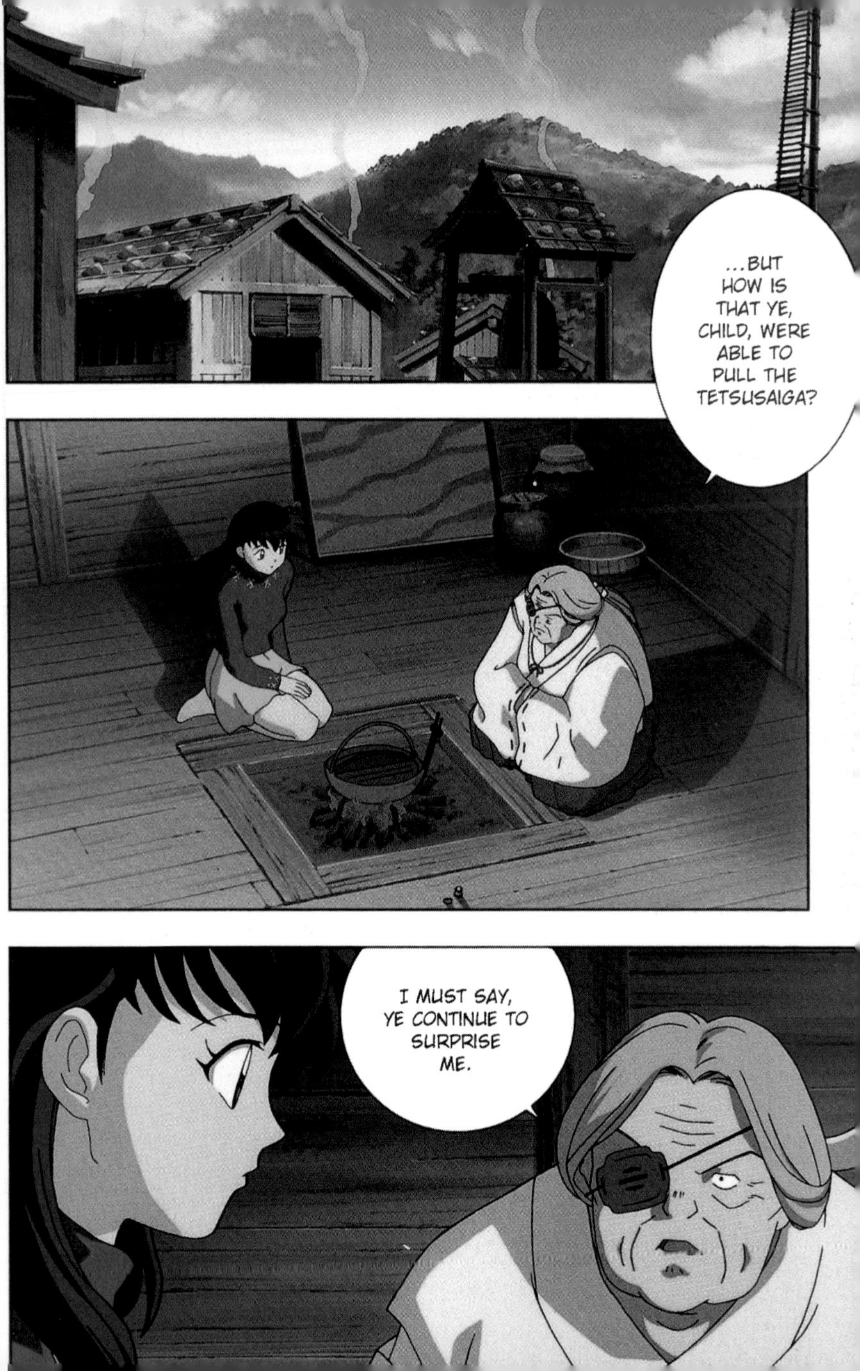
...BUT HOW IS THAT YE, CHILD, WERE ABLE TO PULL THE TETSUSAIGA?
I MUST SAY, YE CONTINUE TO SURPRISE ME.

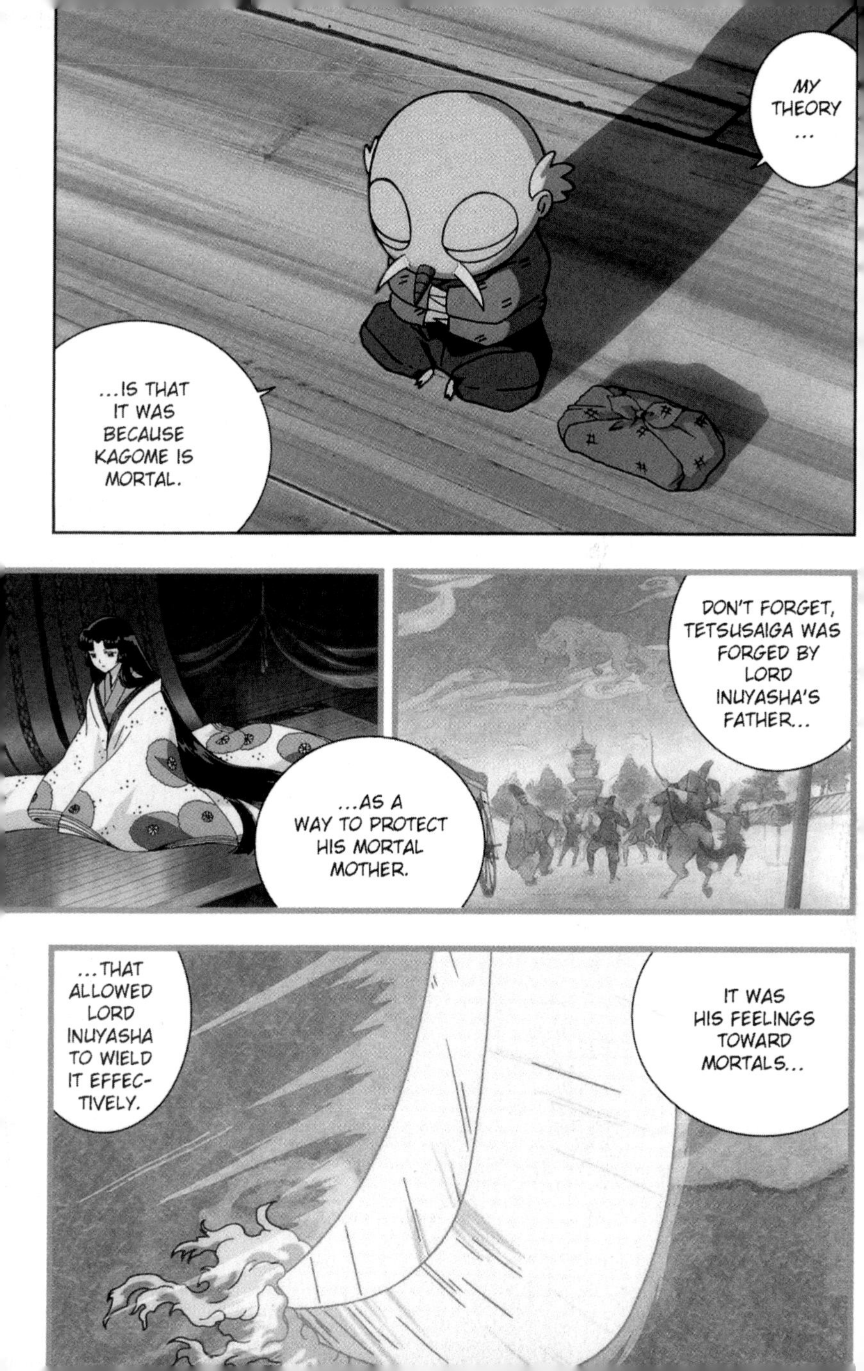
MY THEORY ...
...IS THAT IT WAS BECAUSE KAGOME IS MORTAL.
DON'T FORGET, TETSUSAIGA WAS FORGED BY LORD INUYASHA'S FATHER...
...AS A WAY TO PROTECT HIS MORTAL MOTHER.
IT WAS HIS FEELINGS TOWARD MORTALS...
...THAT ALLOWED LORD INUYASHA TO WIELD IT EFFEC-TIVELY.

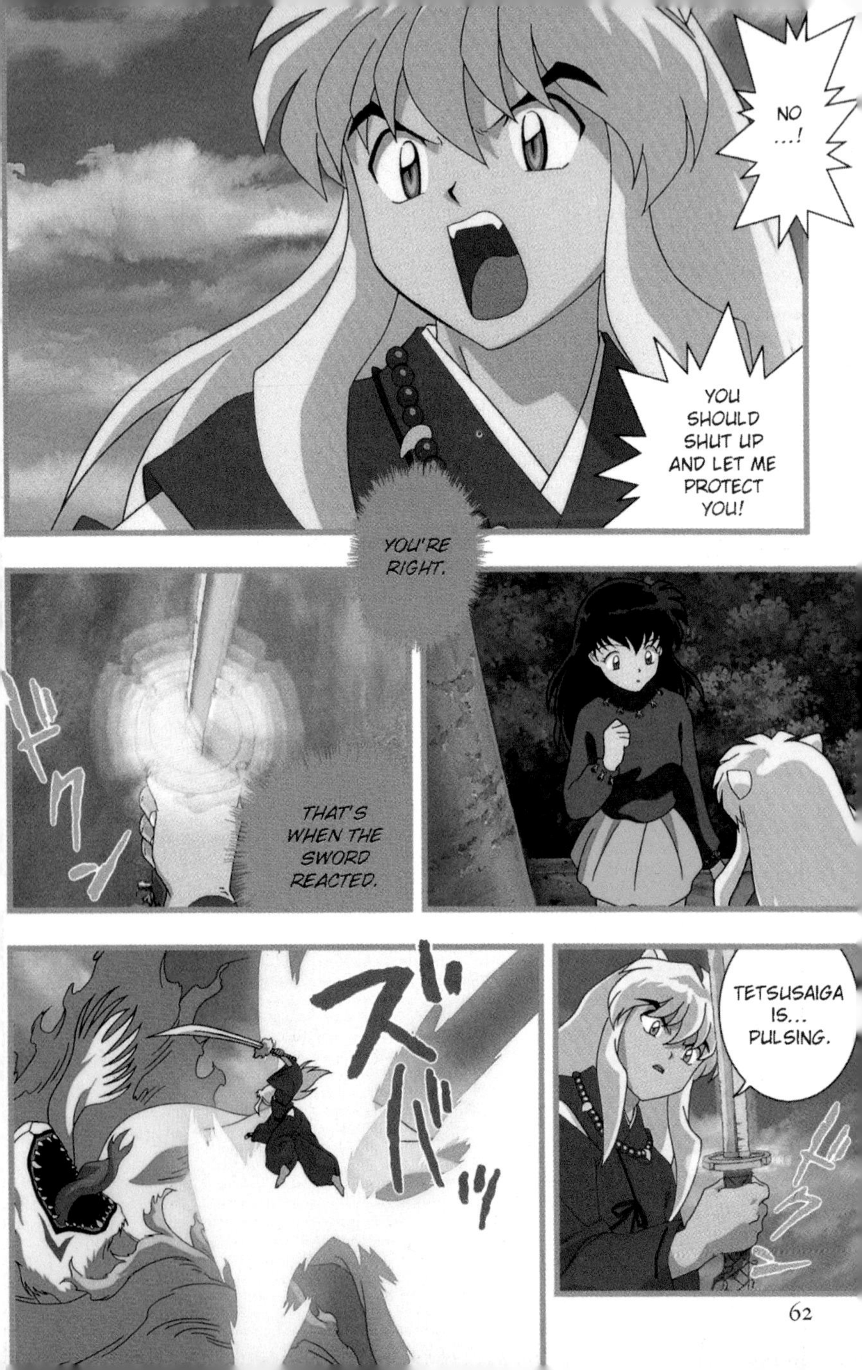
NO ...!
YOU SHOULD SHUT UP AND LET ME PROTECT YOU!
YOU'RE RIGHT.
THAT'S WHEN THE SWORD REACTED.
TETSUSAIGA IS... PULSING.
ズバッ

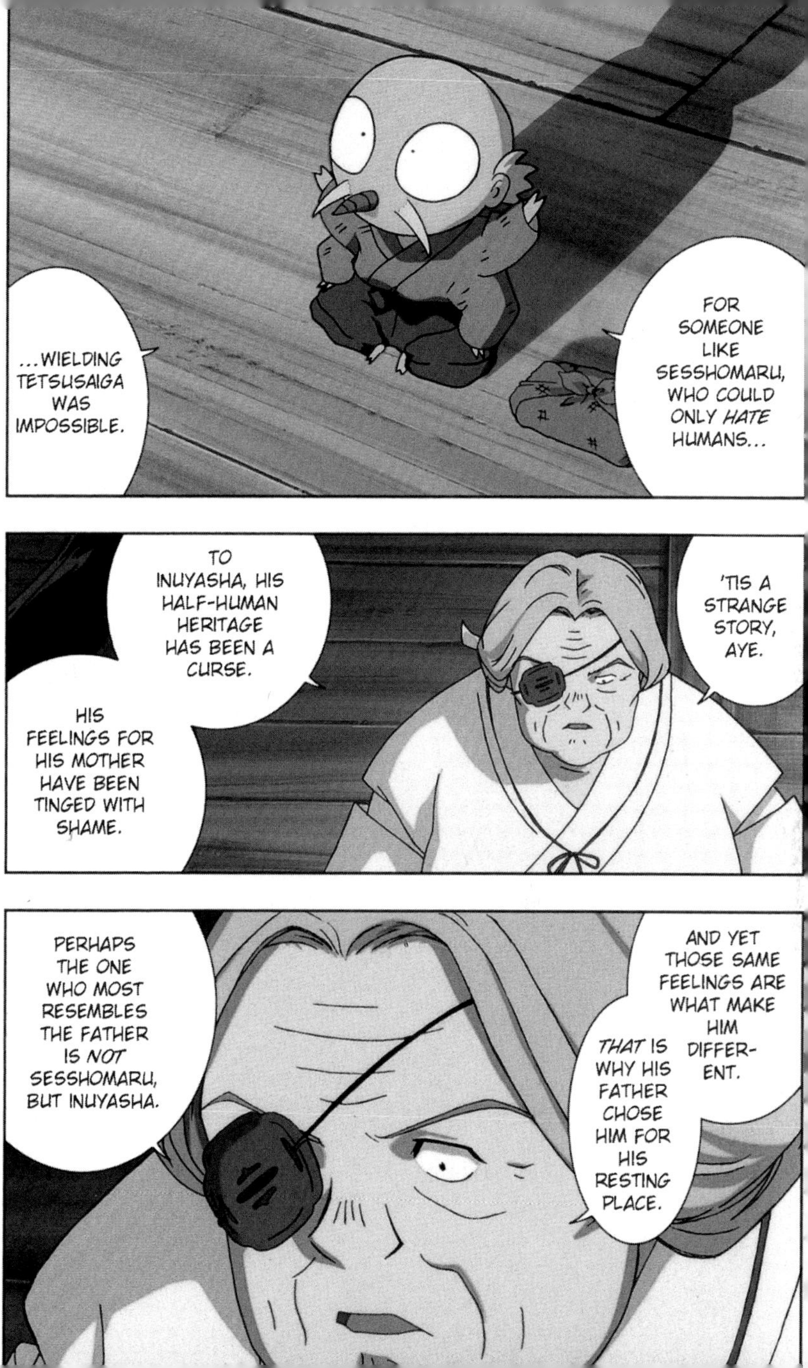
FOR SOMEONE LIKE SESSHOMARU, WHO COULD ONLY *HATE* HUMANS...
...WIELDING TETSUSAIGA WAS IMPOSSIBLE.
'TIS A STRANGE STORY, AYE.
TO INUYASHA, HIS HALF-HUMAN HERITAGE HAS BEEN A CURSE.
HIS FEELINGS FOR HIS MOTHER HAVE BEEN TINGED WITH SHAME.
AND YET THOSE SAME FEELINGS ARE WHAT MAKE HIM DIFFER-ENT.
THAT IS WHY HIS FATHER CHOSE HIM FOR HIS RESTING PLACE.
PERHAPS THE ONE WHO MOST RESEMBLES THE FATHER IS *NOT* SESSHOMARU, BUT INUYASHA.

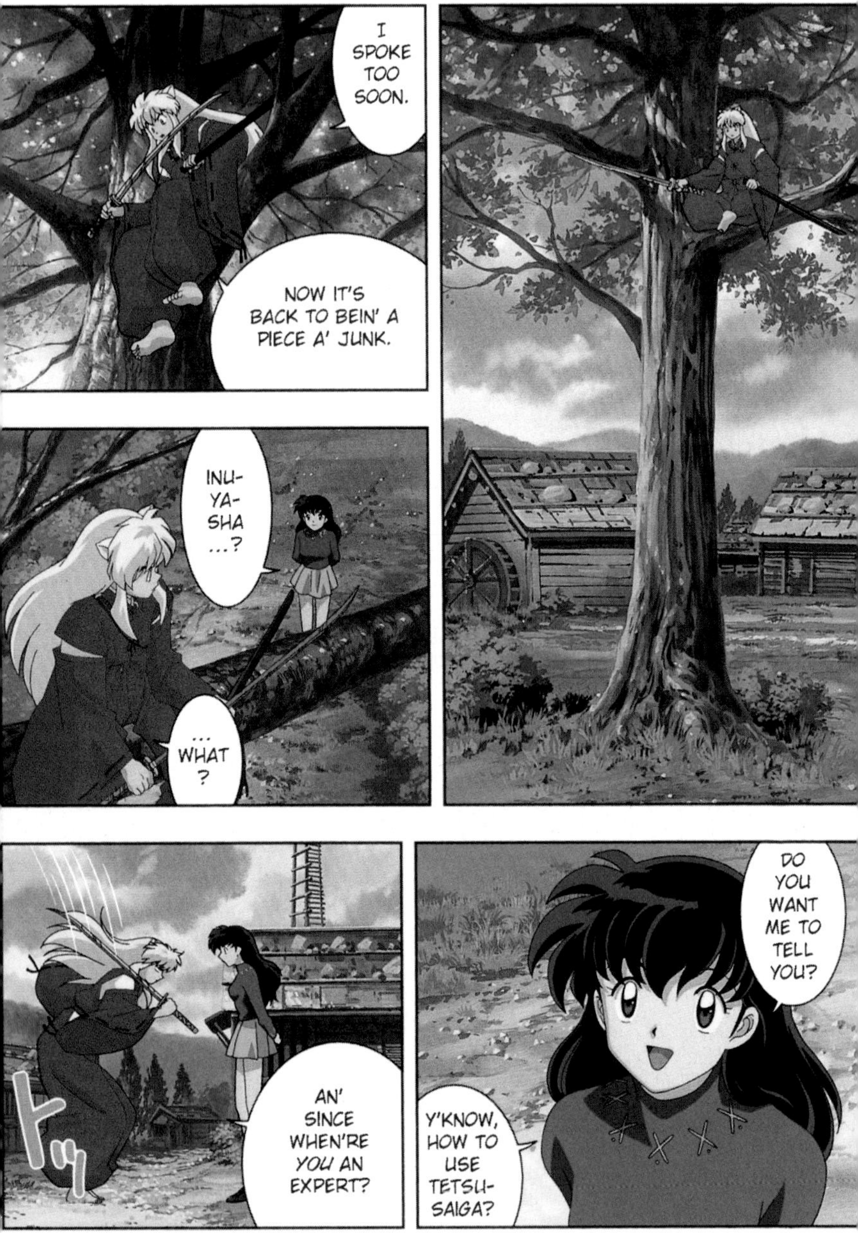
I SPOKE TOO SOON.
NOW IT'S BACK TO BEIN' A PIECE A' JUNK.
INU-YA-SHA ...?
... WHAT ?
DO YOU WANT ME TO TELL YOU?
Y'KNOW, HOW TO USE TETSU-SAIGA?
AN' SINCE WHEN'RE *YOU* AN EXPERT?

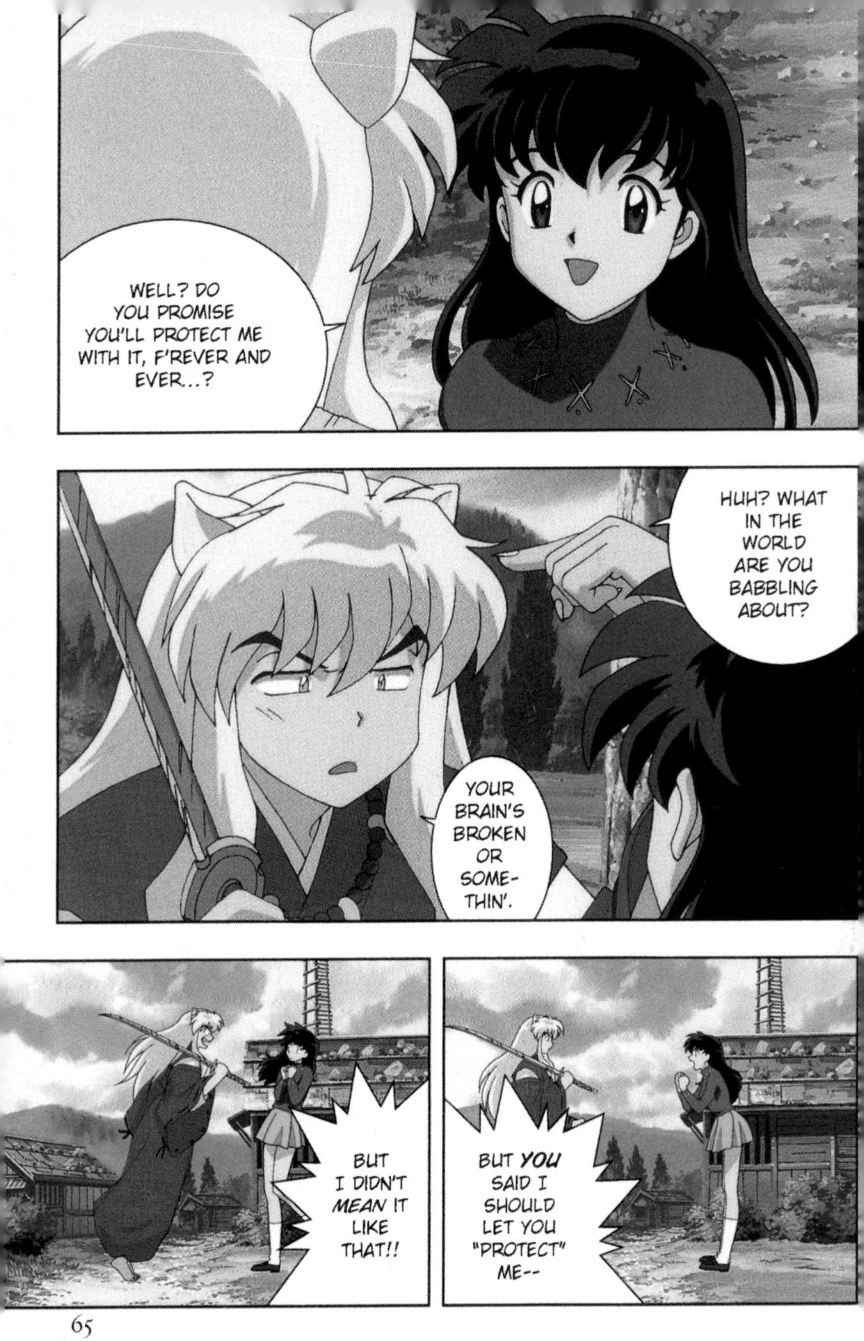
WELL? DO YOU PROMISE YOU'LL PROTECT ME WITH IT, F'REVER AND EVER...?
HUH? WHAT IN THE WORLD ARE YOU BABBLING ABOUT?
YOUR BRAIN'S BROKEN OR SOME-THIN'.
BUT *YOU* SAID I SHOULD LET YOU "PROTECT" ME--
BUT I DIDN'T *MEAN* IT LIKE THAT!!

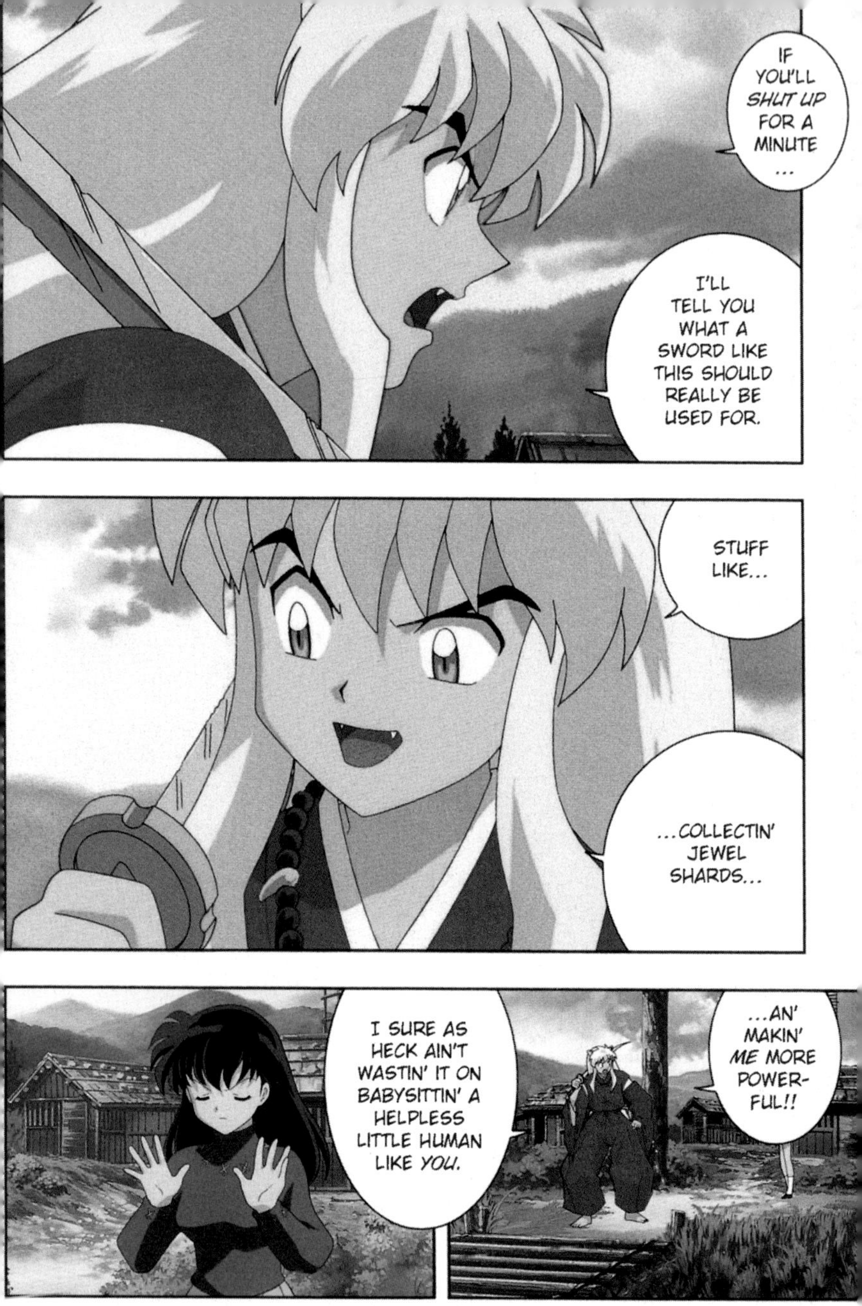
IF YOU'LL *SHUT UP* FOR A MINUTE ...
I'LL TELL YOU WHAT A SWORD LIKE THIS SHOULD REALLY BE USED FOR.
STUFF LIKE...
...COLLECTIN' JEWEL SHARDS...
...AN' MAKIN' *ME* MORE POWER-FUL!!
I SURE AS HECK AIN'T WASTIN' IT ON BABYSITTIN' A HELPLESS LITTLE HUMAN LIKE *YOU*.

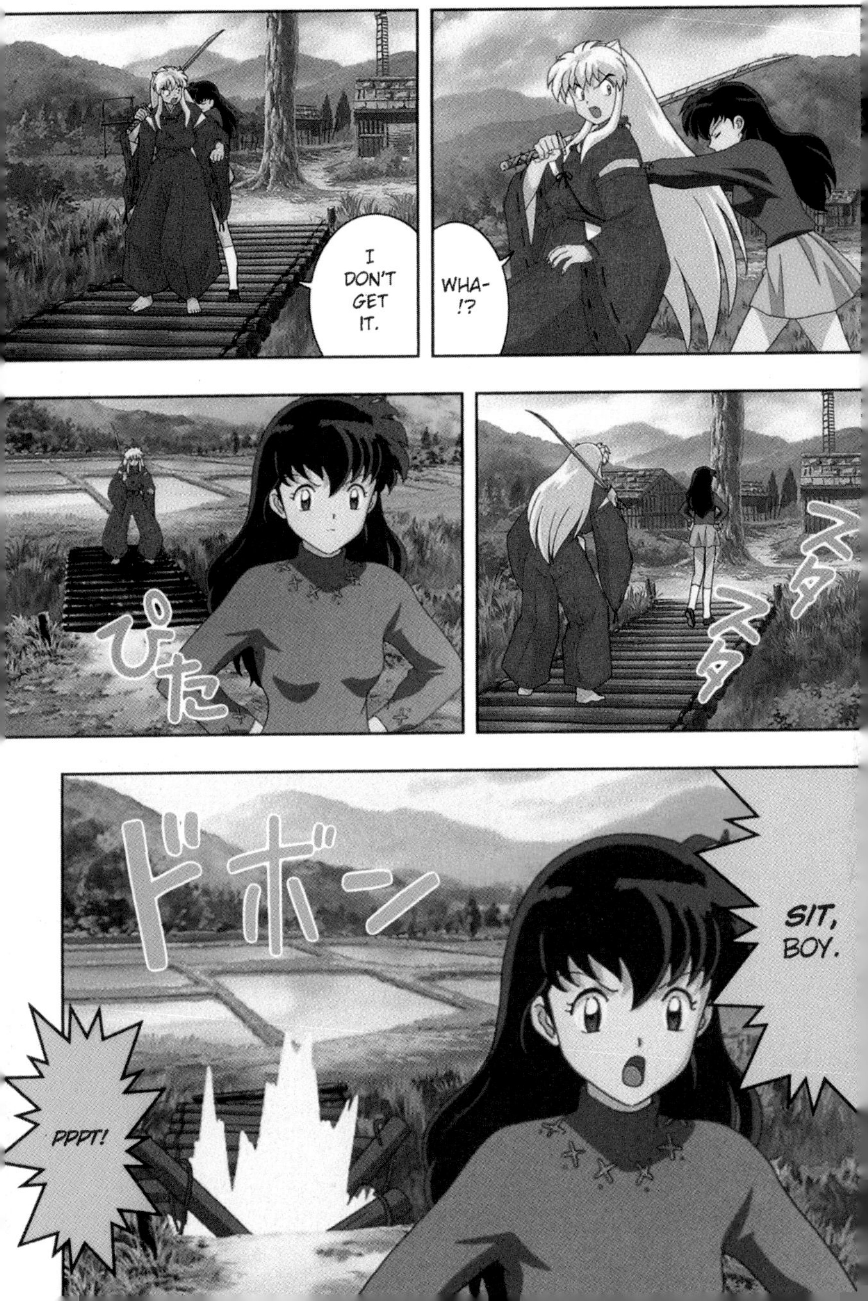
WHA-!?
I DON'T GET IT.
スタスタ
ぴた
SIT, BOY.
ドボン
PPPT!

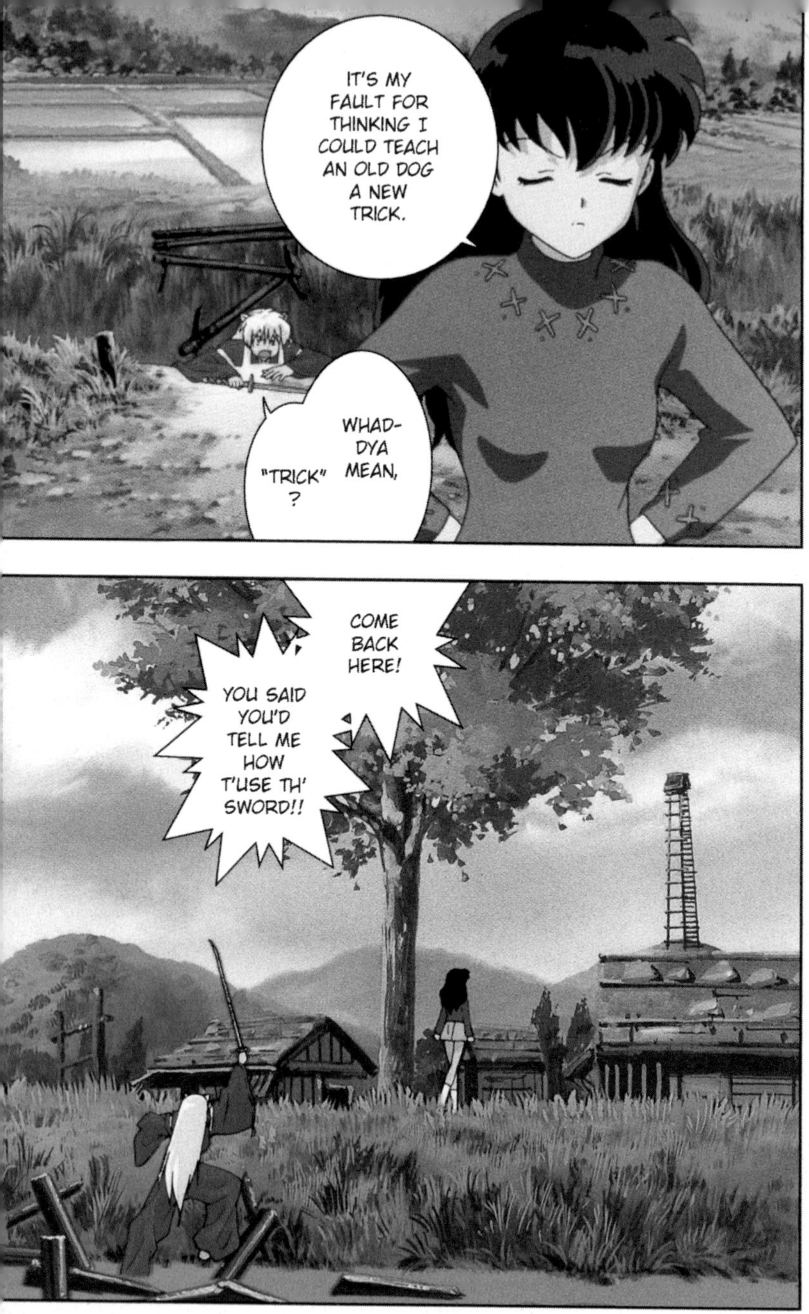
IT'S MY FAULT FOR THINKING I COULD TEACH AN OLD DOG A NEW TRICK.
WHAD-DYA MEAN, "TRICK"?
COME BACK HERE!
YOU SAID YOU'D TELL ME HOW T'USE TH' SWORD!!

8
The Toad Who Would Be Prince

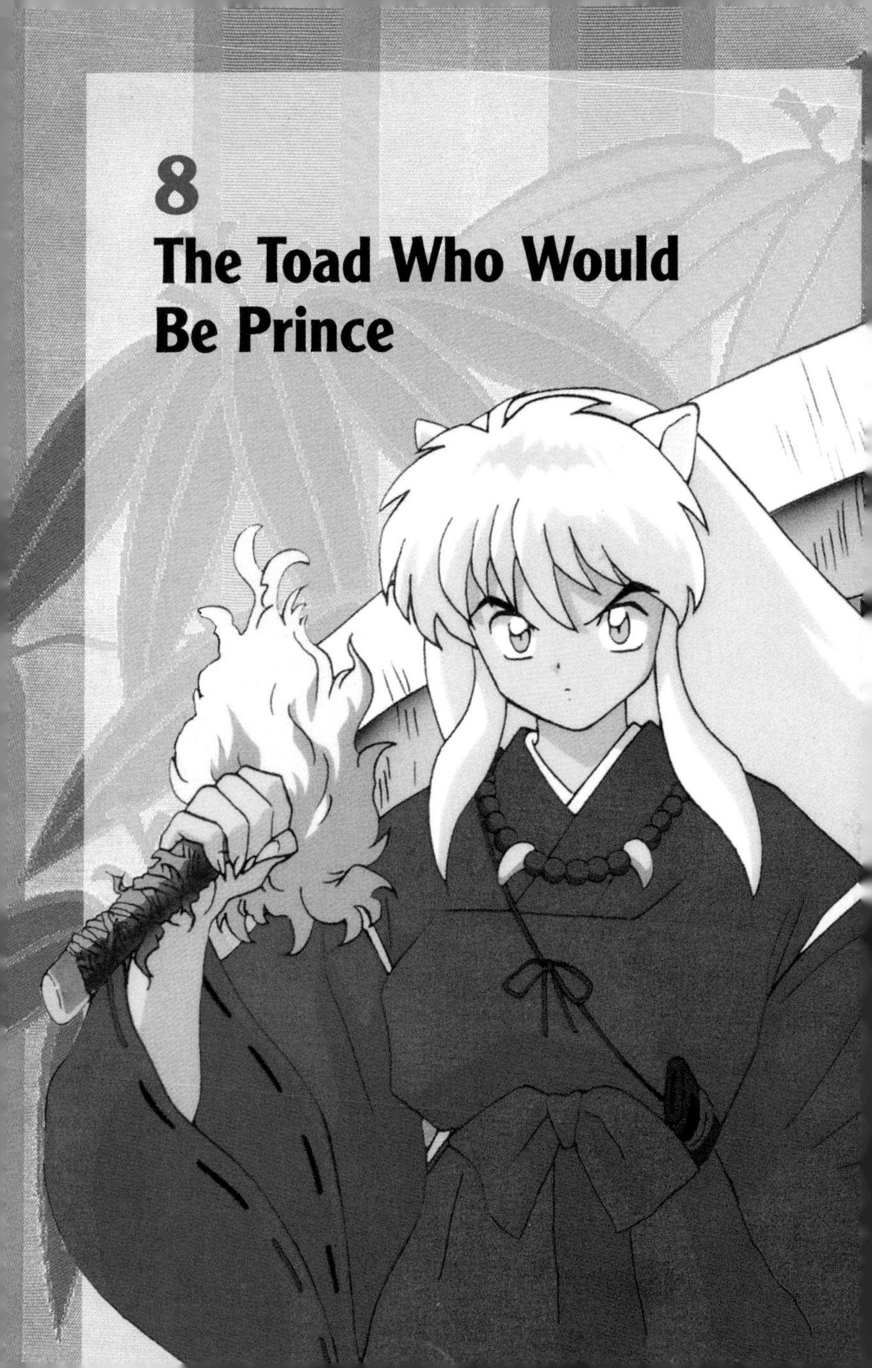

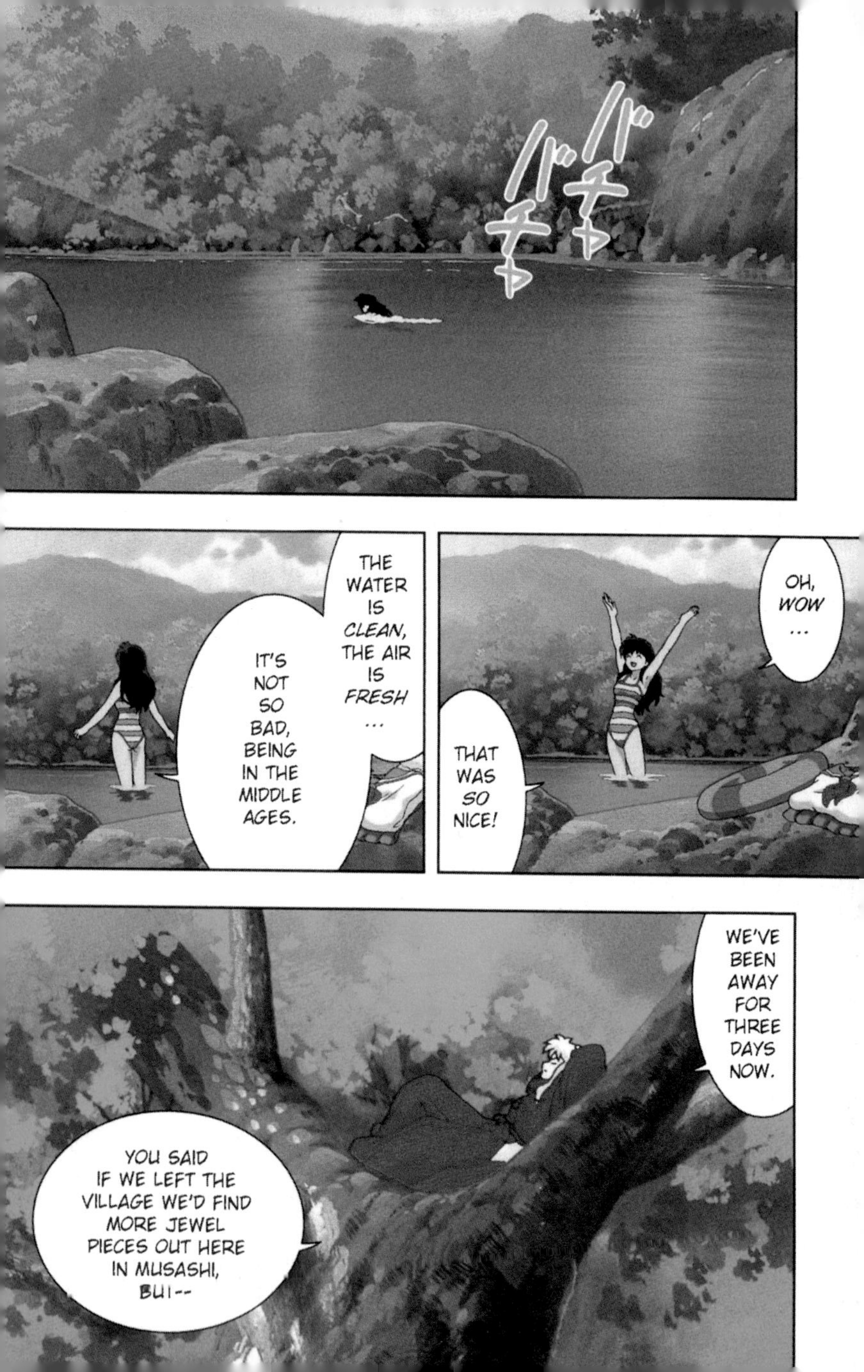
バチャ
バチャ
OH, WOW ...
THAT WAS SO NICE!
THE WATER IS CLEAN, THE AIR IS FRESH ...
IT'S NOT SO BAD, BEING IN THE MIDDLE AGES.
WE'VE BEEN AWAY FOR THREE DAYS NOW.
YOU SAID IF WE LEFT THE VILLAGE WE'D FIND MORE JEWEL PIECES OUT HERE IN MUSASHI, BUT--

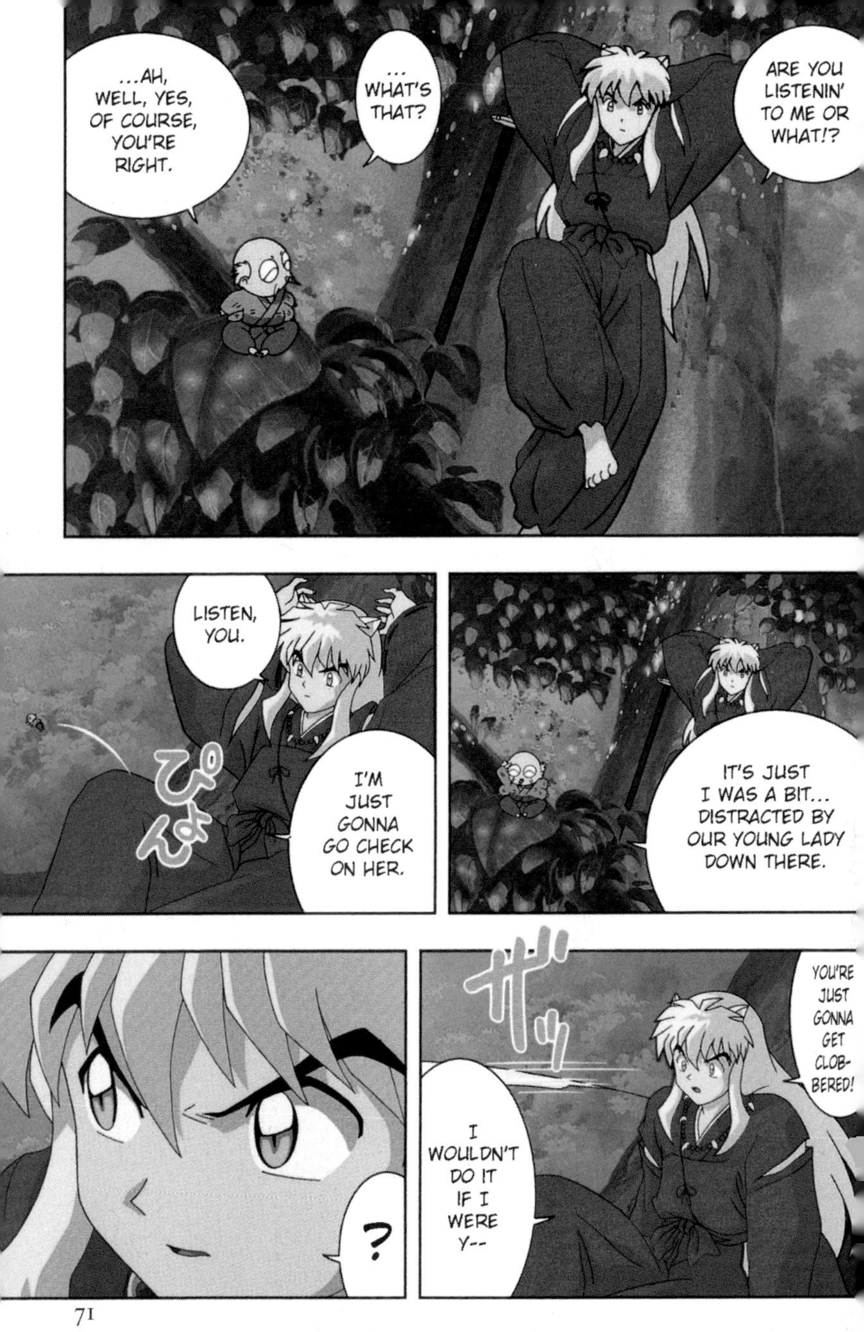
ARE YOU LISTENIN' TO ME OR WHAT!?
... WHAT'S THAT?
...AH, WELL, YES, OF COURSE, YOU'RE RIGHT.
IT'S JUST I WAS A BIT... DISTRACTED BY OUR YOUNG LADY DOWN THERE.
LISTEN, YOU.
ぴょん
I'M JUST GONNA GO CHECK ON HER.
ザッ
YOU'RE JUST GONNA GET CLOB-BERED!
I WOULDN'T DO IT IF I WERE Y--
?

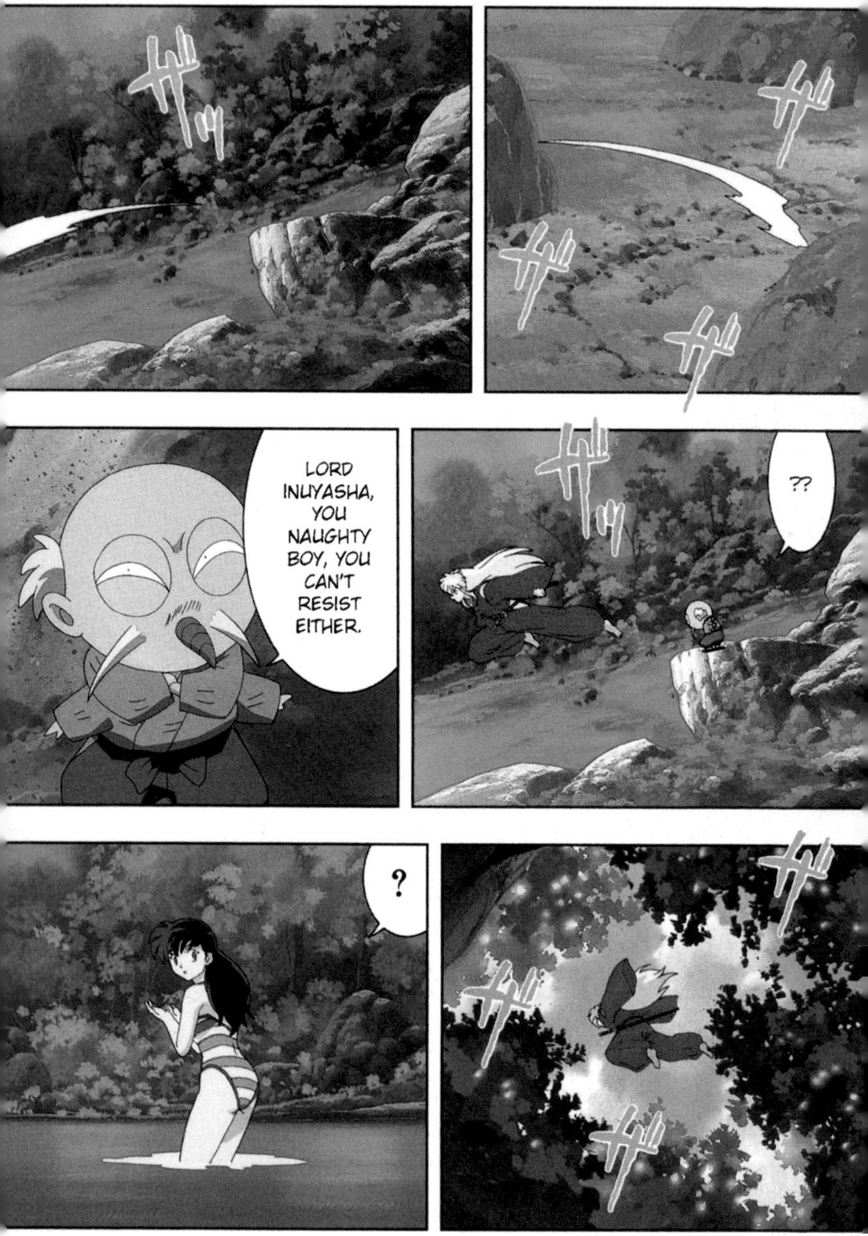
??
LORD INUYASHA, YOU NAUGHTY BOY, YOU CAN'T RESIST EITHER.
?

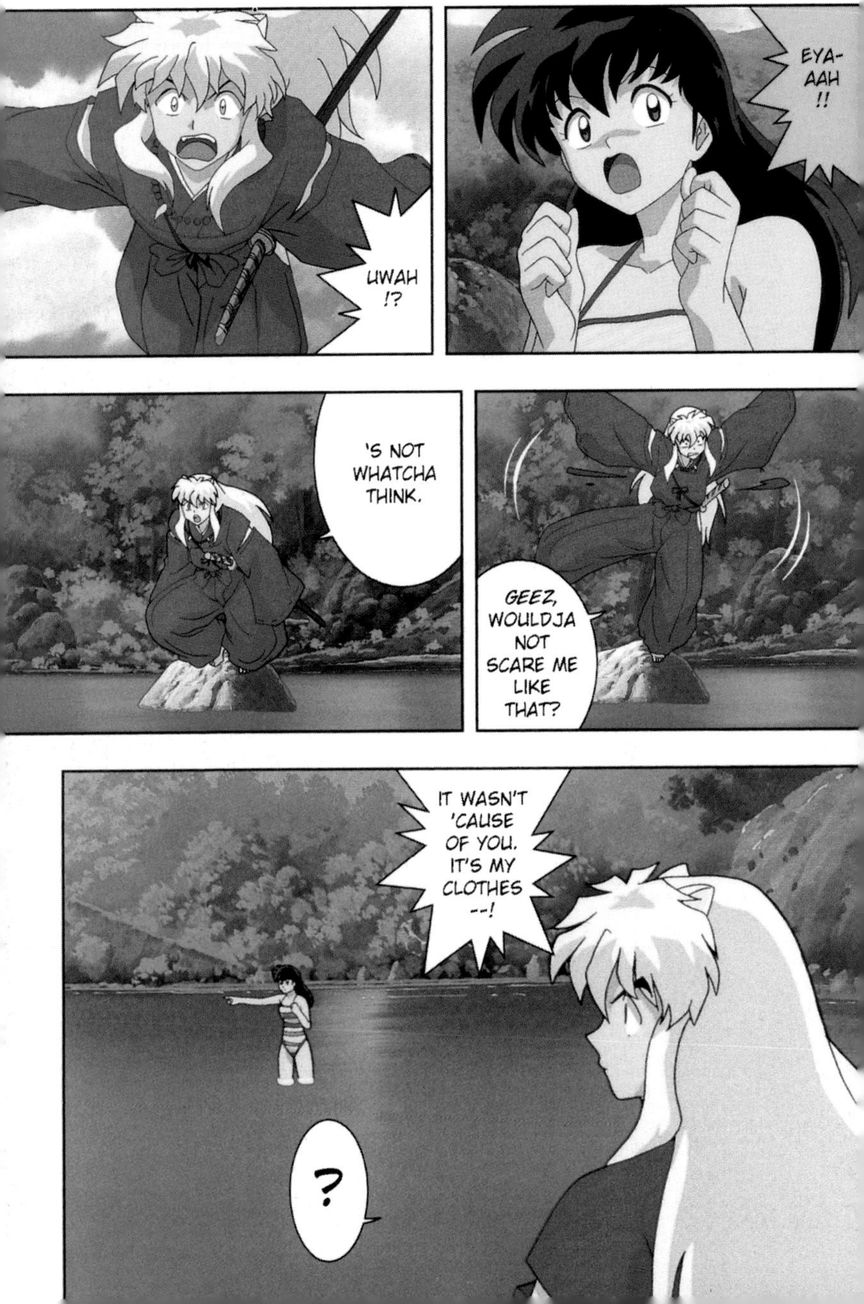
EYA-AAH !!
UWAH !?
GEEZ, WOULDJA NOT SCARE ME LIKE THAT?
'S NOT WHATCHA THINK.
IT WASN'T 'CAUSE OF YOU. IT'S MY CLOTHES --!
?

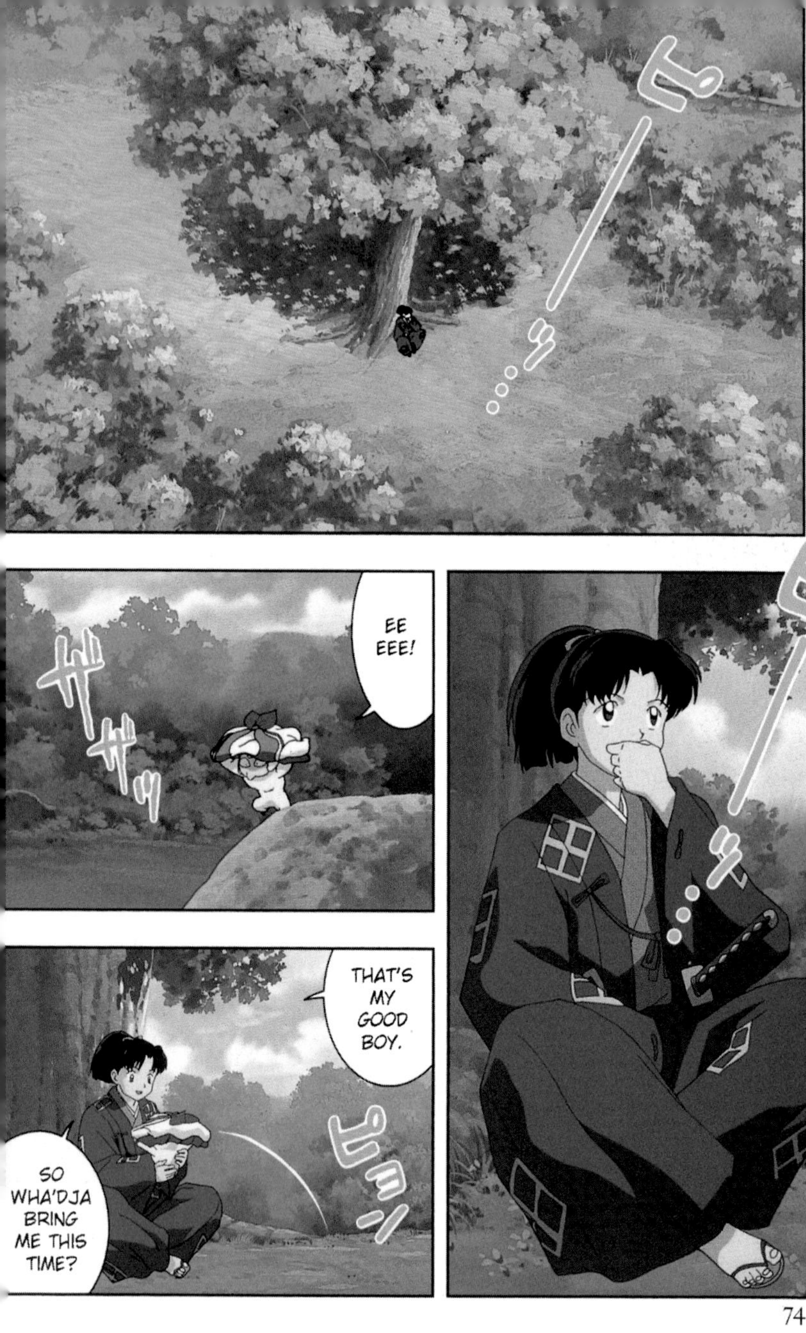
ピーーッ
ピーーッ
EE EEE!
ザザッ
THAT'S MY GOOD BOY.
SO WHA'DJA BRING ME THIS TIME?
ピョン

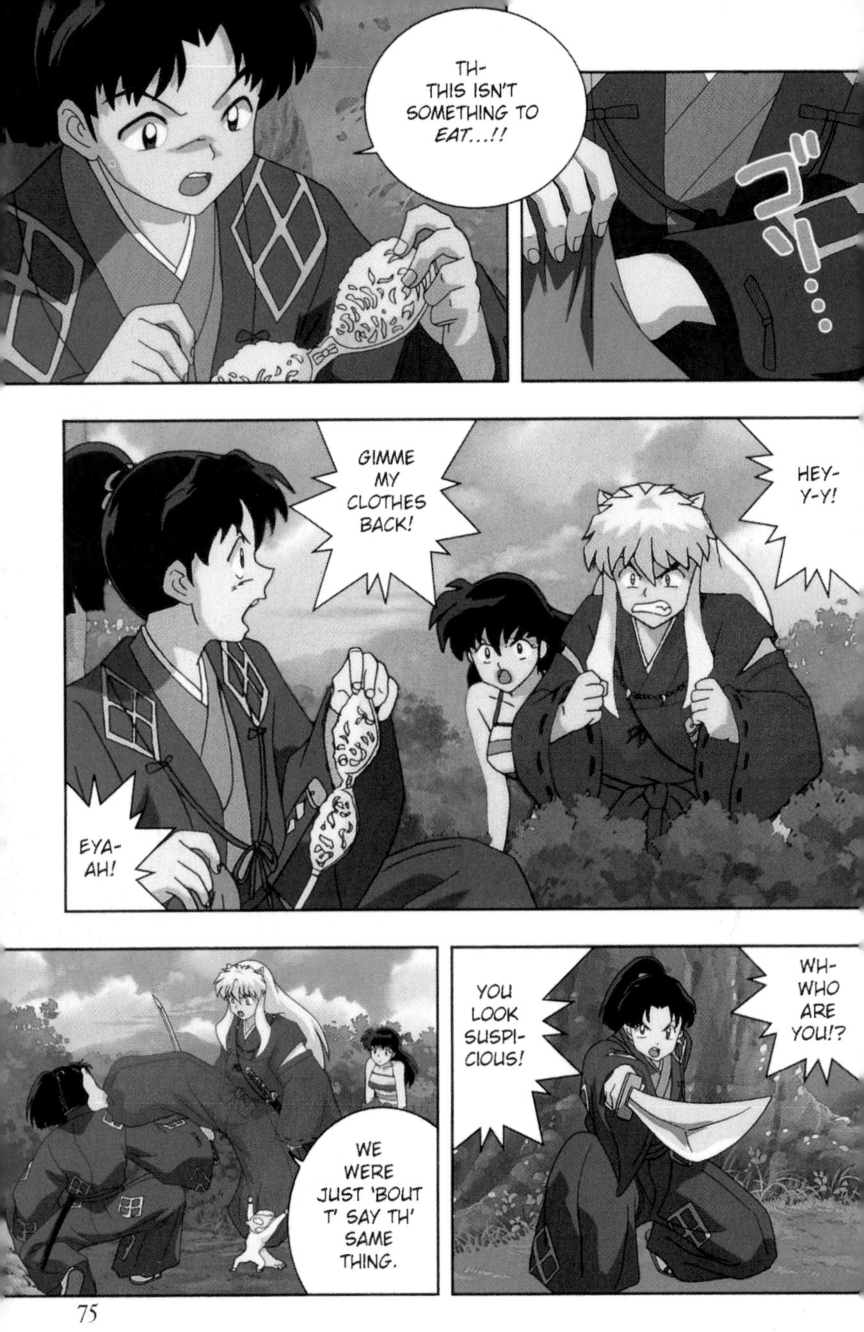
ゴソ…
TH- THIS ISN'T SOMETHING TO EAT...!!
HEY-Y-Y!
GIMME MY CLOTHES BACK!
EYA-AH!
WH- WHO ARE YOU!?
YOU LOOK SUSPI-CIOUS!
WE WERE JUST 'BOUT T' SAY TH' SAME THING.

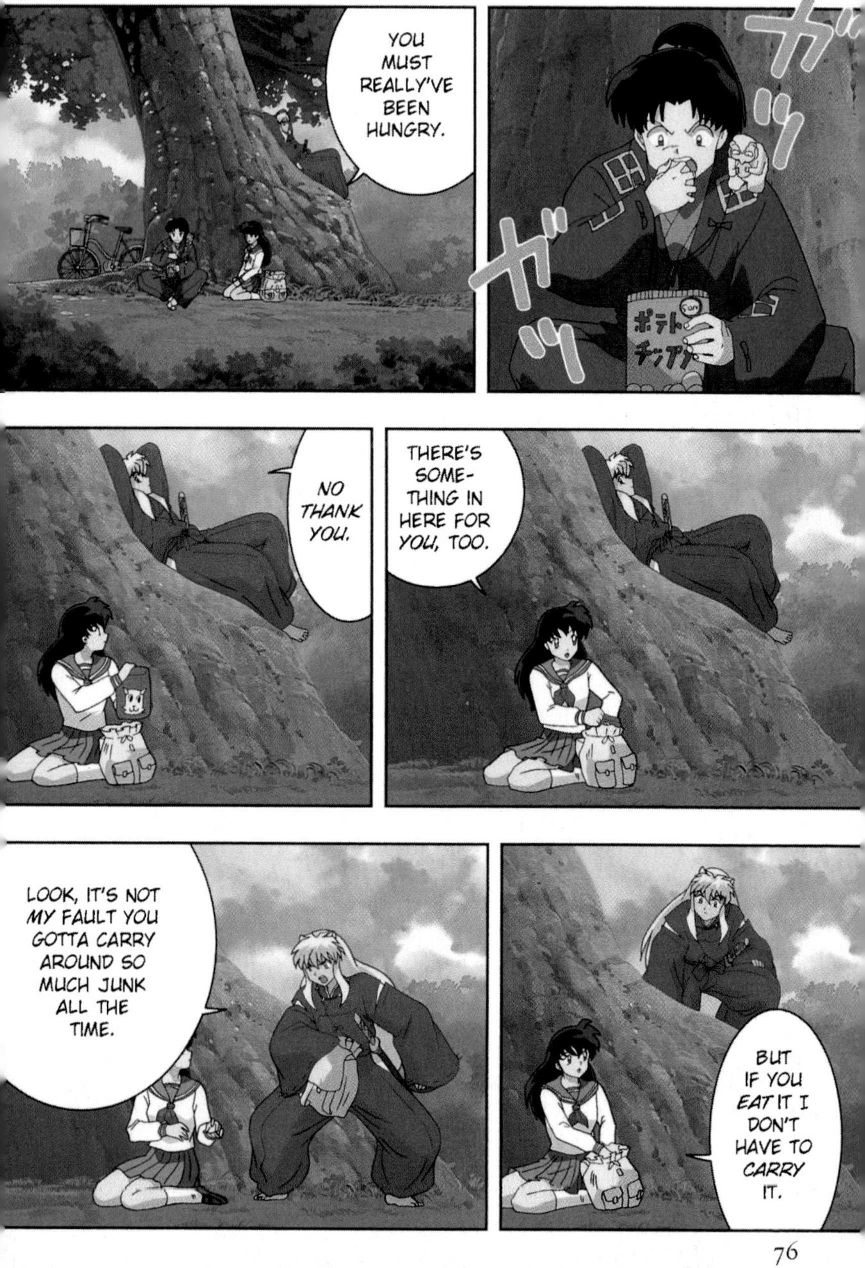
YOU MUST REALLY'VE BEEN HUNGRY.
THERE'S SOME-THING IN HERE FOR *YOU*, TOO.
NO THANK YOU.
BUT IF YOU *EAT* IT I DON'T HAVE TO *CARRY* IT.
LOOK, IT'S NOT *MY* FAULT YOU GOTTA CARRY AROUND SO MUCH JUNK ALL THE TIME.

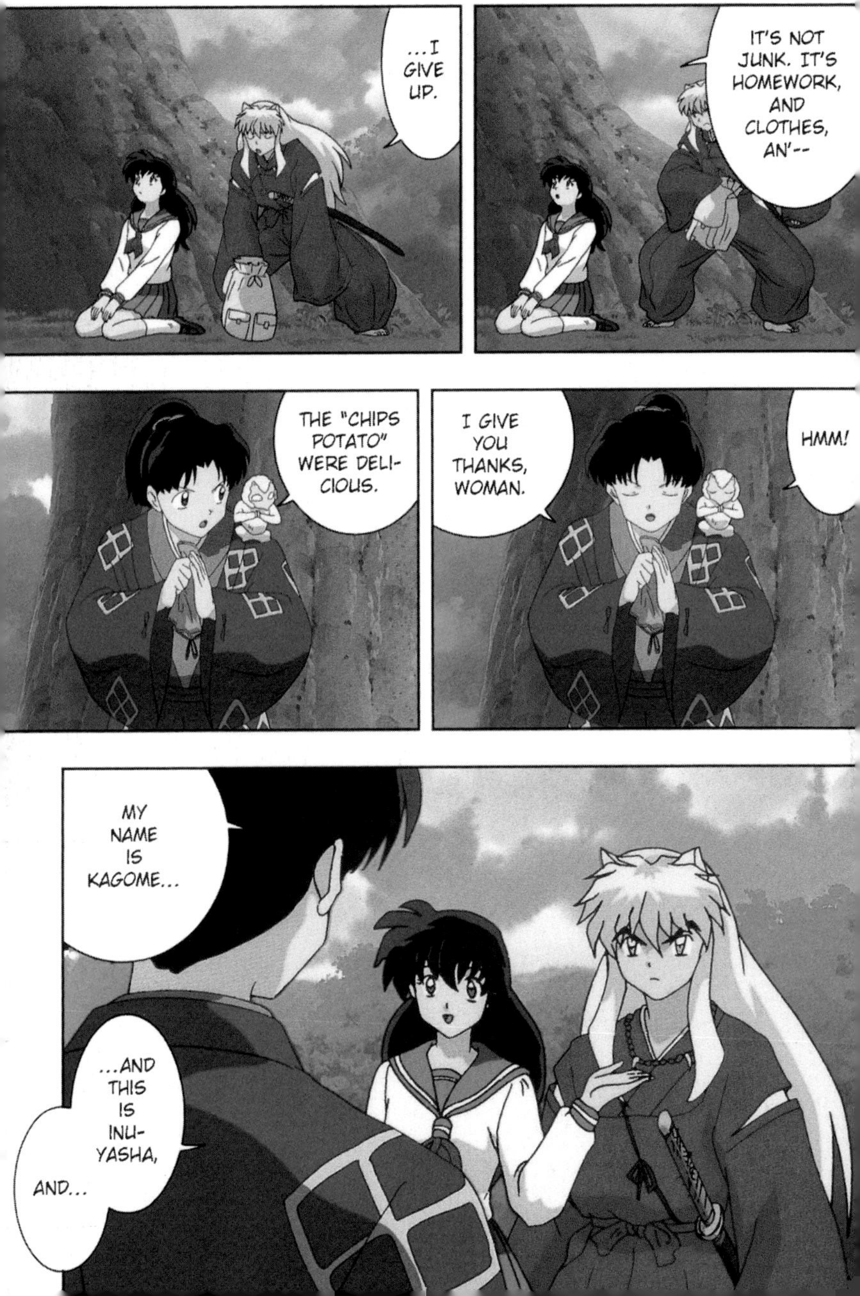

IT'S NOT JUNK. IT'S HOMEWORK, AND CLOTHES, AN'--
...I GIVE UP.
HMM!
I GIVE YOU THANKS, WOMAN.
THE "CHIPS POTATO" WERE DELI-CIOUS.
MY NAME IS KAGOME...
...AND THIS IS INU-YASHA,
AND...

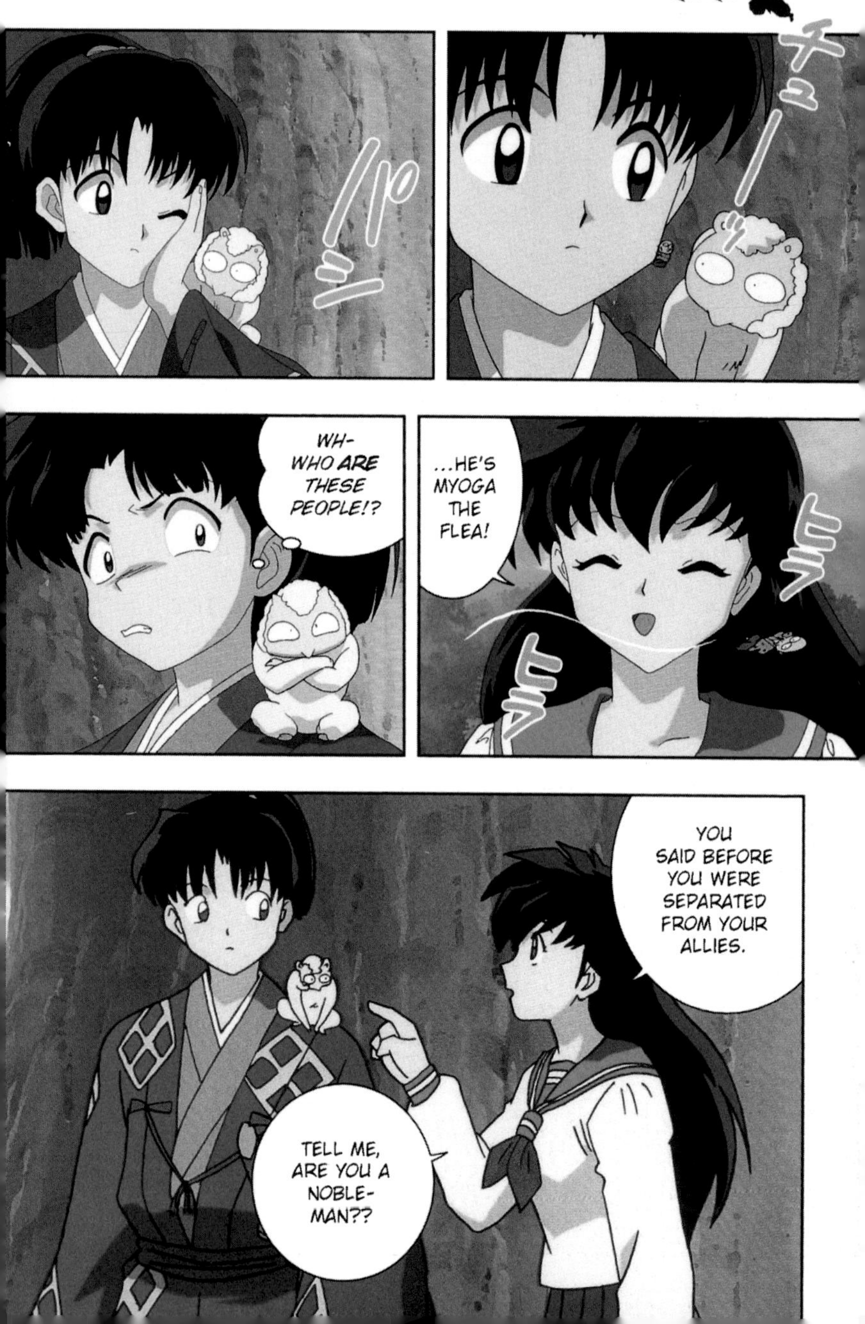
...HE'S MYOGA THE FLEA!
ヒラ
ヒラ
WH- WHO **ARE** THESE PEOPLE!?
YOU SAID BEFORE YOU WERE SEPARATED FROM YOUR ALLIES.
TELL ME, ARE YOU A NOBLE-MAN??

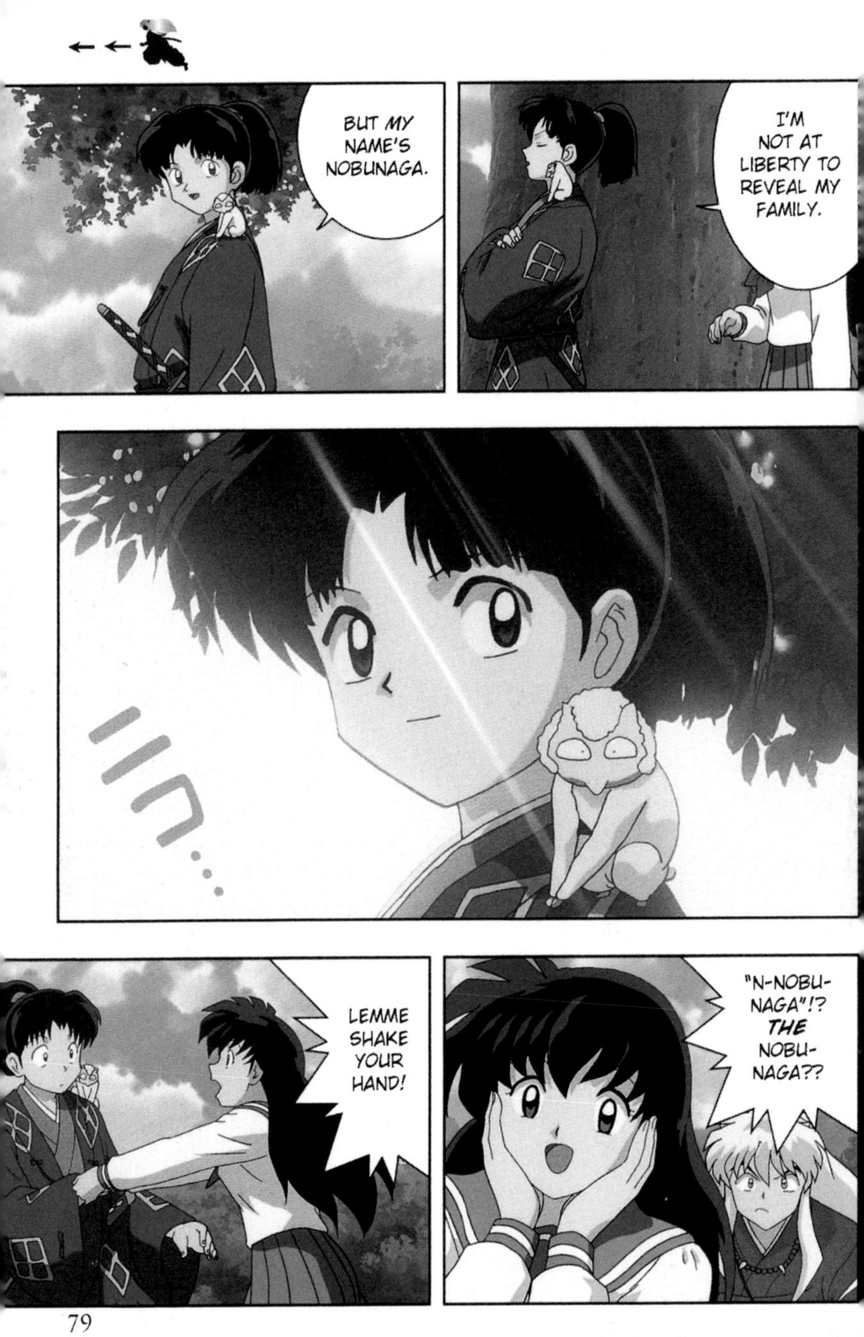
I'M NOT AT LIBERTY TO REVEAL MY FAMILY.
BUT *MY* NAME'S NOBUNAGA.
ニコ...
"N-NOBUNAGA"!? ***THE*** NOBUNAGA??
LEMME SHAKE YOUR HAND!

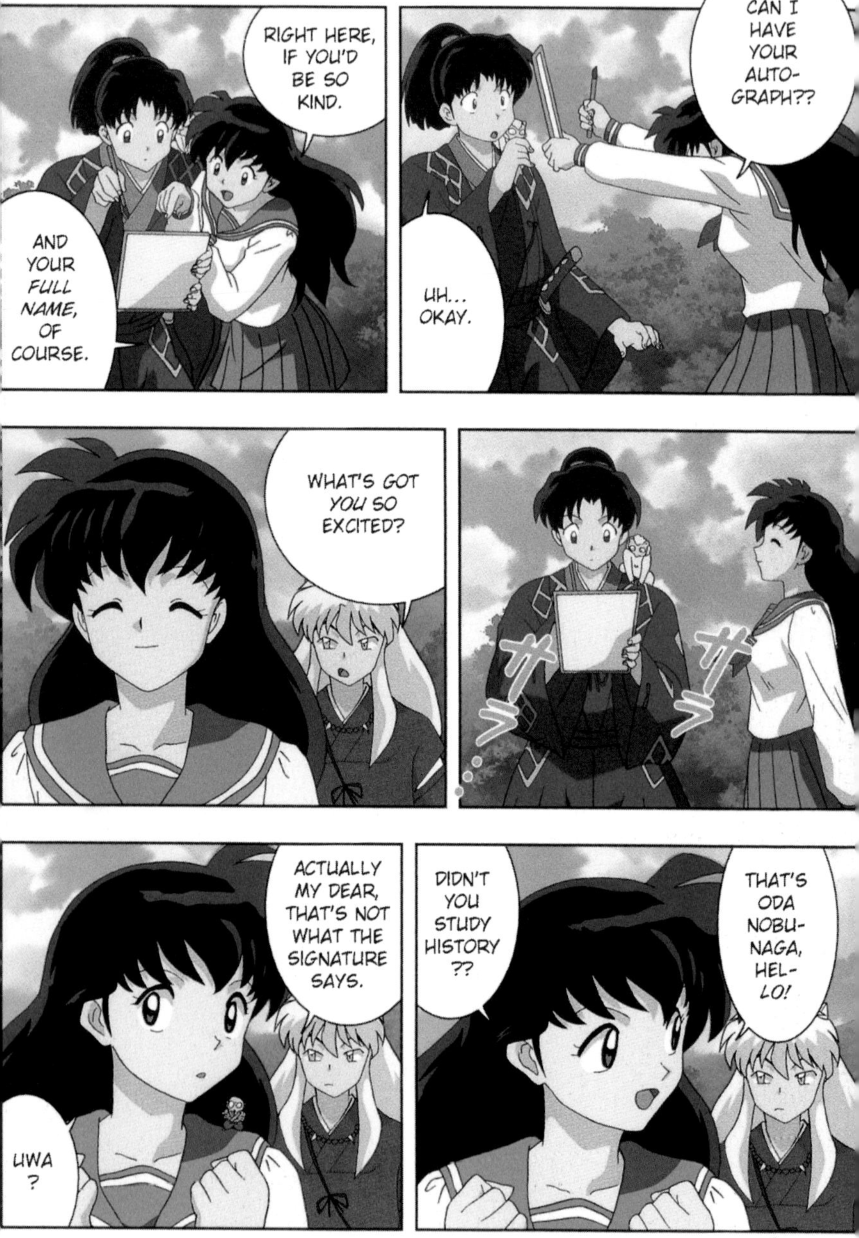
CAN I HAVE YOUR AUTOGRAPH??
UH... OKAY.
RIGHT HERE, IF YOU'D BE SO KIND.
AND YOUR *FULL NAME*, OF COURSE.
サラ
サラ
WHAT'S GOT *YOU* SO EXCITED?
THAT'S ODA NOBUNAGA, HEL-*LO!*
DIDN'T YOU STUDY HISTORY??
ACTUALLY MY DEAR, THAT'S NOT WHAT THE SIGNATURE SAYS.
UWA?

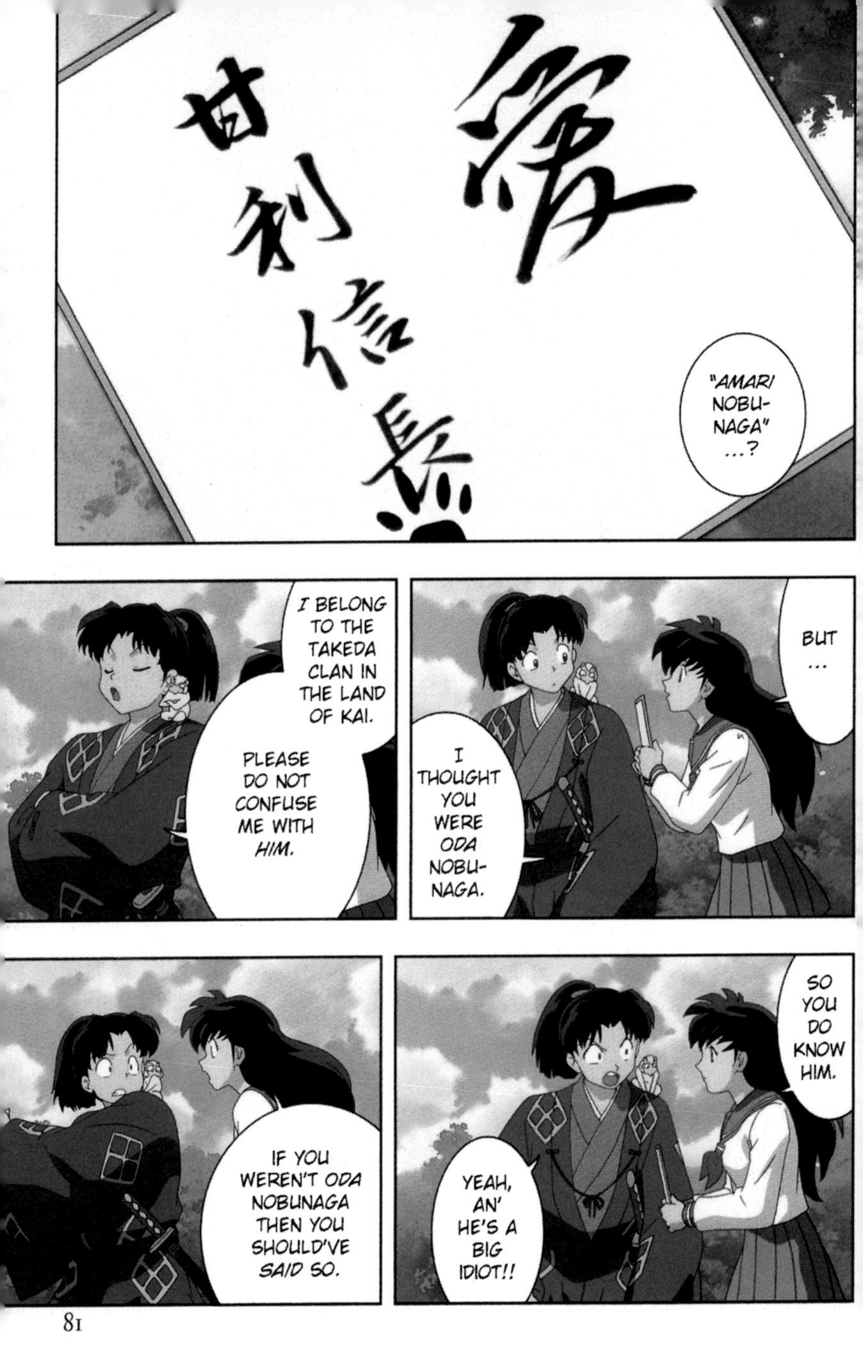
甘利信長
"AMARI NOBUNAGA" ...?
BUT ...
I THOUGHT YOU WERE ODA NOBUNAGA.
I BELONG TO THE TAKEDA CLAN IN THE LAND OF KAI.
PLEASE DO NOT CONFUSE ME WITH HIM.
SO YOU DO KNOW HIM.
YEAH, AN' HE'S A BIG IDIOT!!
IF YOU WEREN'T ODA NOBUNAGA THEN YOU SHOULD'VE SAID SO.

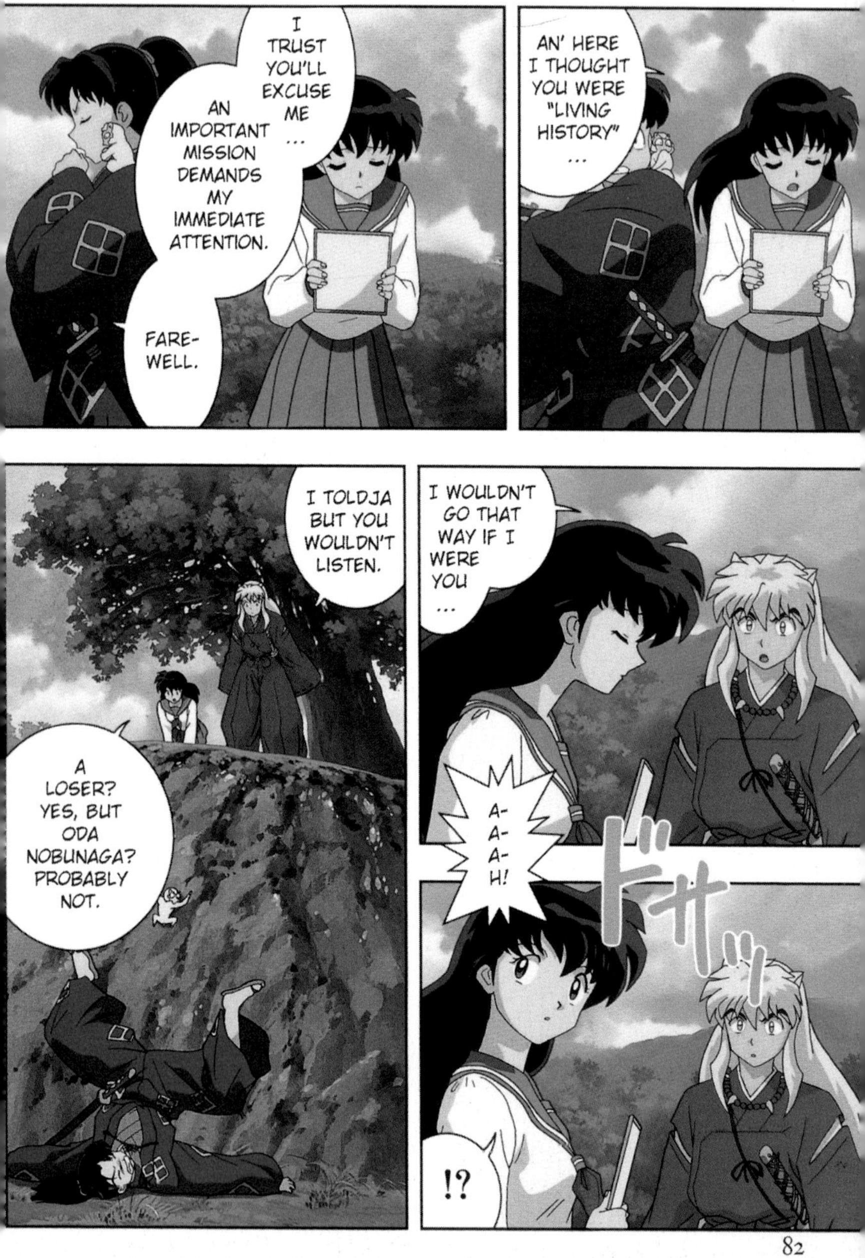
AN' HERE I THOUGHT YOU WERE "LIVING HISTORY" ...
I TRUST YOU'LL EXCUSE ME ...
AN IMPORTANT MISSION DEMANDS MY IMMEDIATE ATTENTION.
FARE-WELL.
I WOULDN'T GO THAT WAY IF I WERE YOU ...
A-A-A-H!
ドサッ
!?
I TOLDJA BUT YOU WOULDN'T LISTEN.
A LOSER? YES, BUT ODA NOBUNAGA? PROBABLY NOT.

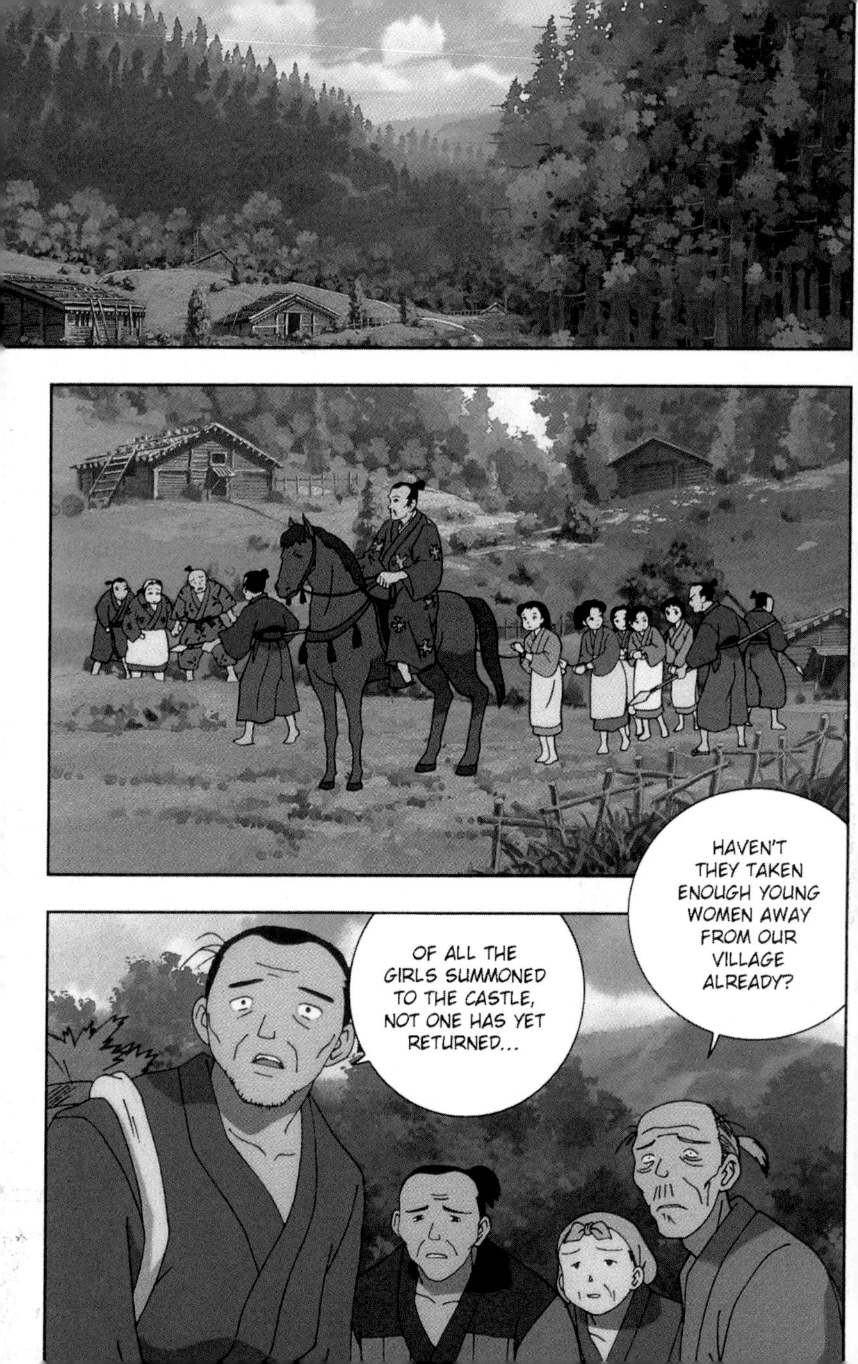
HAVEN'T THEY TAKEN ENOUGH YOUNG WOMEN AWAY FROM OUR VILLAGE ALREADY?
OF ALL THE GIRLS SUMMONED TO THE CASTLE, NOT ONE HAS YET RETURNED...

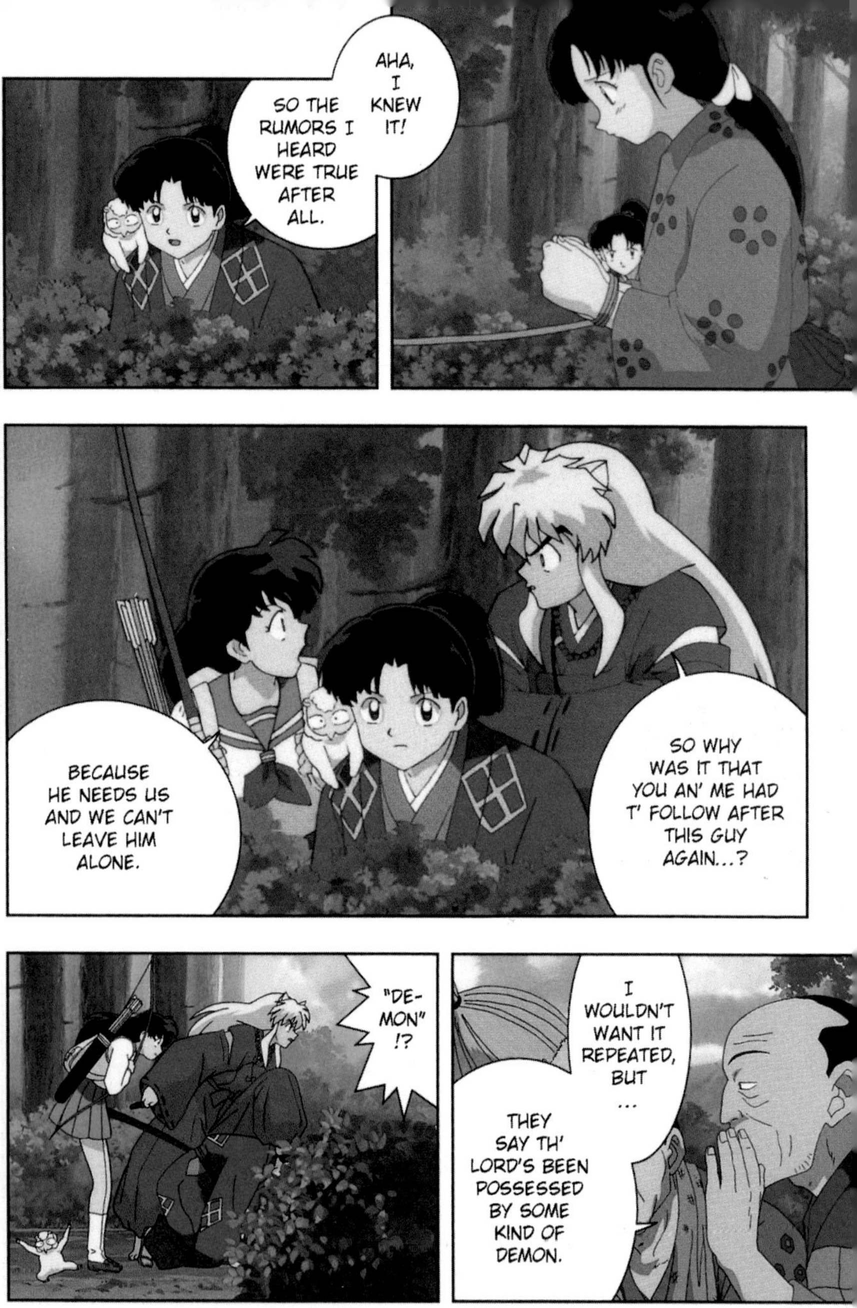
AHA, I KNEW IT!
SO THE RUMORS I HEARD WERE TRUE AFTER ALL.
SO WHY WAS IT THAT YOU AN' ME HAD T' FOLLOW AFTER THIS GUY AGAIN...?
BECAUSE HE NEEDS US AND WE CAN'T LEAVE HIM ALONE.
I WOULDN'T WANT IT REPEATED, BUT ...
THEY SAY TH' LORD'S BEEN POSSESSED BY SOME KIND OF DEMON.
"DE-MON" !?

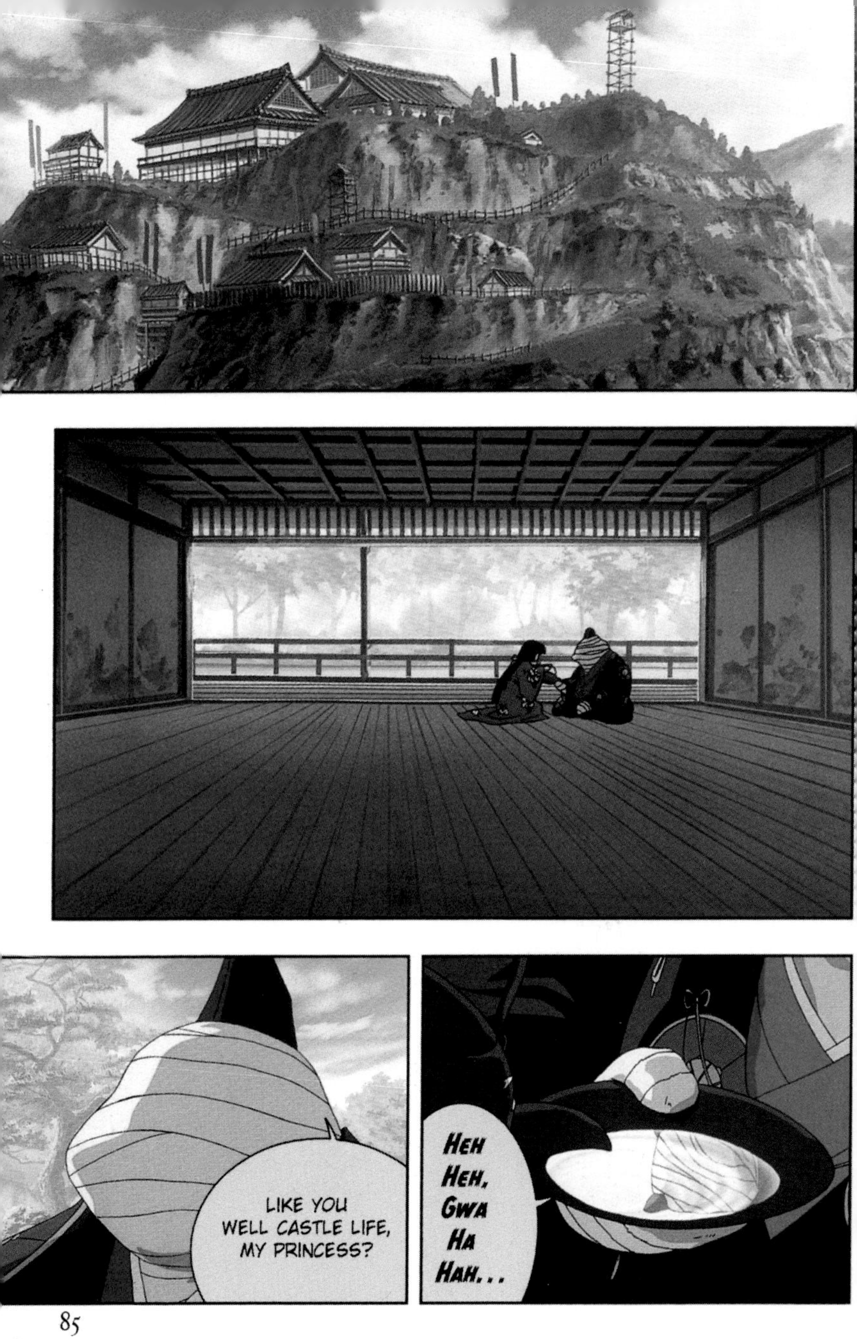
HEH HEH, GWA HA HAH...
LIKE YOU WELL CASTLE LIFE, MY PRINCESS?

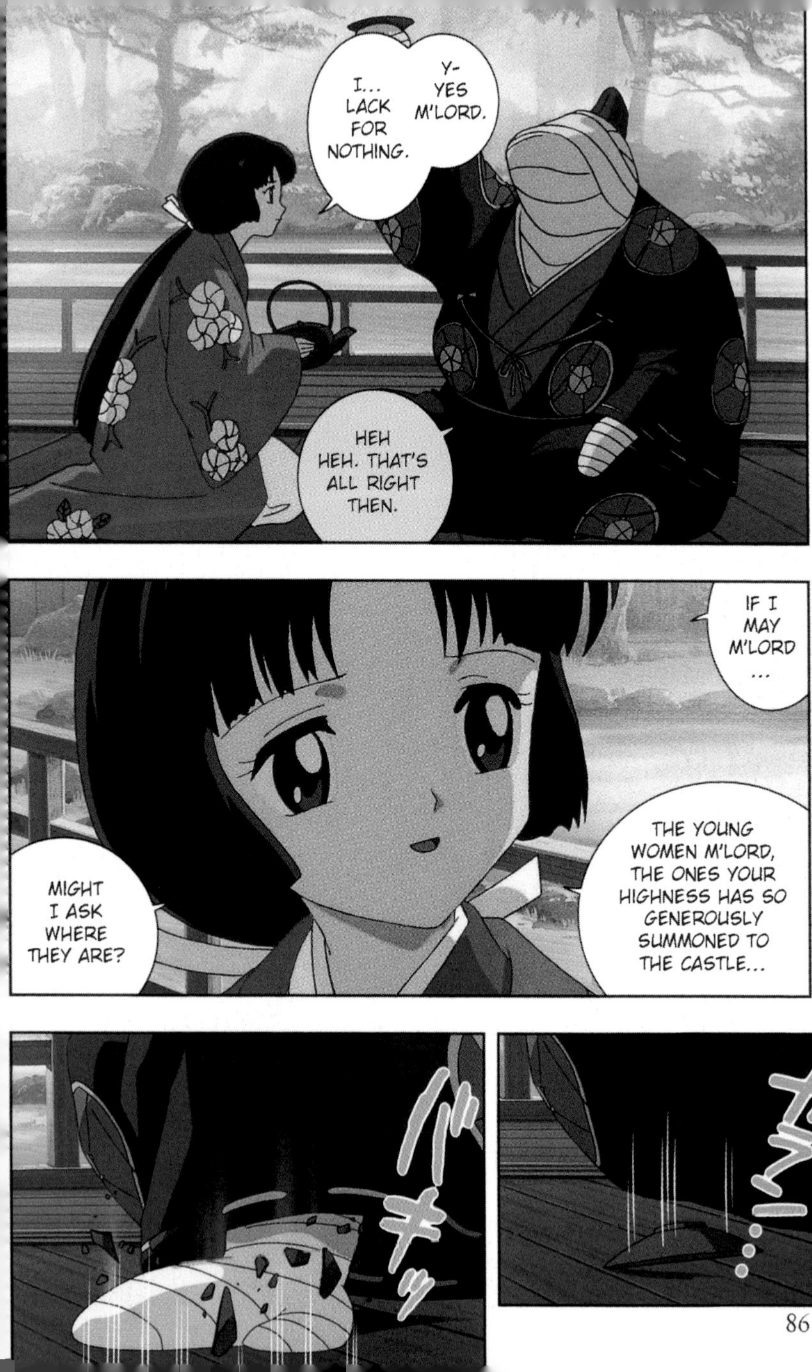
Y- YES M'LORD.
I... LACK FOR NOTHING.
HEH HEH. THAT'S ALL RIGHT THEN.
IF I MAY M'LORD ...
THE YOUNG WOMEN M'LORD, THE ONES YOUR HIGHNESS HAS SO GENEROUSLY SUMMONED TO THE CASTLE...
MIGHT I ASK WHERE THEY ARE?

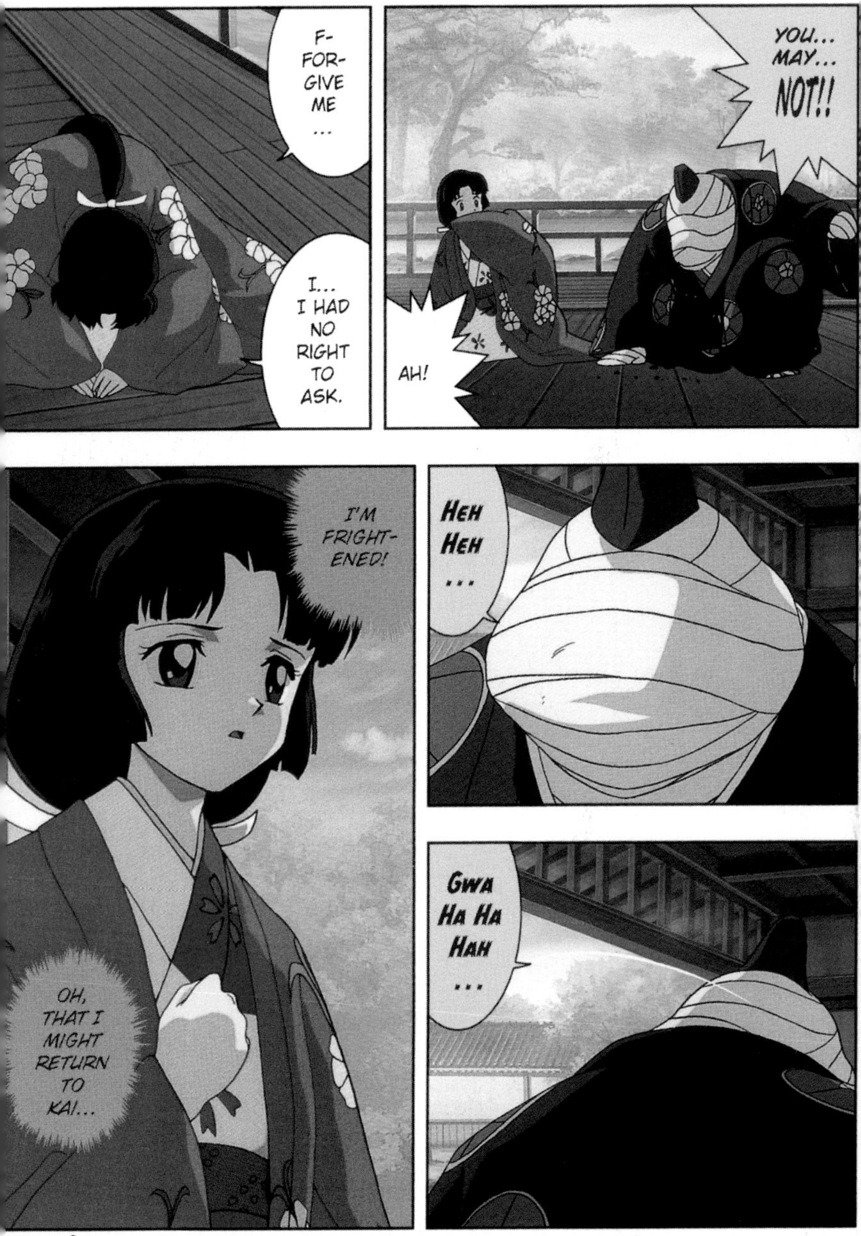
YOU... MAY... NOT!!
AH!
F-FORGIVE ME...
I... I HAD NO RIGHT TO ASK.
HEH HEH...
GWA HA HA HAH...
I'M FRIGHTENED!
OH, THAT I MIGHT RETURN TO KAI...

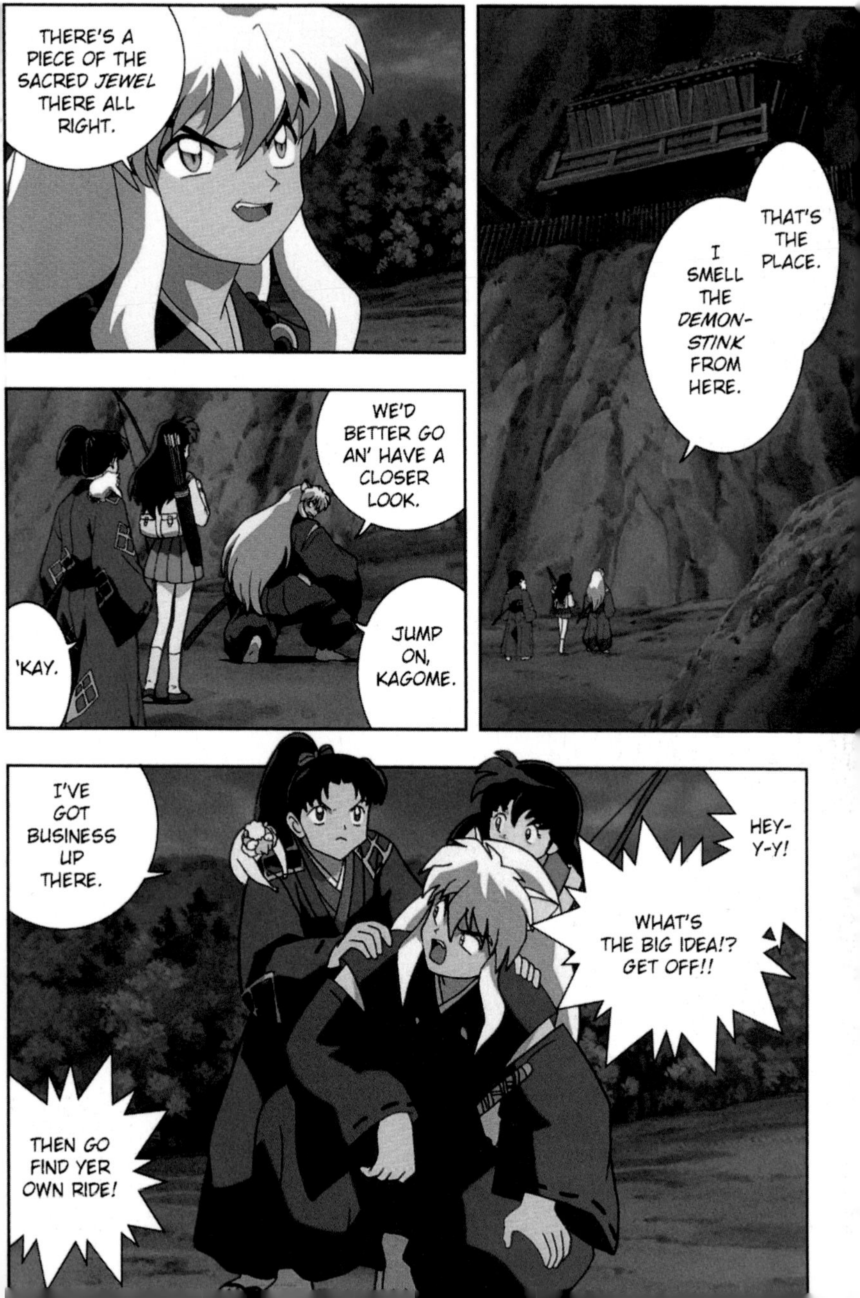
THAT'S THE PLACE.
I SMELL THE DEMON-STINK FROM HERE.
THERE'S A PIECE OF THE SACRED JEWEL THERE ALL RIGHT.
WE'D BETTER GO AN' HAVE A CLOSER LOOK.
JUMP ON, KAGOME.
'KAY.
HEY-Y-Y!
WHAT'S THE BIG IDEA!? GET OFF!!
I'VE GOT BUSINESS UP THERE.
THEN GO FIND YER OWN RIDE!

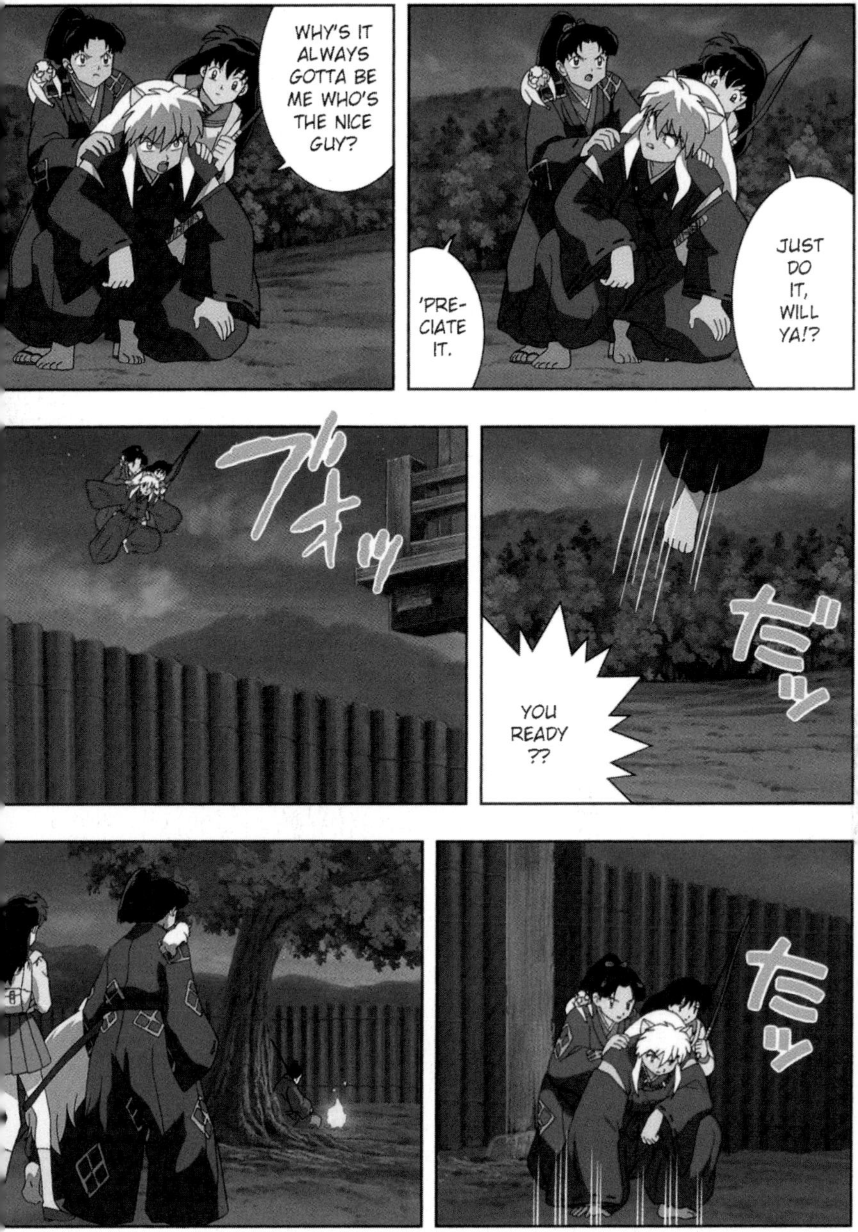
JUST DO IT, WILL YA!?
'PRE-CIATE IT.
WHY'S IT ALWAYS GOTTA BE ME WHO'S THE NICE GUY?
だッ
YOU READY??
ブオッ
たッ

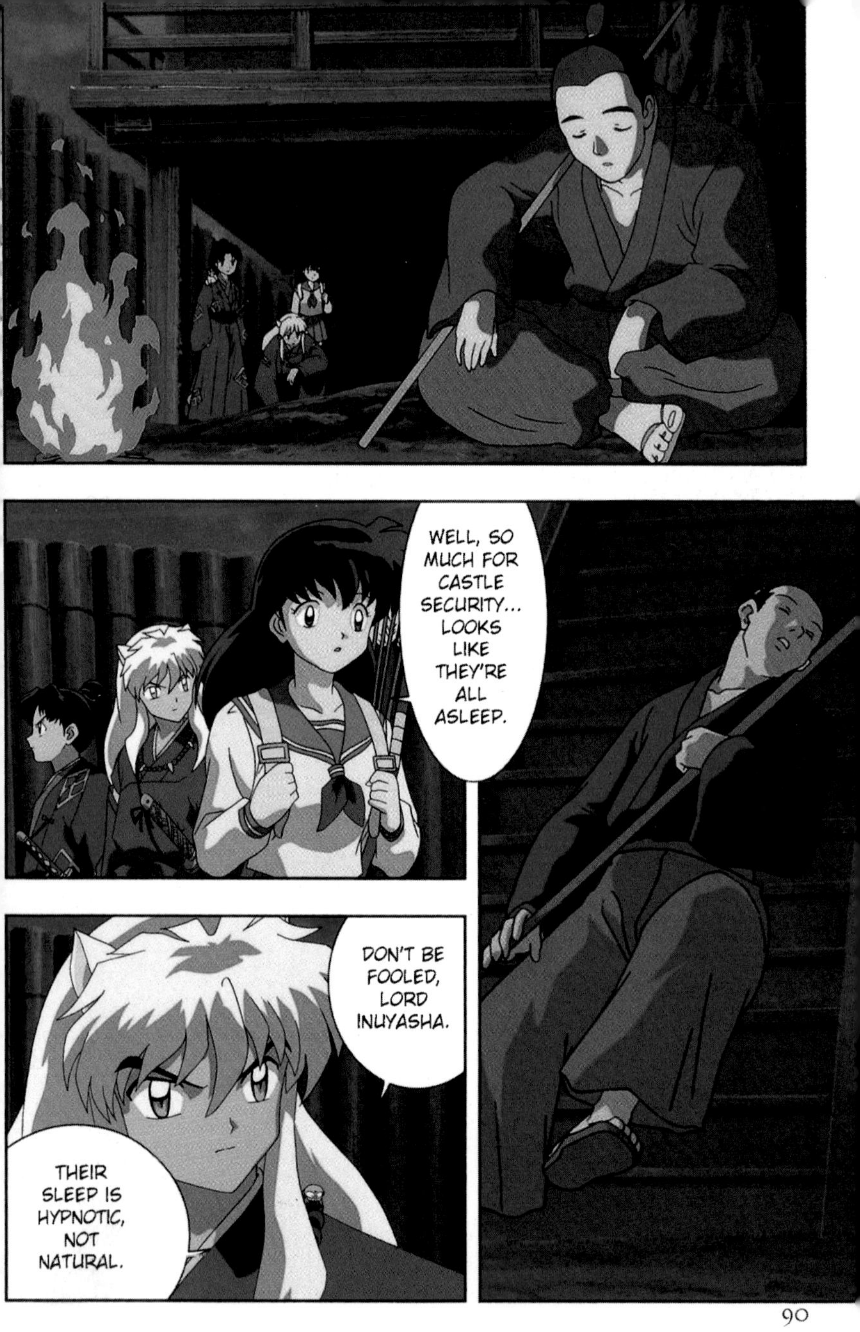
WELL, SO MUCH FOR CASTLE SECURITY... LOOKS LIKE THEY'RE ALL ASLEEP.
DON'T BE FOOLED, LORD INUYASHA.
THEIR SLEEP IS HYPNOTIC, NOT NATURAL.

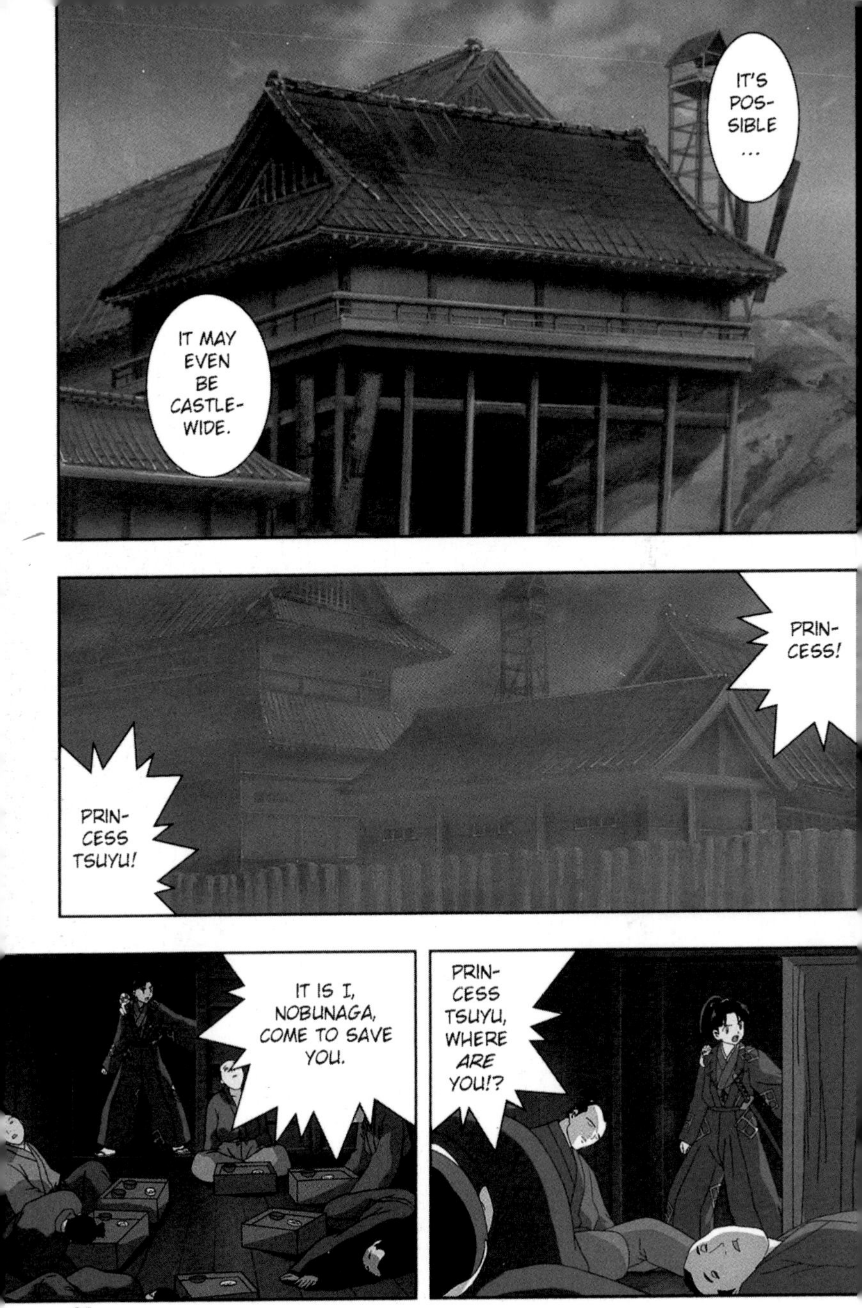
IT'S POS-SIBLE ...
IT MAY EVEN BE CASTLE-WIDE.
PRIN-CESS!
PRIN-CESS TSUYU!
PRIN-CESS TSUYU, WHERE *ARE* YOU!?
IT IS I, NOBUNAGA, COME TO SAVE YOU.

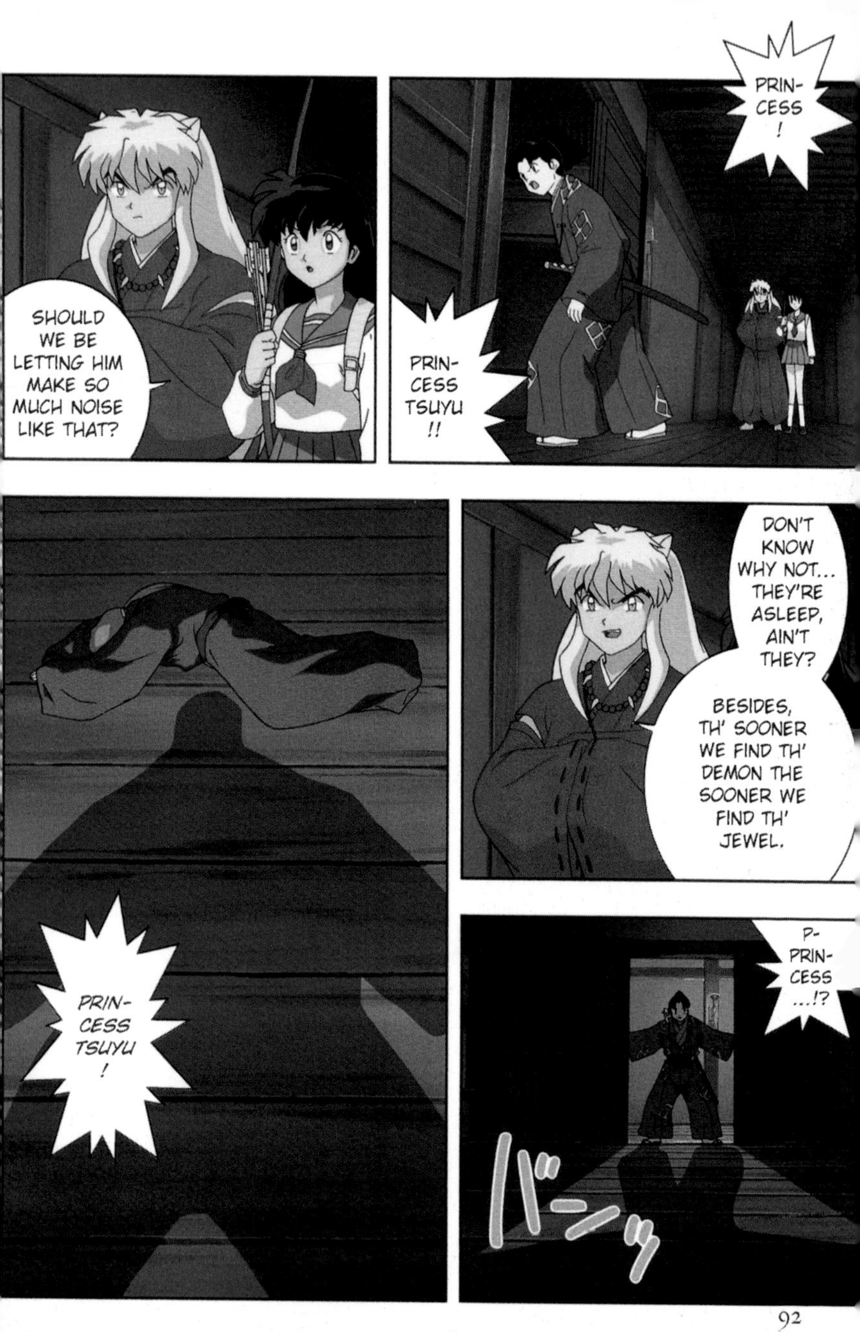
PRIN-CESS!
PRIN-CESS TSUYU!!
SHOULD WE BE LETTING HIM MAKE SO MUCH NOISE LIKE THAT?
DON'T KNOW WHY NOT... THEY'RE ASLEEP, AIN'T THEY?
BESIDES, TH' SOONER WE FIND TH' DEMON THE SOONER WE FIND TH' JEWEL.
P-PRIN-CESS...!?
バーンッ
PRIN-CESS TSUYU!

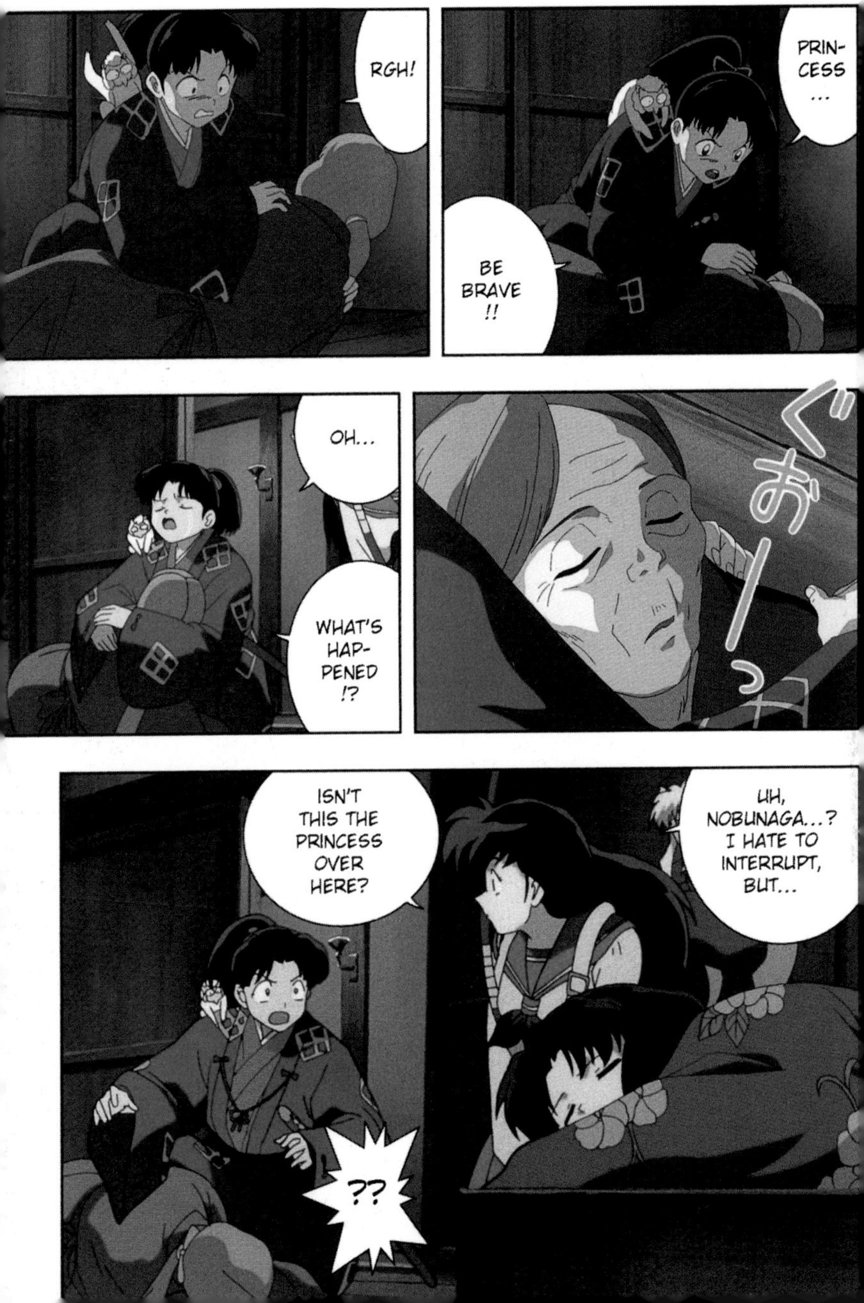
PRIN-CESS...
BE BRAVE!!
RGH!
ぐおーっ
OH...
WHAT'S HAP-PENED!?
UH, NOBUNAGA...? I HATE TO INTERRUPT, BUT...
ISN'T THIS THE PRINCESS OVER HERE?
??

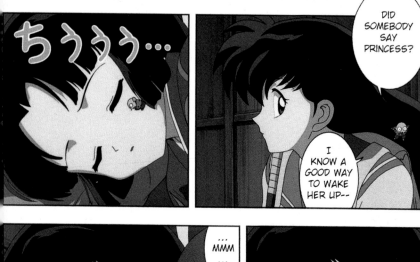

ちうぅぅ…

DID SOMEBODY SAY PRINCESS?

I KNOW A GOOD WAY TO WAKE HER UP--

...MMM...

はらり

ぱし

N-NOBU-NAGA...?

WHY'RE YOU HERE??

PRINCESS!

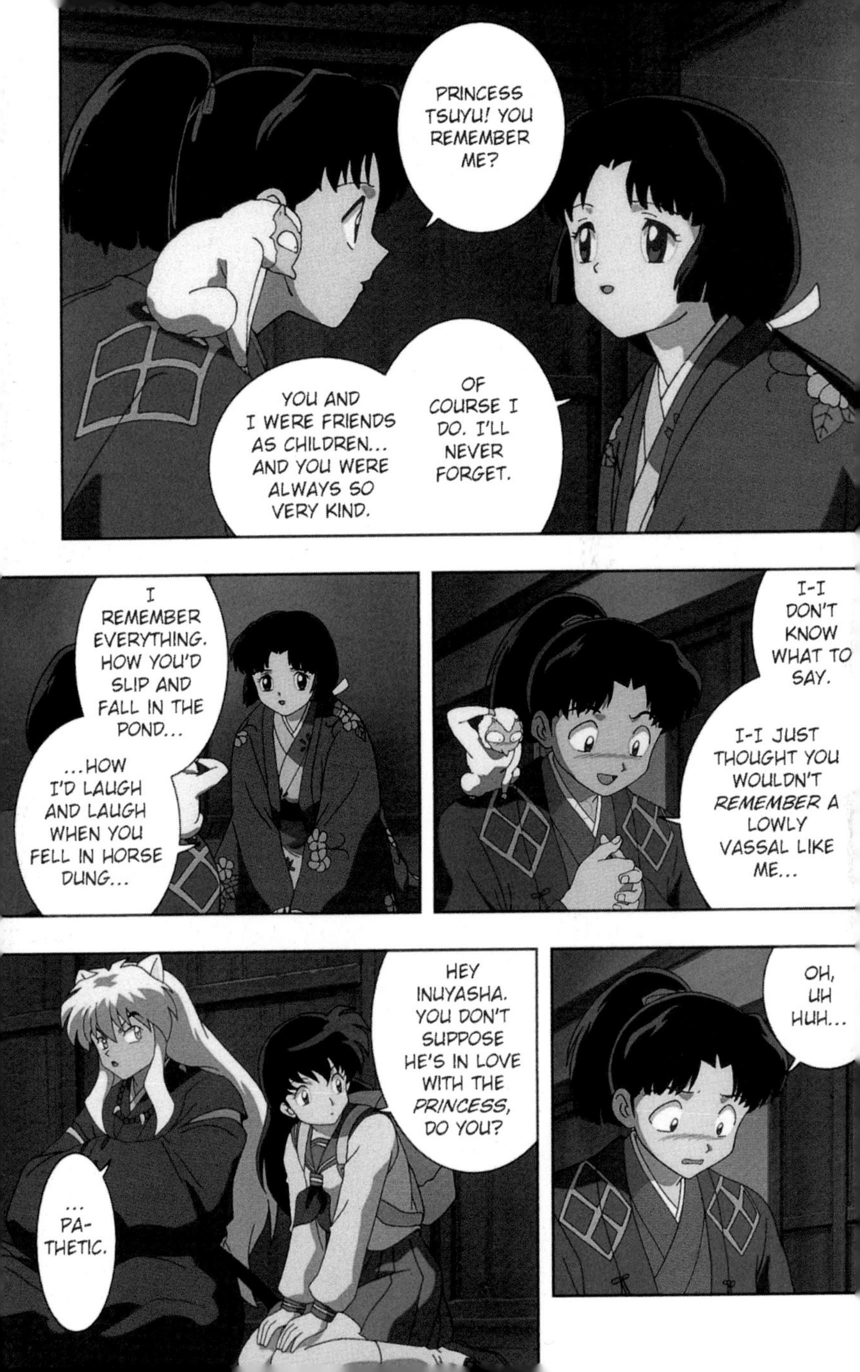
PRINCESS TSUYU! YOU REMEMBER ME?
OF COURSE I DO. I'LL NEVER FORGET.
YOU AND I WERE FRIENDS AS CHILDREN... AND YOU WERE ALWAYS SO VERY KIND.
I-I DON'T KNOW WHAT TO SAY.
I-I JUST THOUGHT YOU WOULDN'T *REMEMBER* A LOWLY VASSAL LIKE ME...
I REMEMBER EVERYTHING. HOW YOU'D SLIP AND FALL IN THE POND...
...HOW I'D LAUGH AND LAUGH WHEN YOU FELL IN HORSE DUNG...
OH, UH HUH...
HEY INUYASHA. YOU DON'T SUPPOSE HE'S IN LOVE WITH THE *PRINCESS*, DO YOU?
... PA-THETIC.

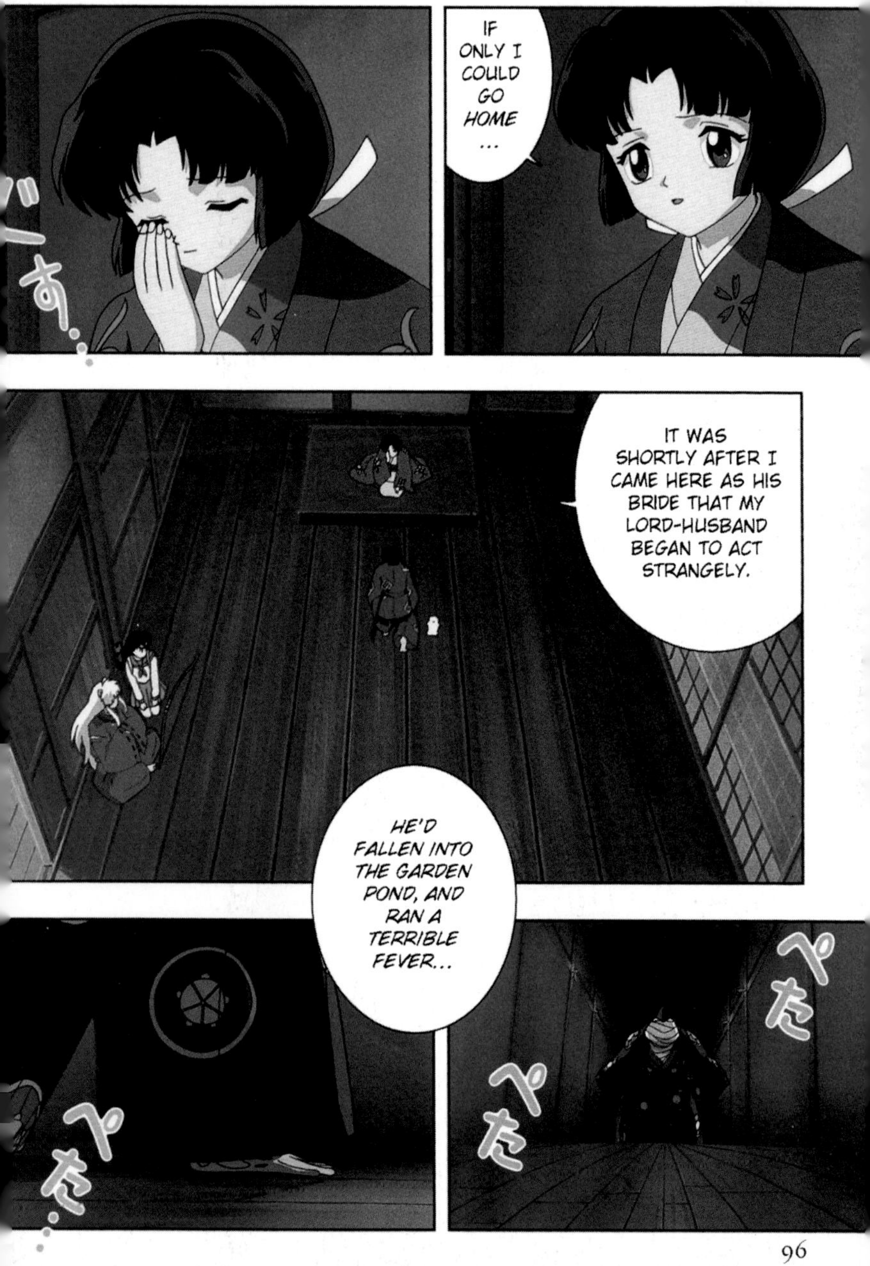
IF ONLY I COULD GO HOME...
IT WAS SHORTLY AFTER I CAME HERE AS HIS BRIDE THAT MY LORD-HUSBAND BEGAN TO ACT STRANGELY.
HE'D FALLEN INTO THE GARDEN POND, AND RAN A TERRIBLE FEVER...
ぺた
ぺた
ぺた...

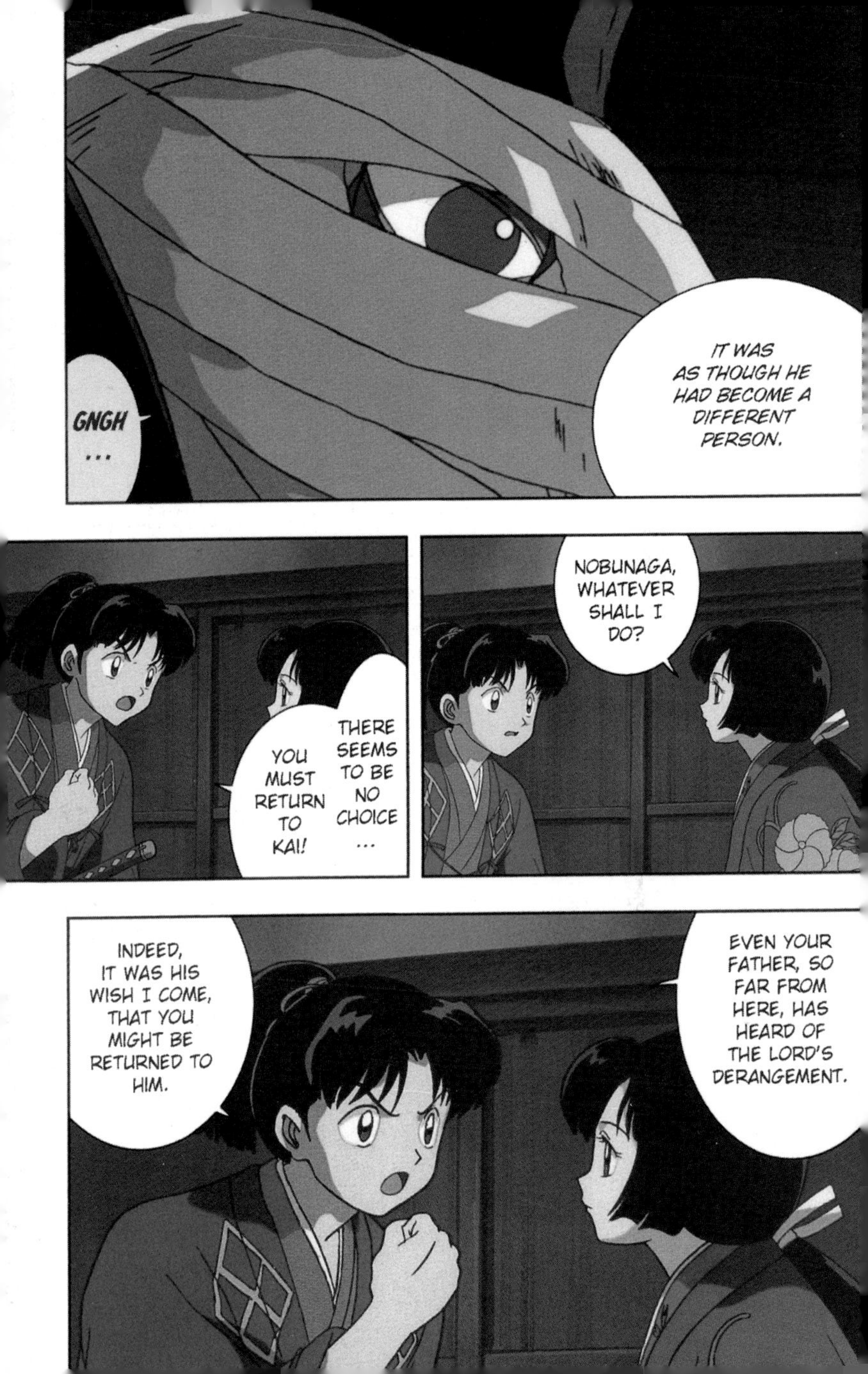
IT WAS AS THOUGH HE HAD BECOME A DIFFERENT PERSON.
GNGH ...
NOBUNAGA, WHATEVER SHALL I DO?
THERE SEEMS TO BE NO CHOICE ...
YOU MUST RETURN TO KAI!
EVEN YOUR FATHER, SO FAR FROM HERE, HAS HEARD OF THE LORD'S DERANGEMENT.
INDEED, IT WAS HIS WISH I COME, THAT YOU MIGHT BE RETURNED TO HIM.

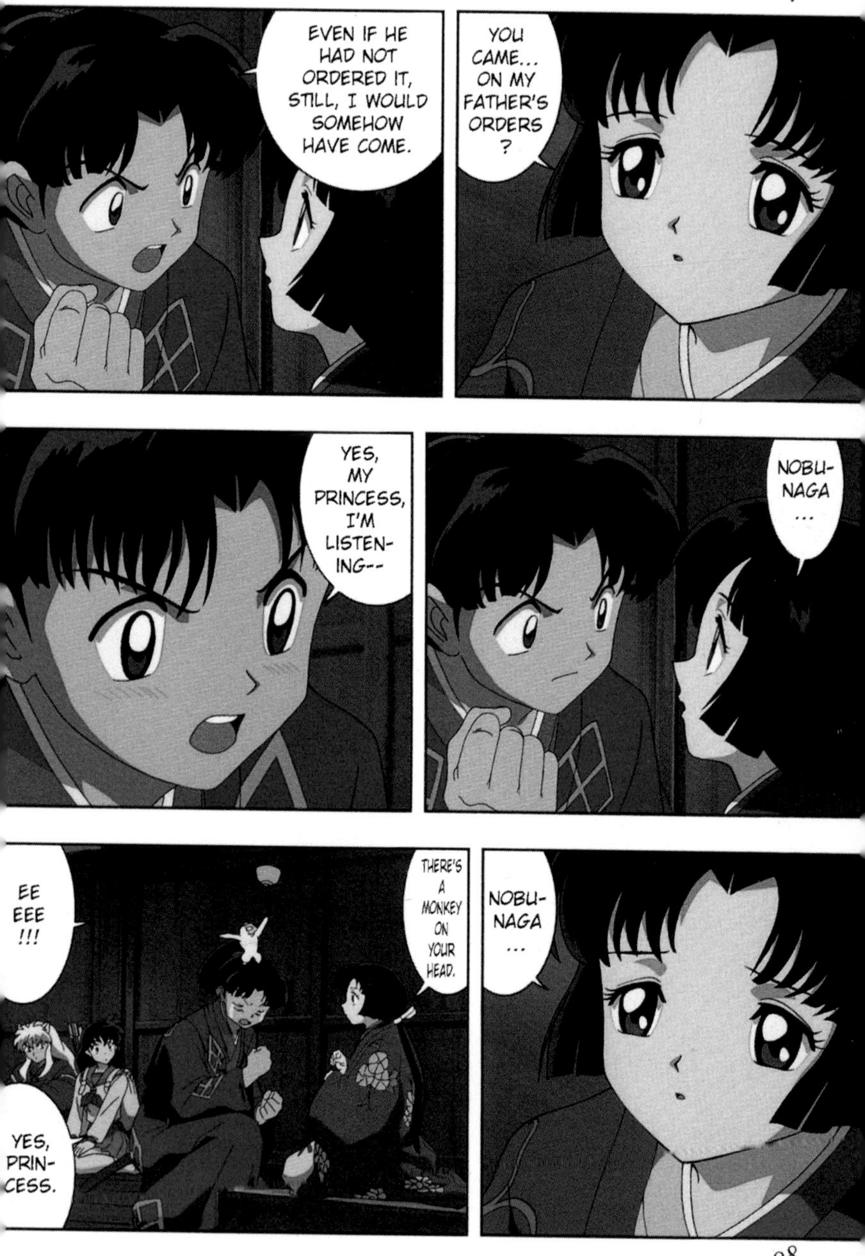
YOU CAME... ON MY FATHER'S ORDERS ?
EVEN IF HE HAD NOT ORDERED IT, STILL, I WOULD SOMEHOW HAVE COME.
NOBU-NAGA ...
YES, MY PRINCESS, I'M LISTEN-ING--
NOBU-NAGA ...
THERE'S A MONKEY ON YOUR HEAD.
EE EEE !!!
YES, PRIN-CESS.

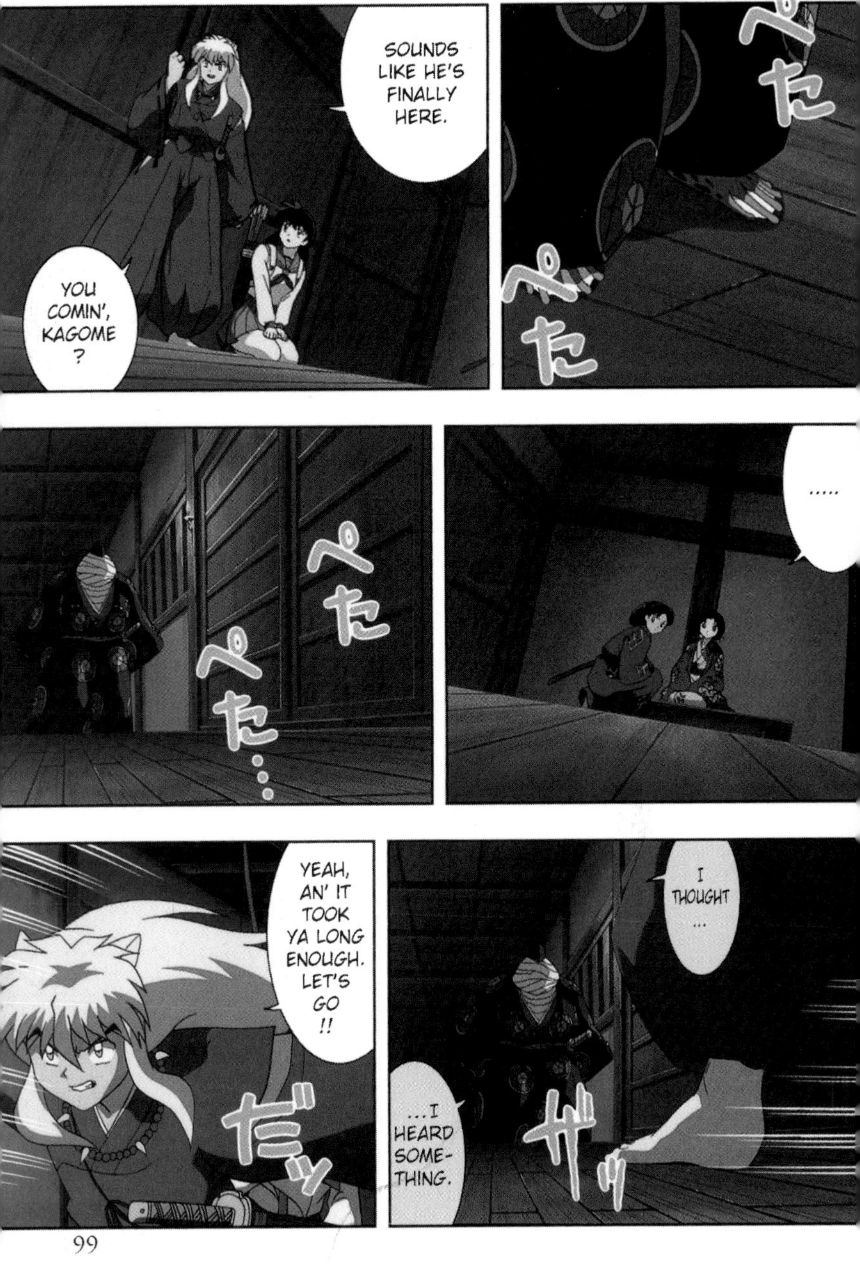
ぺた
ぺた
SOUNDS LIKE HE'S FINALLY HERE.
YOU COMIN', KAGOME?
.....
ぺた
ぺた...
I THOUGHT...
...I HEARD SOME-THING.
ザッ
YEAH, AN' IT TOOK YA LONG ENOUGH. LET'S GO!!
だッ

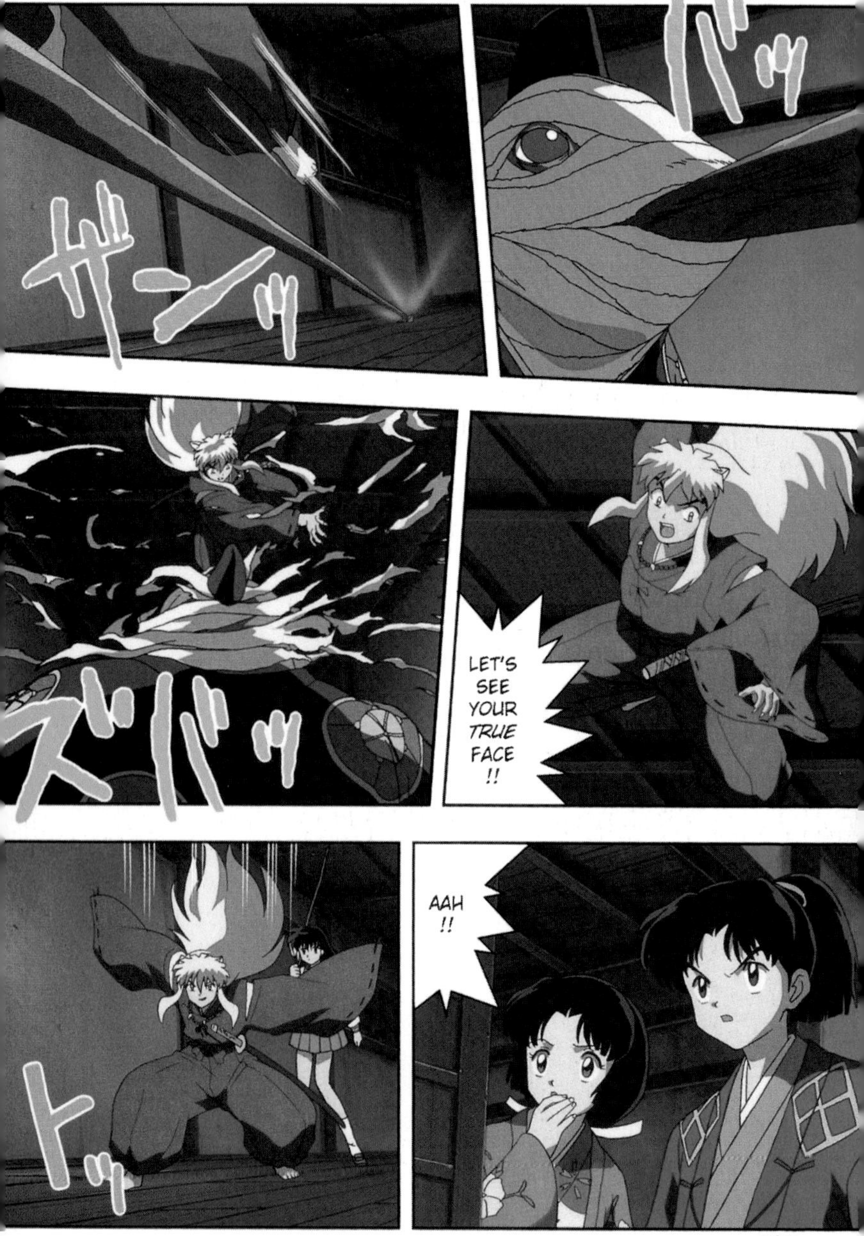
バッ
ザーンッ
LET'S SEE YOUR *TRUE* FACE !!
ズバッ
AAH !!
トッ

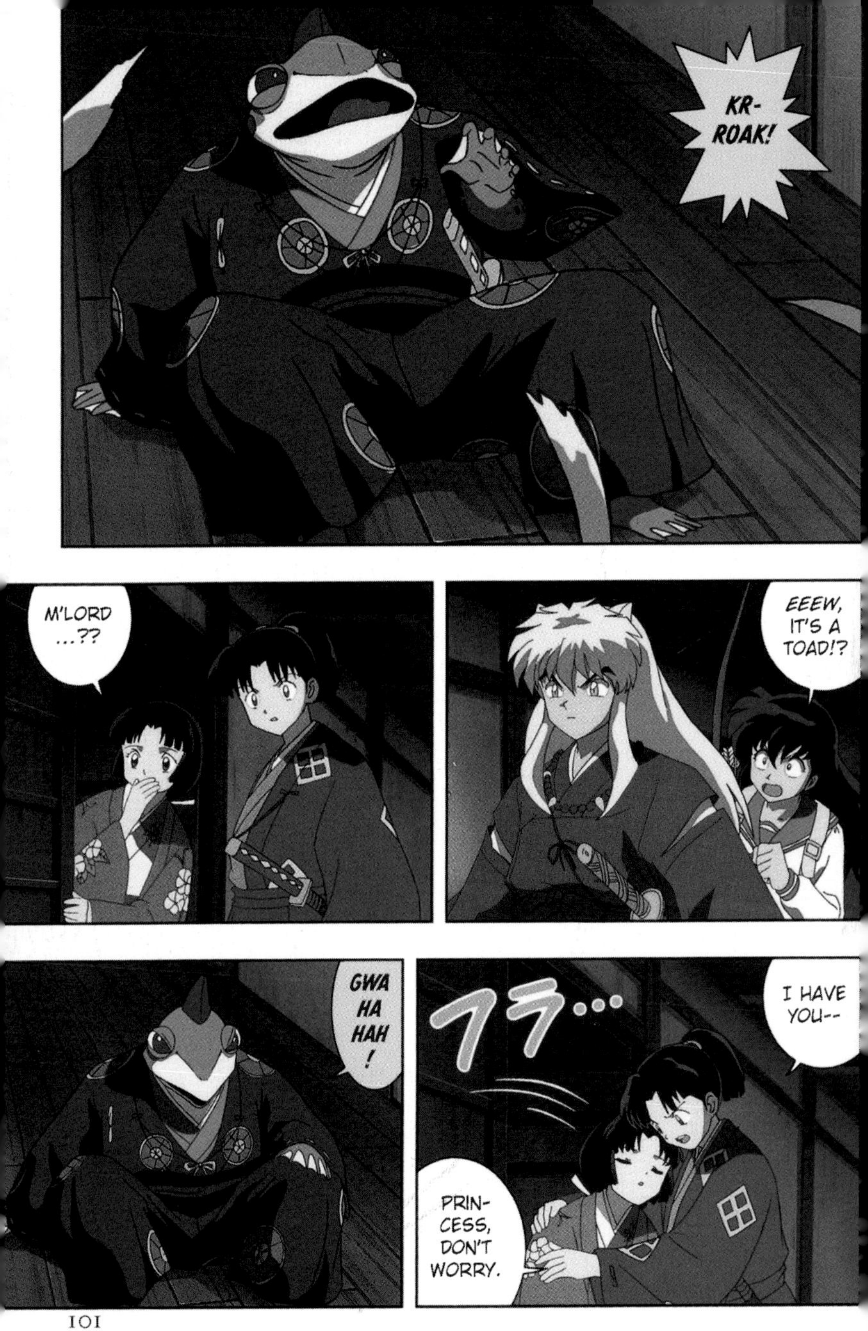
KR-ROAK!
EEEW, IT'S A TOAD!?
M'LORD ...??
I HAVE YOU--
フラ...
PRIN-CESS, DON'T WORRY.
GWA HA HAH!

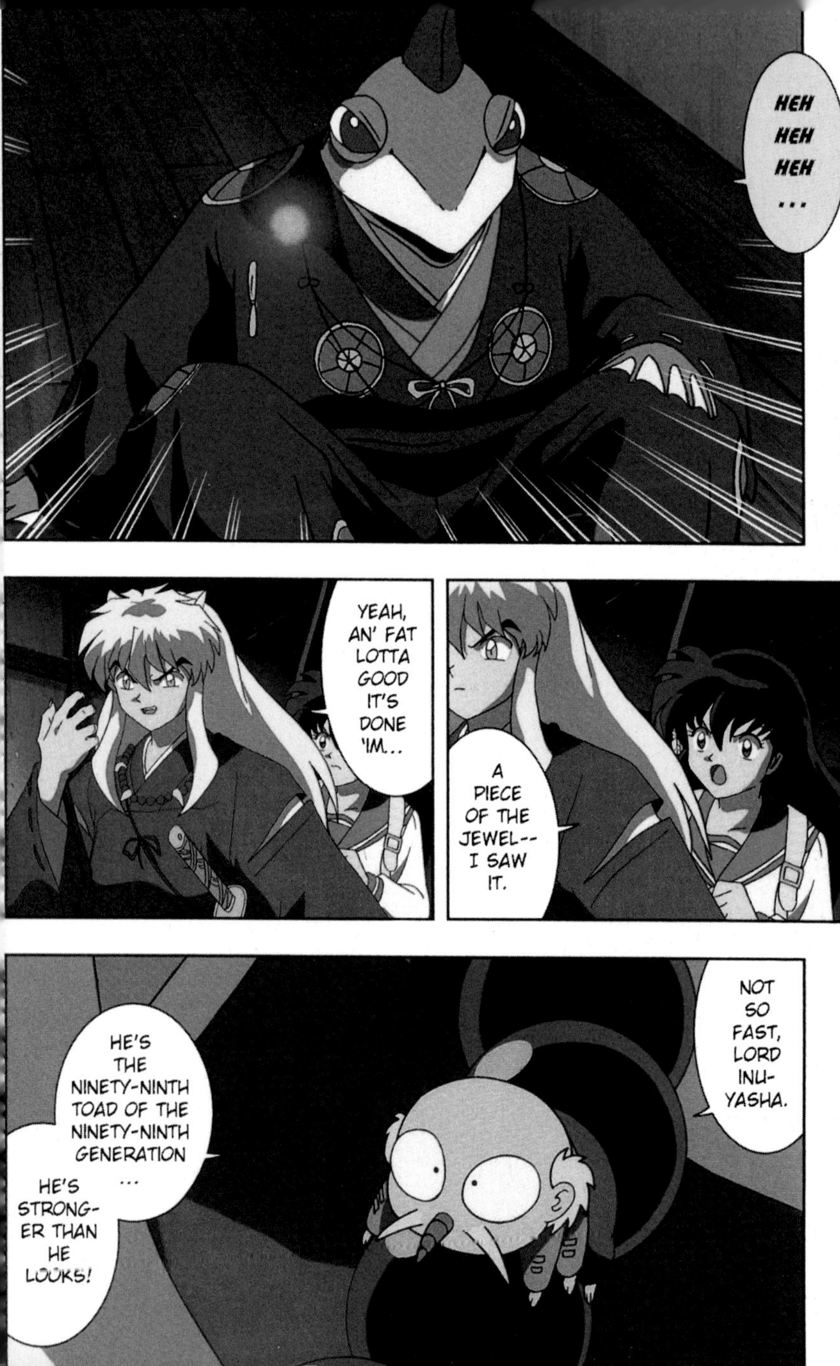
HEH HEH HEH ...
A PIECE OF THE JEWEL-- I SAW IT.
YEAH, AN' FAT LOTTA GOOD IT'S DONE 'IM...
NOT SO FAST, LORD INU-YASHA.
HE'S THE NINETY-NINTH TOAD OF THE NINETY-NINTH GENERATION ...
HE'S STRONGER THAN HE LOOKS!

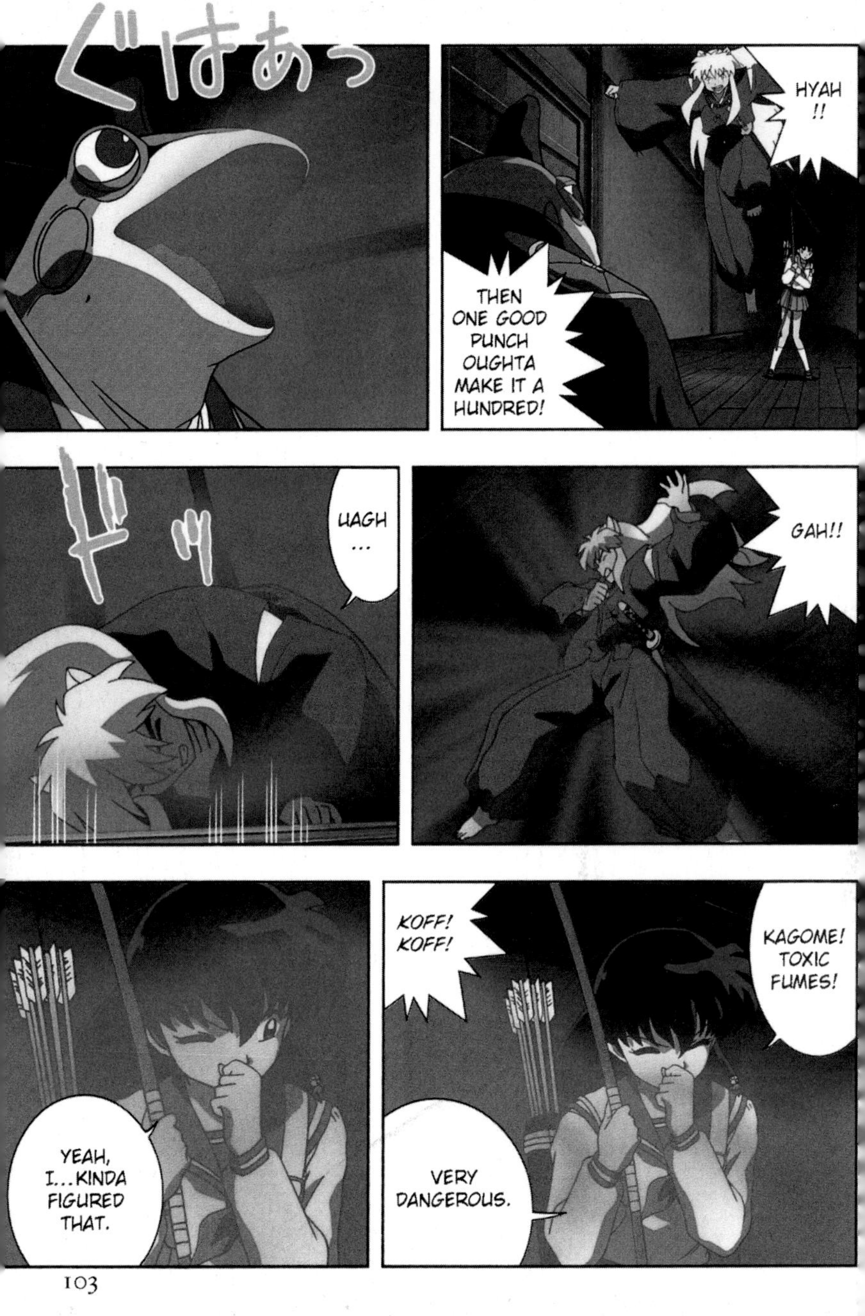
HYAH !!
THEN ONE GOOD PUNCH OUGHTA MAKE IT A HUNDRED!
ぐはあっ
GAH!!
ドッ
UAGH ...
KAGOME! TOXIC FUMES!
KOFF! KOFF!
VERY DANGEROUS.
YEAH, I...KINDA FIGURED THAT.

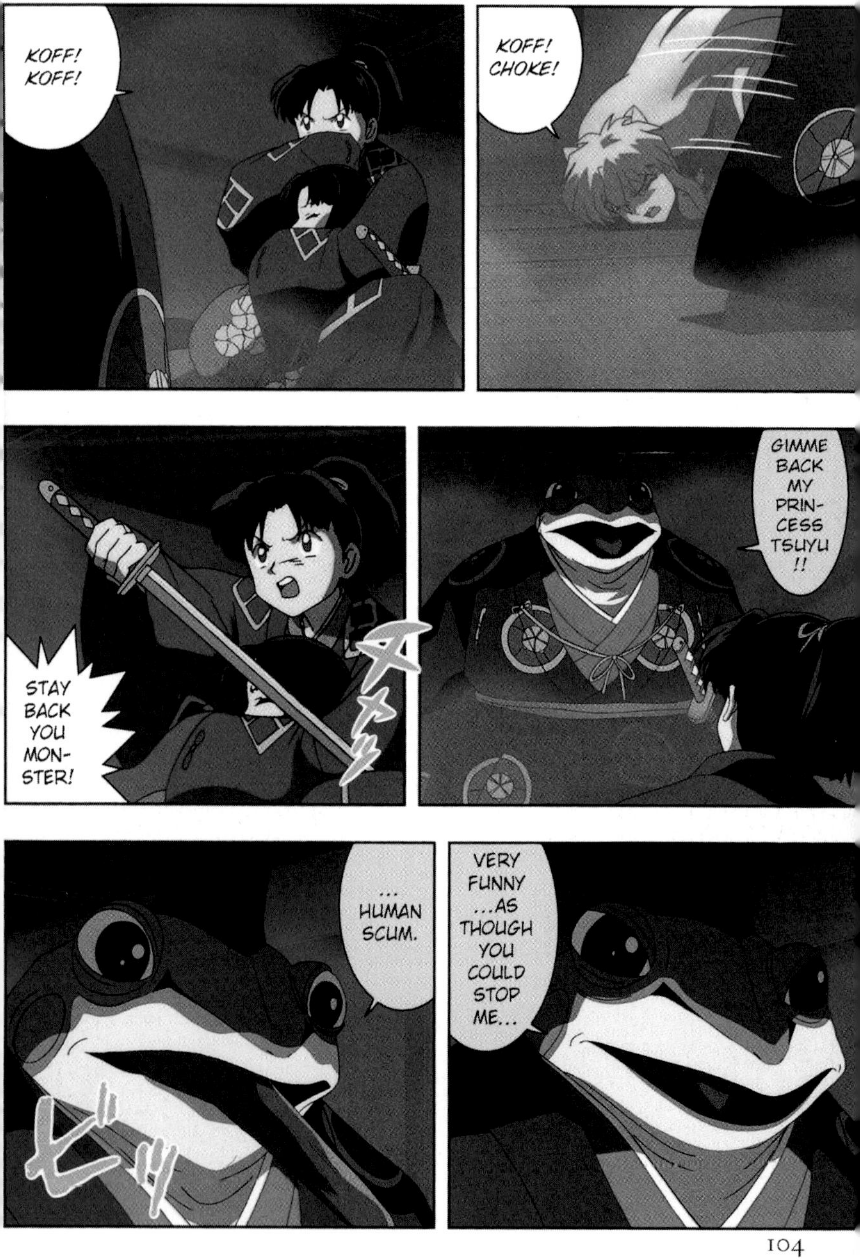
KOFF! CHOKE!
KOFF! KOFF!
GIMME BACK MY PRINCESS TSUYU!!
STAY BACK YOU MONSTER!
VERY FUNNY ...AS THOUGH YOU COULD STOP ME...
... HUMAN SCUM.

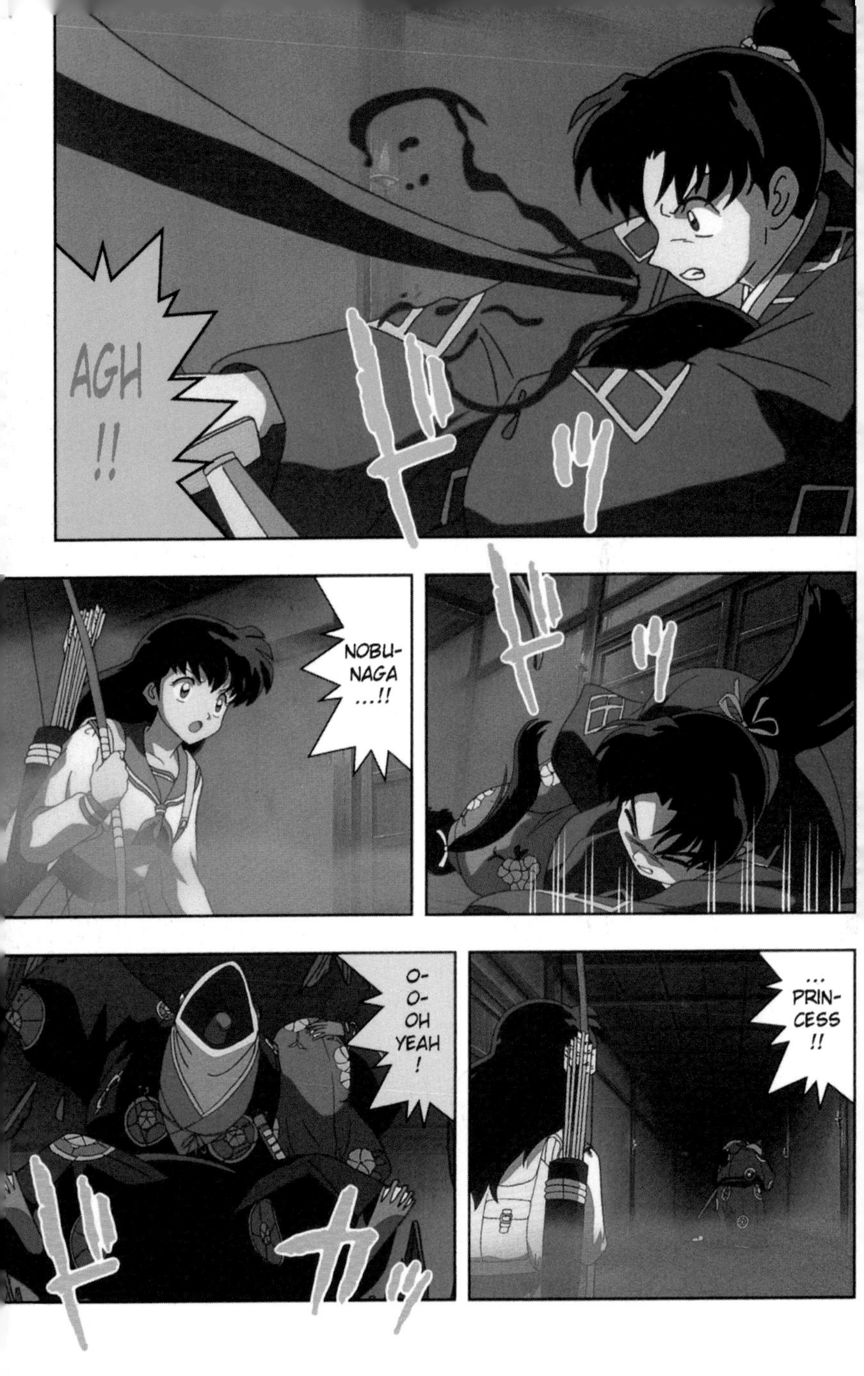
AGH!!
ドッ
ドッ
NOBU-NAGA...!!
...PRIN-CESS!!
O-O-OH YEAH!
ドカッ

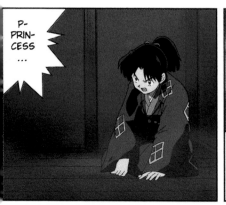

NYAH HA HA!
ぺた
HA HAH.
ぺた
P-PRINCESS...
NOBUNAGA, STAY STILL...
YOUR SHOULDER...
IT DOESN'T MATTER WHAT HAPPENS TO ME...
PLEASE, YOU'VE GOTTA SAVE THE PRINCESS!
I KNEW IT.
SO YOU *ARE* IN LOVE WITH THE PRINCESS THEN, *AREN'T* YOU NOBUNAGA?
H-HOW COULD YOU TELL...?
YOU MEAN IT WAS A SECRET?

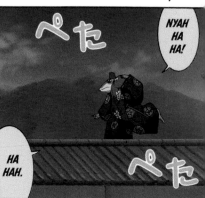

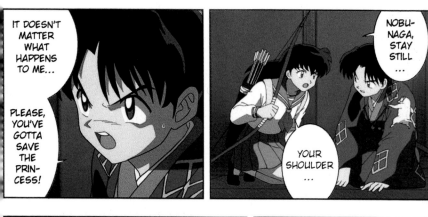

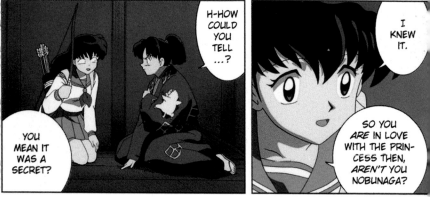

LOUSY STINKIN' TOAD!
NO WAY IS HE GETTIN' AWAY.
YAH !!
I'M GOIN' AHEAD !!
だッ
COME BACK!
たたた…
HEY! HEY!!

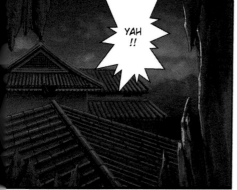

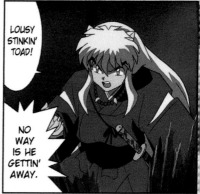

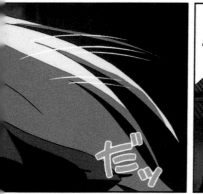

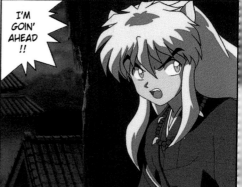

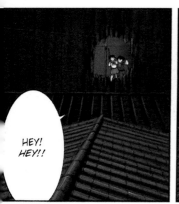

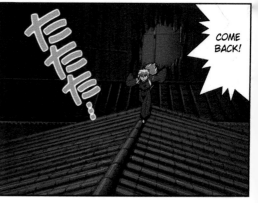

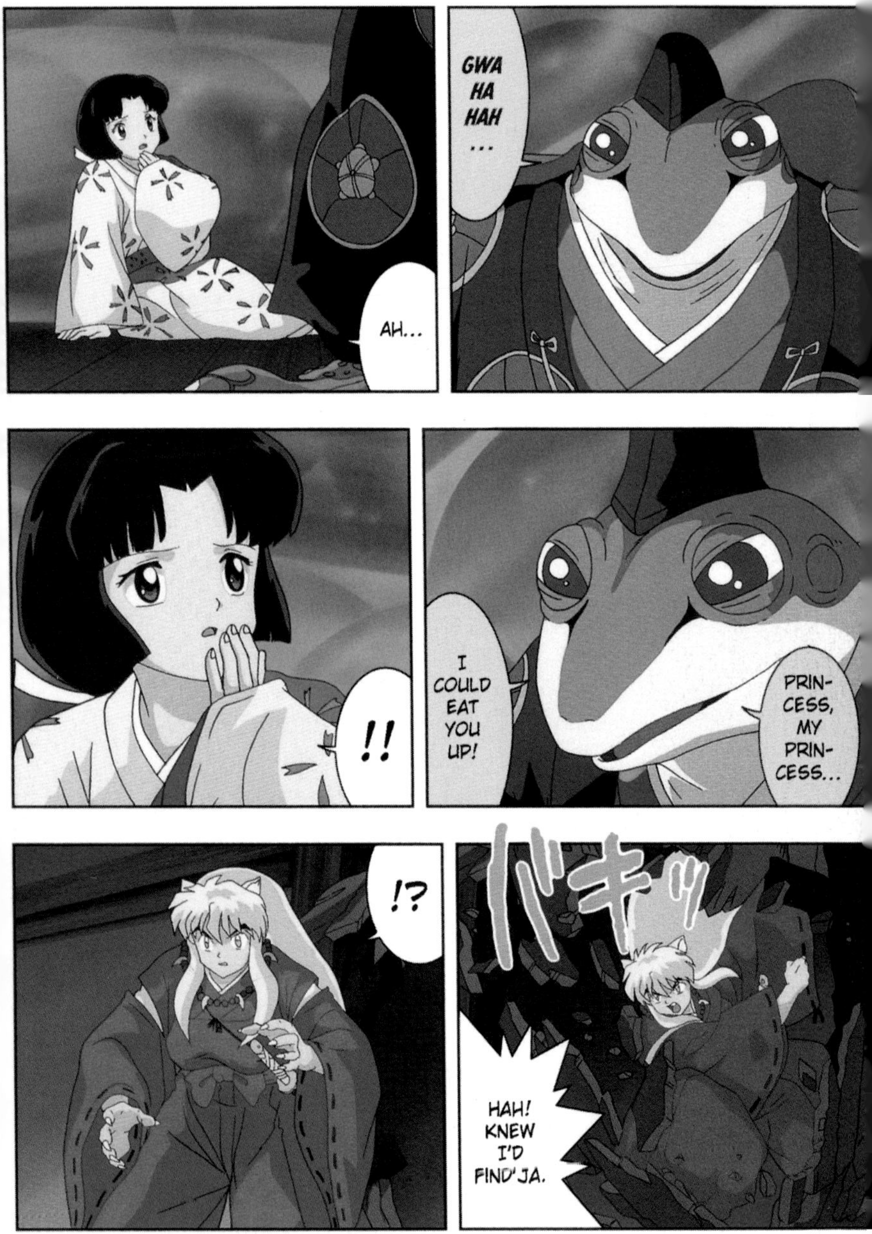
GWA HA HAH ...
AH...
PRIN-CESS, MY PRIN-CESS...
I COULD EAT YOU UP!
!!
バキッ
HAH! KNEW I'D FIND'JA.
!?

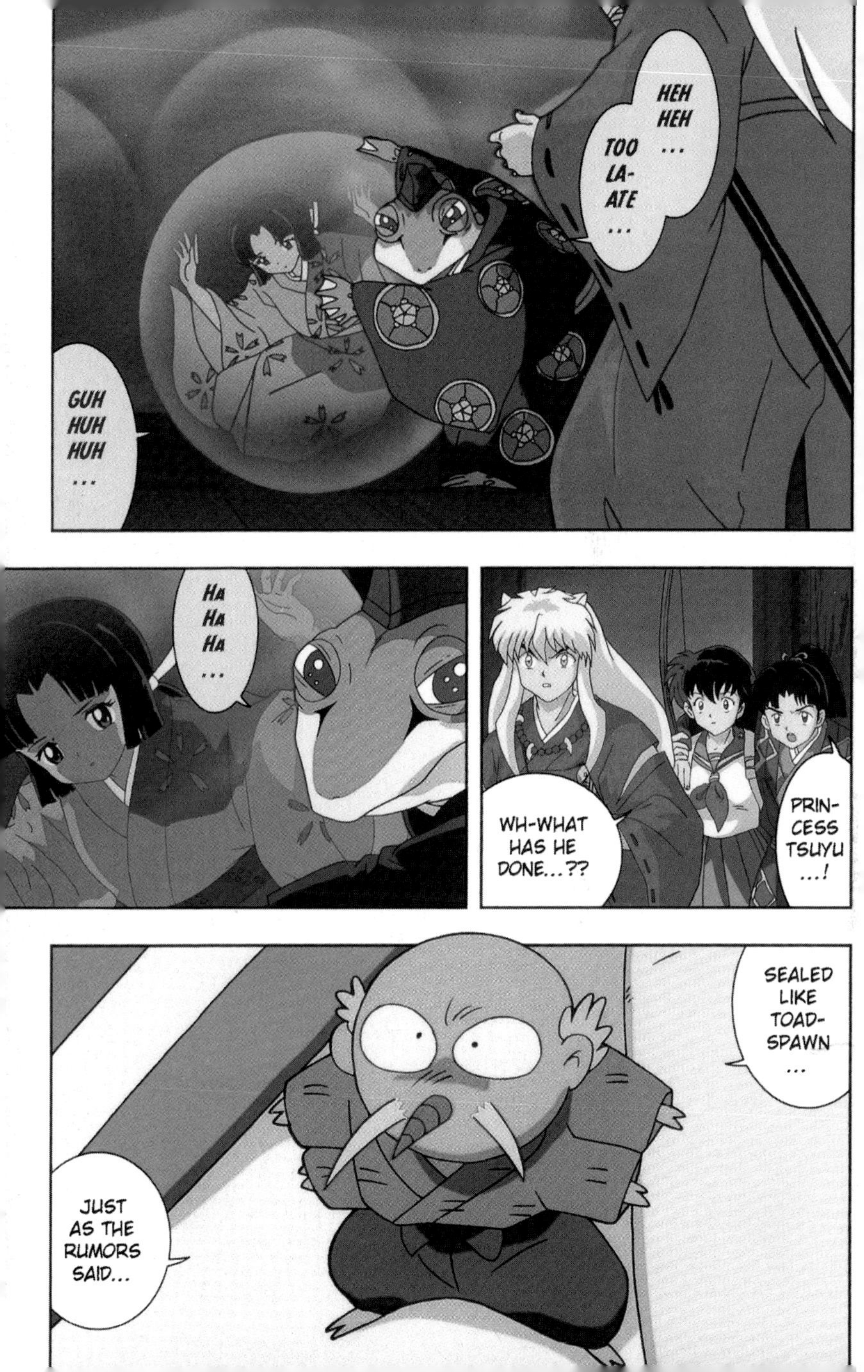
HEH HEH... TOO LA-ATE...
GUH HUH HUH...
PRIN-CESS TSUYU...!
WH-WHAT HAS HE DONE...??
HA HA HA...
SEALED LIKE TOAD-SPAWN...
JUST AS THE RUMORS SAID...

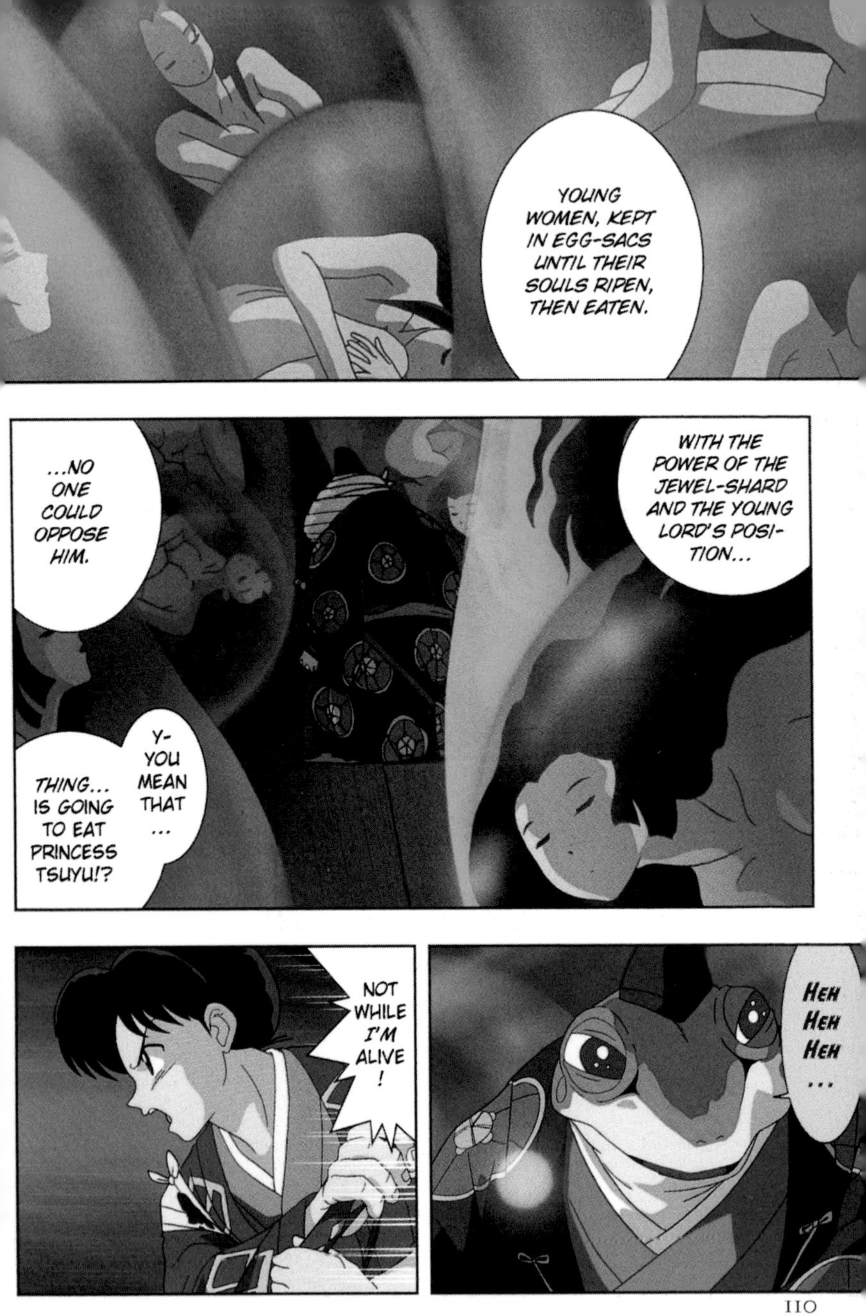
YOUNG WOMEN, KEPT IN EGG-SACS UNTIL THEIR SOULS RIPEN, THEN EATEN.
WITH THE POWER OF THE JEWEL-SHARD AND THE YOUNG LORD'S POSITION...
...NO ONE COULD OPPOSE HIM.
Y-YOU MEAN THAT ...
THING... IS GOING TO EAT PRINCESS TSUYU!?
HEH HEH HEH ...
NOT WHILE I'M ALIVE !

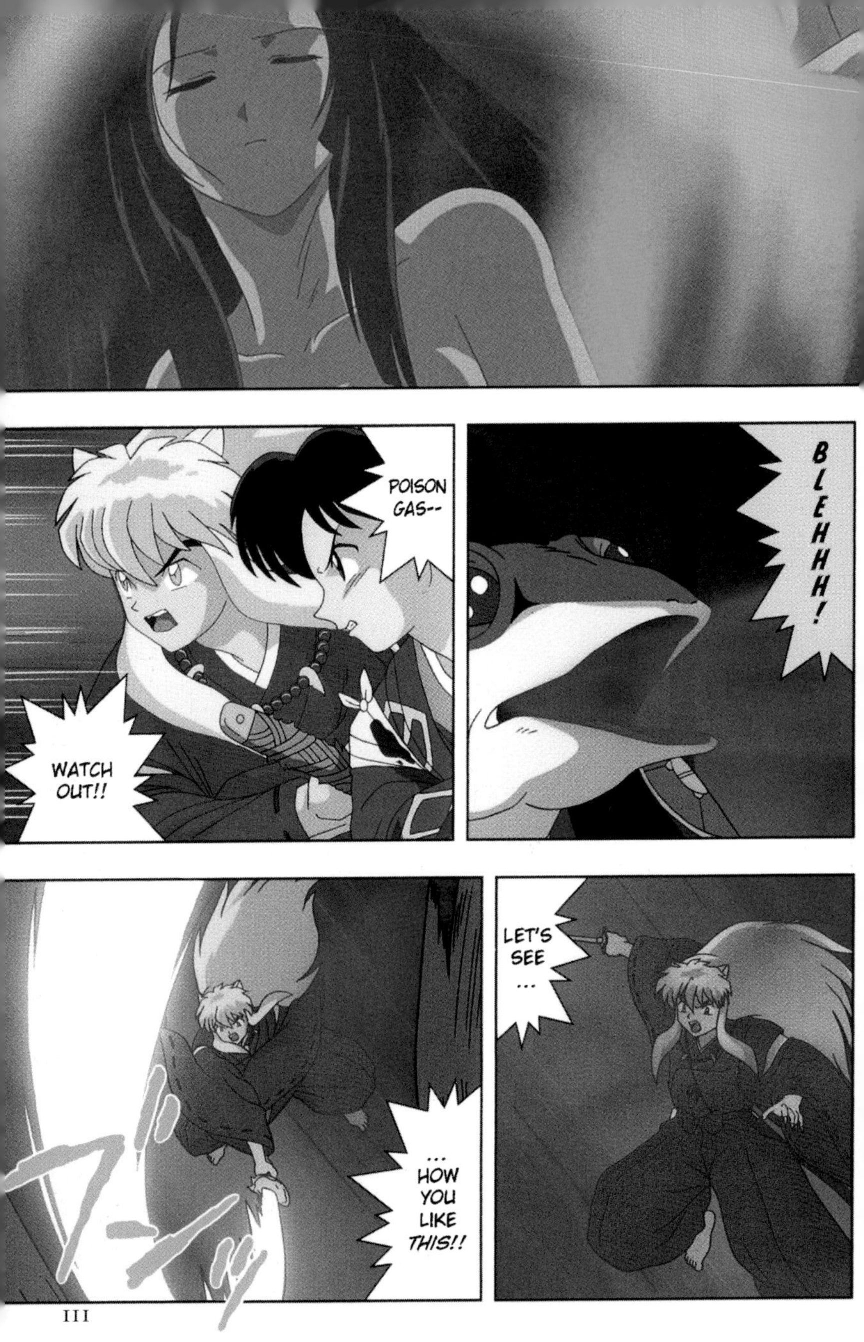
BLEHHHH!
POISON GAS--
WATCH OUT!!
LET'S SEE ...
... HOW YOU LIKE THIS!!

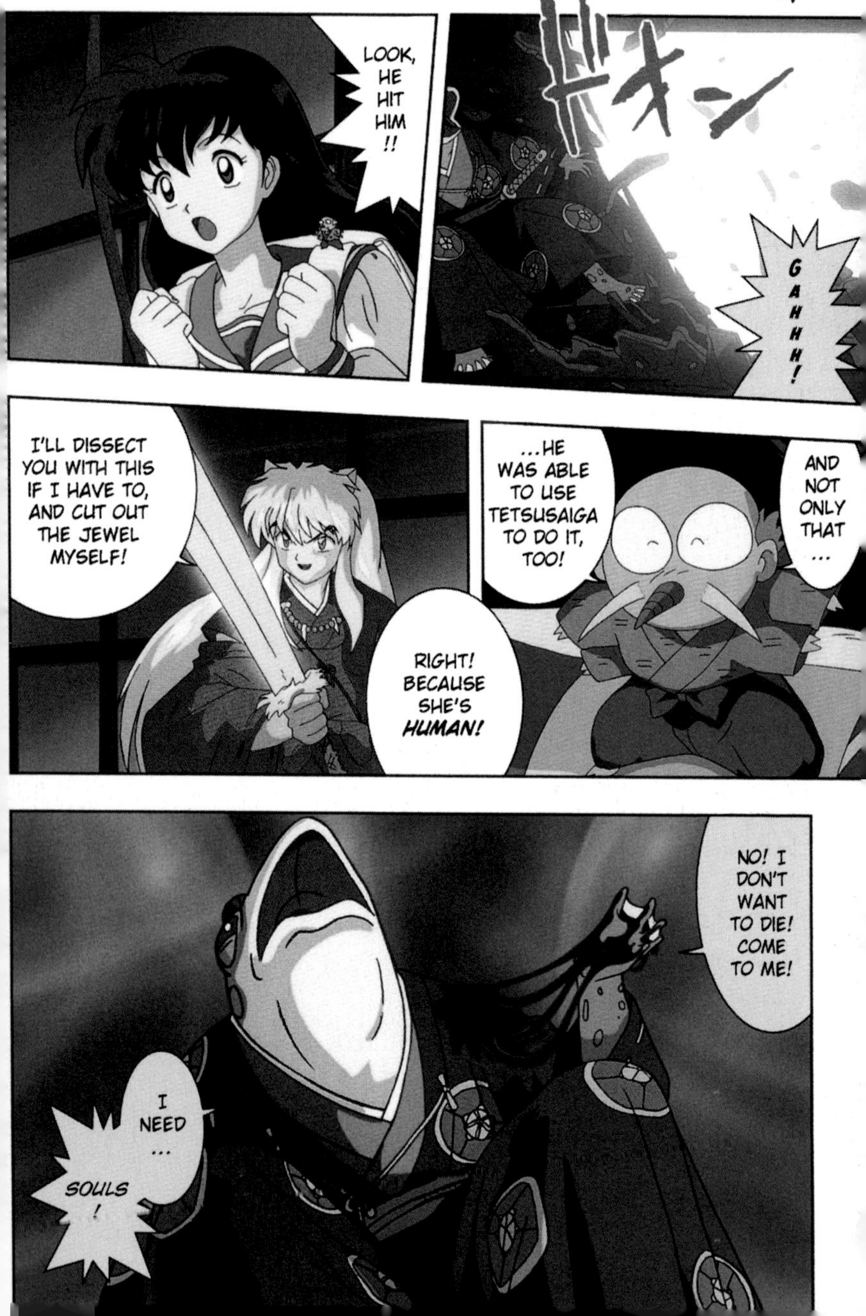
ドオン
GAHHHH!
LOOK, HE HIT HIM!!
AND NOT ONLY THAT...
...HE WAS ABLE TO USE TETSUSAIGA TO DO IT, TOO!
I'LL DISSECT YOU WITH THIS IF I HAVE TO, AND CUT OUT THE JEWEL MYSELF!
RIGHT! BECAUSE SHE'S *HUMAN!*
NO! I DON'T WANT TO DIE! COME TO ME!
I NEED... SOULS!

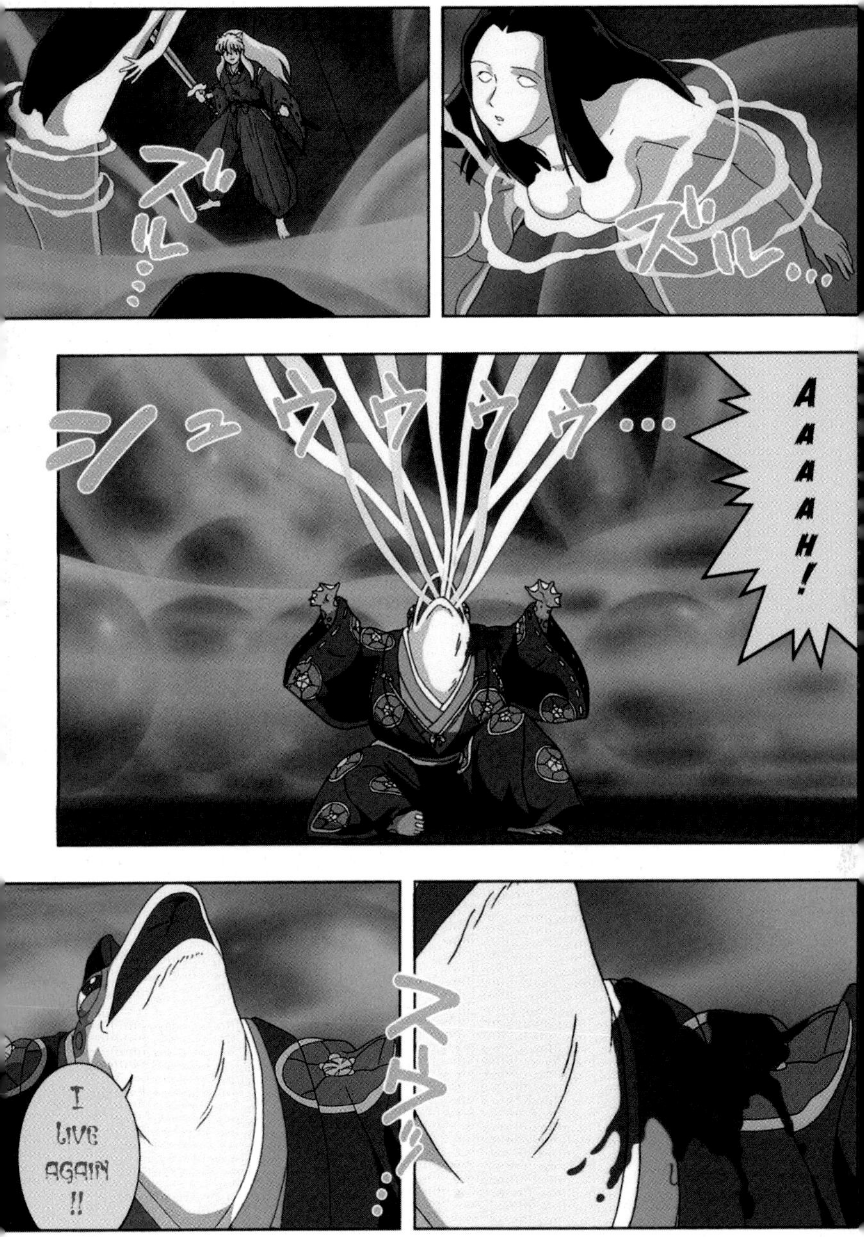
ズル...
ズル...
シュウウウ...
AAAAAH!
スゥッ...
I LIVE AGAIN !!

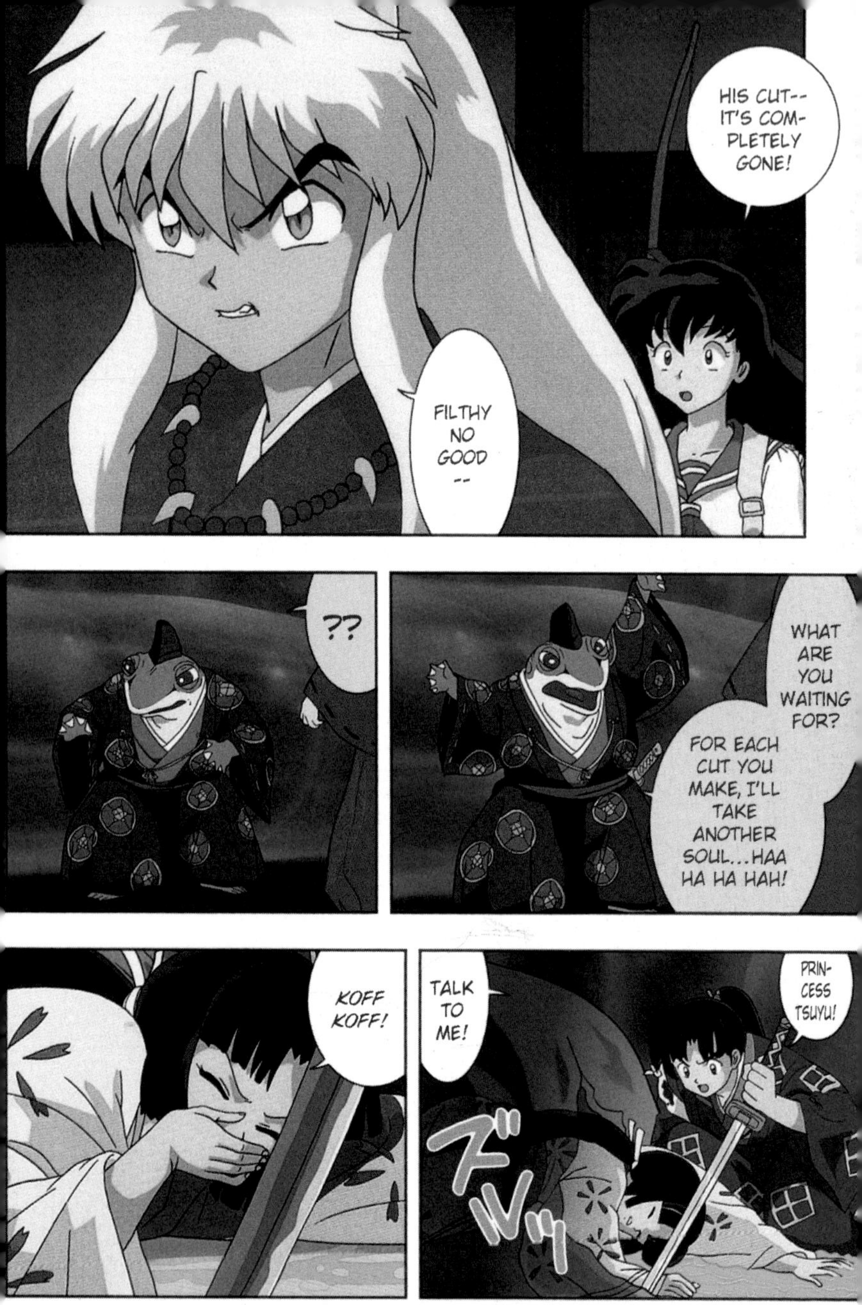
HIS CUT-- IT'S COM-PLETELY GONE!
FILTHY NO GOOD --
WHAT ARE YOU WAITING FOR?
FOR EACH CUT YOU MAKE, I'LL TAKE ANOTHER SOUL...HAA HA HA HAH!
??
PRIN-CESS TSUYU!
TALK TO ME!
KOFF KOFF!

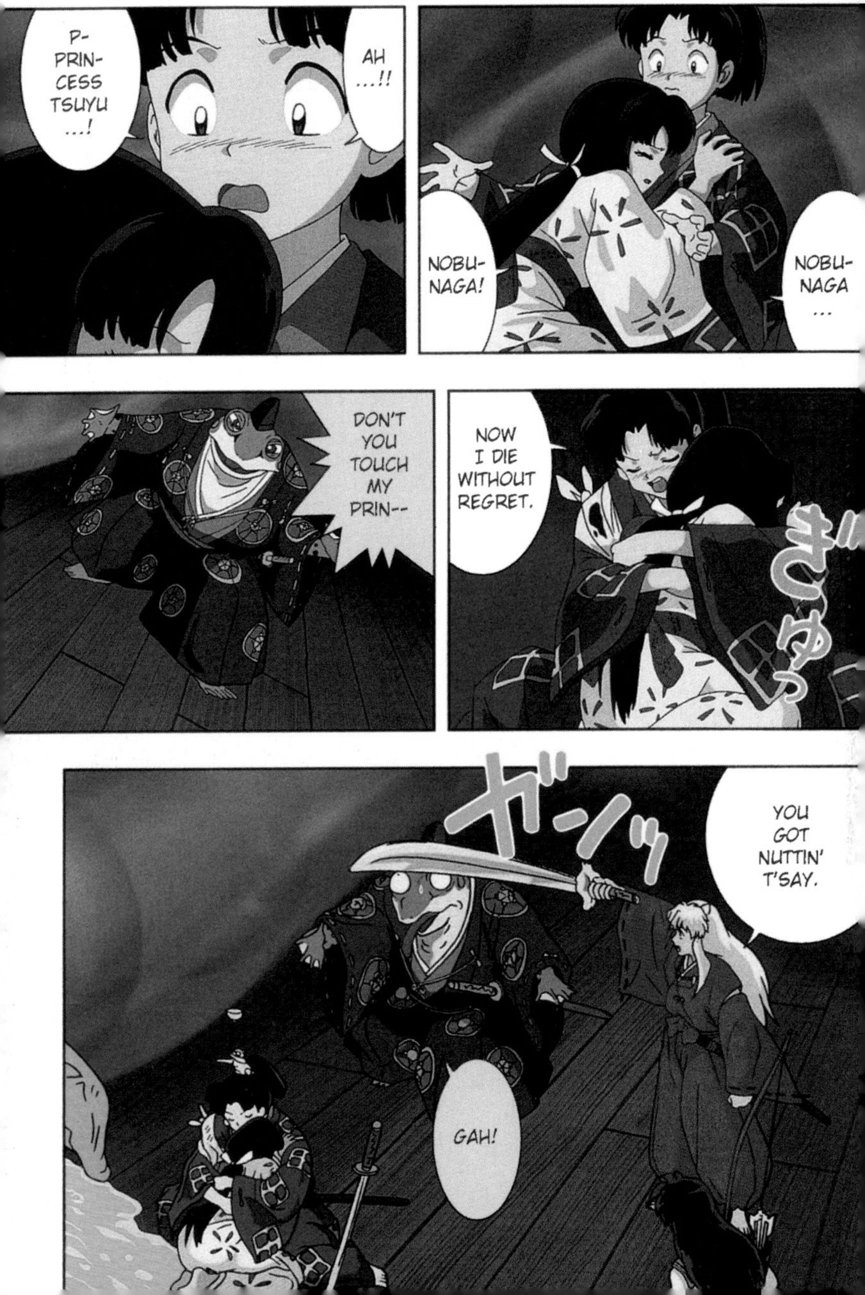
NOBU-NAGA ...
NOBU-NAGA!
AH ...!!
P-PRIN-CESS TSUYU ...!
NOW I DIE WITHOUT REGRET.
ぎゅっ
DON'T YOU TOUCH MY PRIN--
YOU GOT NUTTIN' T'SAY.
ガーンッ
GAH!

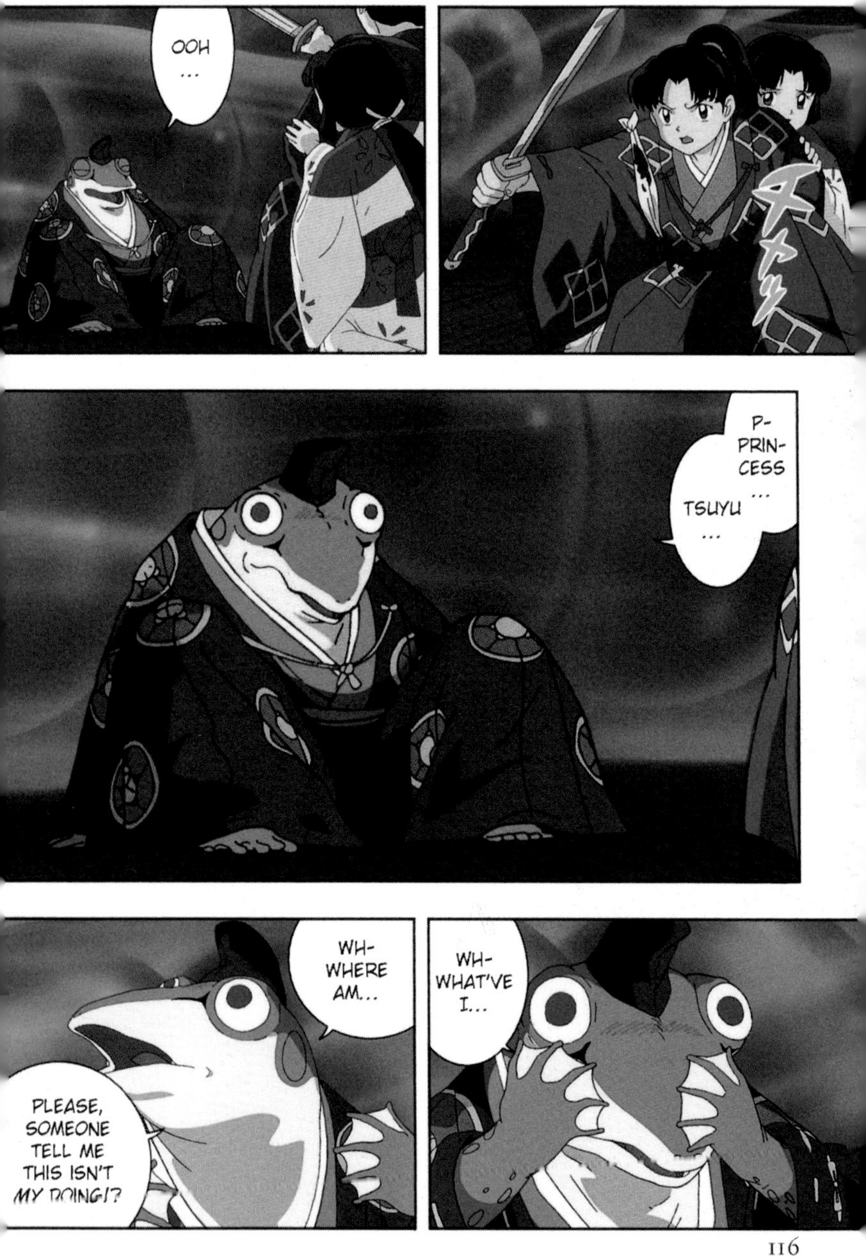
チャッ
OOH ...
P-PRINCESS ... TSUYU ...
WH-WHAT'VE I...
WH-WHERE AM...
PLEASE, SOMEONE TELL ME THIS ISN'T MY DOING!?

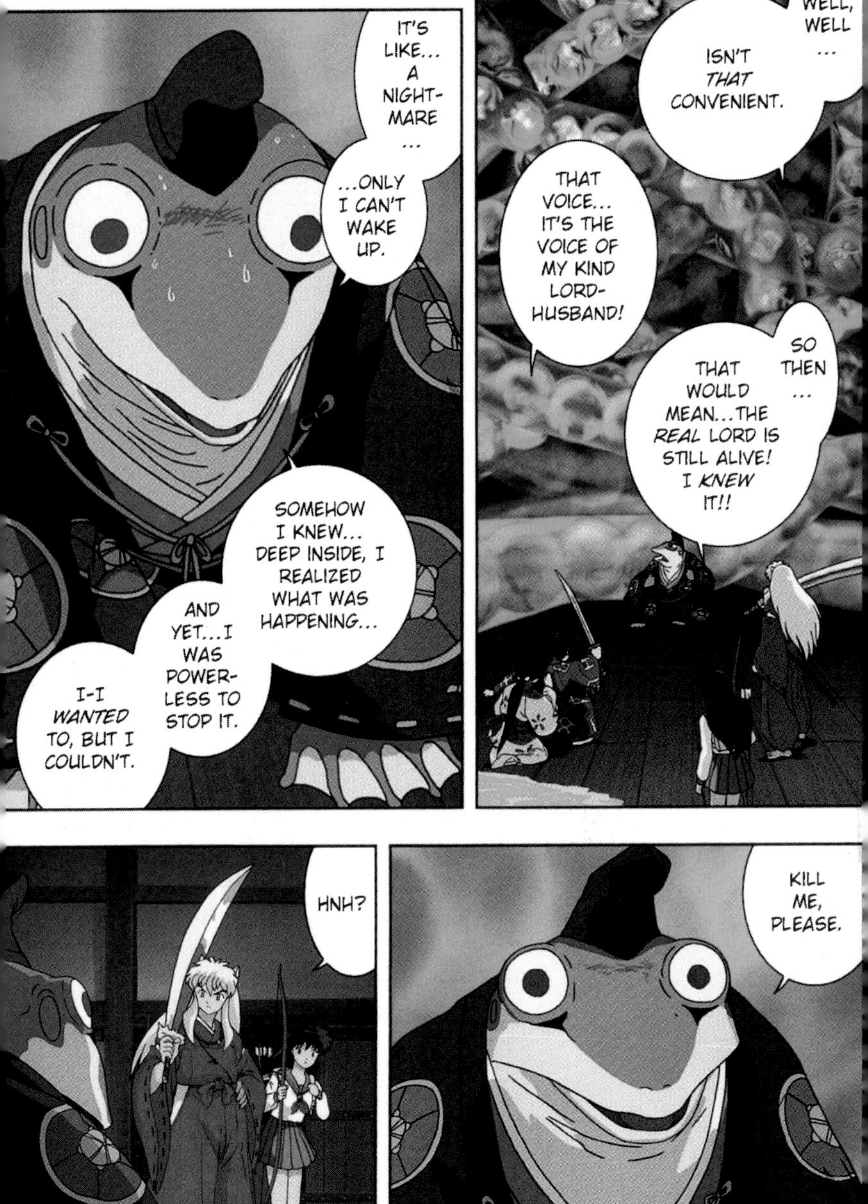
WELL, WELL...
ISN'T *THAT* CONVENIENT.
THAT VOICE... IT'S THE VOICE OF MY KIND LORD-HUSBAND!
SO THEN...
THAT WOULD MEAN...THE *REAL* LORD IS STILL ALIVE! I *KNEW* IT!!
IT'S LIKE... A NIGHT-MARE...
...ONLY I CAN'T WAKE UP.
SOMEHOW I KNEW... DEEP INSIDE, I REALIZED WHAT WAS HAPPENING...
AND YET...I WAS POWER-LESS TO STOP IT.
I-I *WANTED* TO, BUT I COULDN'T.
KILL ME, PLEASE.
HNH?

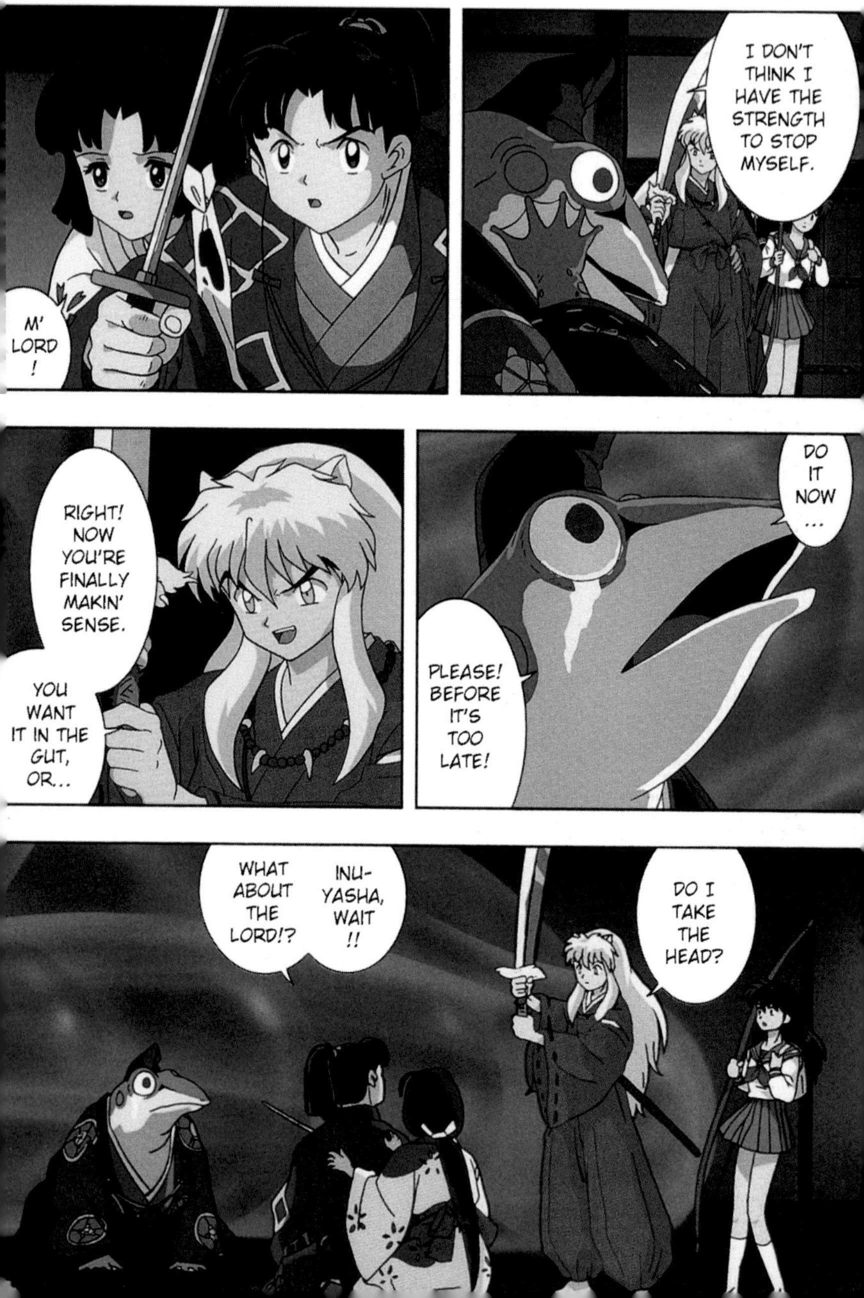
I DON'T THINK I HAVE THE STRENGTH TO STOP MYSELF.
M' LORD!
DO IT NOW...
PLEASE! BEFORE IT'S TOO LATE!
RIGHT! NOW YOU'RE FINALLY MAKIN' SENSE.
YOU WANT IT IN THE GUT, OR...
DO I TAKE THE HEAD?
INU-YASHA, WAIT!!
WHAT ABOUT THE LORD!?

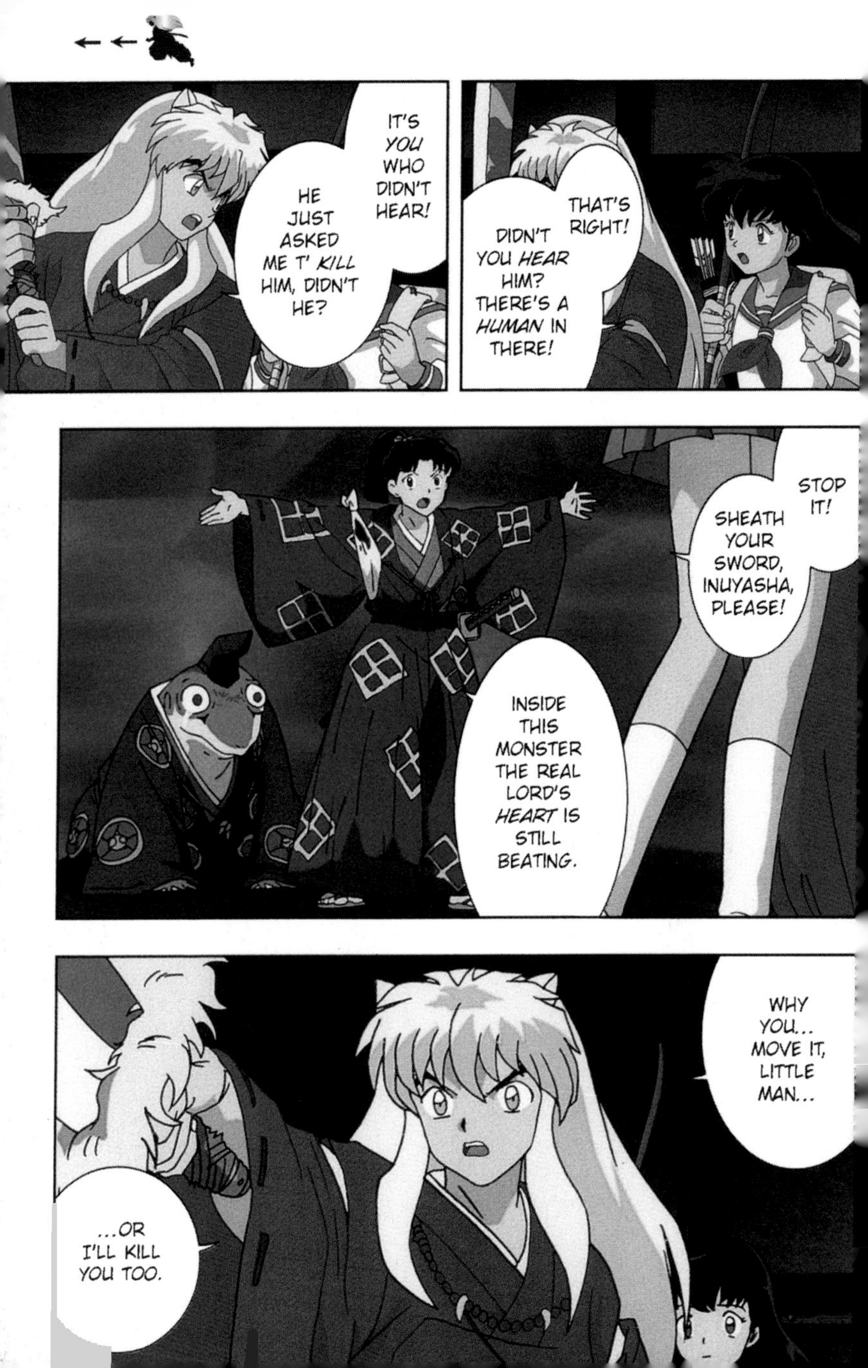
THAT'S RIGHT!
DIDN'T YOU *HEAR* HIM? THERE'S A *HUMAN* IN THERE!
IT'S *YOU* WHO DIDN'T HEAR!
HE JUST ASKED ME T' *KILL* HIM, DIDN'T HE?
STOP IT!
SHEATH YOUR SWORD, INUYASHA, PLEASE!
INSIDE THIS MONSTER THE REAL LORD'S *HEART* IS STILL BEATING.
WHY YOU... MOVE IT, LITTLE MAN...
...OR I'LL KILL YOU TOO.

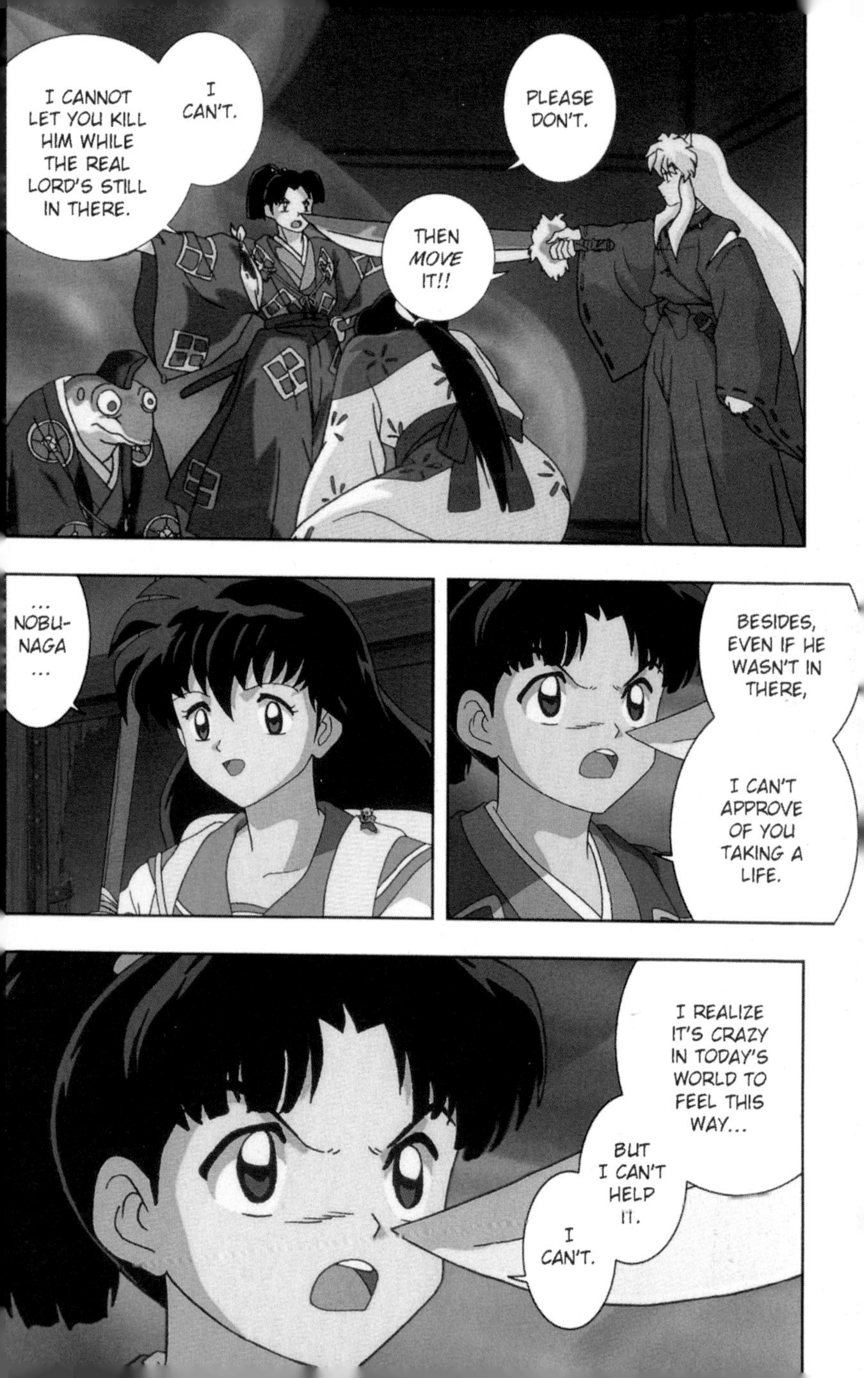
PLEASE DON'T.
I CAN'T.
I CANNOT LET YOU KILL HIM WHILE THE REAL LORD'S STILL IN THERE.
THEN *MOVE* IT!!
BESIDES, EVEN IF HE WASN'T IN THERE,
I CAN'T APPROVE OF YOU TAKING A LIFE.
...NOBU-NAGA...
I REALIZE IT'S CRAZY IN TODAY'S WORLD TO FEEL THIS WAY...
BUT I CAN'T HELP IT.
I CAN'T.

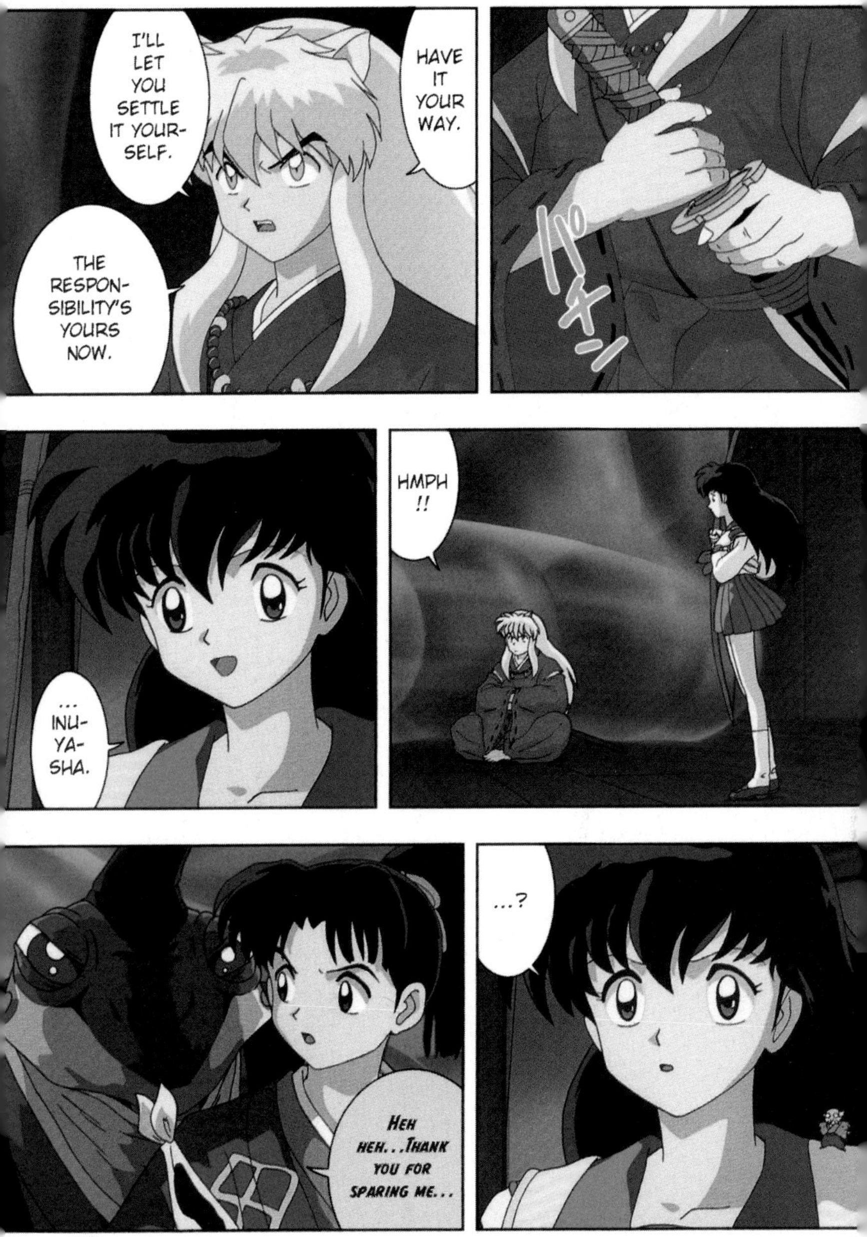
パキン
HAVE IT YOUR WAY.
I'LL LET YOU SETTLE IT YOUR-SELF.
THE RESPON-SIBILITY'S YOURS NOW.
HMPH !!
... INU-YA-SHA.
...?
HEH HEH...THANK YOU FOR SPARING ME...

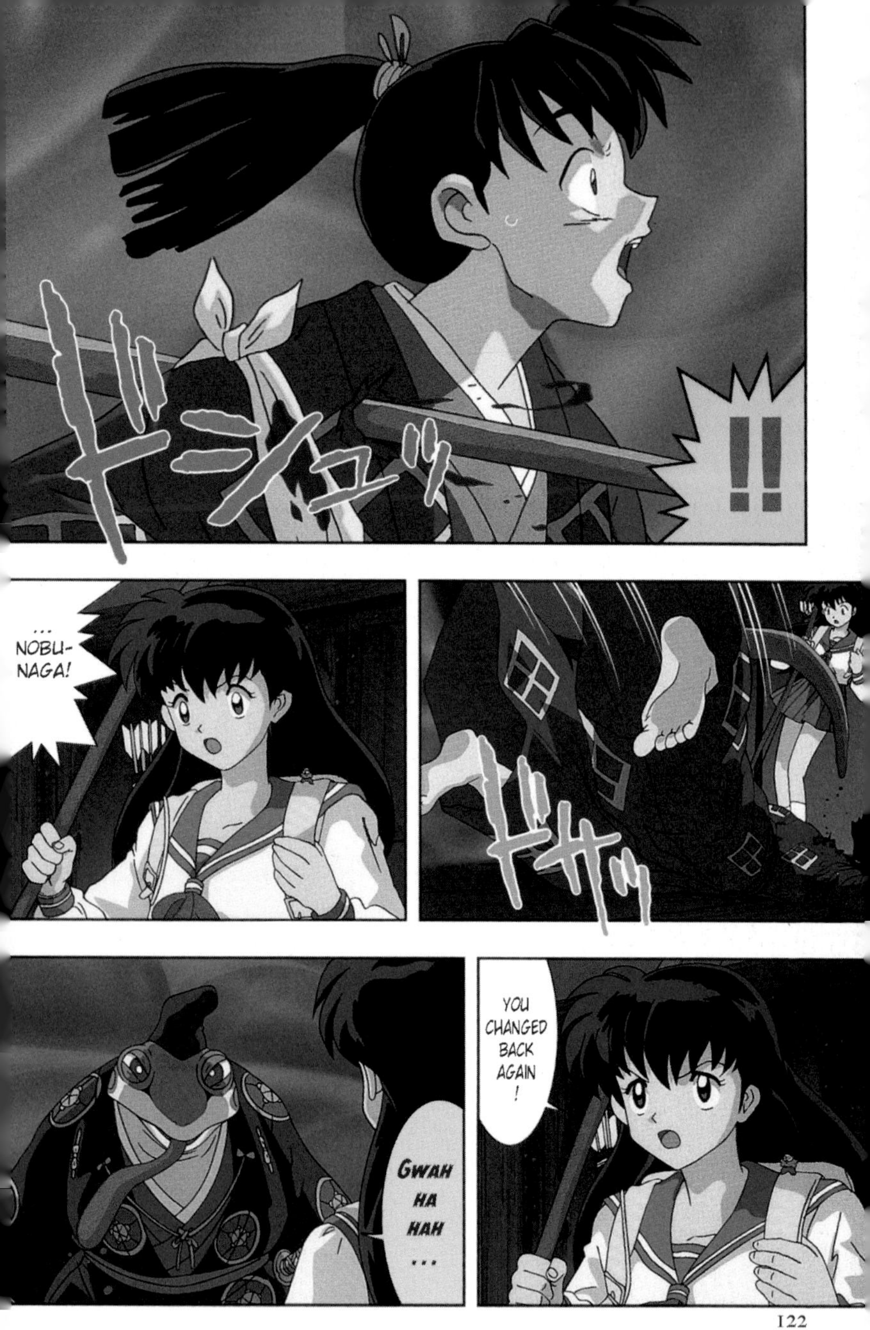
ドシュッ
!!
ドサッ
... NOBU-NAGA!
YOU CHANGED BACK AGAIN !
GWAH HA HAH ...

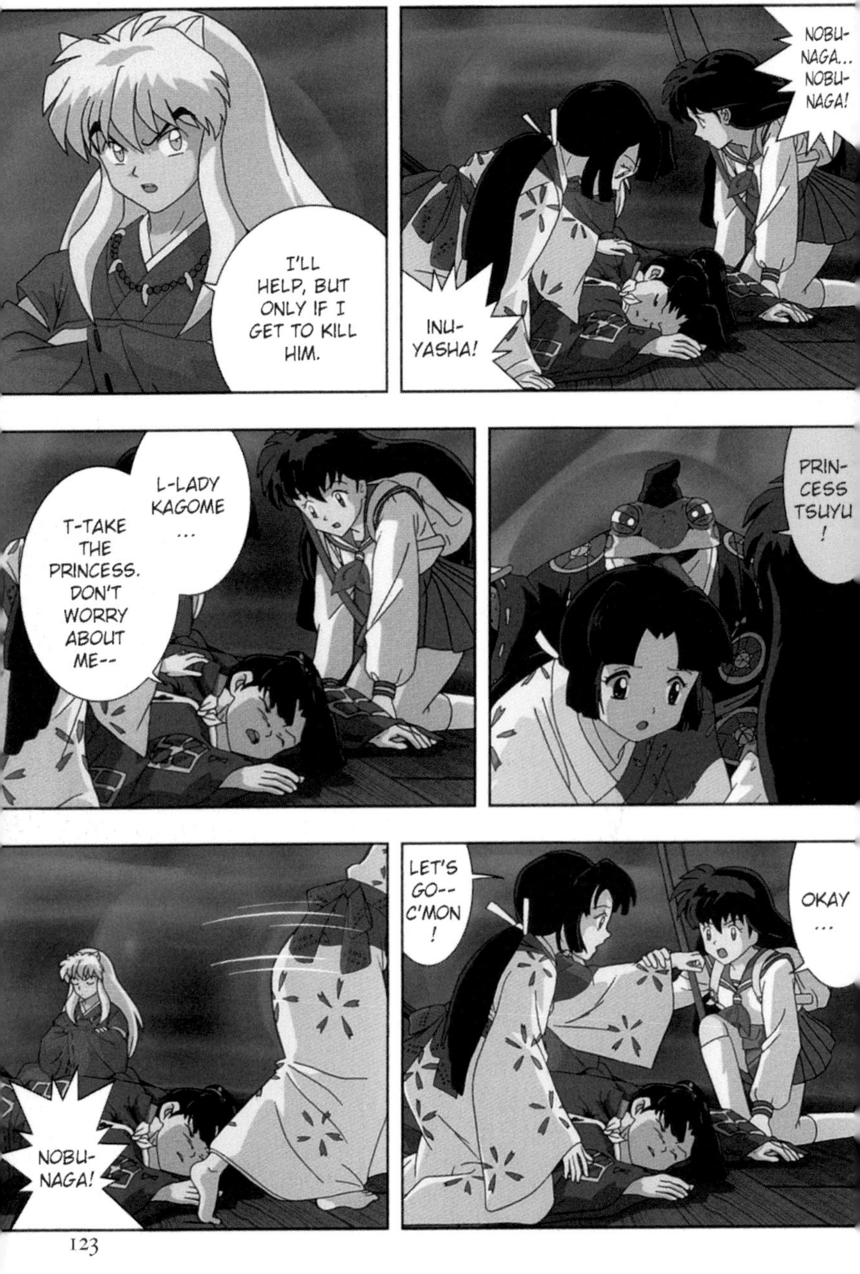
NOBU-NAGA... NOBU-NAGA!
INU-YASHA!
I'LL HELP, BUT ONLY IF I GET TO KILL HIM.
PRIN-CESS TSUYU!
L-LADY KAGOME...
T-TAKE THE PRINCESS. DON'T WORRY ABOUT ME--
OKAY...
LET'S GO-- C'MON!
NOBU-NAGA!

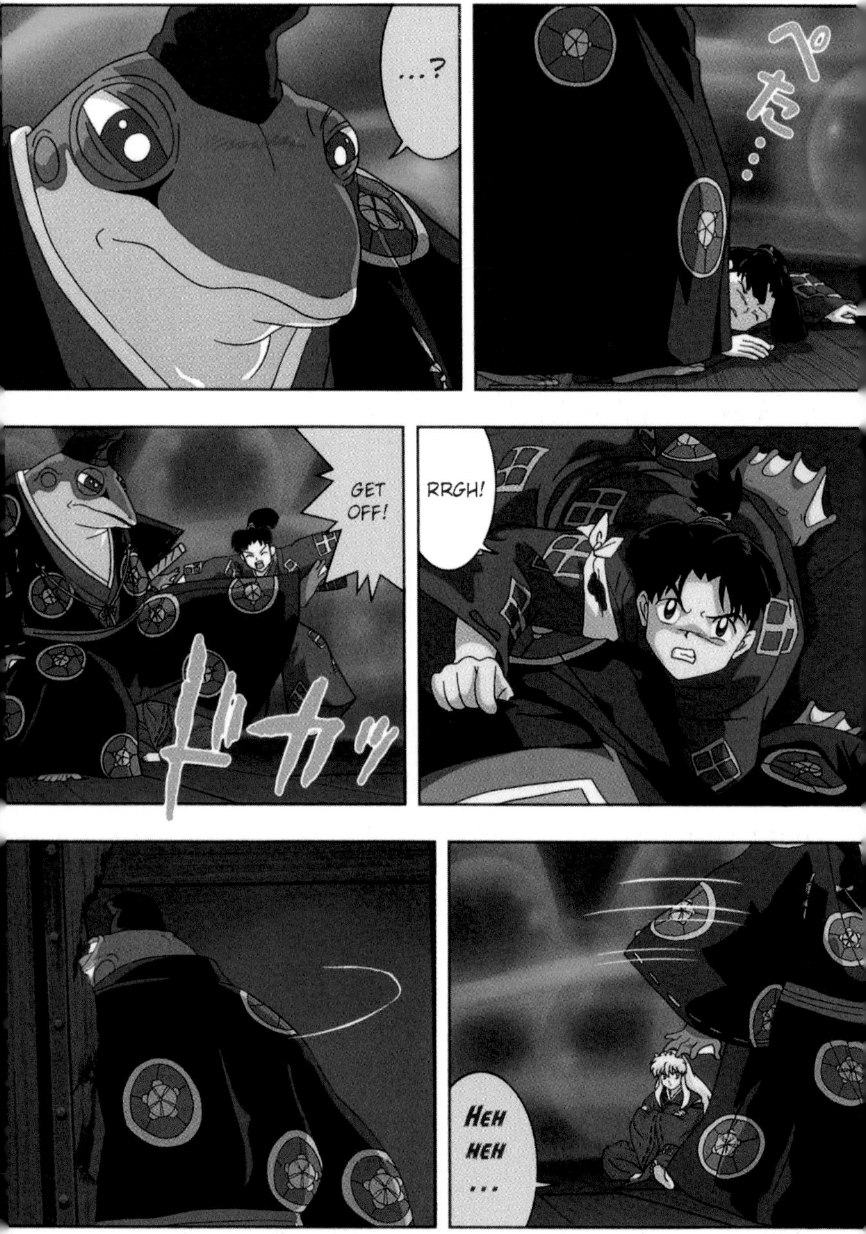
ぺた…
...?
RRGH!
GET OFF!
ドカッ
HEH HEH ...

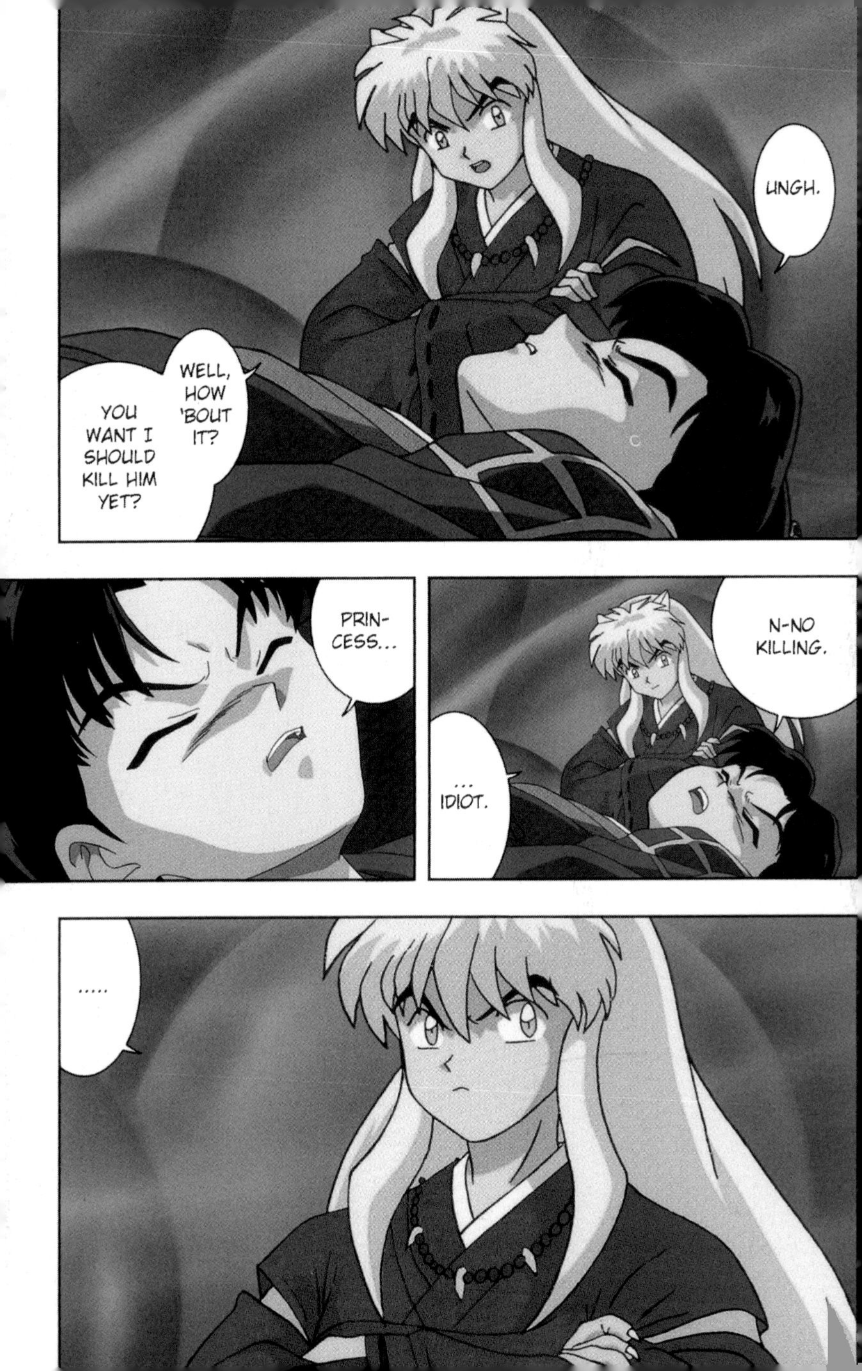
UNGH.
WELL, HOW 'BOUT IT?
YOU WANT I SHOULD KILL HIM YET?
N-NO KILLING.
...IDIOT.
PRIN-CESS...
.....

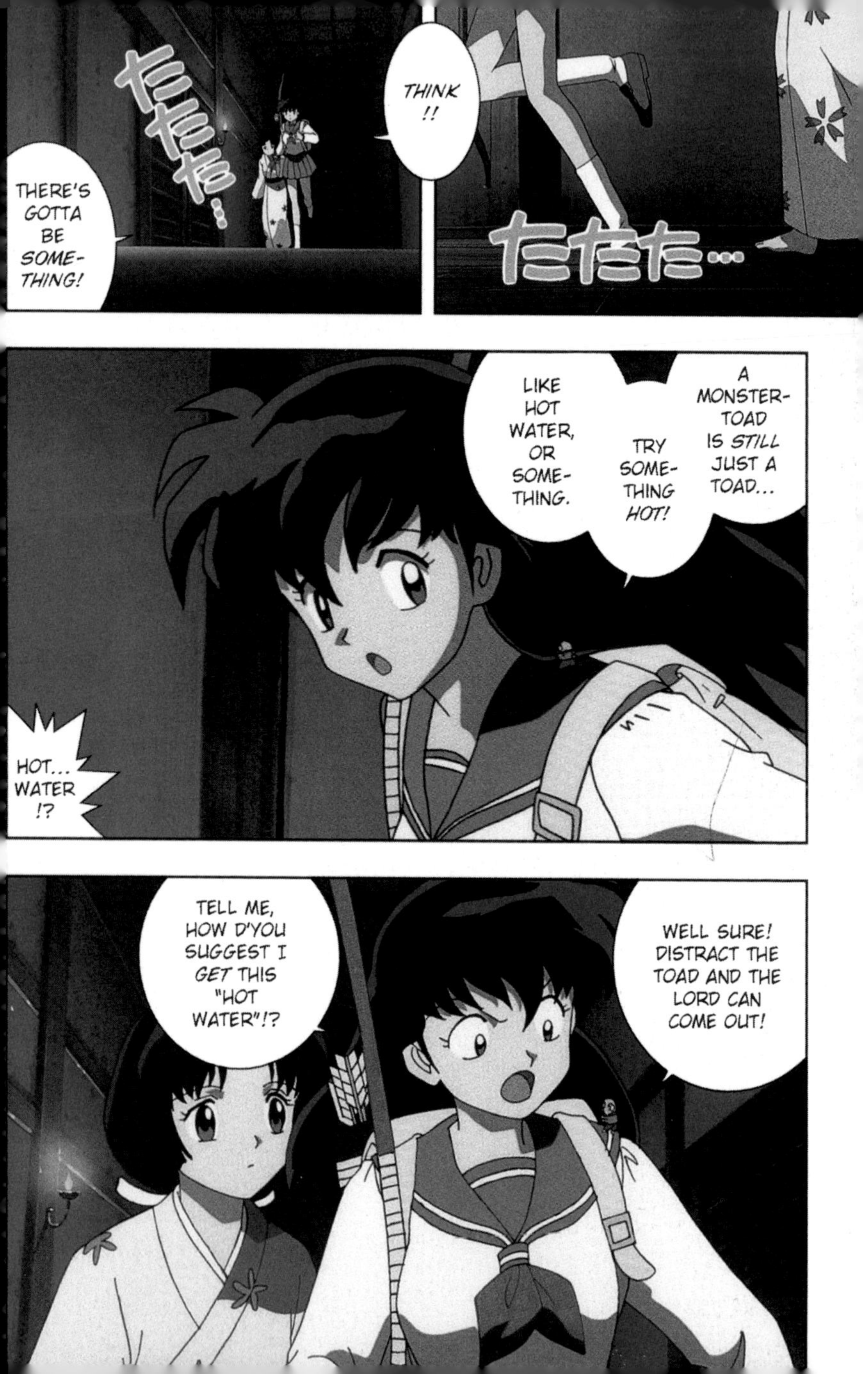
THINK !!
たたた…
たたた…
THERE'S GOTTA BE SOMETHING!
A MONSTER-TOAD IS STILL JUST A TOAD...
TRY SOMETHING HOT!
LIKE HOT WATER, OR SOMETHING.
HOT... WATER !?
WELL SURE! DISTRACT THE TOAD AND THE LORD CAN COME OUT!
TELL ME, HOW D'YOU SUGGEST I GET THIS "HOT WATER"!?

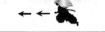

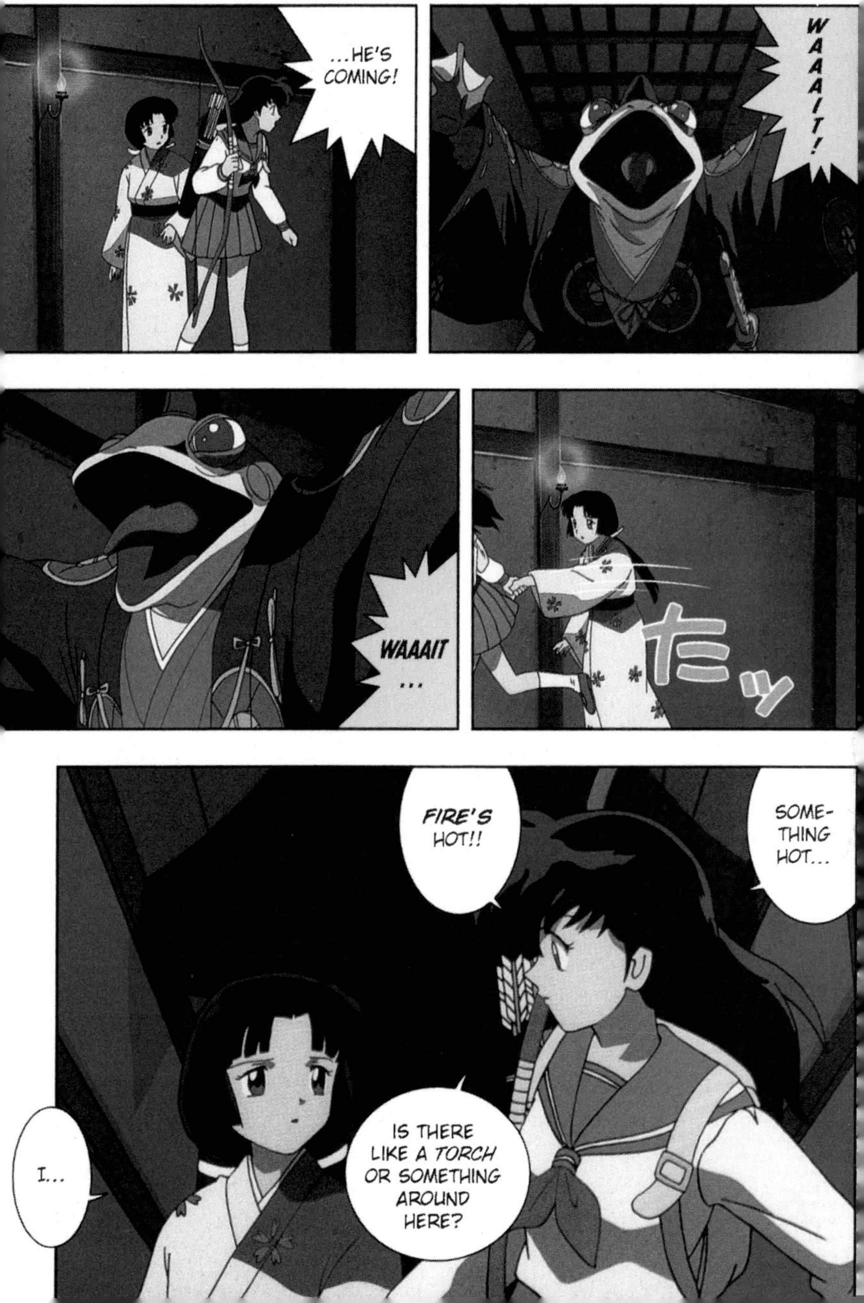
WAAAIT!
...HE'S COMING!
たッ
WAAAIT ...
SOME-THING HOT...
FIRE'S HOT!!
IS THERE LIKE A TORCH OR SOMETHING AROUND HERE?
I...

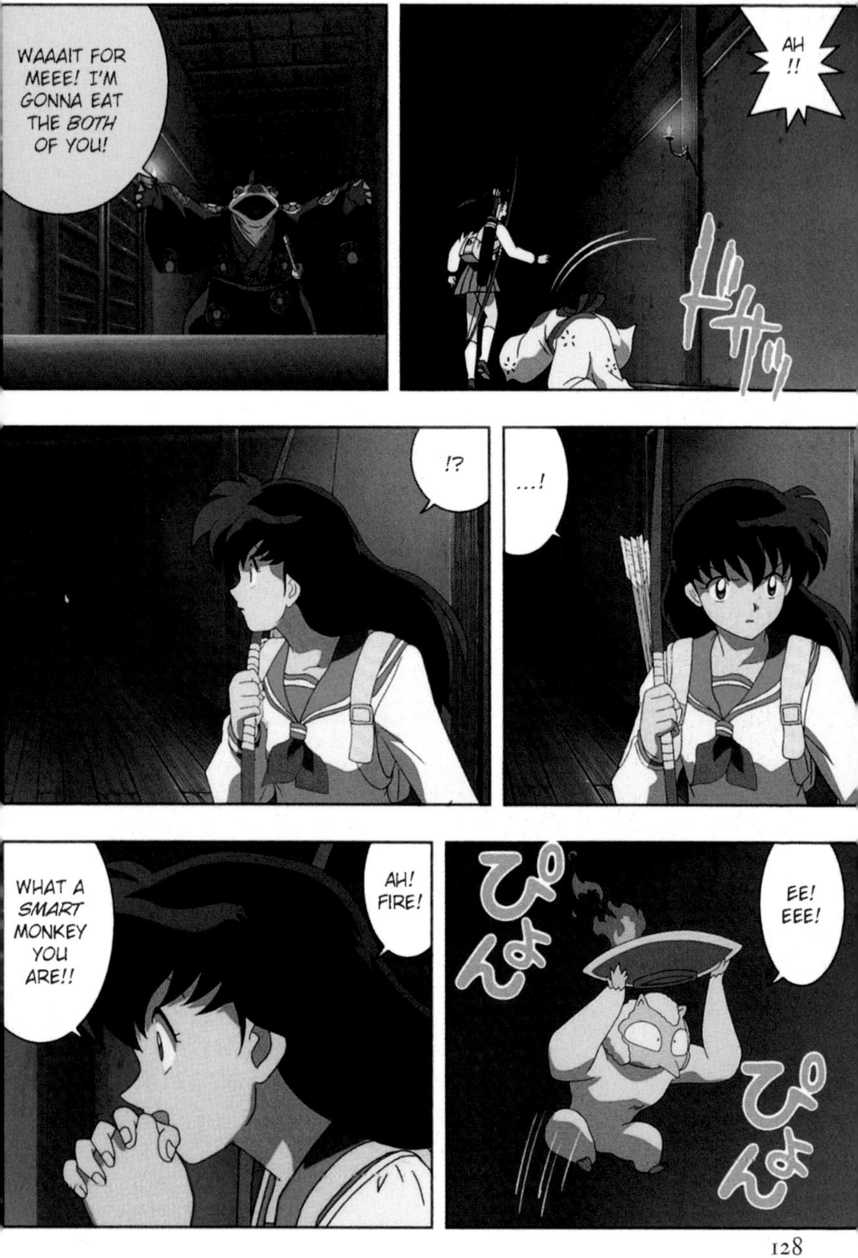
AH !!
ドサッ
WAAAIT FOR MEEE! I'M GONNA EAT THE *BOTH* OF YOU!
...!
!?
EE! EEE!
ぴょん
ぴょん
AH! FIRE!
WHAT A *SMART* MONKEY YOU ARE!!

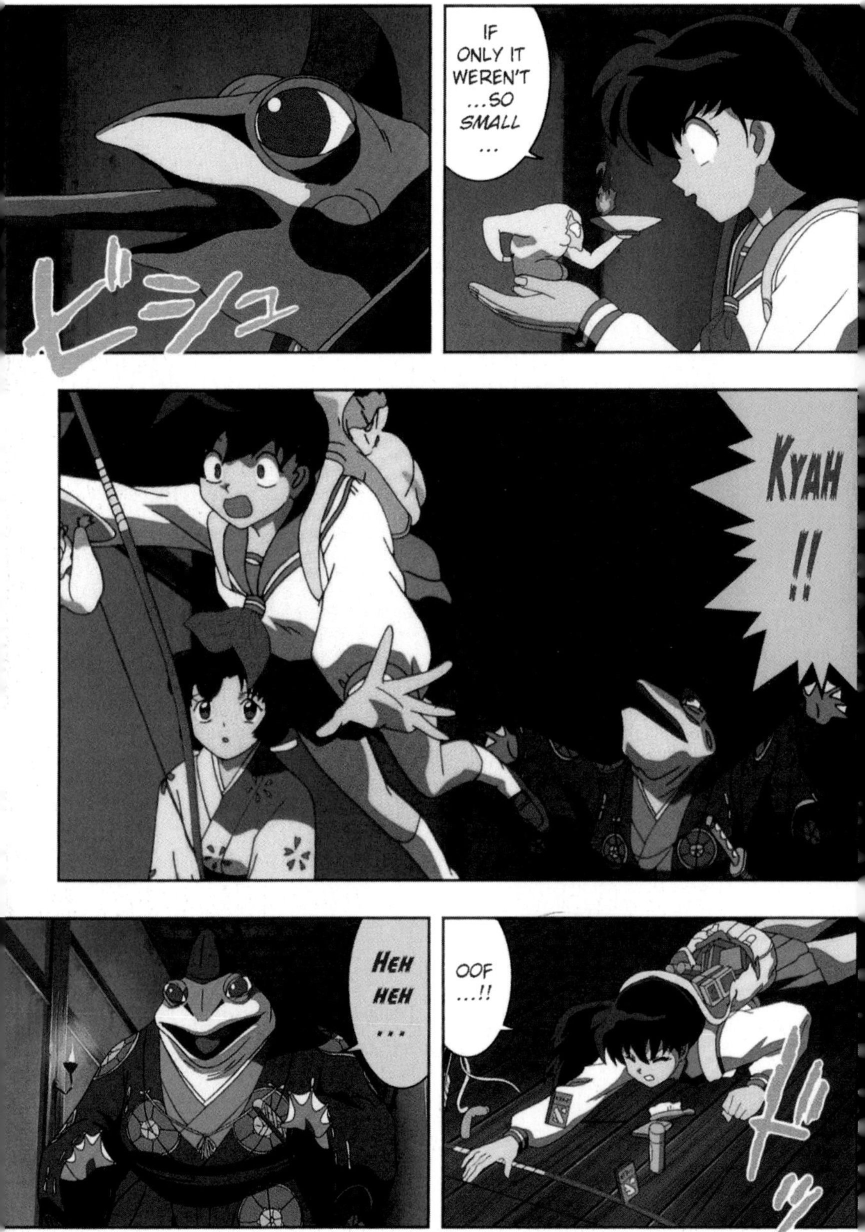
IF ONLY IT WEREN'T ...SO SMALL ...
ビシュ
KYAH !!
OOF ...!!
HEH HEH ...

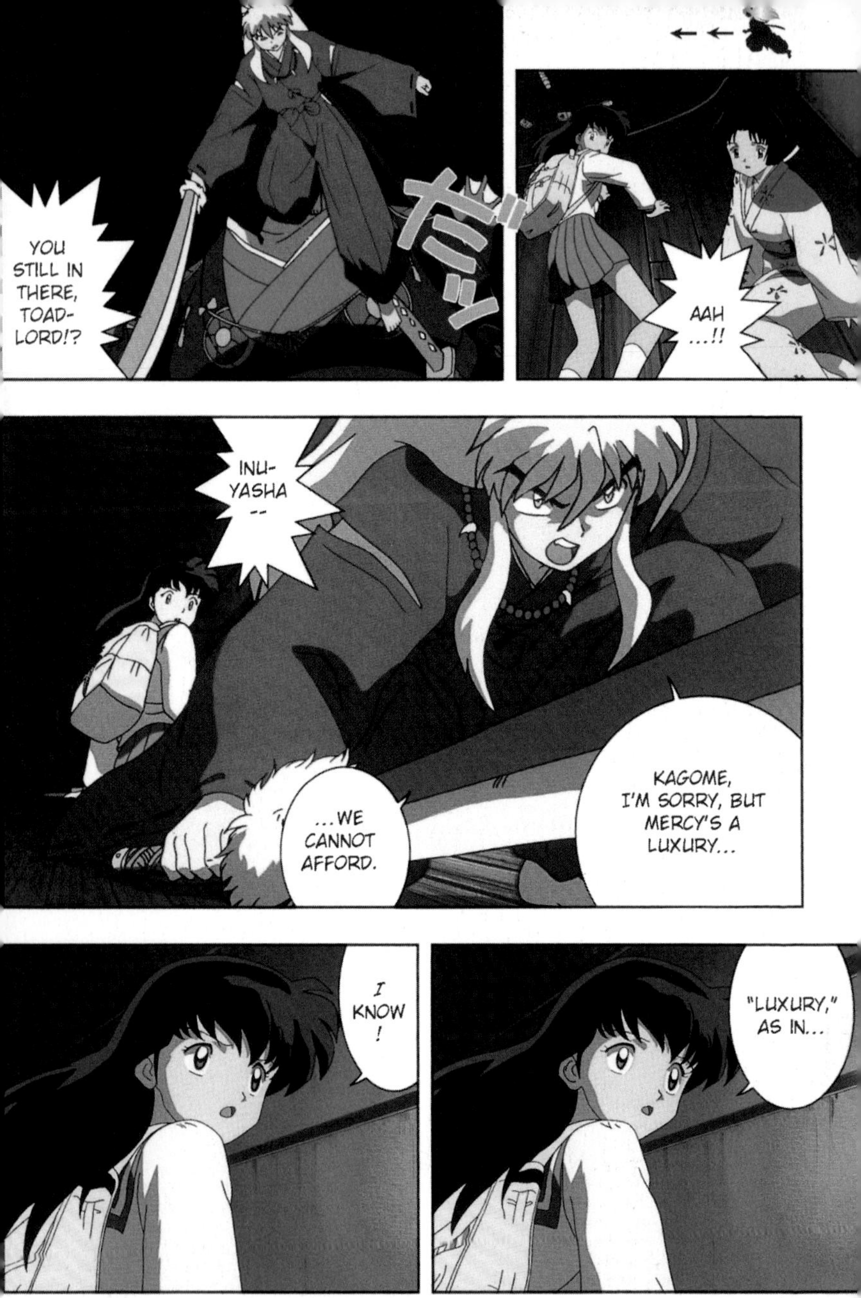
AAH ...!!
YOU STILL IN THERE, TOAD-LORD!?
ダッ
INU-YASHA --
KAGOME, I'M SORRY, BUT MERCY'S A LUXURY...
...WE CANNOT AFFORD.
"LUXURY," AS IN...
I KNOW!

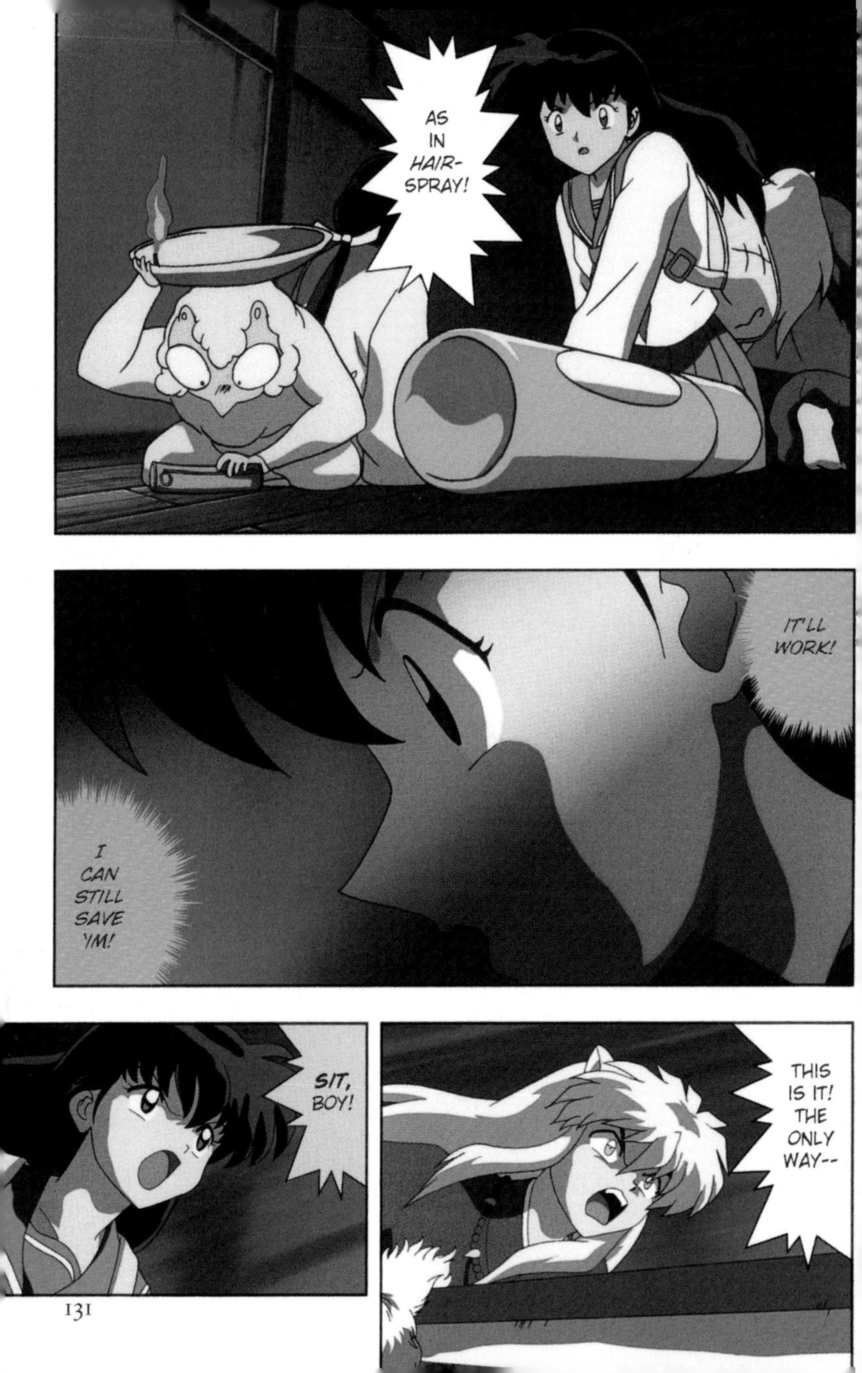
AS IN HAIR-SPRAY!
IT'LL WORK!
I CAN STILL SAVE 'IM!
THIS IS IT! THE ONLY WAY--
SIT, BOY!

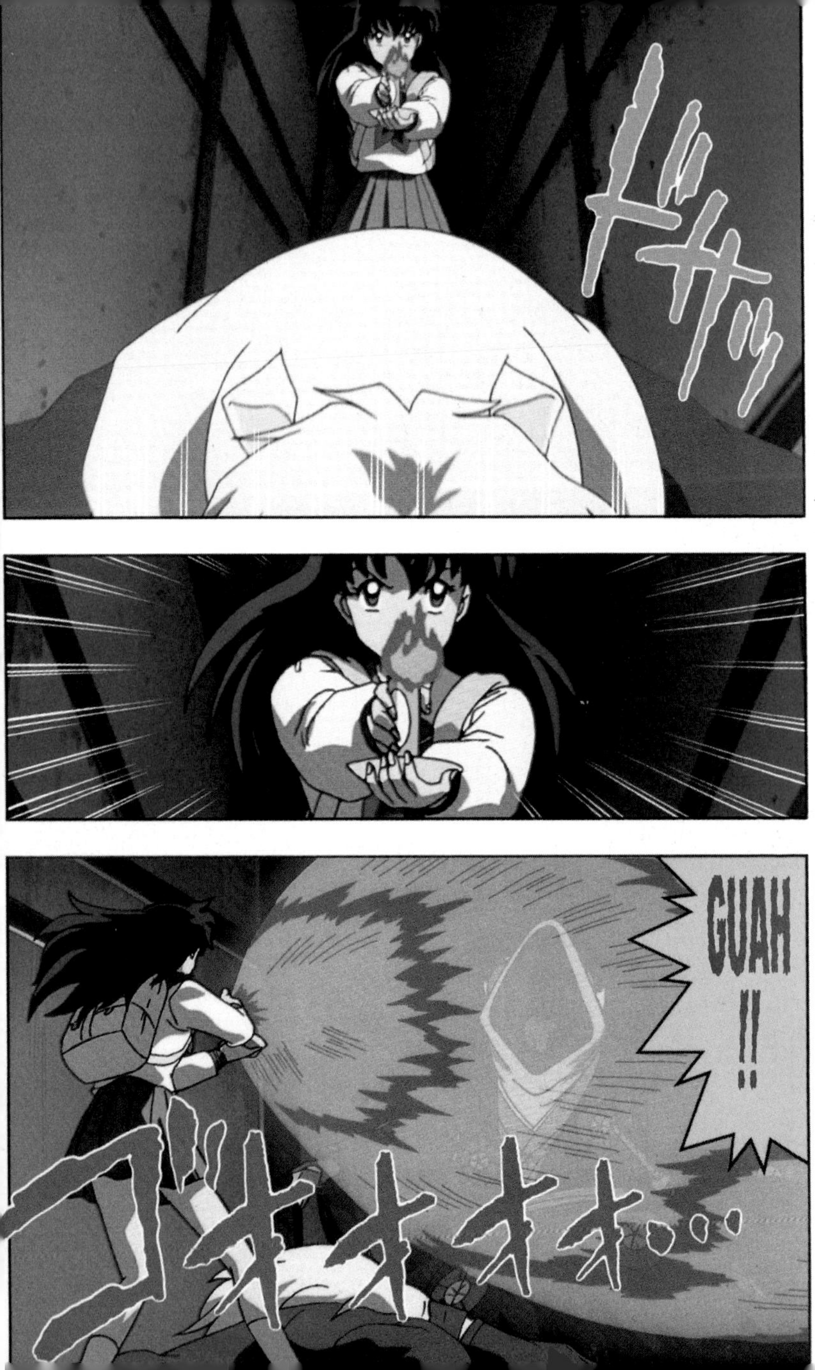
ドサッ
GUAH!!

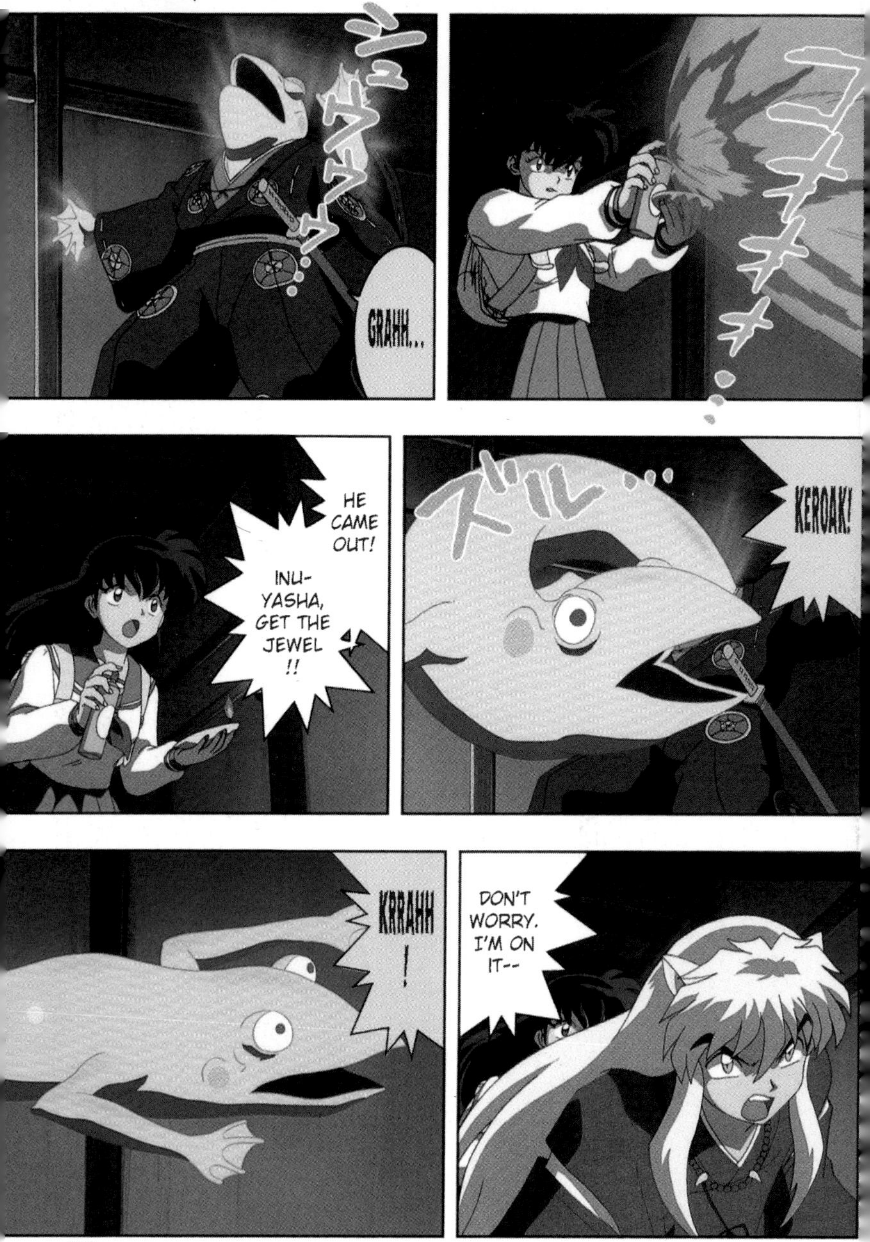
GRAHH...
ズル...
KEROAK!
HE CAME OUT!
INU-YASHA, GET THE JEWEL!!
DON'T WORRY. I'M ON IT--
KRRAHH!

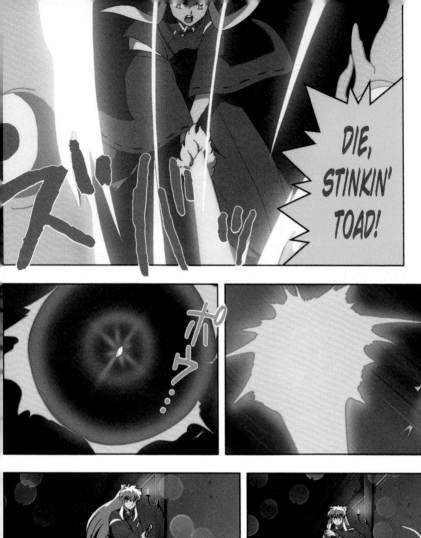

DIE, STINKIN' TOAD!

134

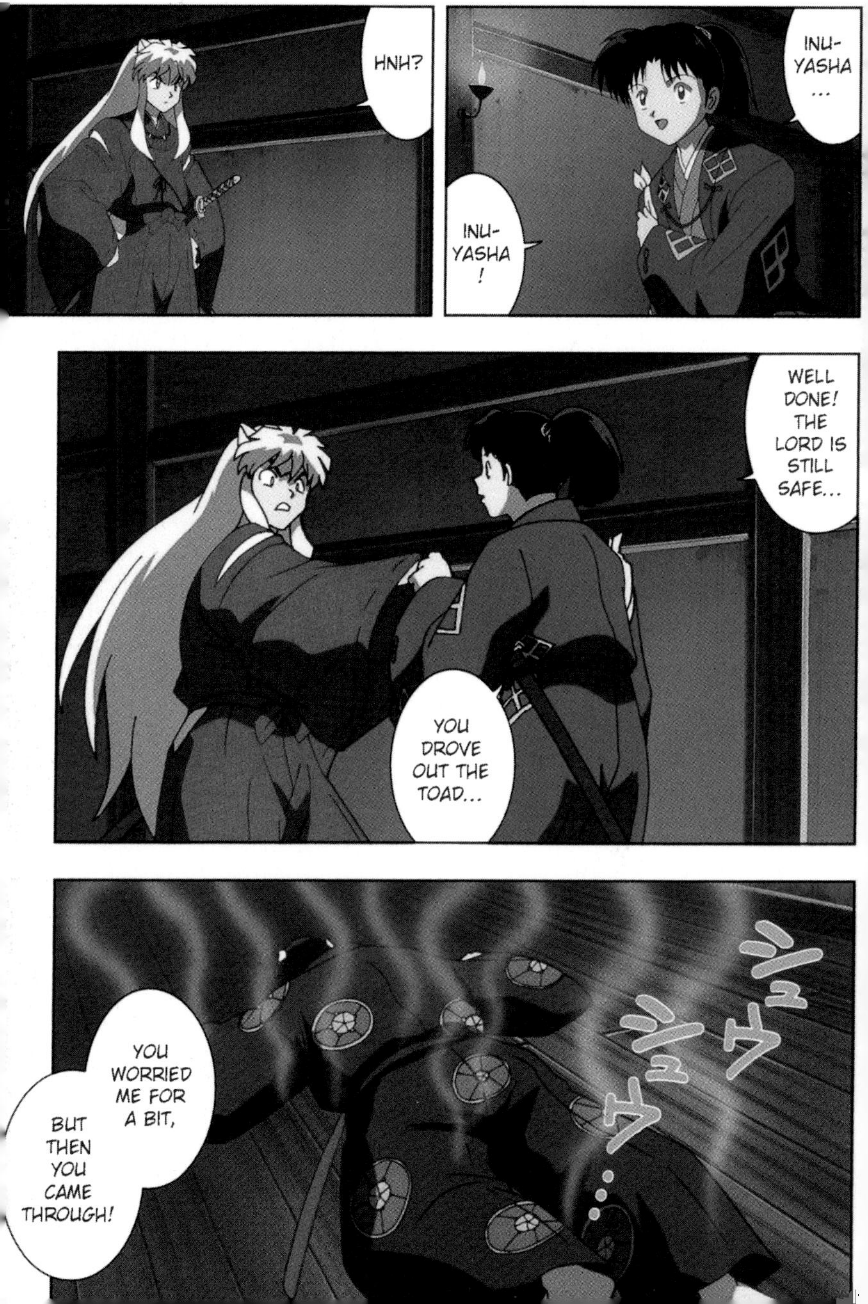
INU-YASHA ...
INU-YASHA !
HNH?
WELL DONE! THE LORD IS STILL SAFE...
YOU DROVE OUT THE TOAD...
YOU WORRIED ME FOR A BIT,
BUT THEN YOU CAME THROUGH!

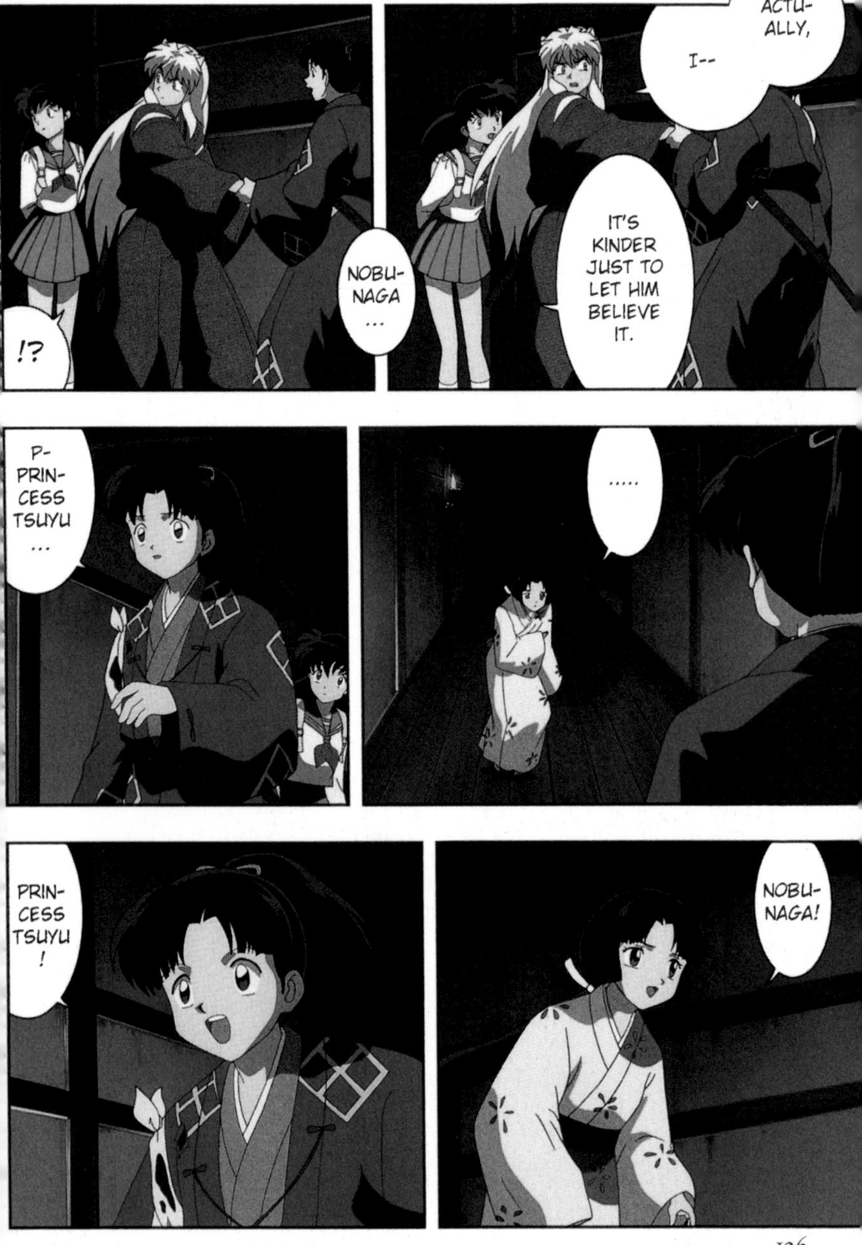
ACTU-ALLY,
I--
IT'S KINDER JUST TO LET HIM BELIEVE IT.
NOBU-NAGA ...
!?
.....
P-PRINCESS TSUYU ...
NOBU-NAGA!
PRIN-CESS TSUYU !

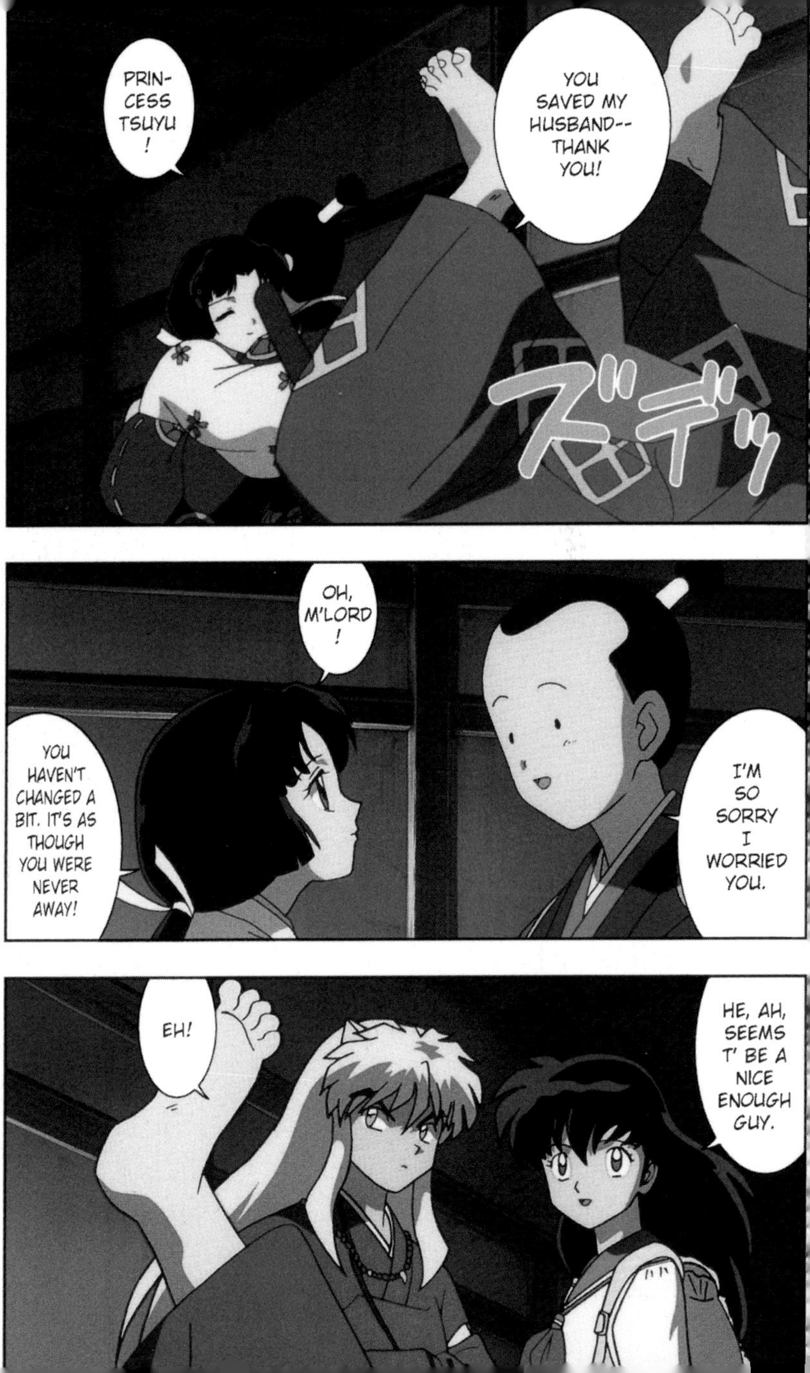
YOU SAVED MY HUSBAND-- THANK YOU!
PRIN-CESS TSUYU!
ズデッ
OH, M'LORD!
I'M SO SORRY I WORRIED YOU.
YOU HAVEN'T CHANGED A BIT. IT'S AS THOUGH YOU WERE NEVER AWAY!
HE, AH, SEEMS T' BE A NICE ENOUGH GUY.
EH!

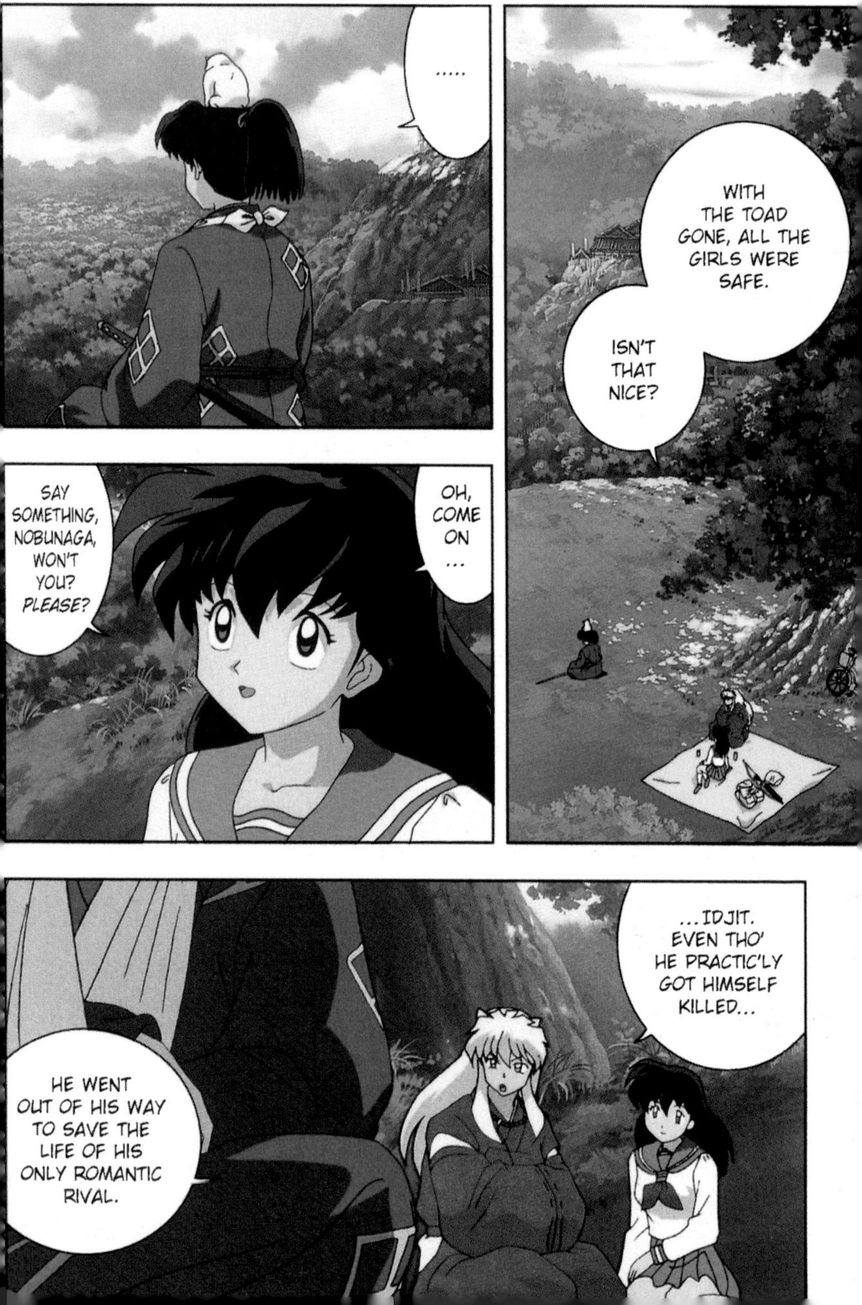
WITH THE TOAD GONE, ALL THE GIRLS WERE SAFE.
ISN'T THAT NICE?
.....
OH, COME ON ...
SAY SOMETHING, NOBUNAGA, WON'T YOU? *PLEASE?*
...IDJIT. EVEN THO' HE PRACTIC'LY GOT HIMSELF KILLED...
HE WENT OUT OF HIS WAY TO SAVE THE LIFE OF HIS ONLY ROMANTIC RIVAL.

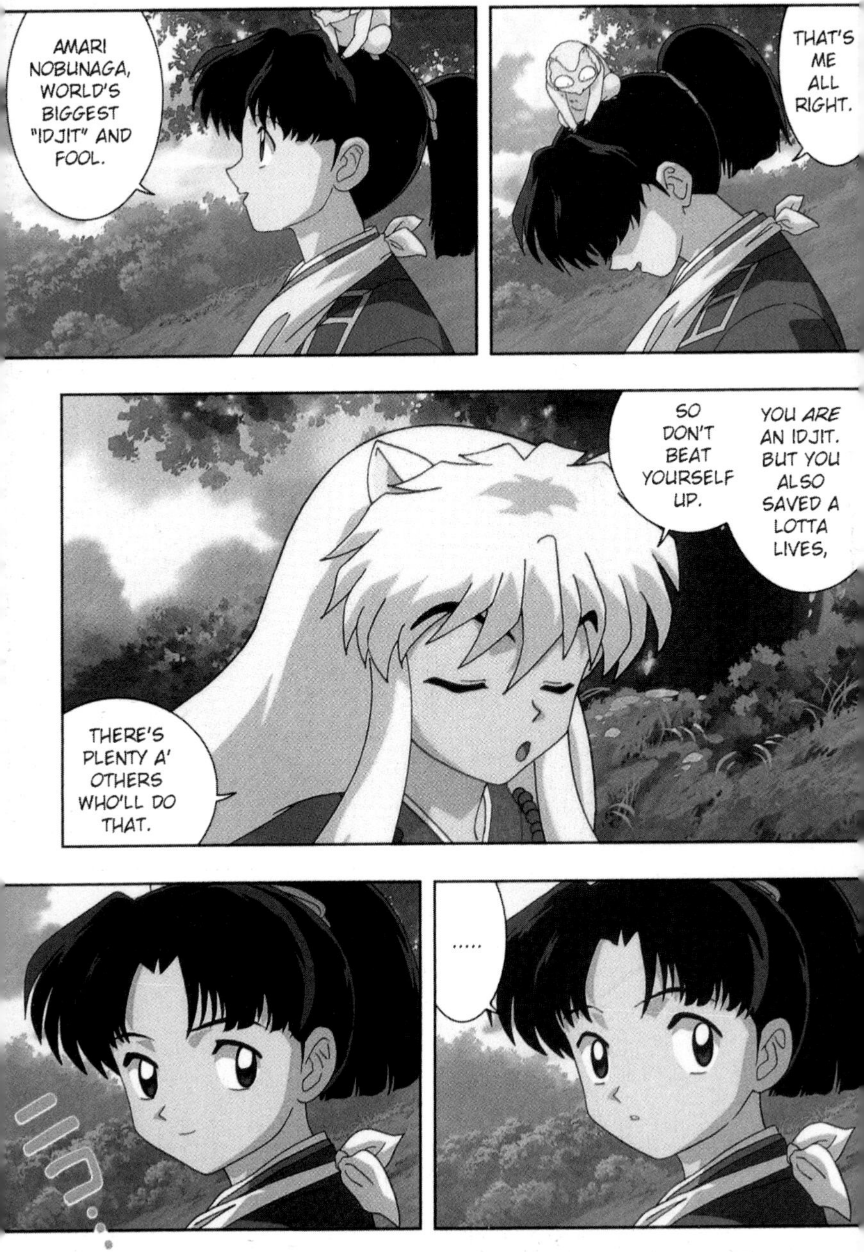
AMARI NOBUNAGA, WORLD'S BIGGEST "IDJIT" AND FOOL.
THAT'S ME ALL RIGHT.
YOU *ARE* AN IDJIT. BUT YOU ALSO SAVED A LOTTA LIVES,
SO DON'T BEAT YOURSELF UP.
THERE'S PLENTY A' OTHERS WHO'LL DO THAT.
.....

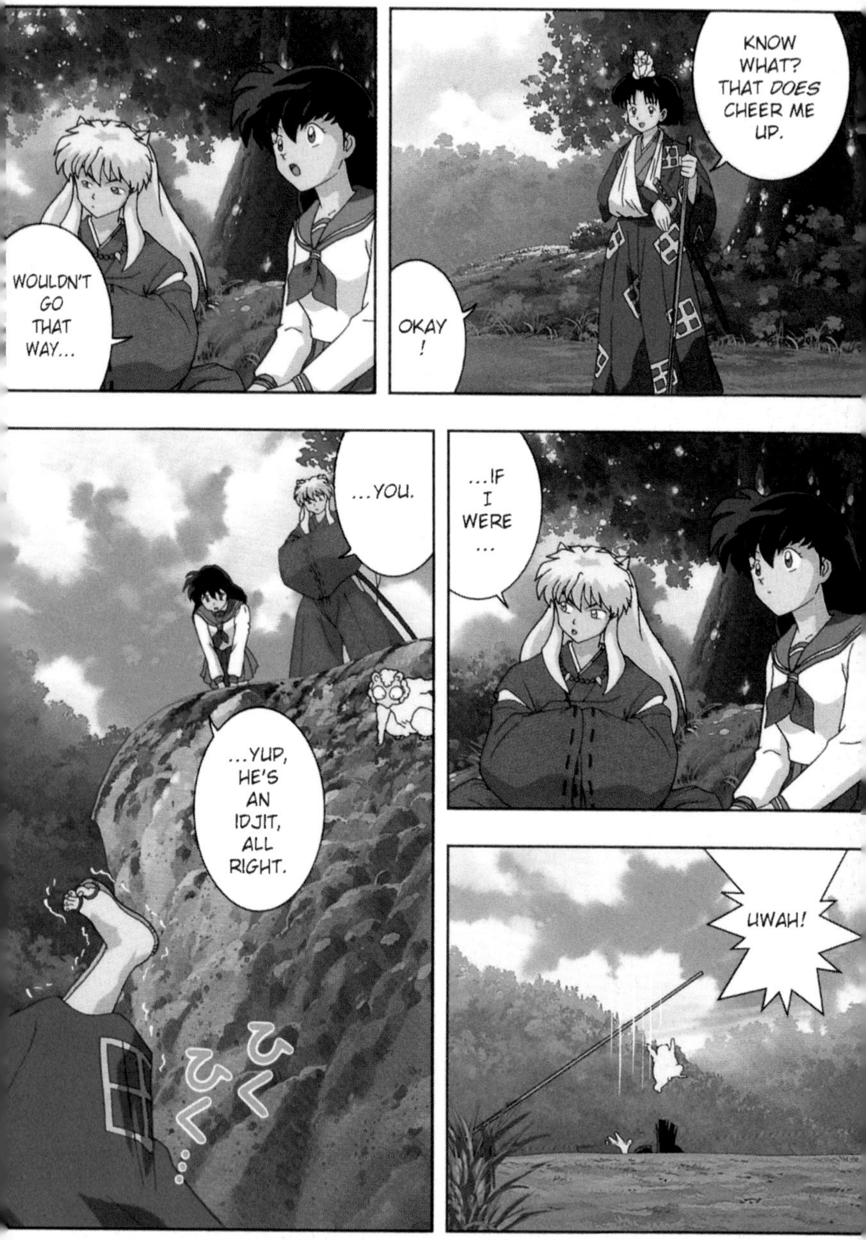
KNOW WHAT? THAT *DOES* CHEER ME UP.
OKAY!
WOULDN'T GO THAT WAY...
...IF I WERE...
UWAH!
...YOU.
...YUP, HE'S AN IDJIT, ALL RIGHT.
ひくひく

9
Shippo and the Thunder Brothers

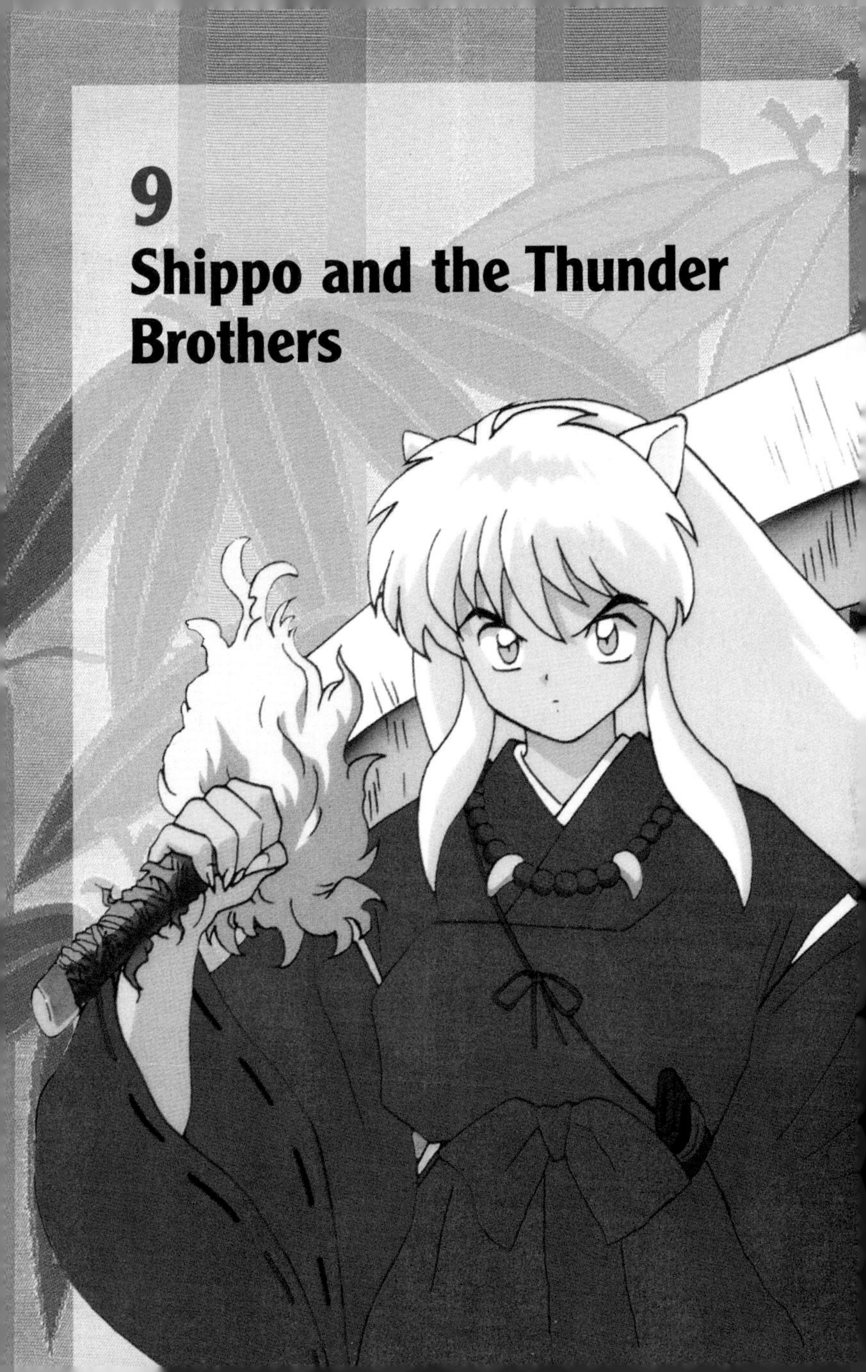

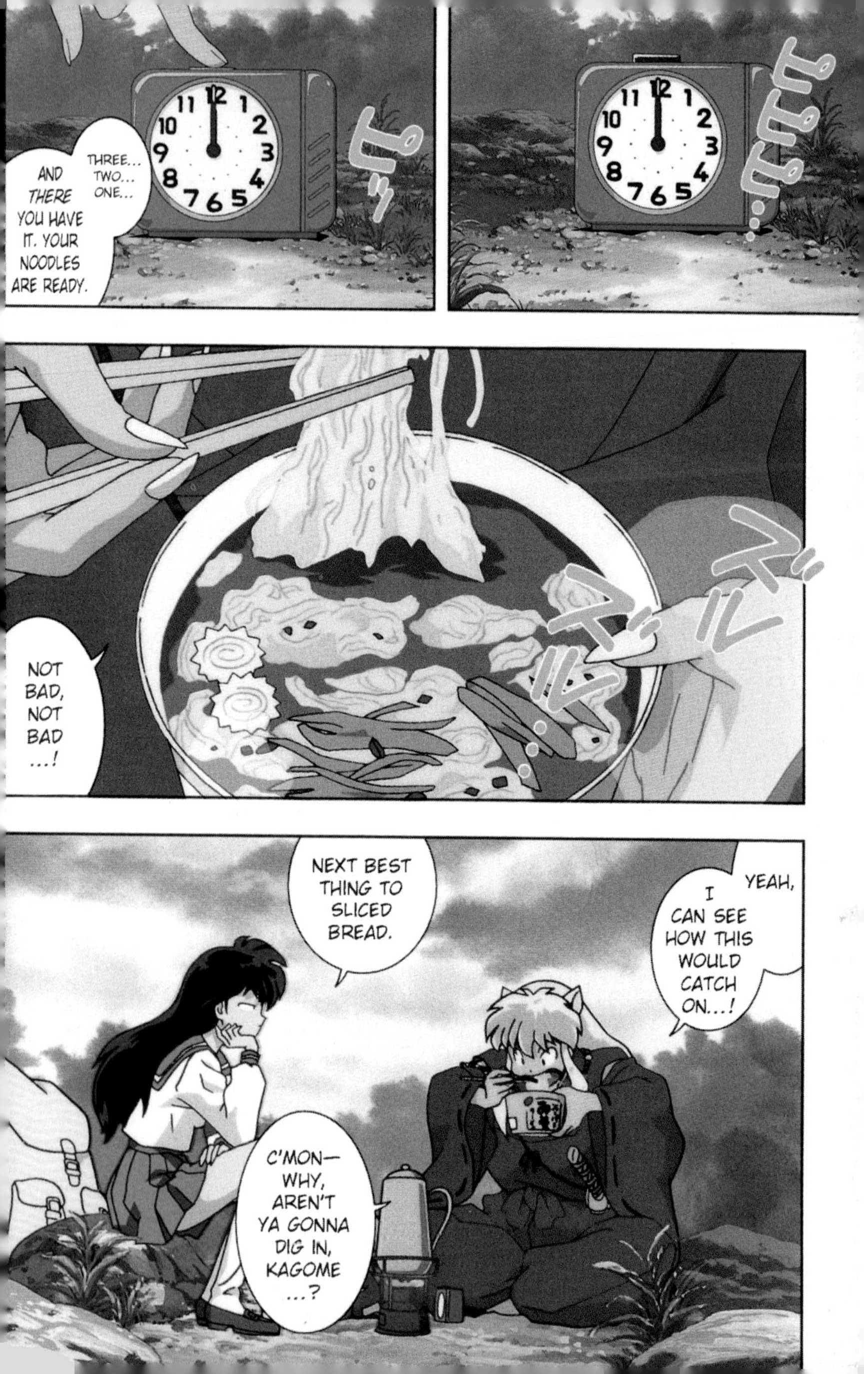
ピピピ…
ピッ
THREE... TWO... ONE...
AND THERE YOU HAVE IT. YOUR NOODLES ARE READY.
NOT BAD, NOT BAD ...!
YEAH, I CAN SEE HOW THIS WOULD CATCH ON...!
NEXT BEST THING TO SLICED BREAD.
C'MON— WHY, AREN'T YA GONNA DIG IN, KAGOME ...?

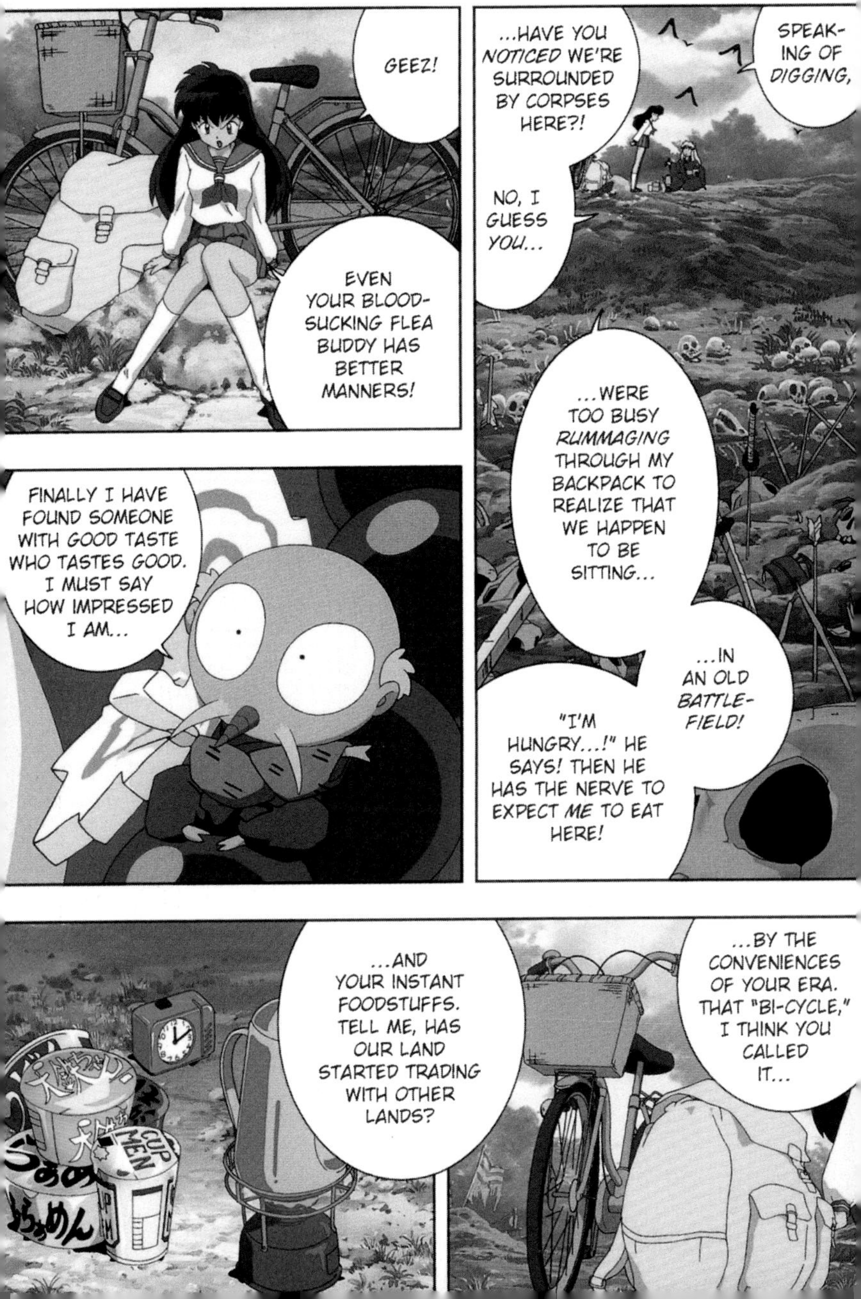
SPEAKING OF DIGGING,
...HAVE YOU NOTICED WE'RE SURROUNDED BY CORPSES HERE?!
NO, I GUESS YOU...
...WERE TOO BUSY RUMMAGING THROUGH MY BACKPACK TO REALIZE THAT WE HAPPEN TO BE SITTING...
...IN AN OLD BATTLE-FIELD!
"I'M HUNGRY...!" HE SAYS! THEN HE HAS THE NERVE TO EXPECT ME TO EAT HERE!
GEEZ!
EVEN YOUR BLOOD-SUCKING FLEA BUDDY HAS BETTER MANNERS!
FINALLY I HAVE FOUND SOMEONE WITH GOOD TASTE WHO TASTES GOOD. I MUST SAY HOW IMPRESSED I AM...
...BY THE CONVENIENCES OF YOUR ERA. THAT "BI-CYCLE," I THINK YOU CALLED IT...
...AND YOUR INSTANT FOODSTUFFS. TELL ME, HAS OUR LAND STARTED TRADING WITH OTHER LANDS?

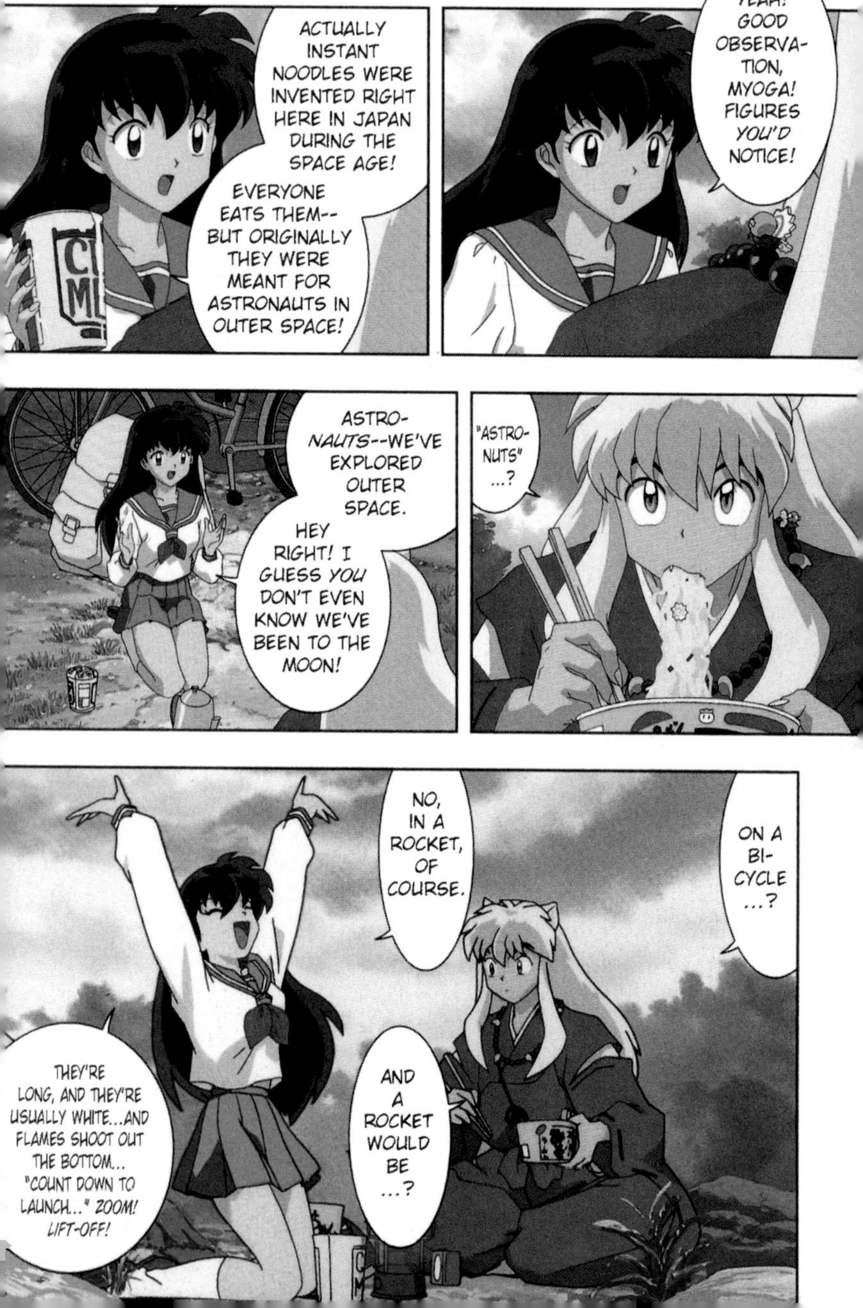
YEAH! GOOD OBSERVATION, MYOGA! FIGURES *YOU'D* NOTICE!
ACTUALLY INSTANT NOODLES WERE INVENTED RIGHT HERE IN JAPAN DURING THE SPACE AGE!
EVERYONE EATS THEM-- BUT ORIGINALLY THEY WERE MEANT FOR ASTRONAUTS IN OUTER SPACE!
"ASTRONUTS" ...?
ASTRO-*NAUTS*--WE'VE EXPLORED OUTER SPACE.
HEY RIGHT! I GUESS *YOU* DON'T EVEN KNOW WE'VE BEEN TO THE MOON!
ON A BICYCLE ...?
NO, IN A ROCKET, OF COURSE.
AND A ROCKET WOULD BE ...?
THEY'RE LONG, AND THEY'RE USUALLY WHITE...AND FLAMES SHOOT OUT THE BOTTOM... "COUNT DOWN TO LAUNCH..." *ZOOM! LIFT-OFF!*

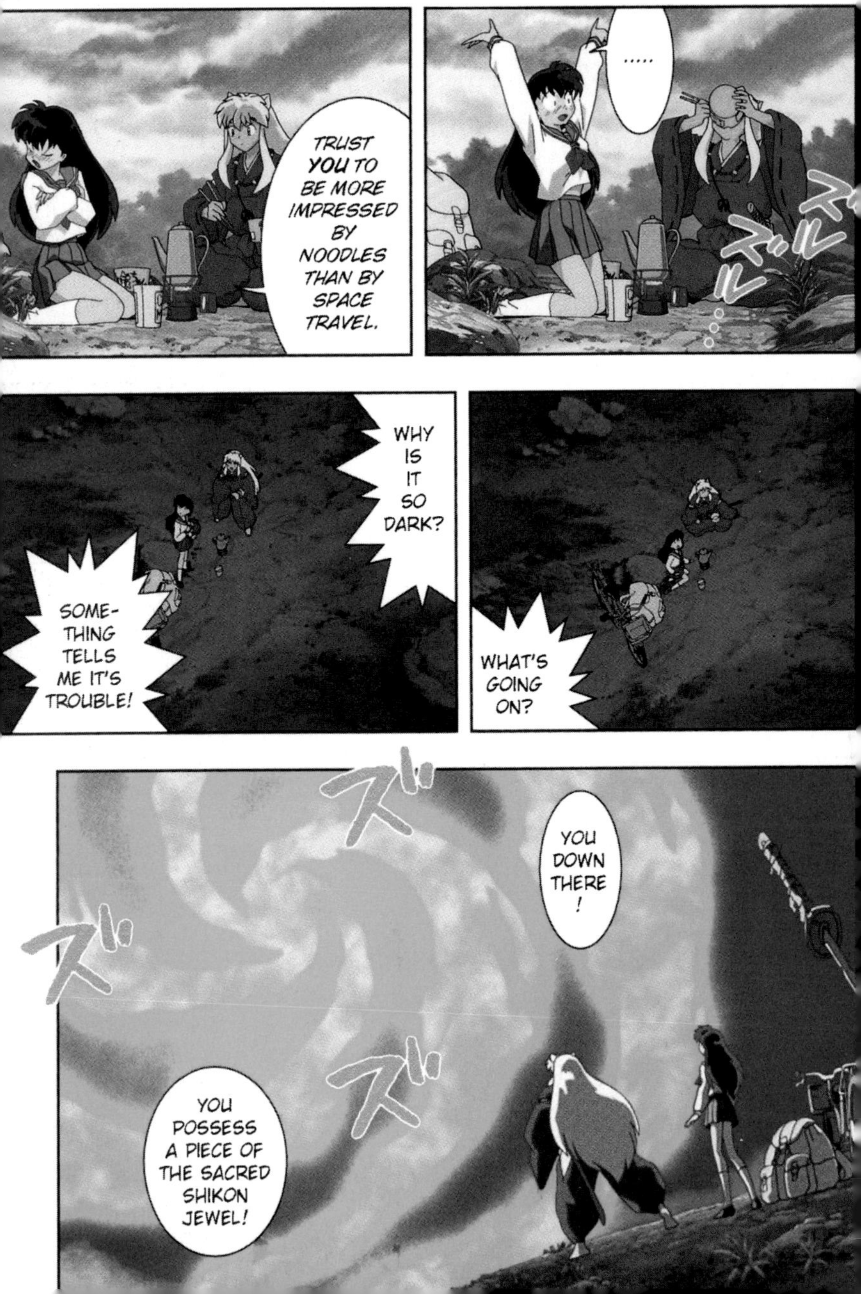
.....
TRUST YOU TO BE MORE IMPRESSED BY NOODLES THAN BY SPACE TRAVEL.
WHAT'S GOING ON?
WHY IS IT SO DARK?
SOME-THING TELLS ME IT'S TROUBLE!
YOU DOWN THERE!
YOU POSSESS A PIECE OF THE SACRED SHIKON JEWEL!

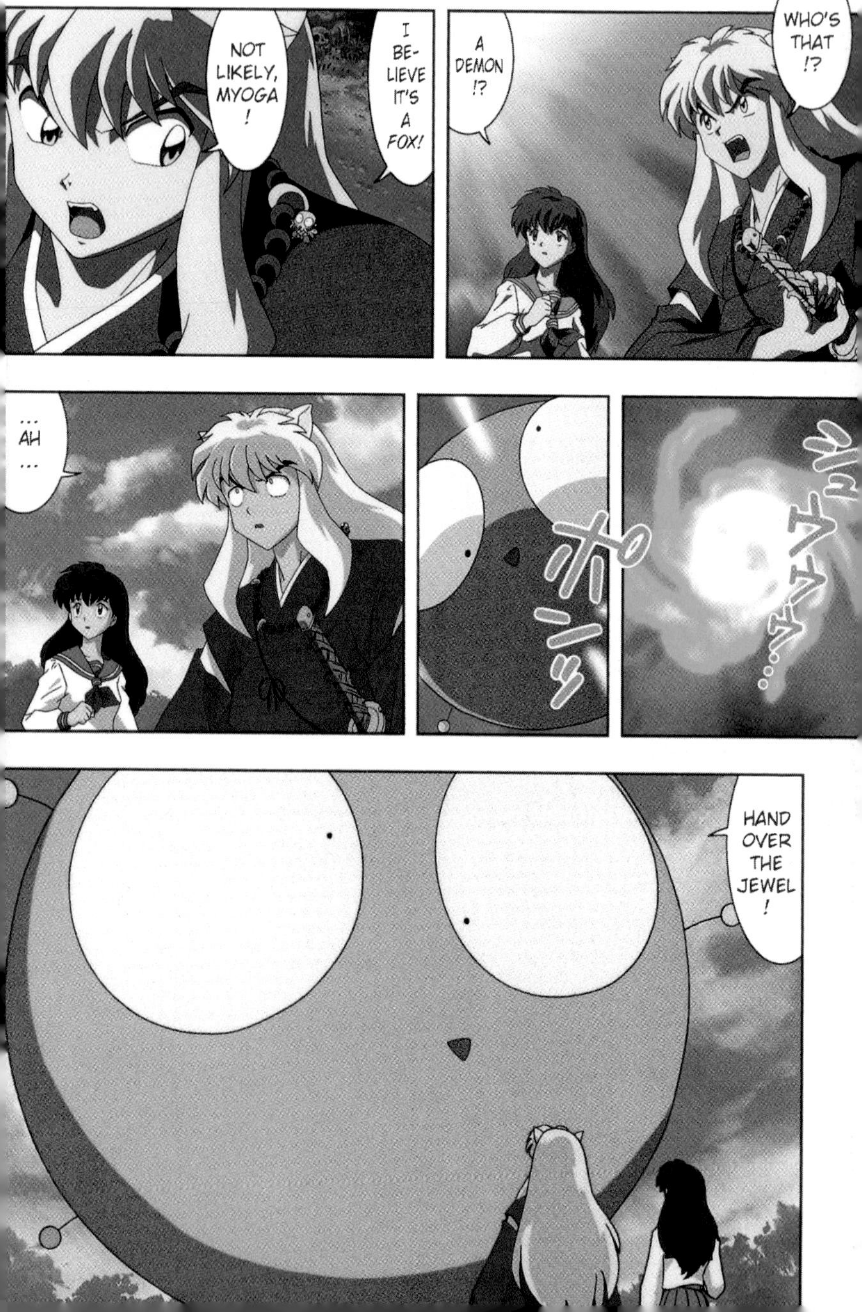
WHO'S THAT !?
A DEMON !?
I BE- LIEVE IT'S A FOX!
NOT LIKELY, MYOGA !
ポンッ
... AH ...
HAND OVER THE JEWEL !

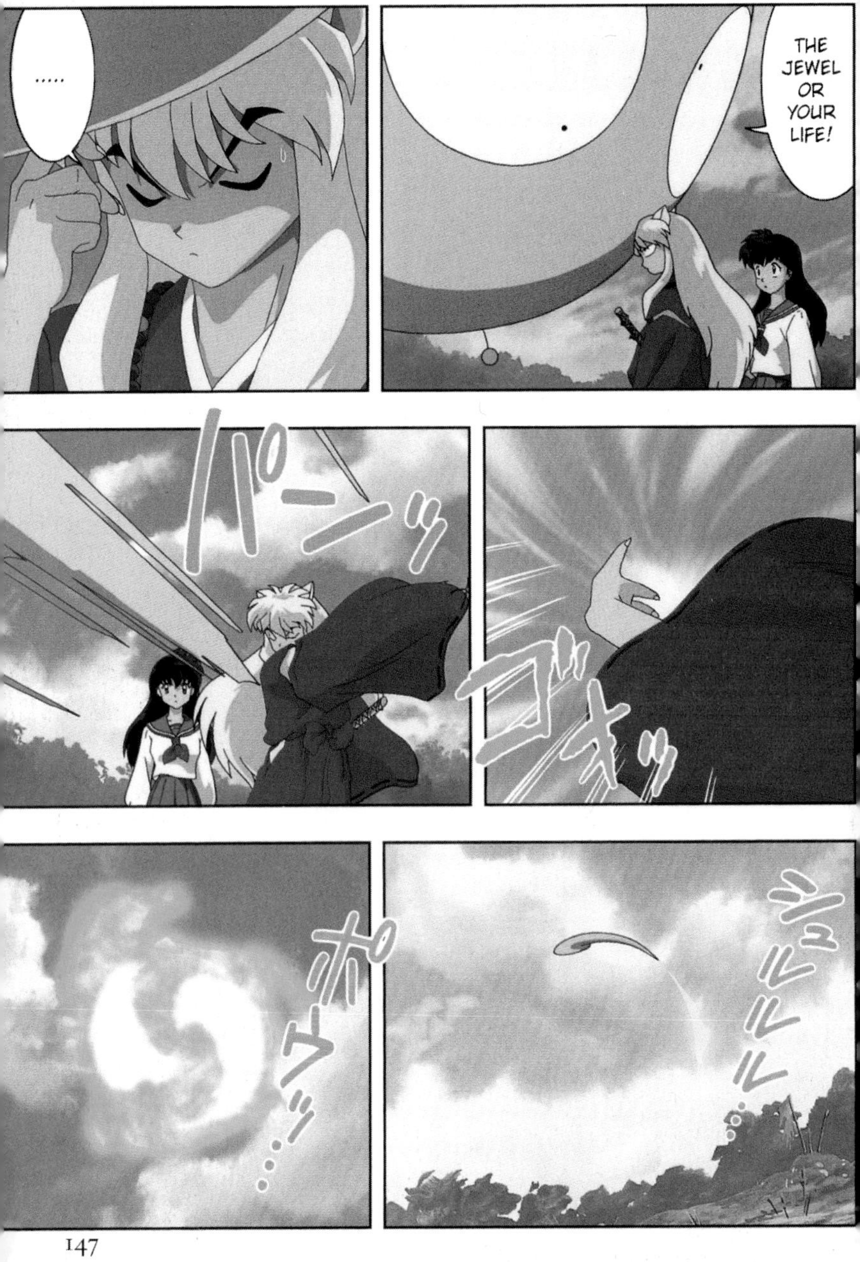
THE JEWEL OR YOUR LIFE!
.....
ゴキッ
パーンッ
シュルルル...
ポワッ...

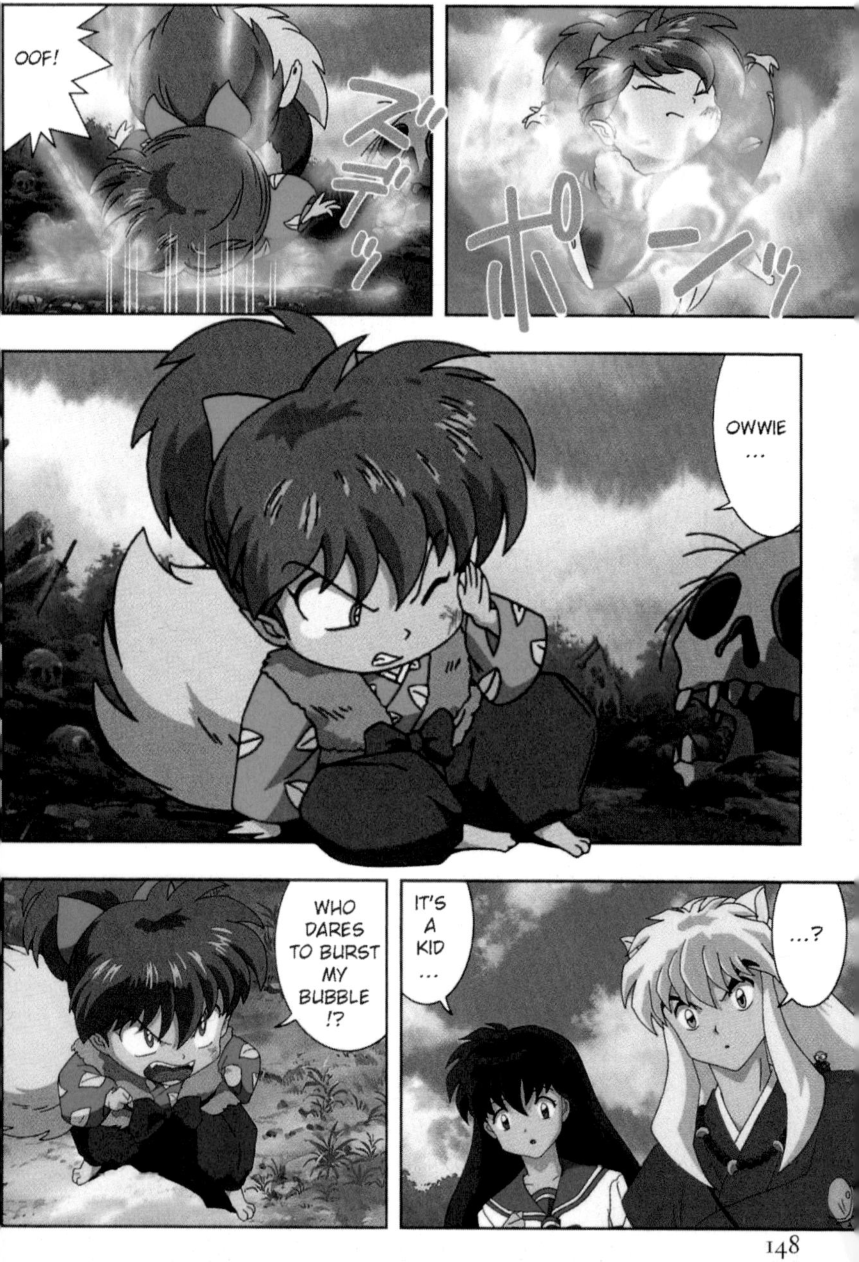
ポーンッ
OOF!
ズデッ
OWWIE ...
...?
IT'S A KID ...
WHO DARES TO BURST MY BUBBLE !?

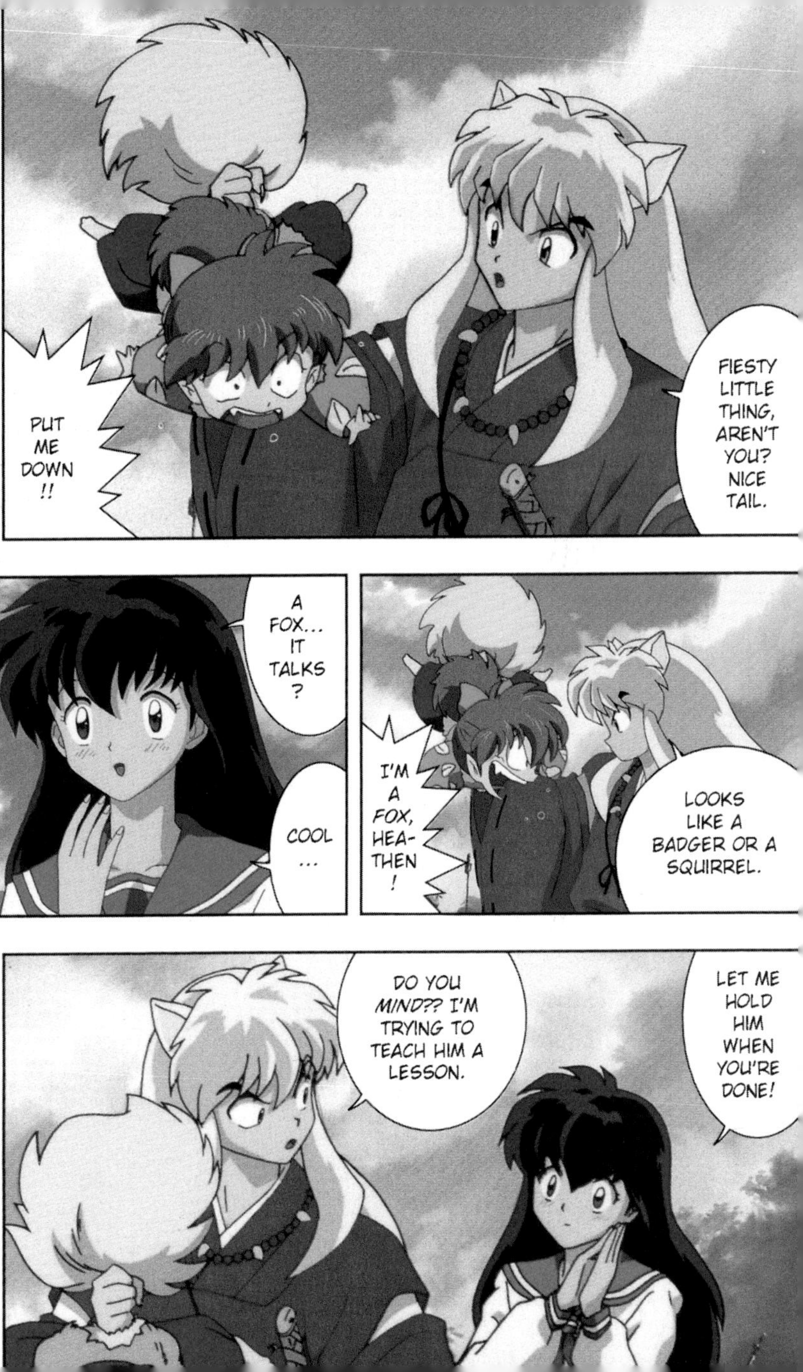
FIESTY LITTLE THING, AREN'T YOU? NICE TAIL.
PUT ME DOWN !!
LOOKS LIKE A BADGER OR A SQUIRREL.
I'M A FOX, HEA-THEN !
A FOX... IT TALKS ?
COOL ...
LET ME HOLD HIM WHEN YOU'RE DONE!
DO YOU *MIND??* I'M TRYING TO TEACH HIM A LESSON.

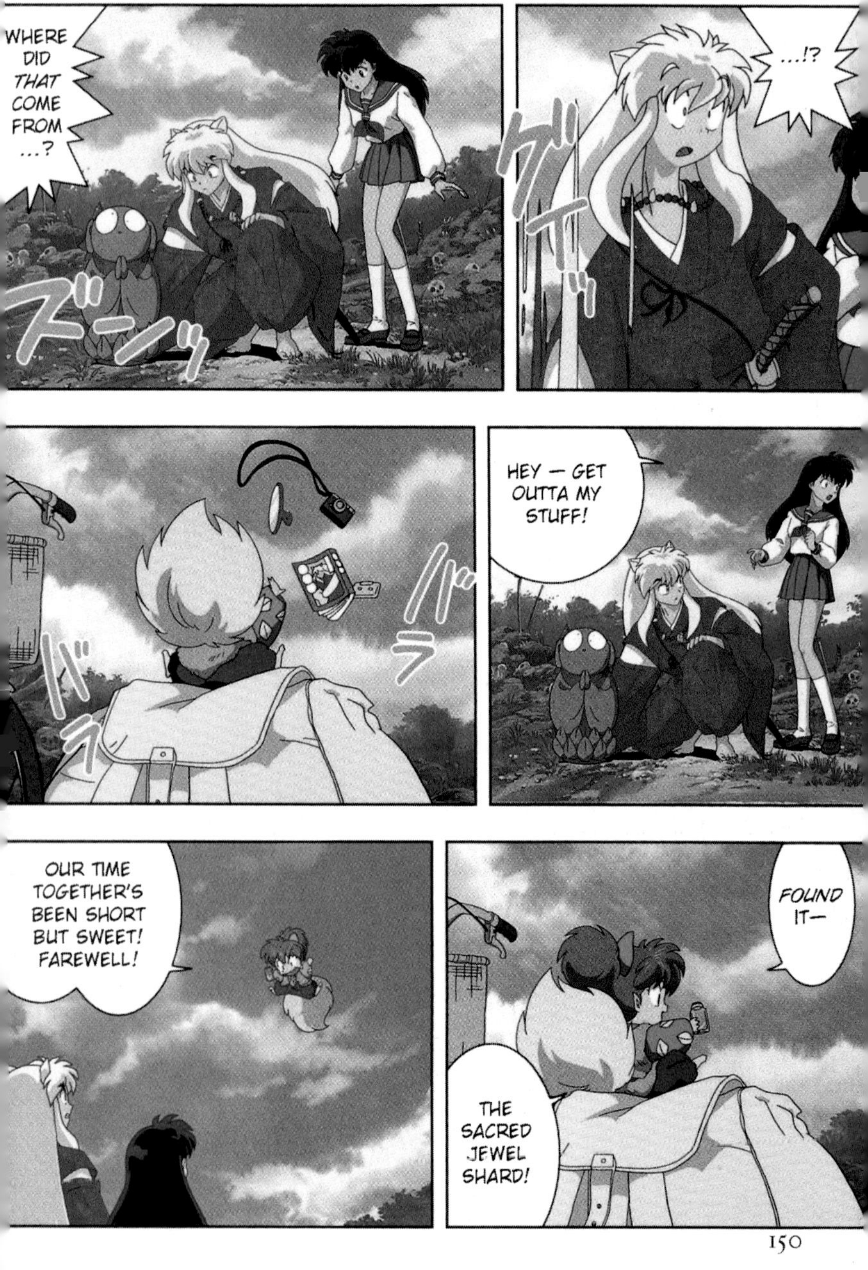
...!?
グイッ
WHERE DID THAT COME FROM ...?
ズーンッ
HEY — GET OUTTA MY STUFF!
バラ
バラ
FOUND IT—
THE SACRED JEWEL SHARD!
OUR TIME TOGETHER'S BEEN SHORT BUT SWEET! FAREWELL!

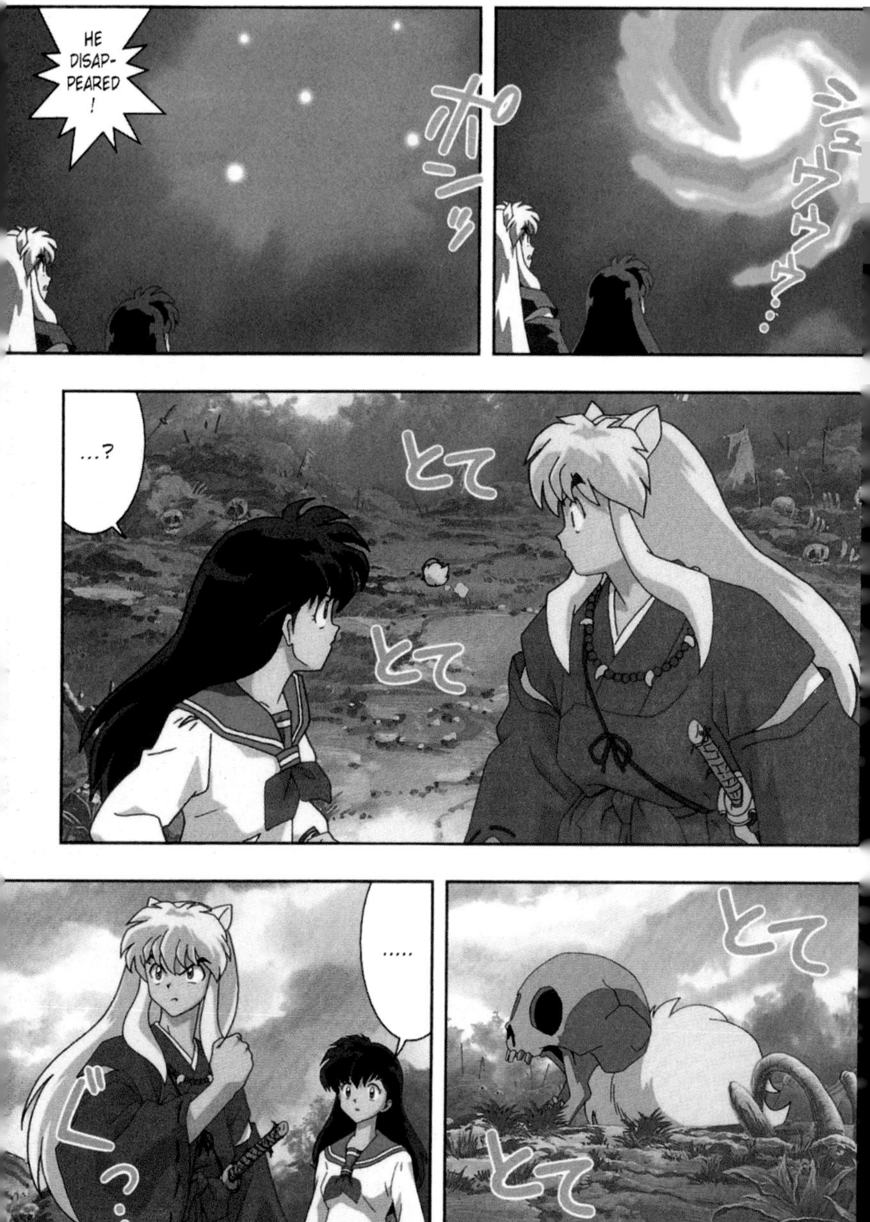
シュヴヴヴ…
HE DISAP-PEARED!
ポンッ
...?
とて
とて
とて
とて
.....
ぐっ…

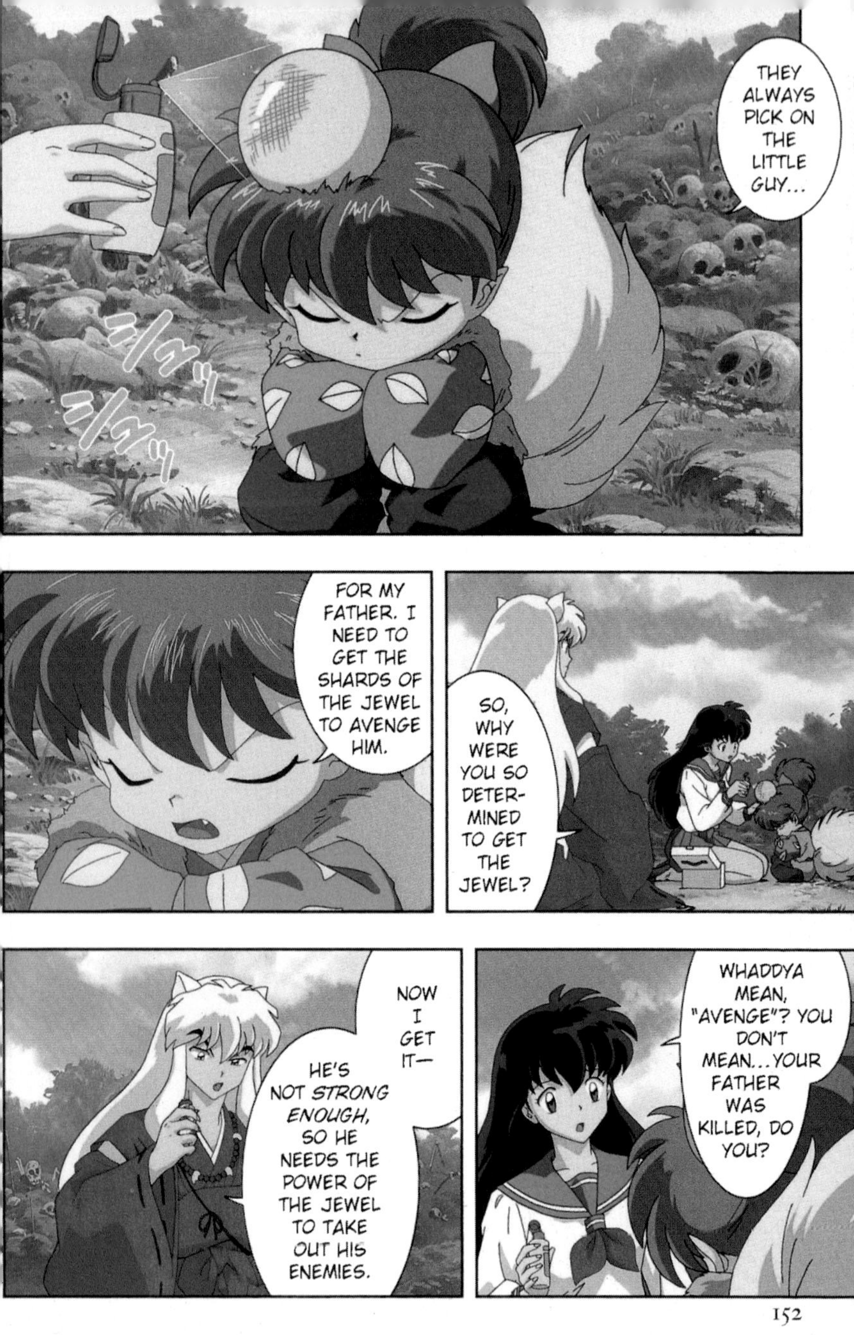
THEY ALWAYS PICK ON THE LITTLE GUY...
SO, WHY WERE YOU SO DETERMINED TO GET THE JEWEL?
FOR MY FATHER. I NEED TO GET THE SHARDS OF THE JEWEL TO AVENGE HIM.
WHADDYA MEAN, "AVENGE"? YOU DON'T MEAN...YOUR FATHER WAS KILLED, DO YOU?
NOW I GET IT—
HE'S NOT *STRONG ENOUGH*, SO HE NEEDS THE POWER OF THE JEWEL TO TAKE OUT HIS ENEMIES.

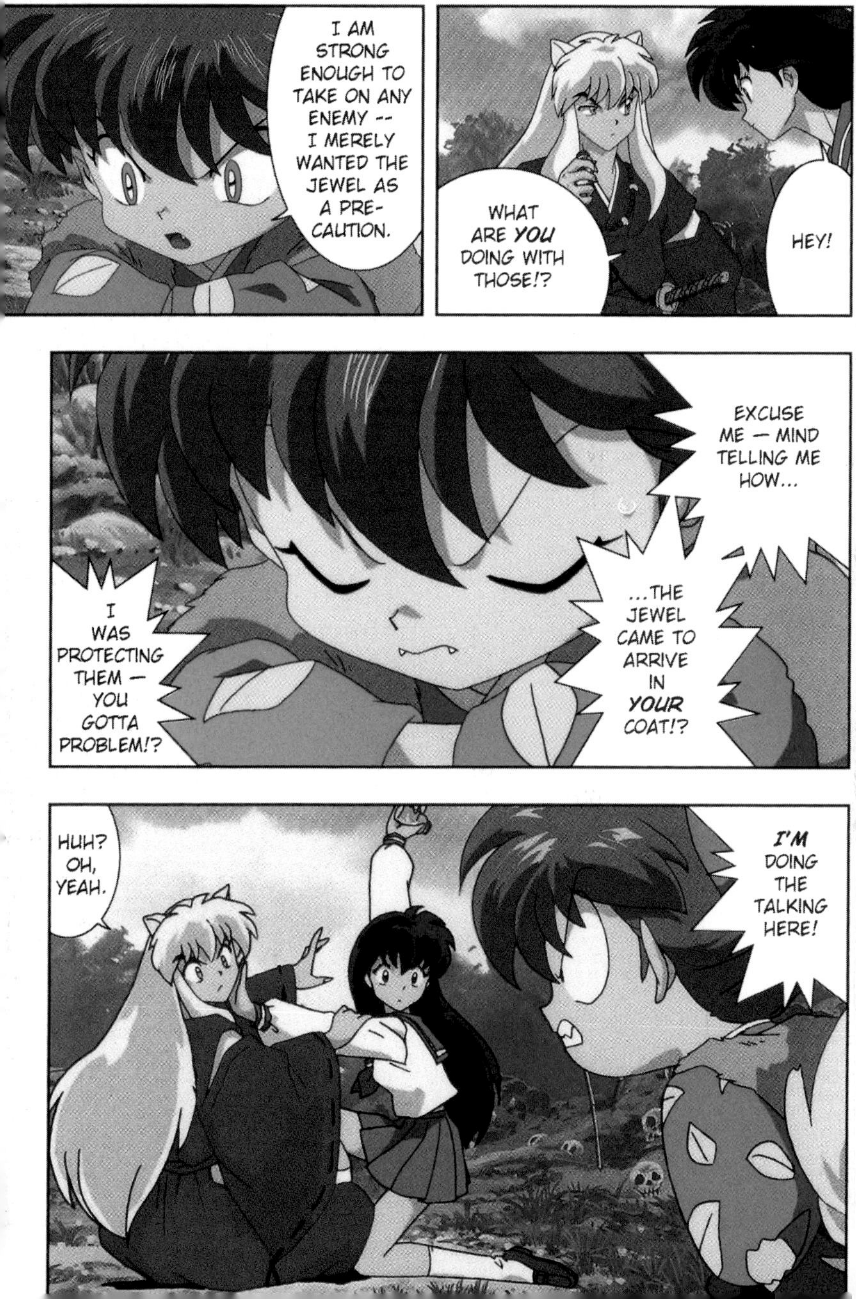
HEY!
WHAT ARE *YOU* DOING WITH THOSE!?
I AM STRONG ENOUGH TO TAKE ON ANY ENEMY -- I MERELY WANTED THE JEWEL AS A PRE-CAUTION.
EXCUSE ME — MIND TELLING ME HOW...
...THE JEWEL CAME TO ARRIVE IN *YOUR* COAT!?
I WAS PROTECTING THEM — YOU GOTTA PROBLEM!?
I'M DOING THE TALKING HERE!
HUH? OH, YEAH.

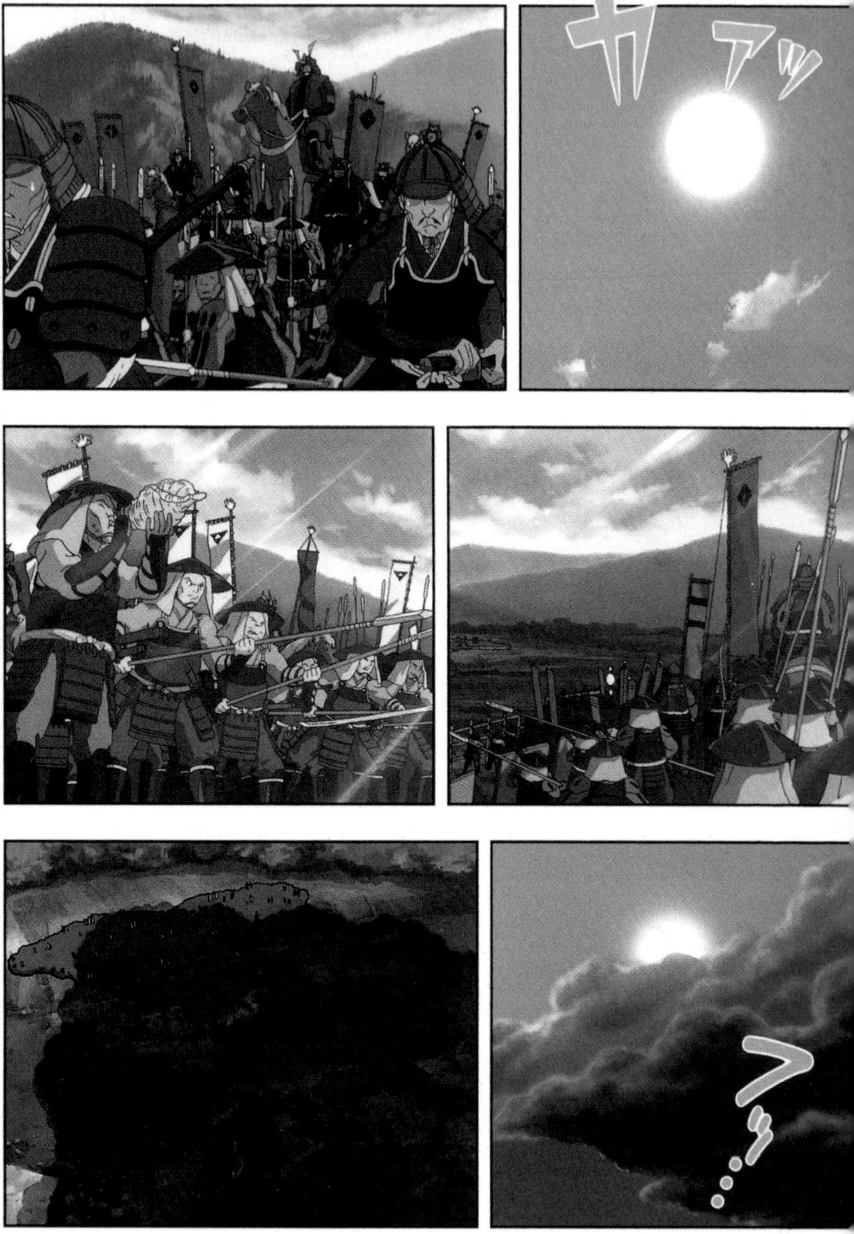
カァッ
フッ…

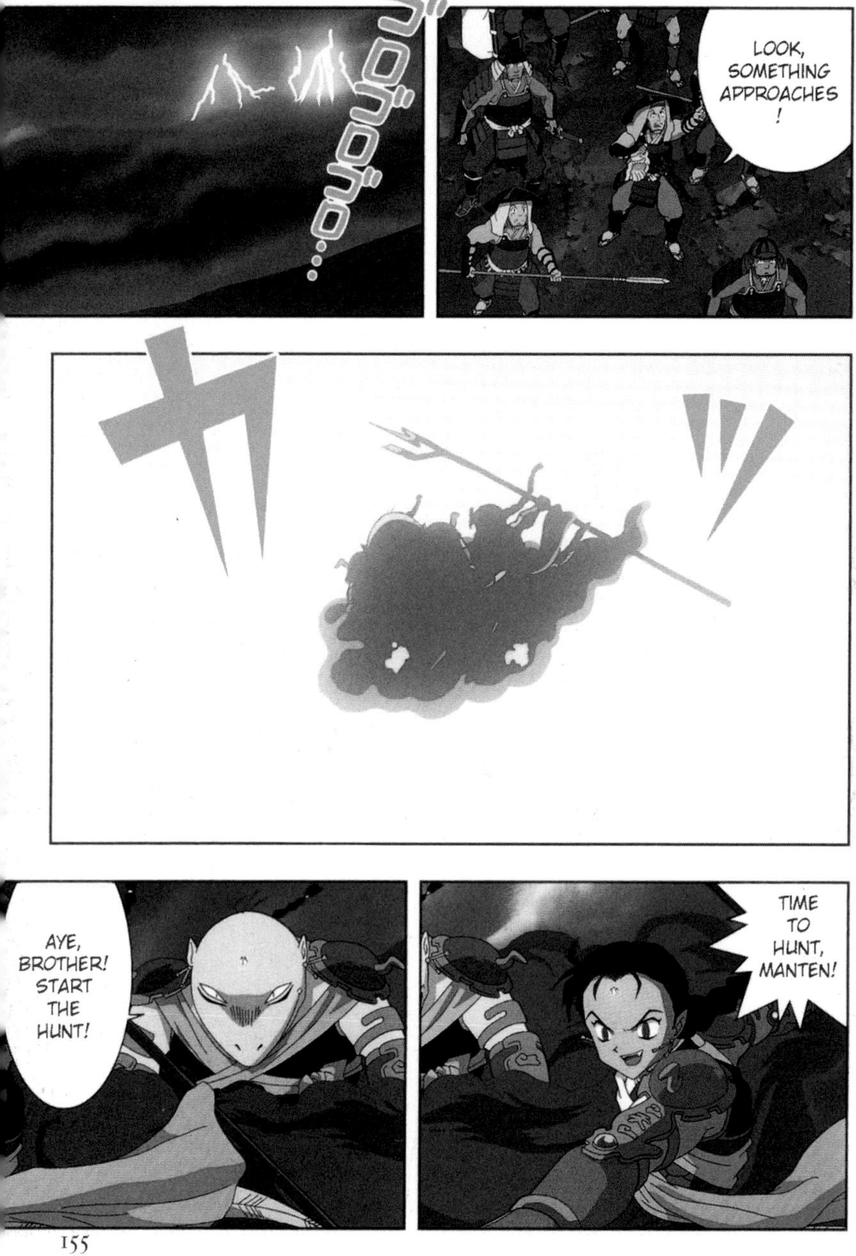
LOOK, SOMETHING APPROACHES!
ゴロゴロゴロ…
ガ
TIME TO HUNT, MANTEN!
AYE, BROTHER! START THE HUNT!

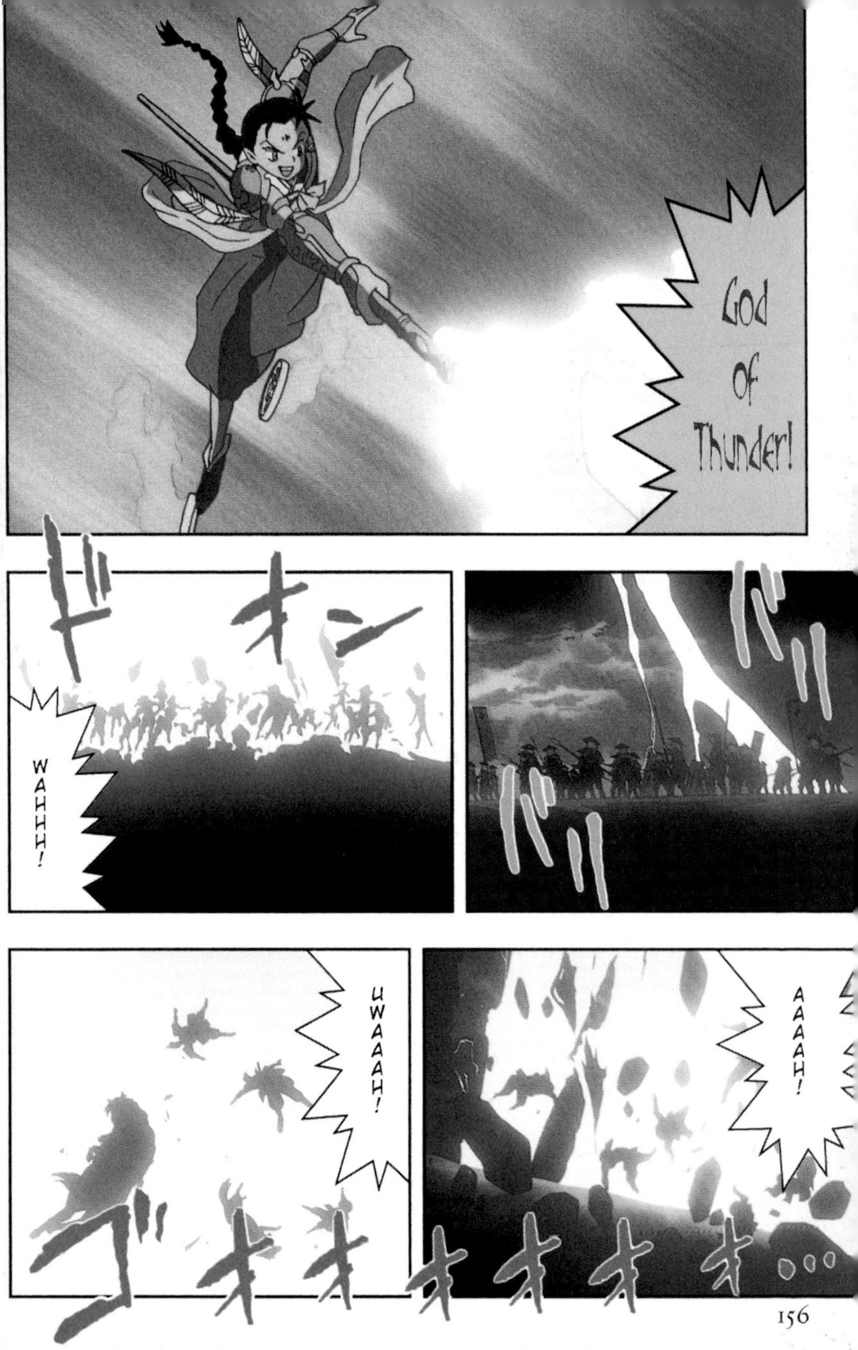

God of Thunder!
バリバリ
ドオン
WAHHH!
AAAAH!
UWAAAAH!
ゴオオオオオ…

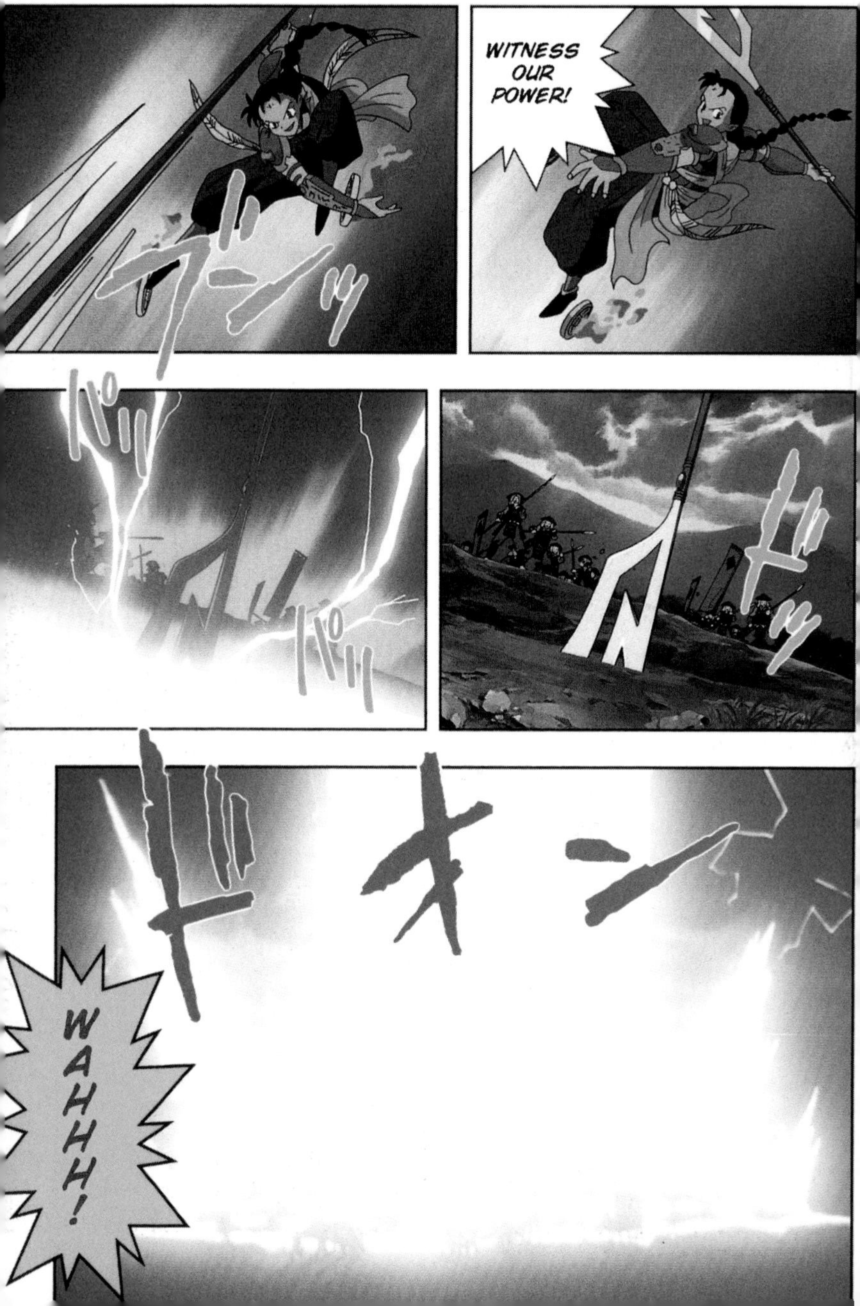
WITNESS OUR POWER!
WAHHH!

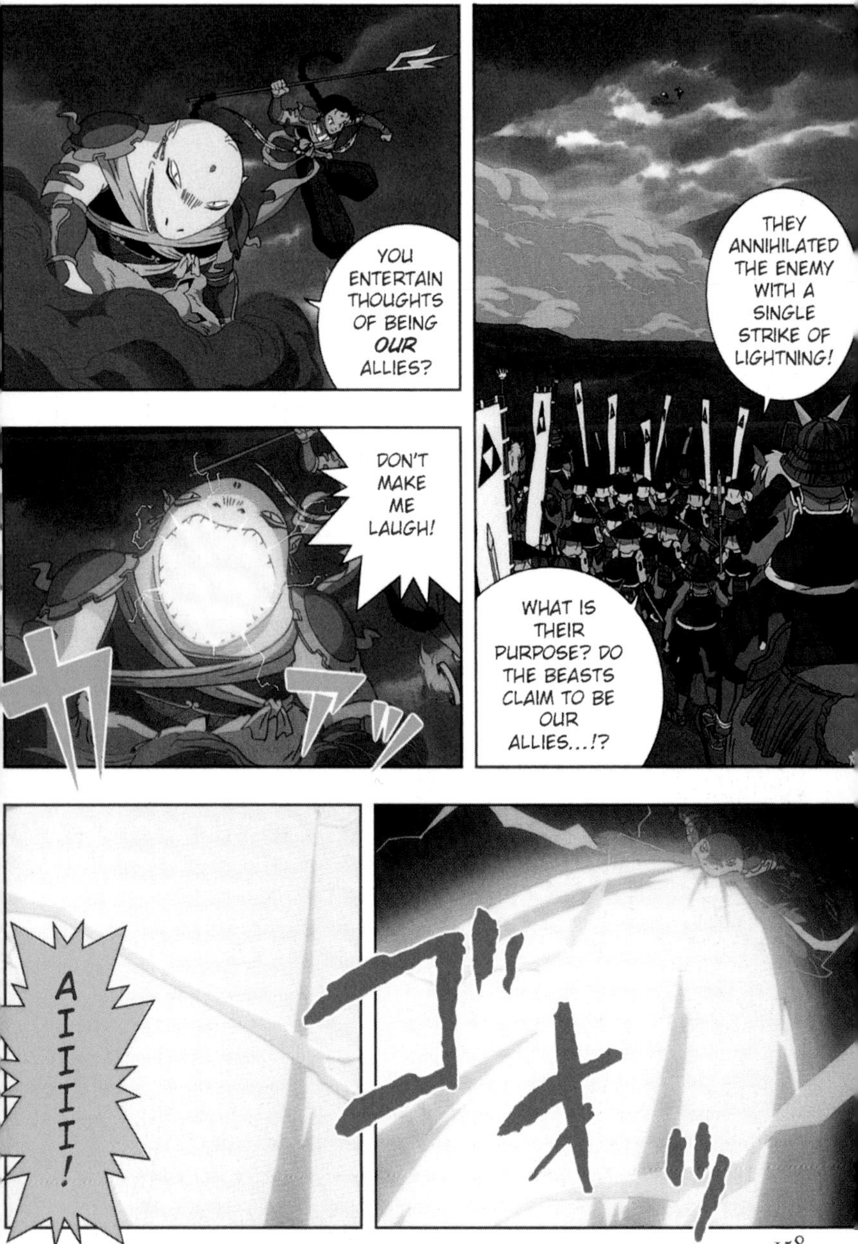
THEY ANNIHILATED THE ENEMY WITH A SINGLE STRIKE OF LIGHTNING!
WHAT IS THEIR PURPOSE? DO THE BEASTS CLAIM TO BE OUR ALLIES...!?
YOU ENTERTAIN THOUGHTS OF BEING OUR ALLIES?
DON'T MAKE ME LAUGH!
ゴオッ
AIIII!

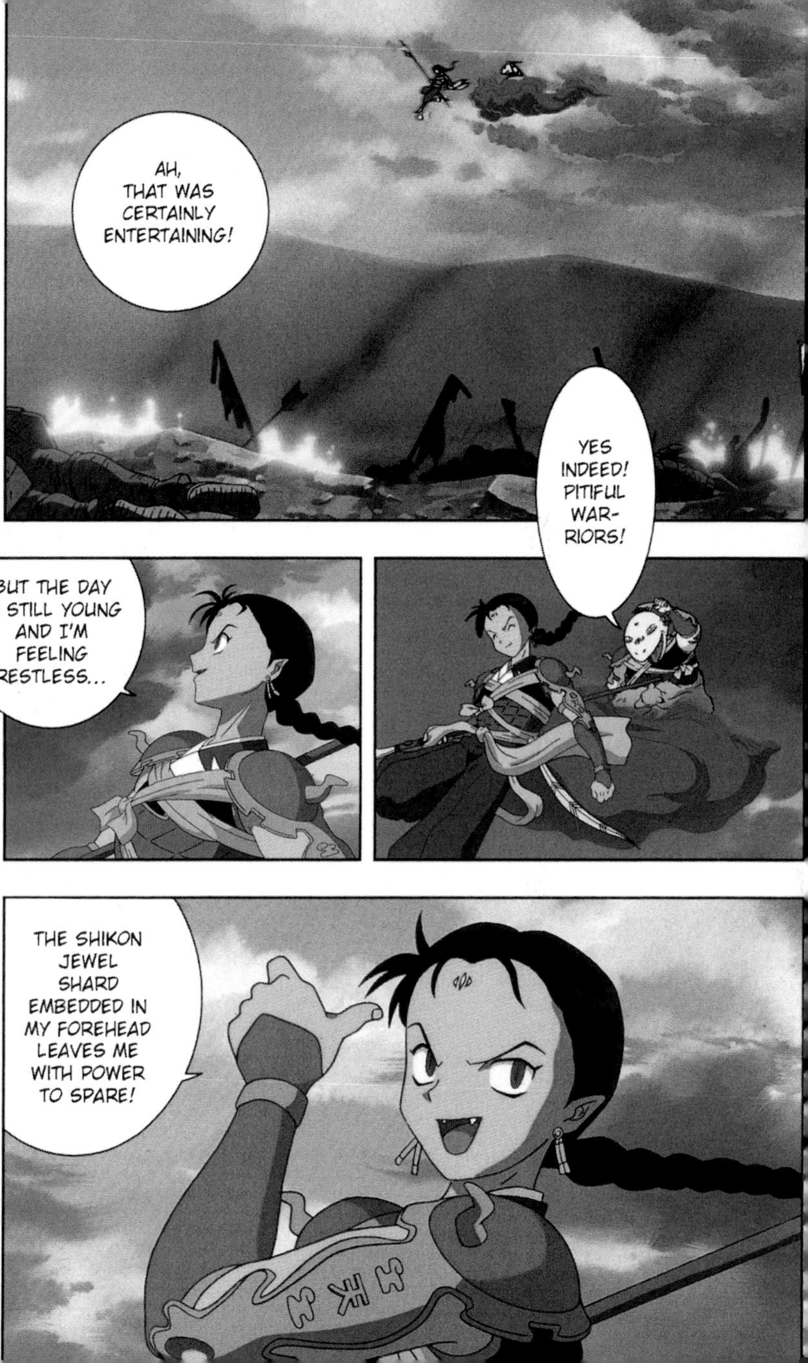
AH, THAT WAS CERTAINLY ENTERTAINING!
YES INDEED! PITIFUL WAR-RIORS!
BUT THE DAY IS STILL YOUNG AND I'M FEELING RESTLESS...
THE SHIKON JEWEL SHARD EMBEDDED IN MY FOREHEAD LEAVES ME WITH POWER TO SPARE!

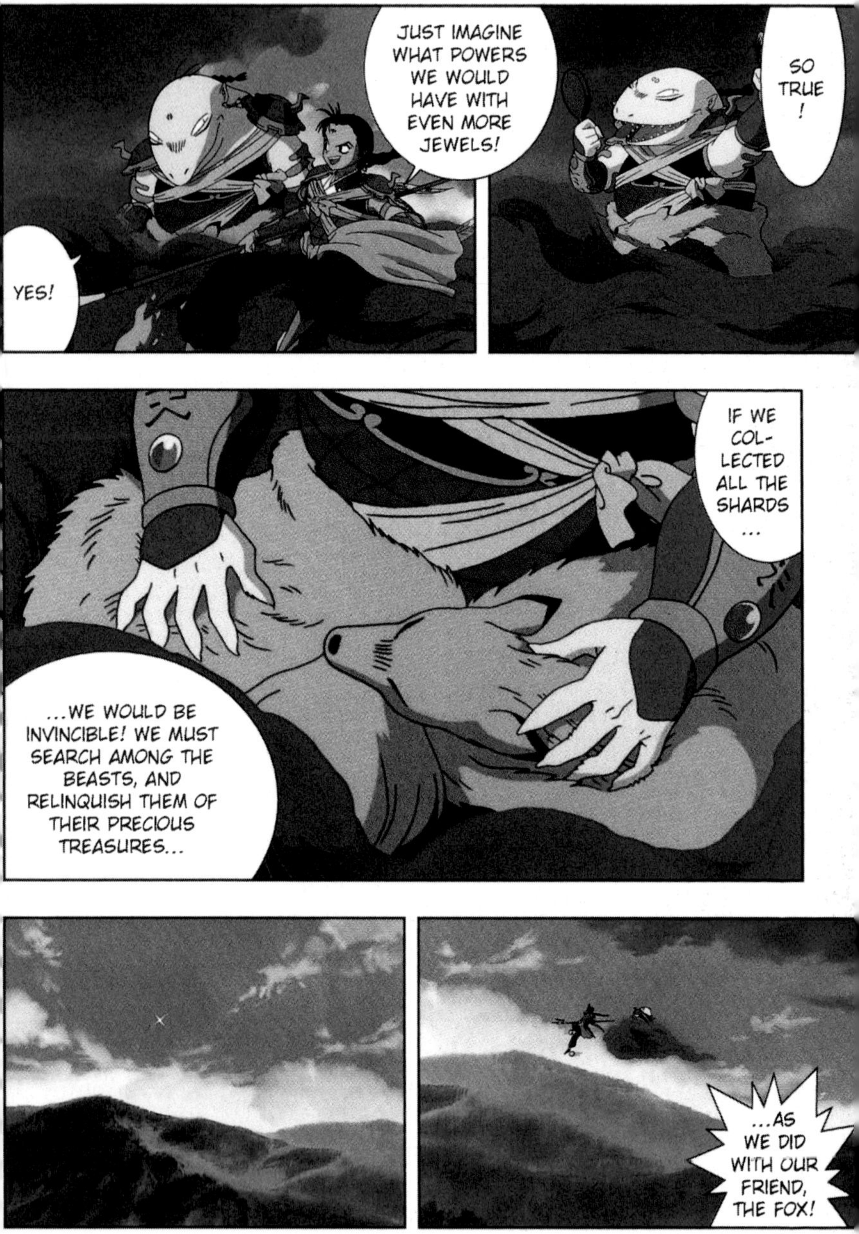
SO TRUE !
JUST IMAGINE WHAT POWERS WE WOULD HAVE WITH EVEN MORE JEWELS!
YES!
IF WE COL-LECTED ALL THE SHARDS ...
...WE WOULD BE INVINCIBLE! WE MUST SEARCH AMONG THE BEASTS, AND RELINQUISH THEM OF THEIR PRECIOUS TREASURES...
...AS WE DID WITH OUR FRIEND, THE FOX!

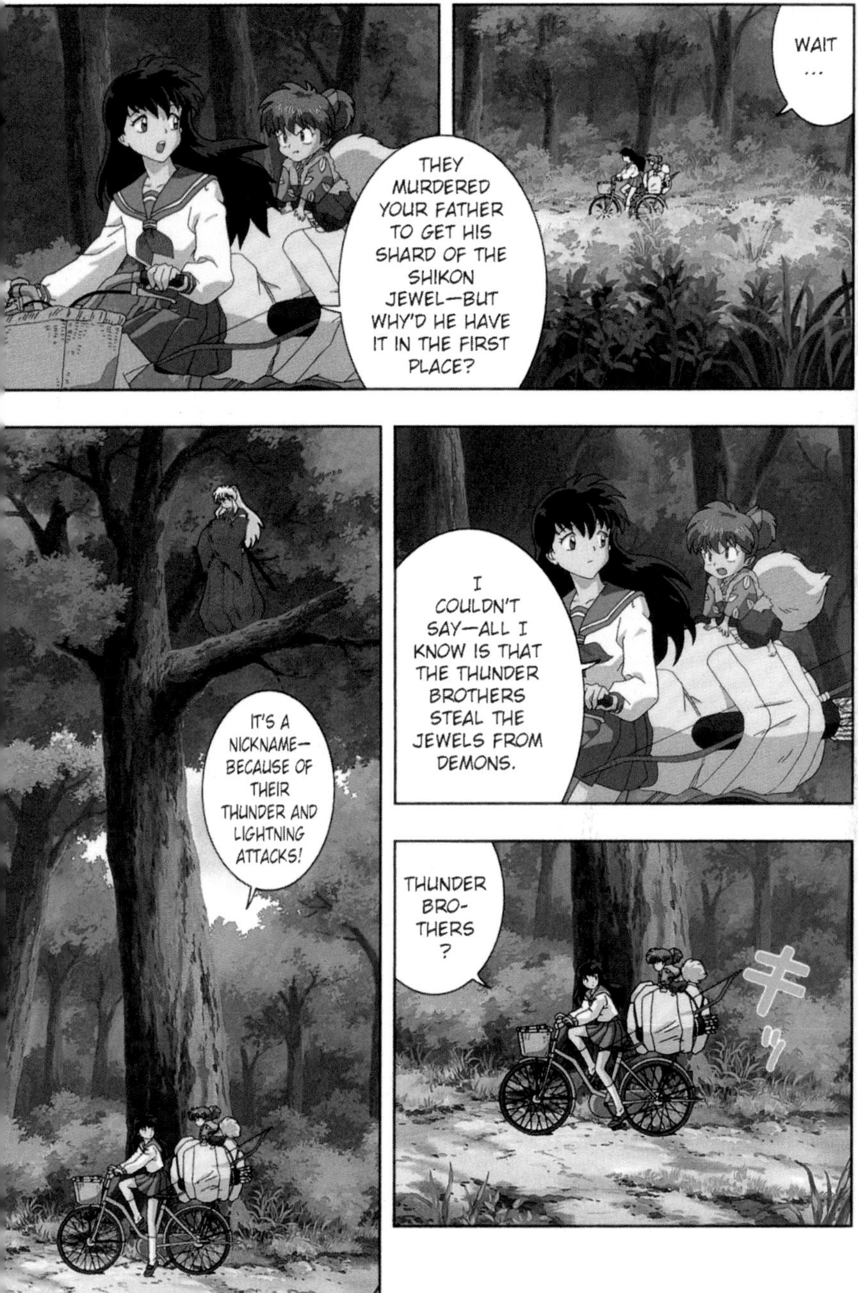
WAIT ...
THEY MURDERED YOUR FATHER TO GET HIS SHARD OF THE SHIKON JEWEL—BUT WHY'D HE HAVE IT IN THE FIRST PLACE?
I COULDN'T SAY—ALL I KNOW IS THAT THE THUNDER BROTHERS STEAL THE JEWELS FROM DEMONS.
THUNDER BRO-THERS ?
キッ
IT'S A NICKNAME—BECAUSE OF THEIR THUNDER AND LIGHTNING ATTACKS!

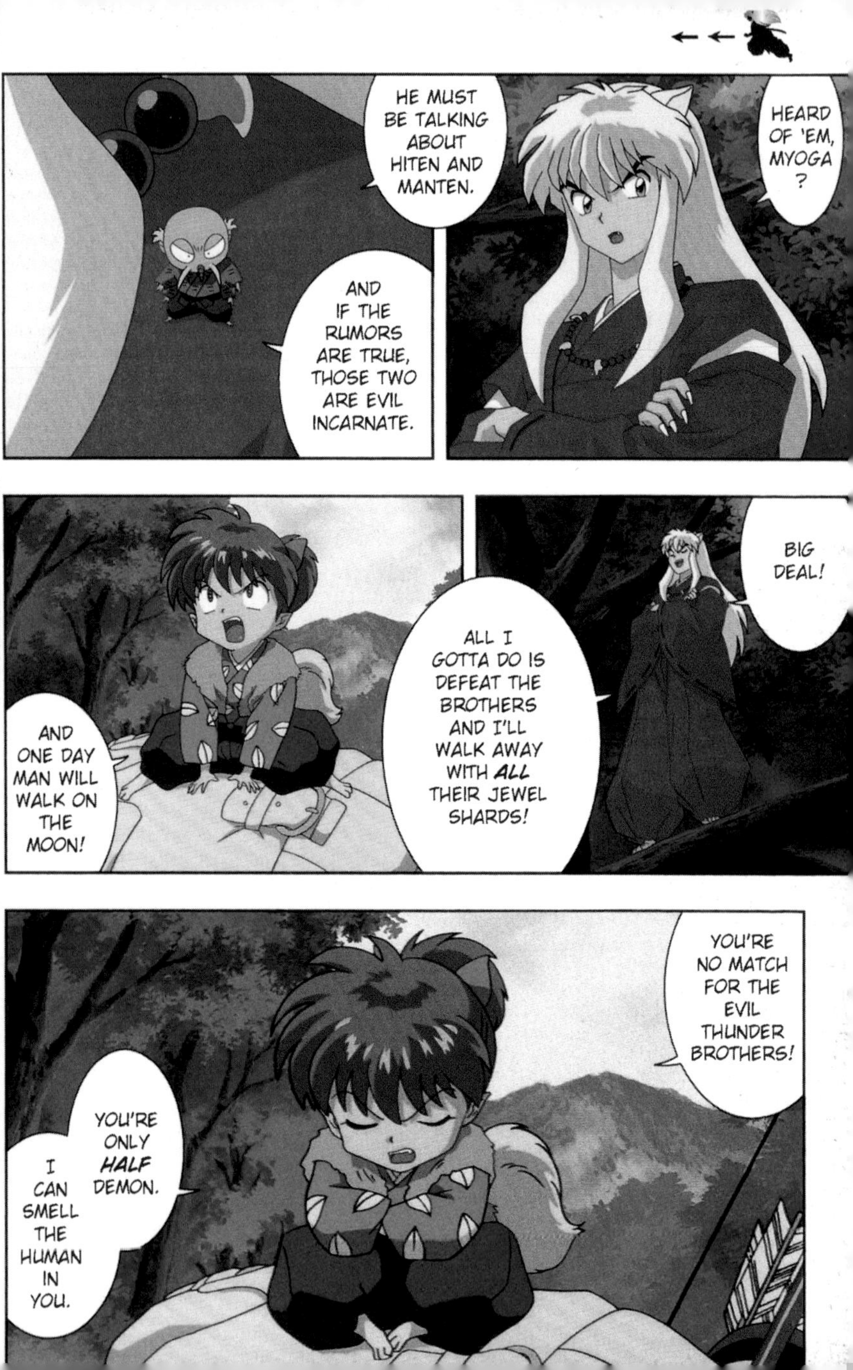
HEARD OF 'EM, MYOGA?
HE MUST BE TALKING ABOUT HITEN AND MANTEN.
AND IF THE RUMORS ARE TRUE, THOSE TWO ARE EVIL INCARNATE.
BIG DEAL!
ALL I GOTTA DO IS DEFEAT THE BROTHERS AND I'LL WALK AWAY WITH ALL THEIR JEWEL SHARDS!
AND ONE DAY MAN WILL WALK ON THE MOON!
YOU'RE NO MATCH FOR THE EVIL THUNDER BROTHERS!
YOU'RE ONLY HALF DEMON.
I CAN SMELL THE HUMAN IN YOU.

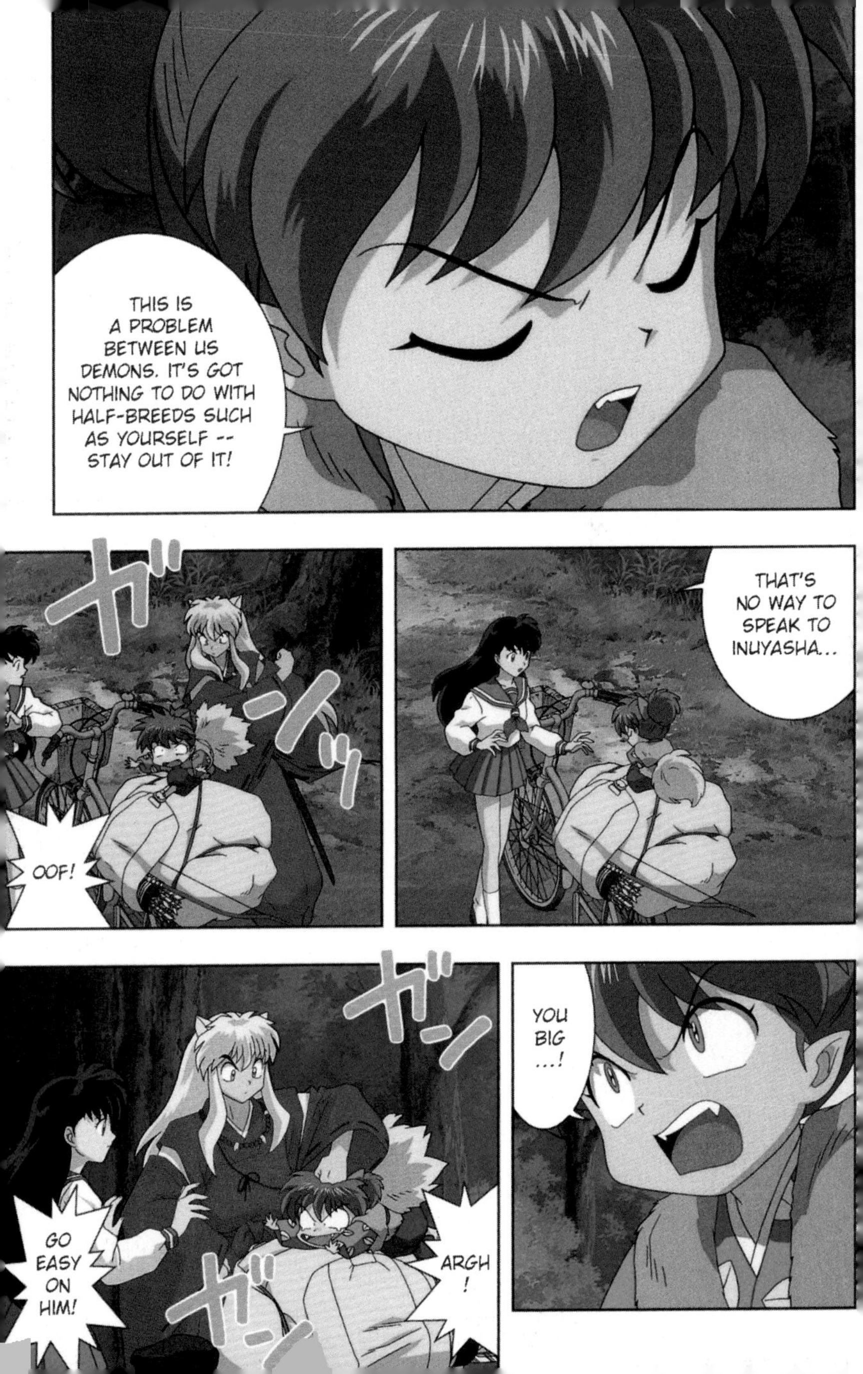
THIS IS A PROBLEM BETWEEN US DEMONS. IT'S GOT NOTHING TO DO WITH HALF-BREEDS SUCH AS YOURSELF -- STAY OUT OF IT!
THAT'S NO WAY TO SPEAK TO INUYASHA...
ガーンッ
OOF!
YOU BIG ...!
ガーン
ARGH!
GO EASY ON HIM!
ガーン

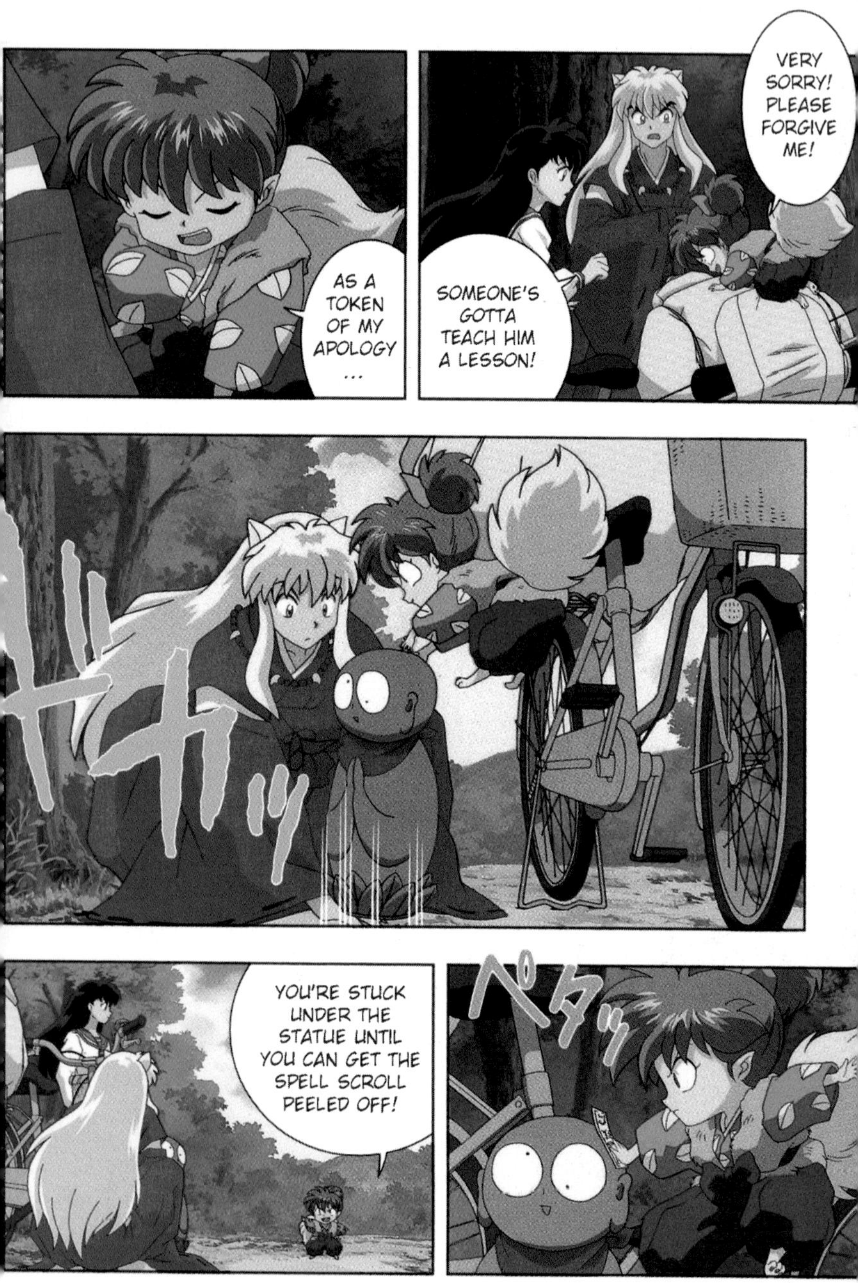
VERY SORRY! PLEASE FORGIVE ME!
SOMEONE'S GOTTA TEACH HIM A LESSON!
AS A TOKEN OF MY APOLOGY ...
ペタッ
YOU'RE STUCK UNDER THE STATUE UNTIL YOU CAN GET THE SPELL SCROLL PEELED OFF!

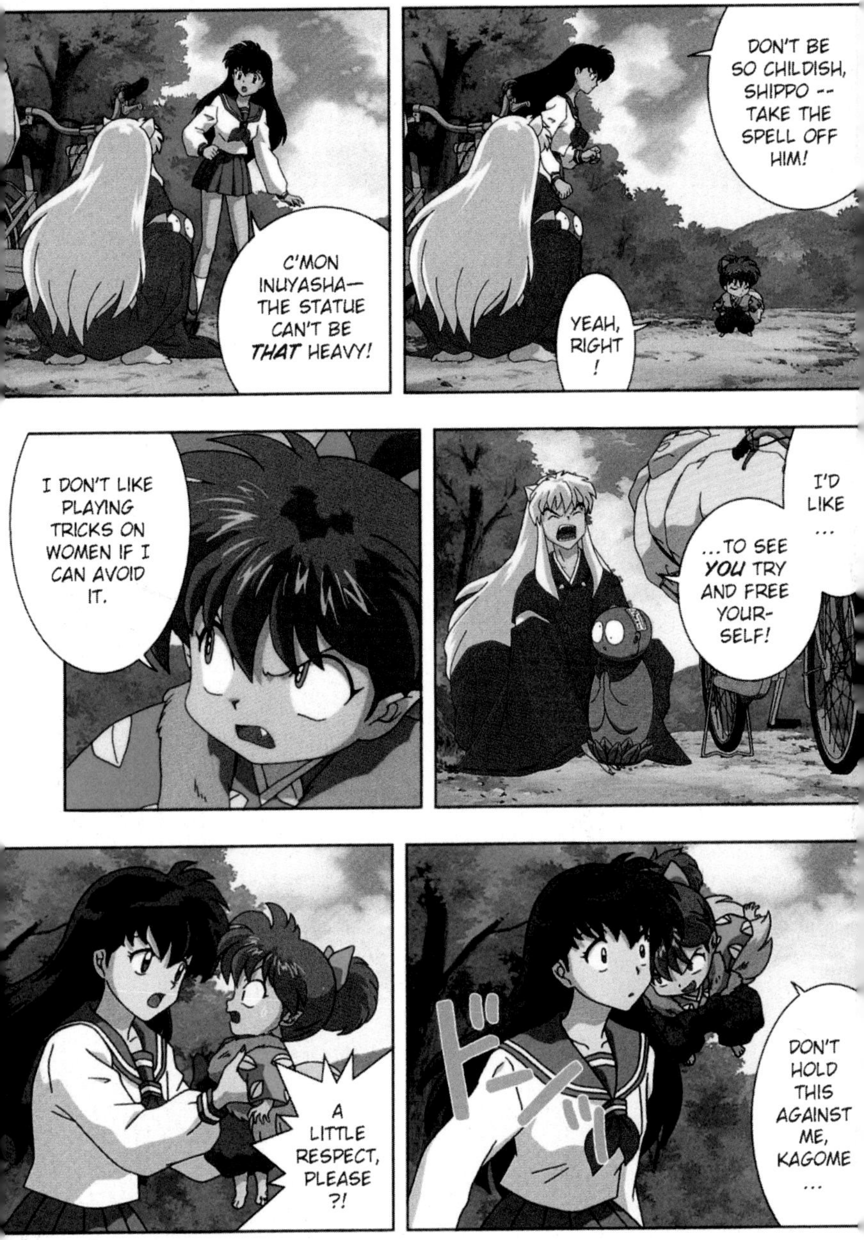
DON'T BE SO CHILDISH, SHIPPO -- TAKE THE SPELL OFF HIM!
YEAH, RIGHT!
C'MON INUYASHA— THE STATUE CAN'T BE THAT HEAVY!
I'D LIKE ...
...TO SEE YOU TRY AND FREE YOUR-SELF!
I DON'T LIKE PLAYING TRICKS ON WOMEN IF I CAN AVOID IT.
DON'T HOLD THIS AGAINST ME, KAGOME ...
A LITTLE RESPECT, PLEASE ?!

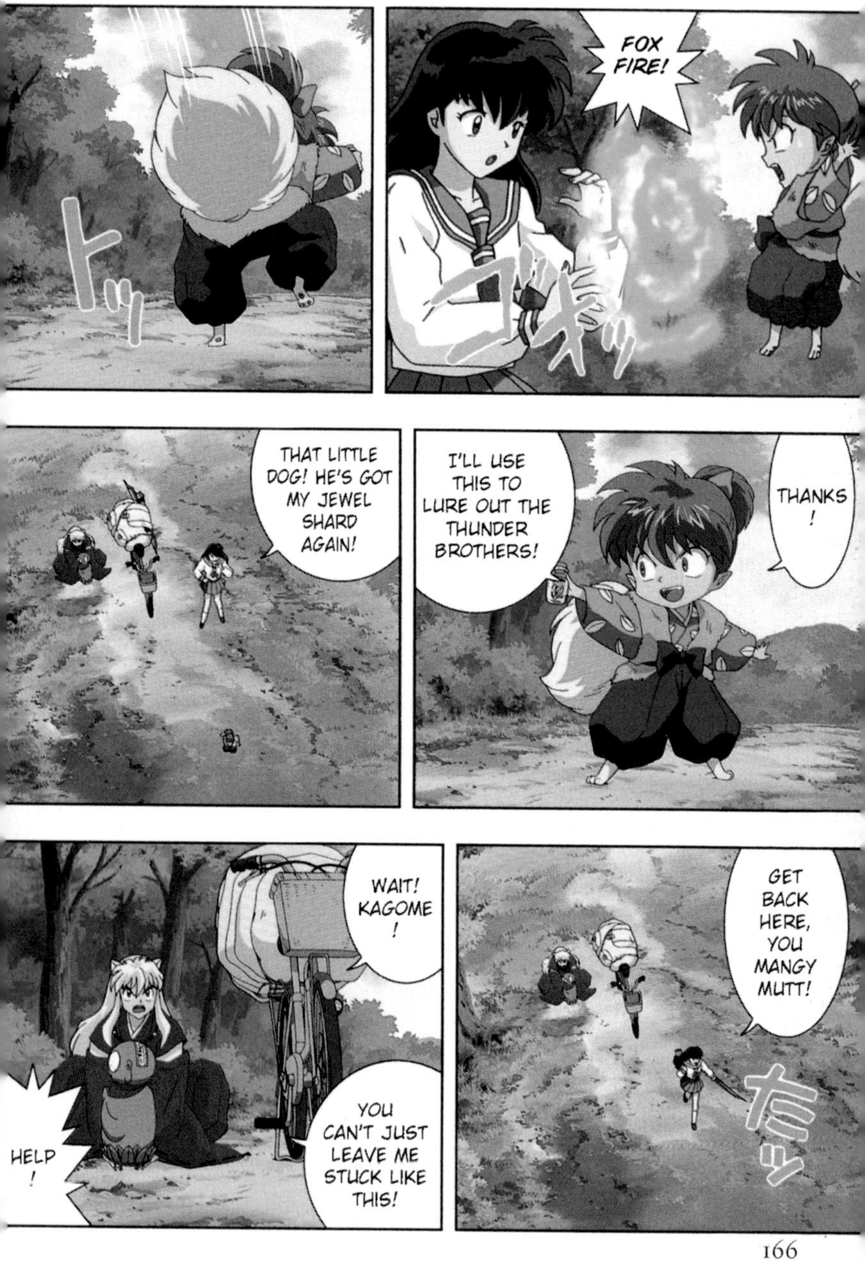
FOX FIRE!
トッ
THANKS!
I'LL USE THIS TO LURE OUT THE THUNDER BROTHERS!
THAT LITTLE DOG! HE'S GOT MY JEWEL SHARD AGAIN!
GET BACK HERE, YOU MANGY MUTT!
WAIT! KAGOME!
YOU CAN'T JUST LEAVE ME STUCK LIKE THIS!
HELP!

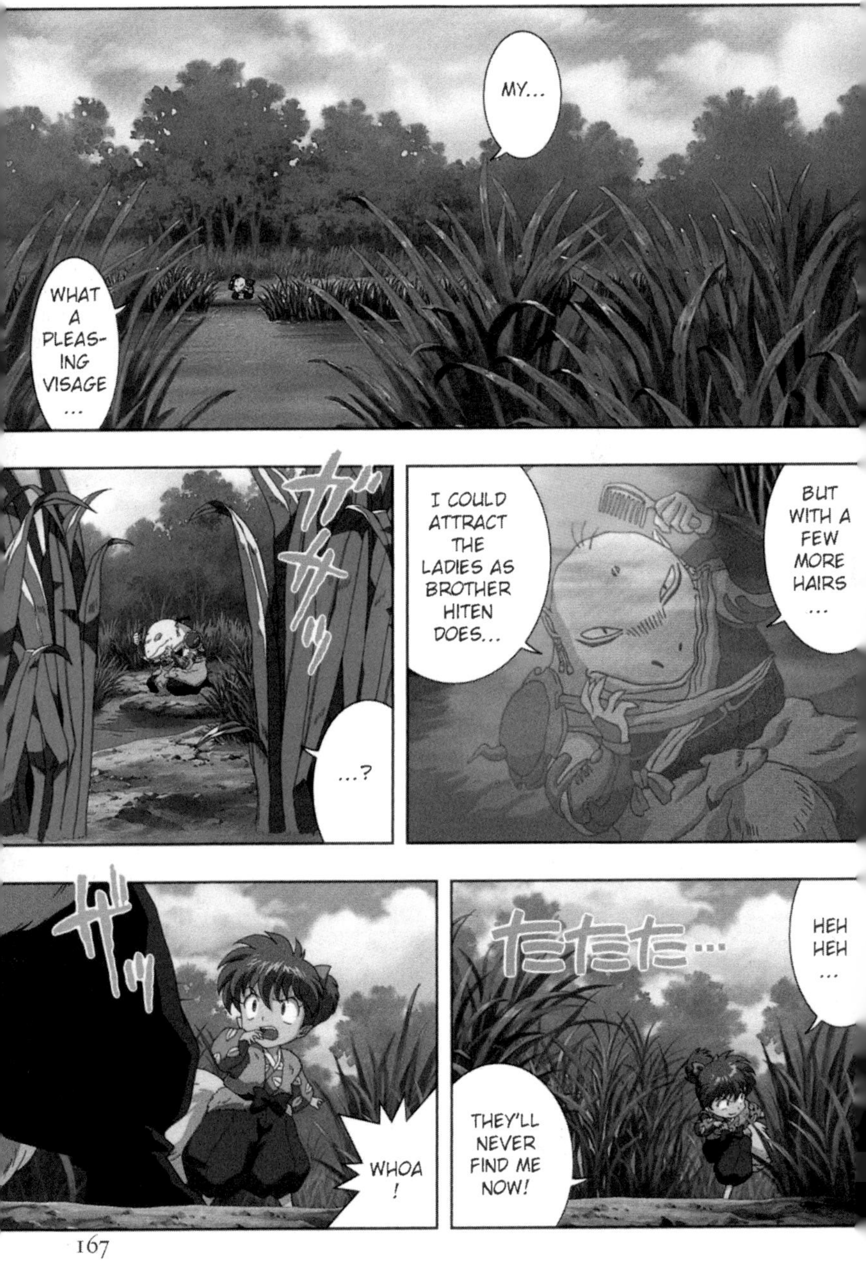
MY...
WHAT A PLEASING-ING VISAGE...
BUT WITH A FEW MORE HAIRS...
I COULD ATTRACT THE LADIES AS BROTHER HITEN DOES...
ガサガサッ
...?
HEH HEH...
たたたた...
THEY'LL NEVER FIND ME NOW!
ザッ
WHOA!

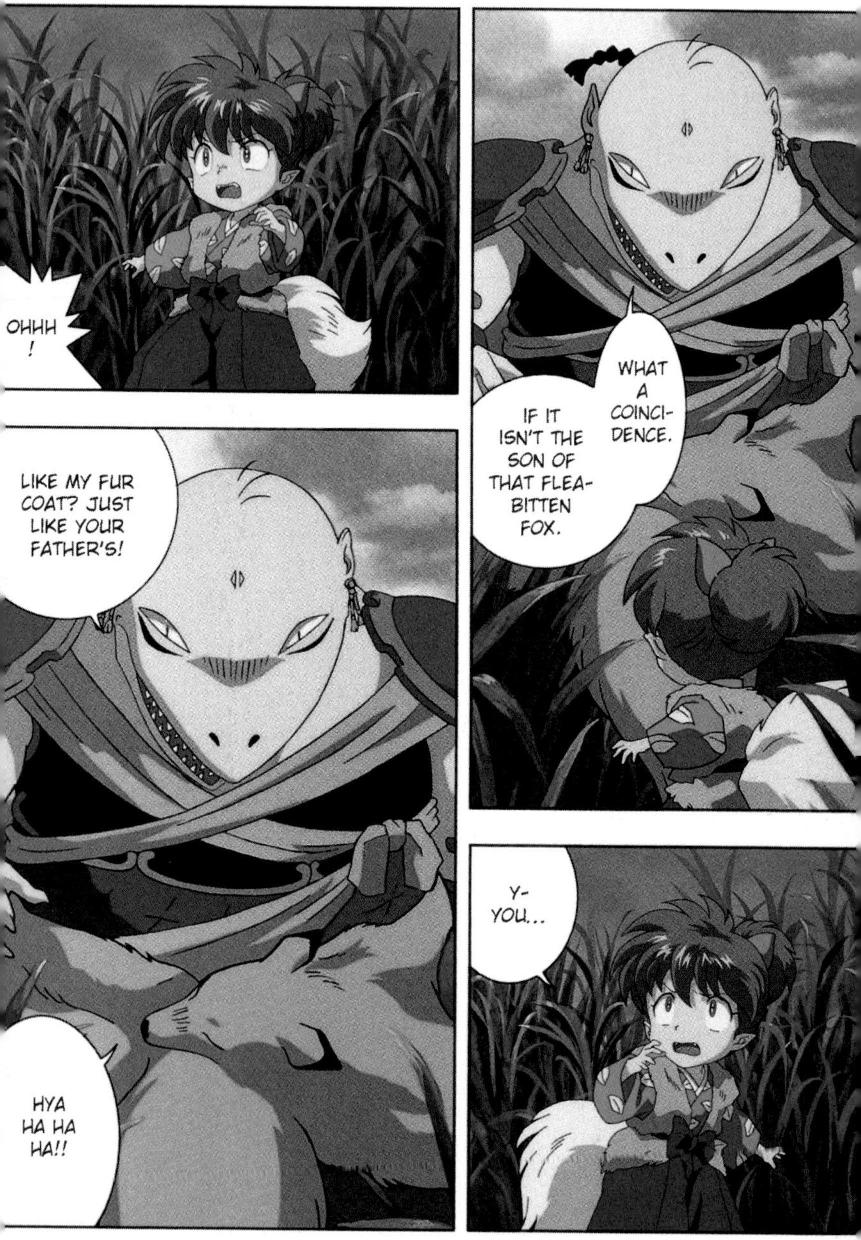
WHAT A COINCIDENCE.
IF IT ISN'T THE SON OF THAT FLEA-BITTEN FOX.
OHHH!
LIKE MY FUR COAT? JUST LIKE YOUR FATHER'S!
HYA HA HA HA!!
Y-YOU...

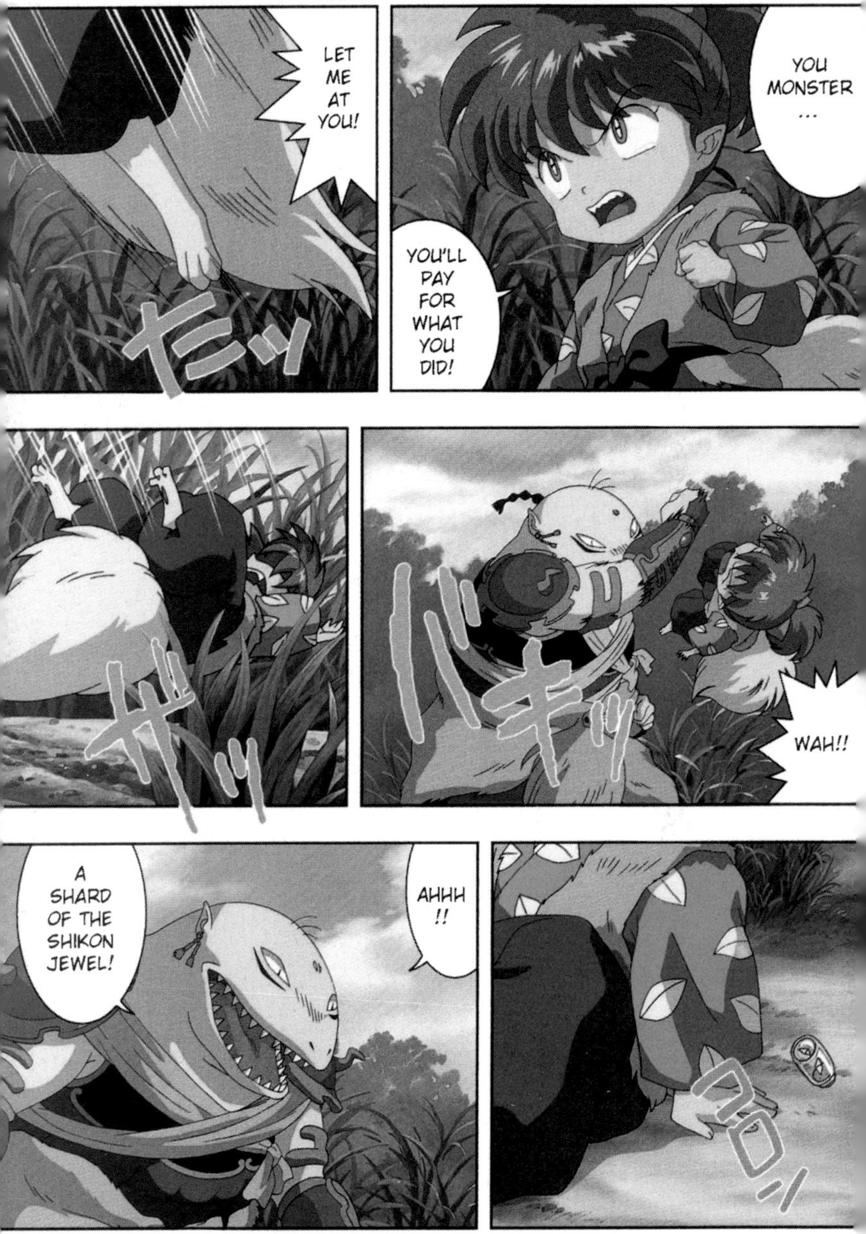
YOU MONSTER ...
YOU'LL PAY FOR WHAT YOU DID!
LET ME AT YOU!
WAH!!
ザッ
バキッ
AHHH!!
A SHARD OF THE SHIKON JEWEL!

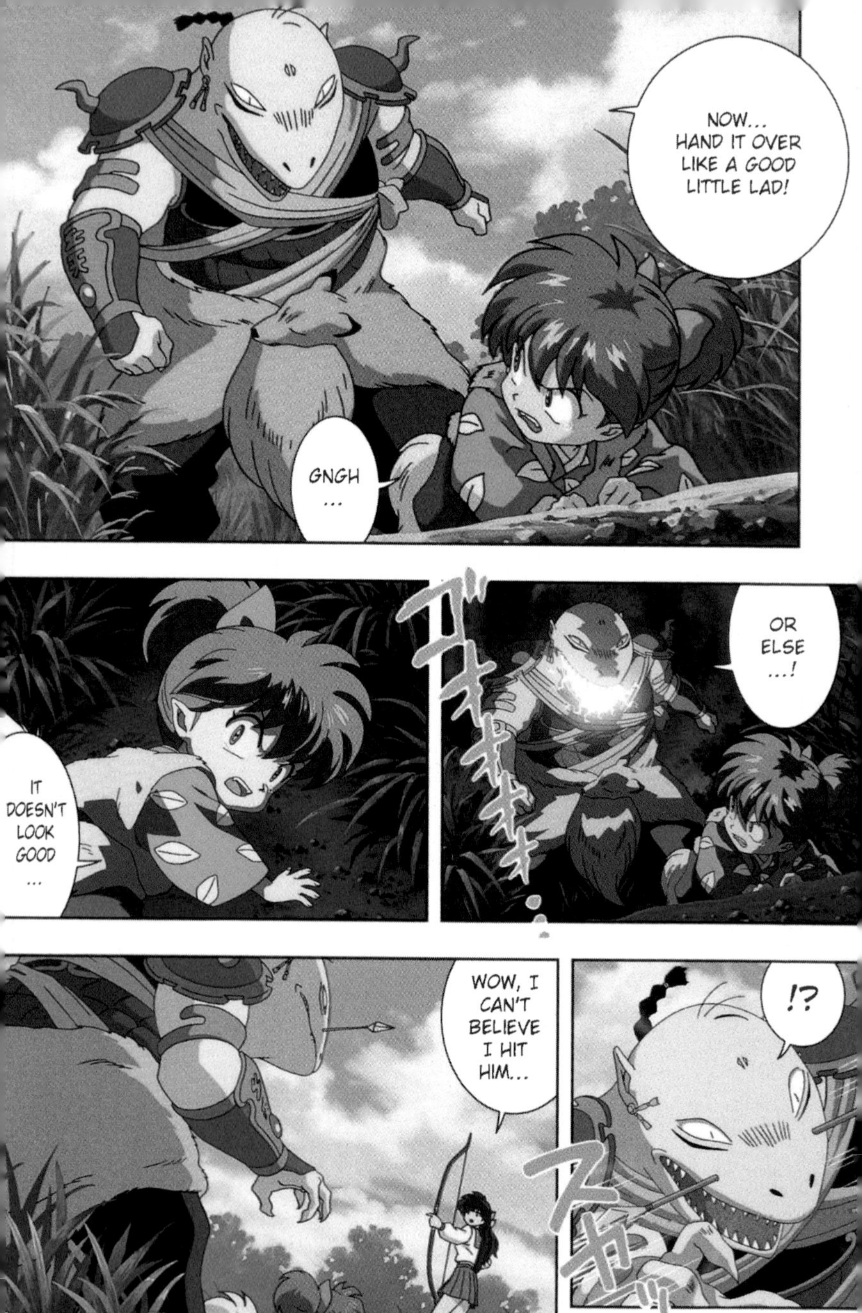
NOW... HAND IT OVER LIKE A GOOD LITTLE LAD!
GNGH ...
OR ELSE ...!
IT DOESN'T LOOK GOOD ...
!?
WOW, I CAN'T BELIEVE I HIT HIM...

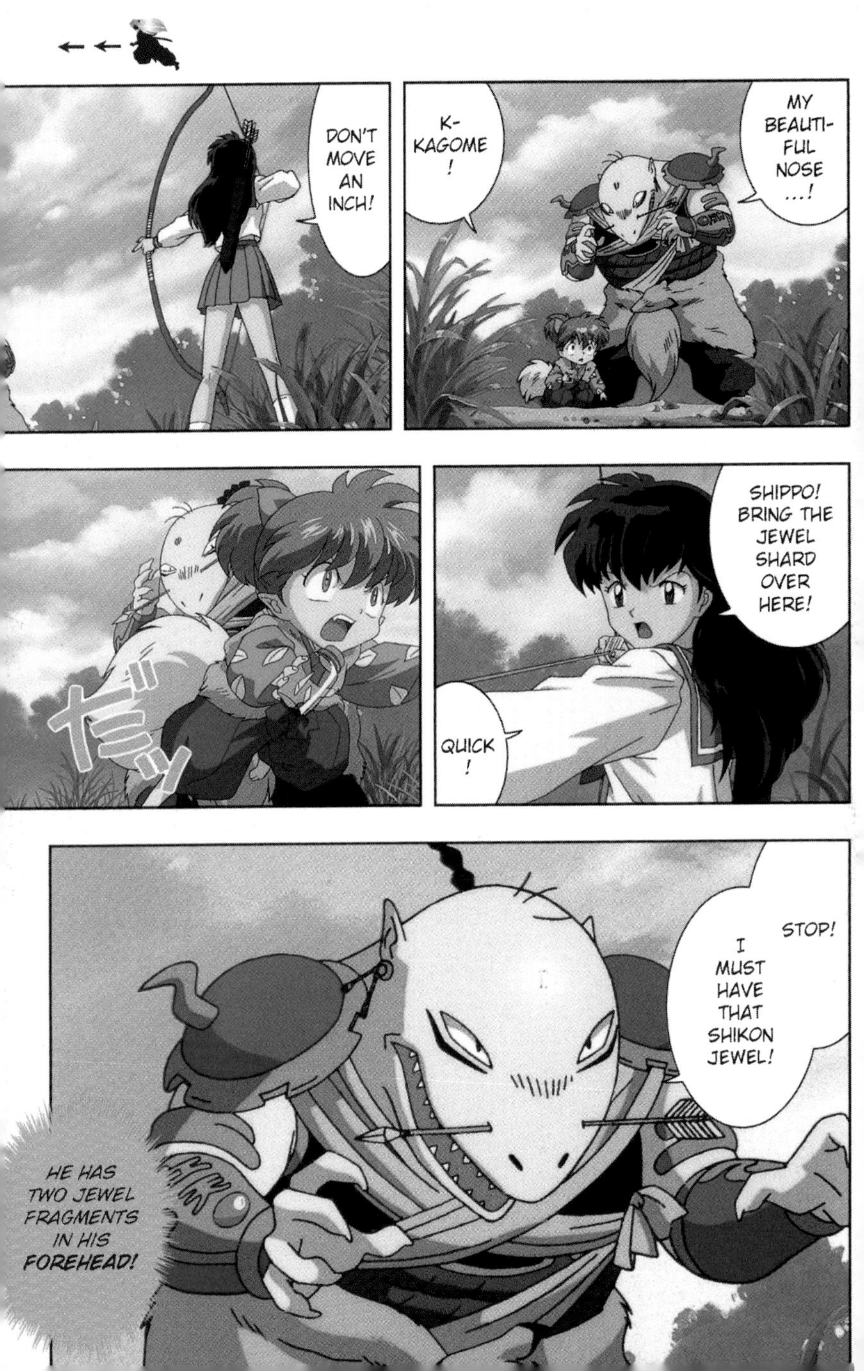
MY BEAUTIFUL NOSE ...!
K-KAGOME!
DON'T MOVE AN INCH!
SHIPPO! BRING THE JEWEL SHARD OVER HERE!
QUICK!
STOP! I MUST HAVE THAT SHIKON JEWEL!
HE HAS TWO JEWEL FRAGMENTS IN HIS FOREHEAD!

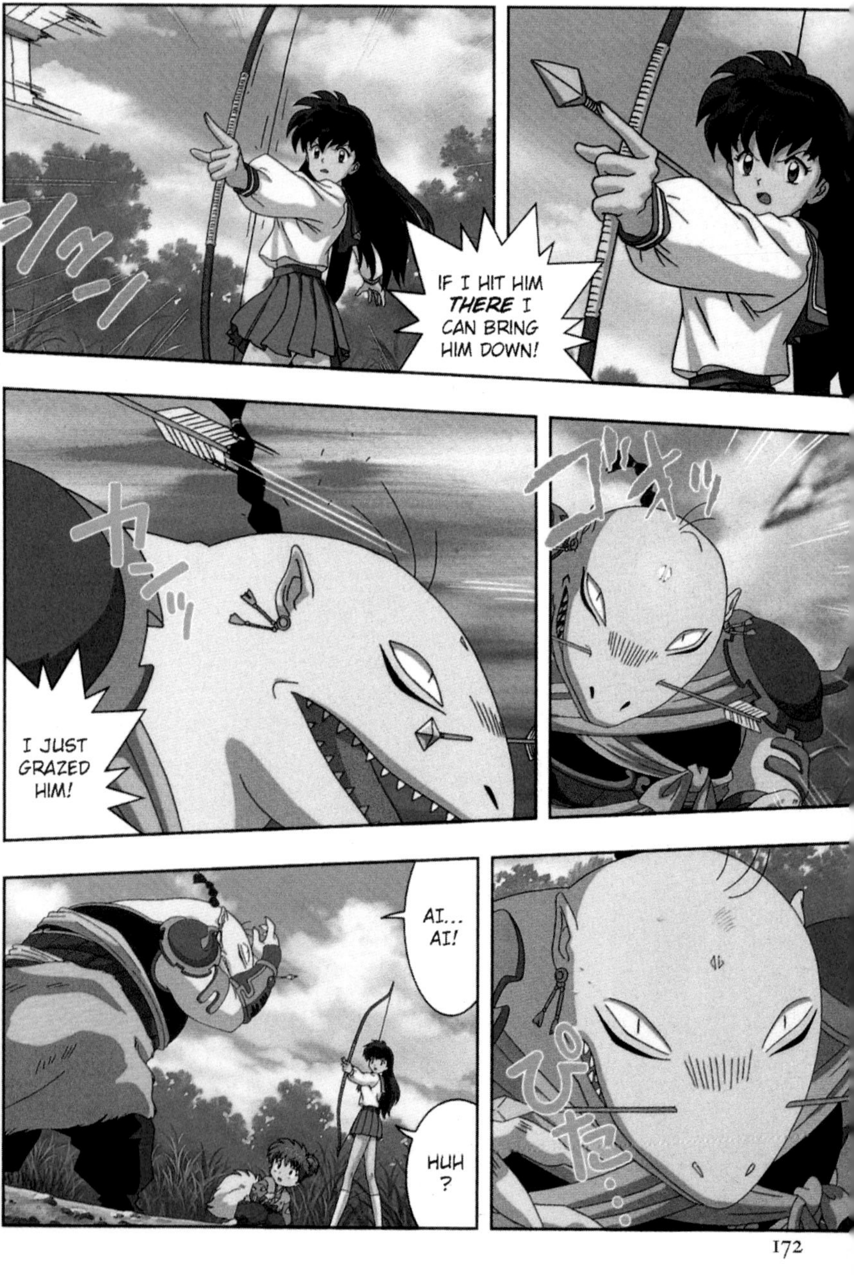
IF I HIT HIM *THERE* I CAN BRING HIM DOWN!
I JUST GRAZED HIM!
AI... AI!
HUH?

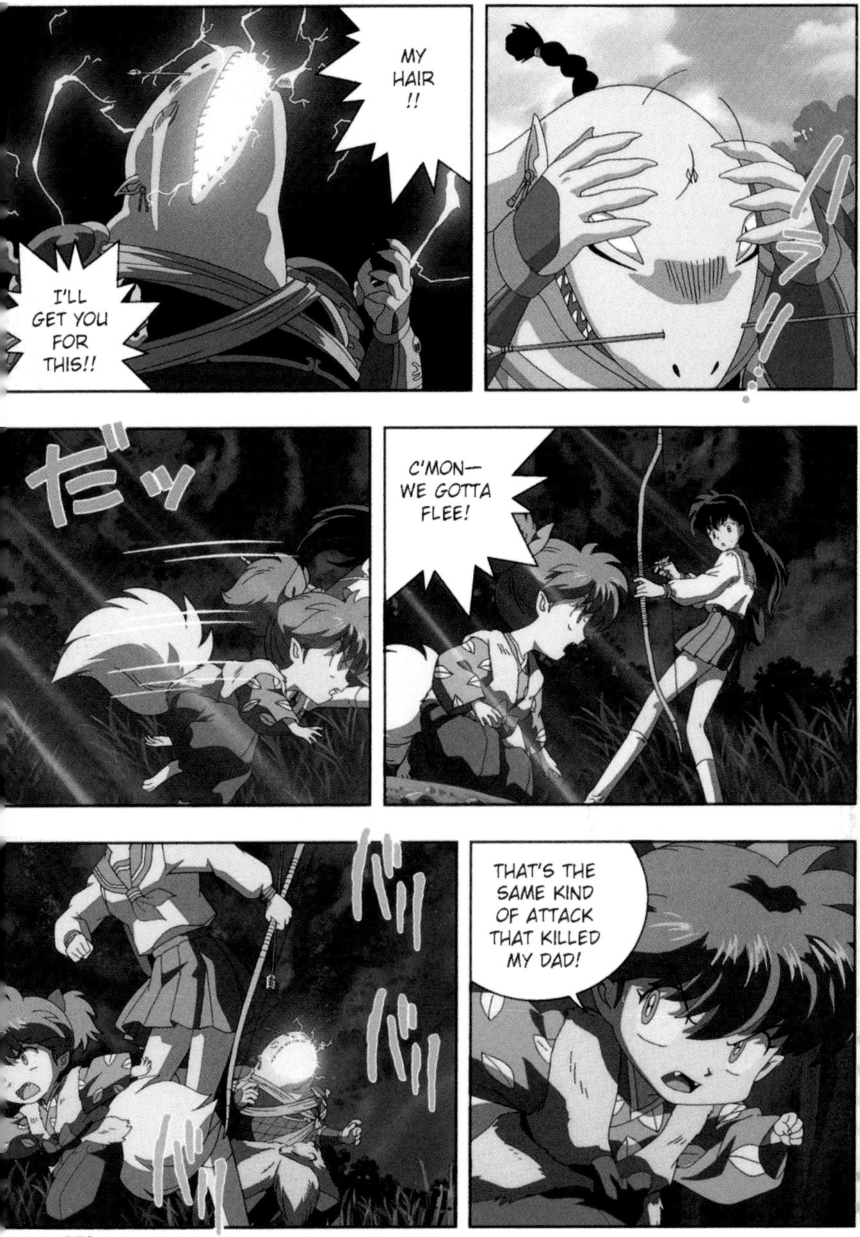
MY HAIR !!
I'LL GET YOU FOR THIS!!
C'MON— WE GOTTA FLEE!
だッ
THAT'S THE SAME KIND OF ATTACK THAT KILLED MY DAD!

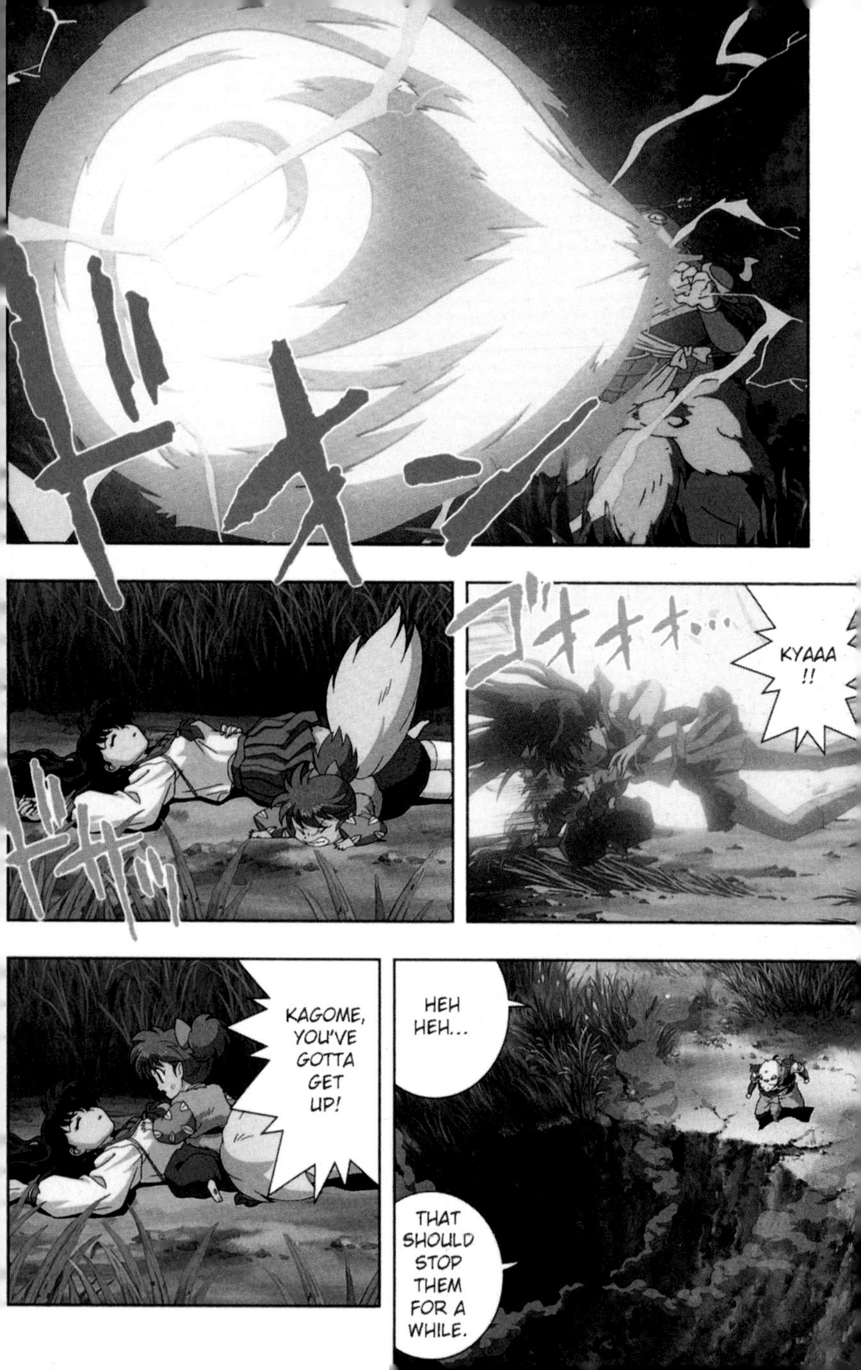
ゴオオオ…
KYAAA !!
HEH HEH...
THAT SHOULD STOP THEM FOR A WHILE.
KAGOME, YOU'VE GOTTA GET UP!

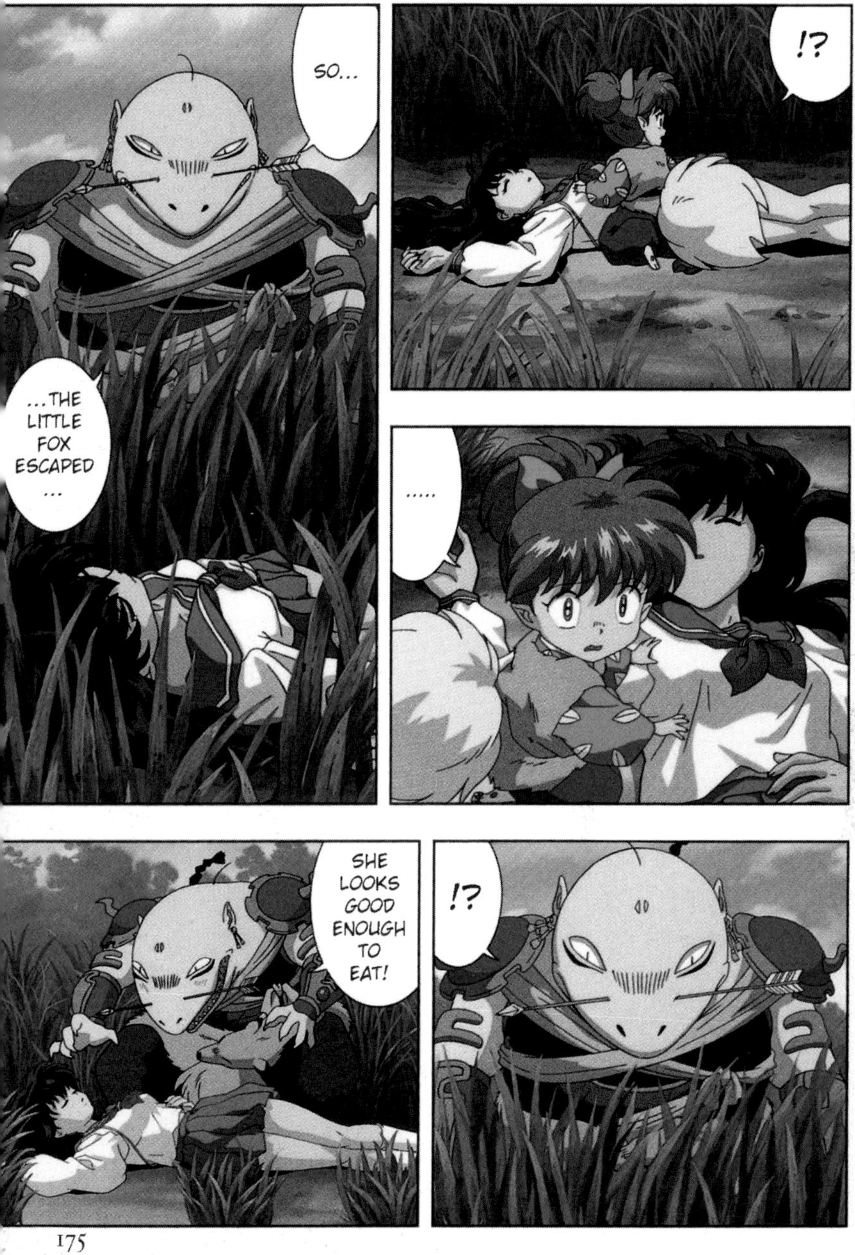
!?
.....
SO...
...THE LITTLE FOX ESCAPED ...
!?
SHE LOOKS GOOD ENOUGH TO EAT!

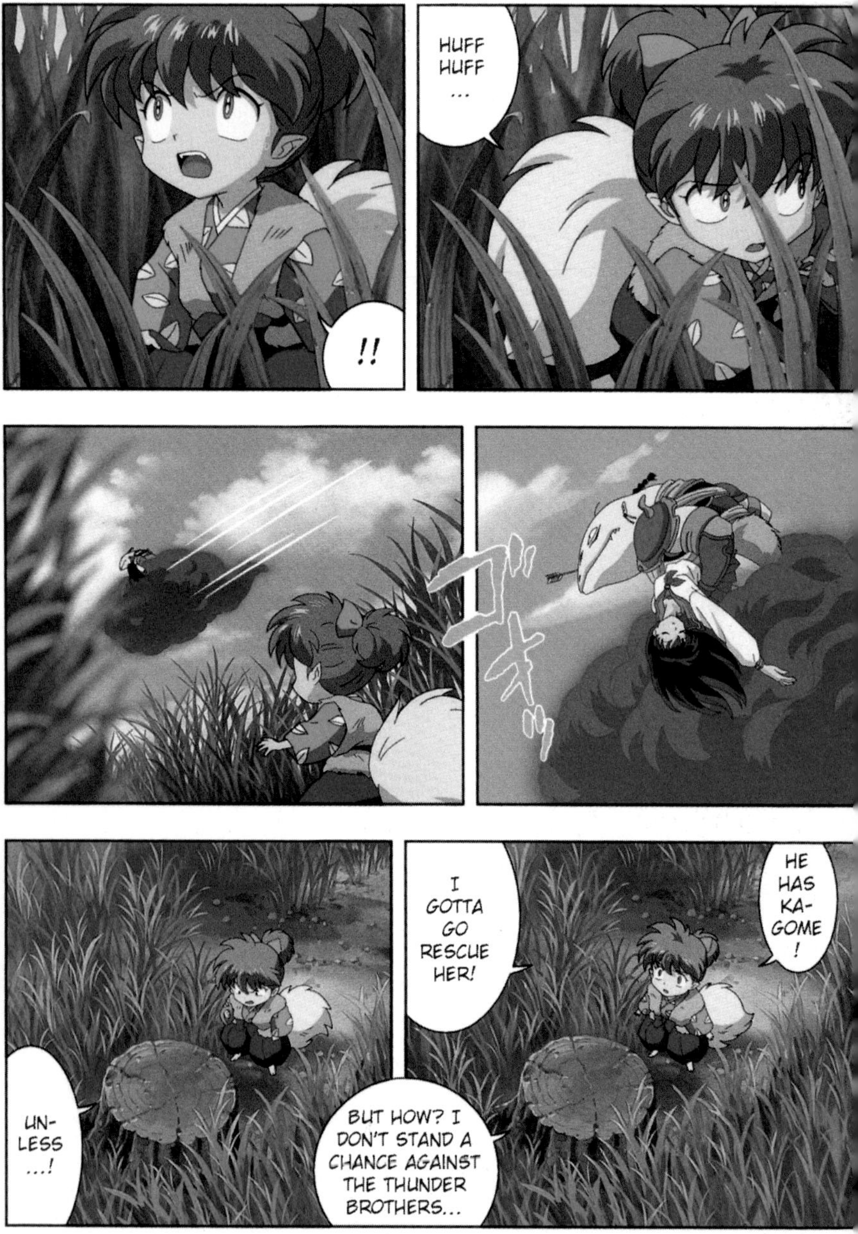
HUFF HUFF ...
!!
HE HAS KA-GOME!
I GOTTA GO RESCUE HER!
BUT HOW? I DON'T STAND A CHANCE AGAINST THE THUNDER BROTHERS...
UN-LESS ...!

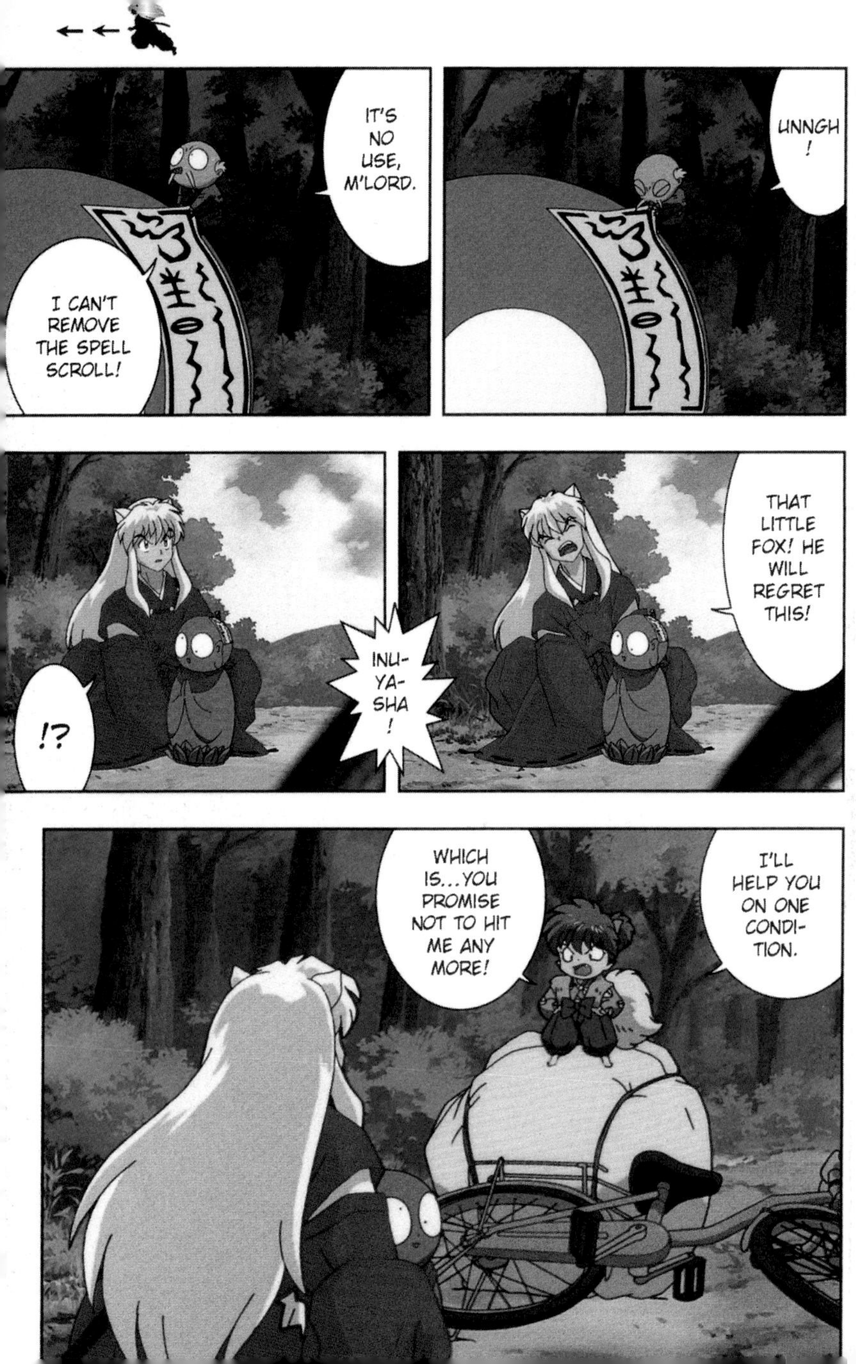
UNNGH!
IT'S NO USE, M'LORD.
I CAN'T REMOVE THE SPELL SCROLL!
THAT LITTLE FOX! HE WILL REGRET THIS!
INU-YASHA!
!?
I'LL HELP YOU ON ONE CONDITION.
WHICH IS...YOU PROMISE NOT TO HIT ME ANY MORE!

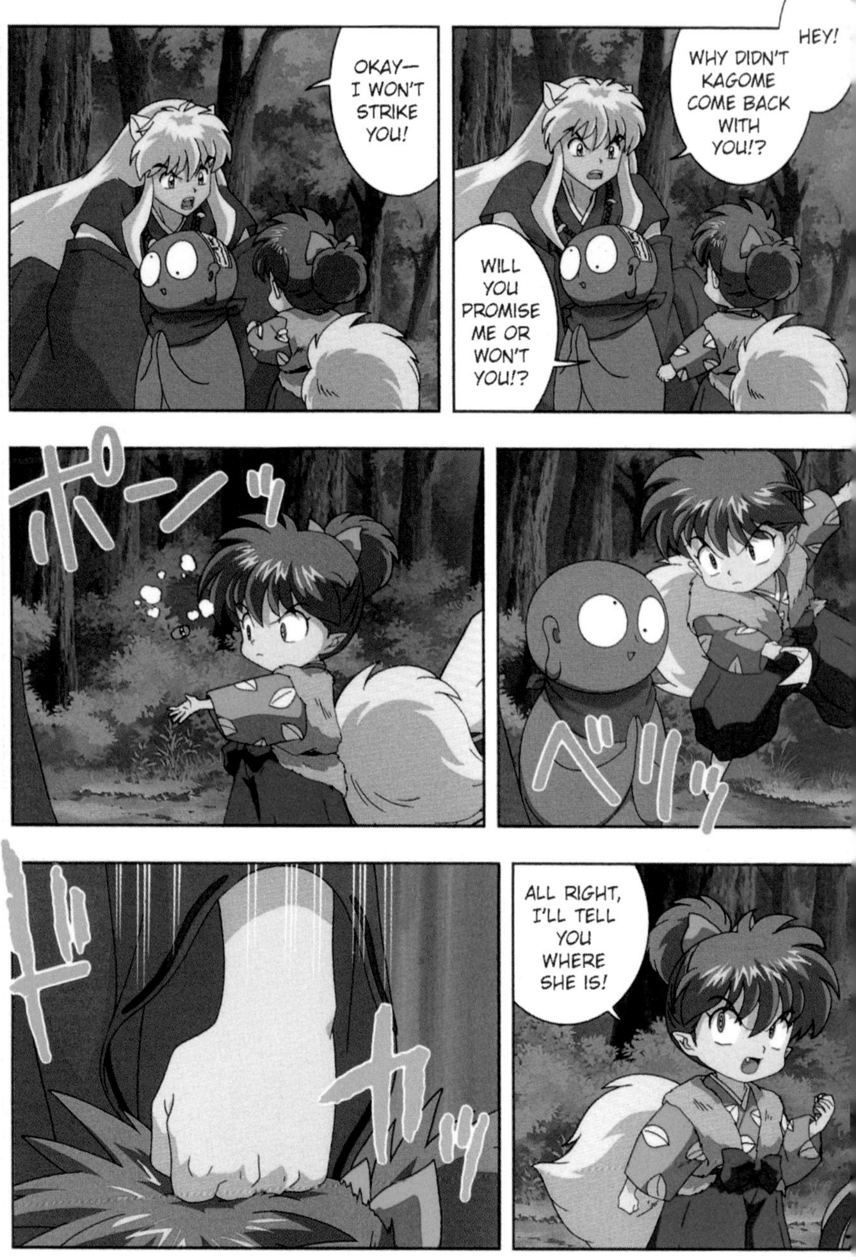
HEY! WHY DIDN'T KAGOME COME BACK WITH YOU!?
WILL YOU PROMISE ME OR WON'T YOU!?
OKAY— I WON'T STRIKE YOU!
ベリッ
ポーンッ
ALL RIGHT, I'LL TELL YOU WHERE SHE IS!
ドカッ

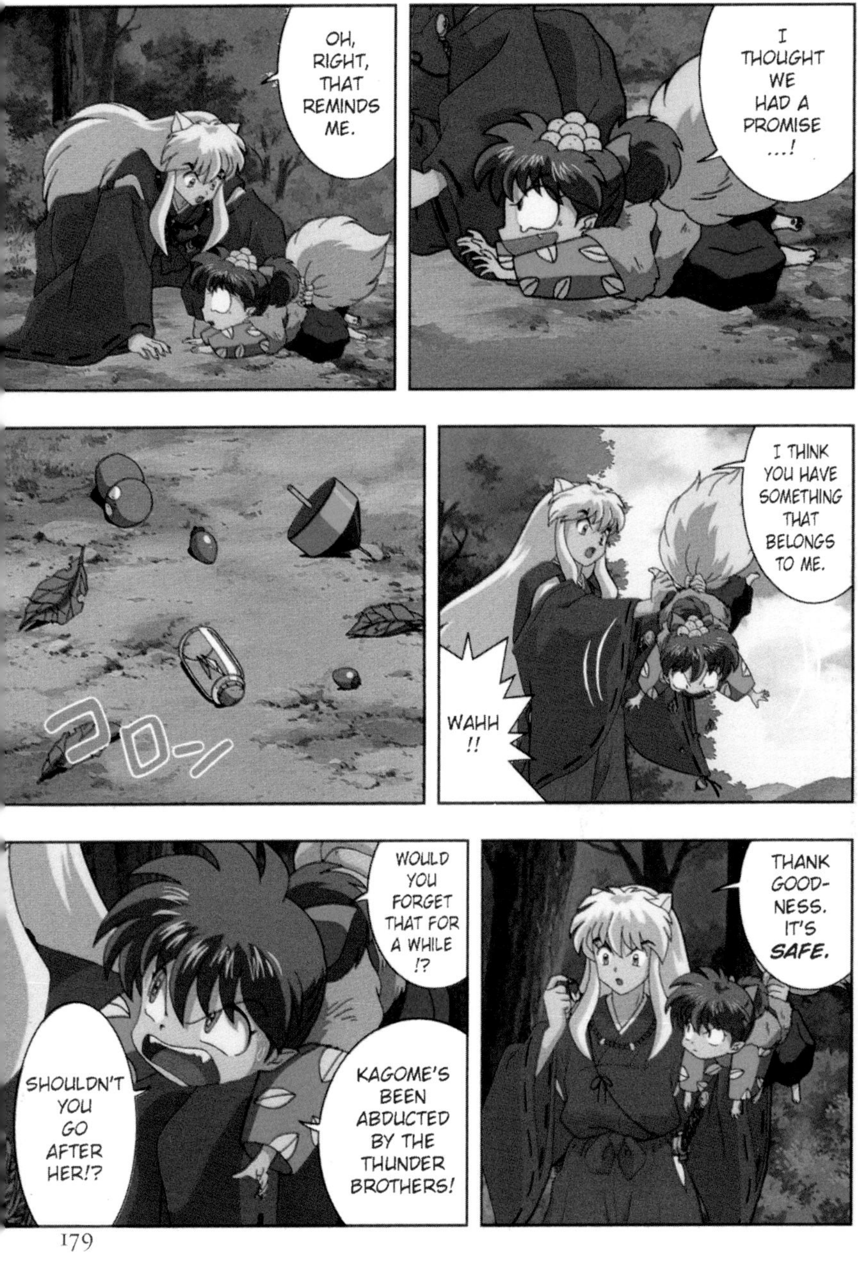
I THOUGHT WE HAD A PROMISE ...!
OH, RIGHT, THAT REMINDS ME.
I THINK YOU HAVE SOMETHING THAT BELONGS TO ME.
WAHH !!
THANK GOODNESS. IT'S *SAFE.*
WOULD YOU FORGET THAT FOR A WHILE !?
KAGOME'S BEEN ABDUCTED BY THE THUNDER BROTHERS!
SHOULDN'T YOU GO AFTER HER!?

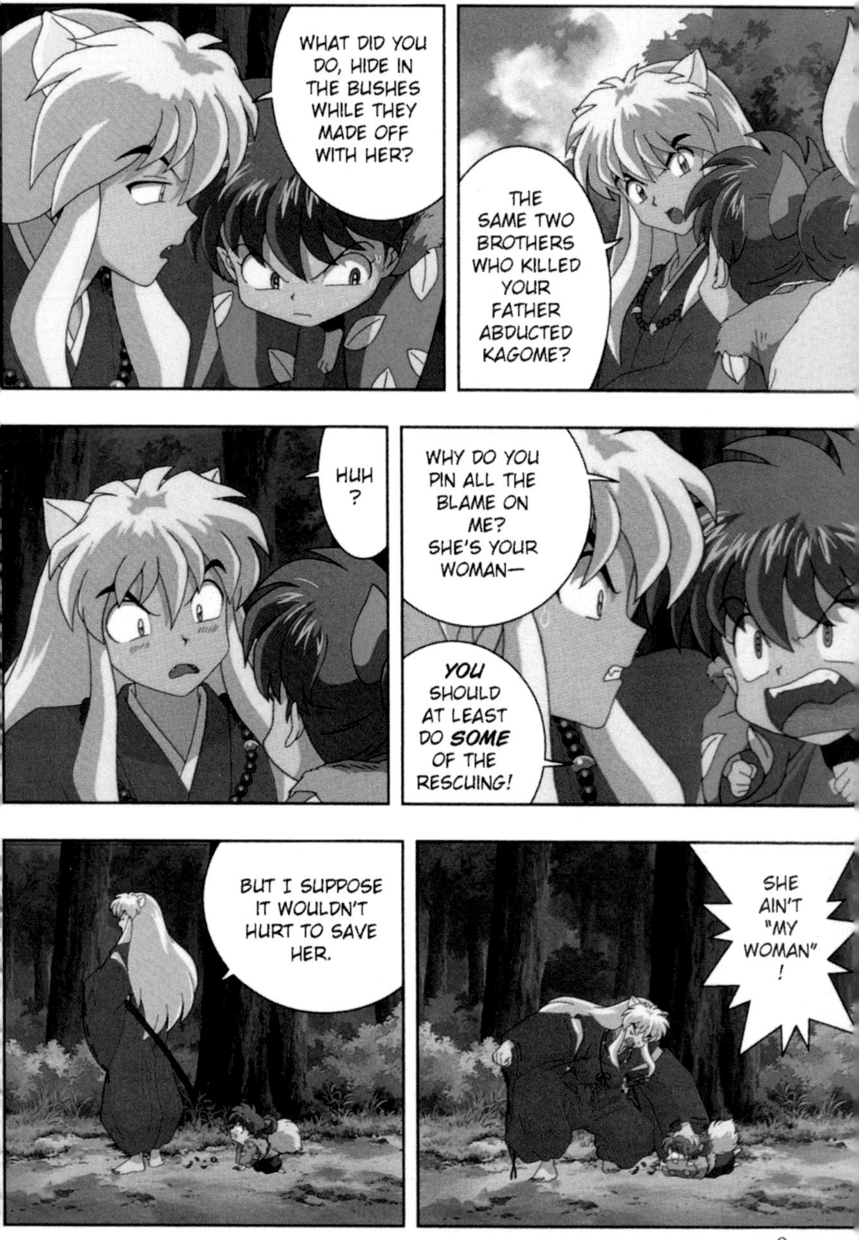
THE SAME TWO BROTHERS WHO KILLED YOUR FATHER ABDUCTED KAGOME?
WHAT DID YOU DO, HIDE IN THE BUSHES WHILE THEY MADE OFF WITH HER?
WHY DO YOU PIN ALL THE BLAME ON ME? SHE'S YOUR WOMAN—
YOU SHOULD AT LEAST DO ***SOME*** OF THE RESCUING!
HUH ?
SHE AIN'T "MY WOMAN" !
BUT I SUPPOSE IT WOULDN'T HURT TO SAVE HER.

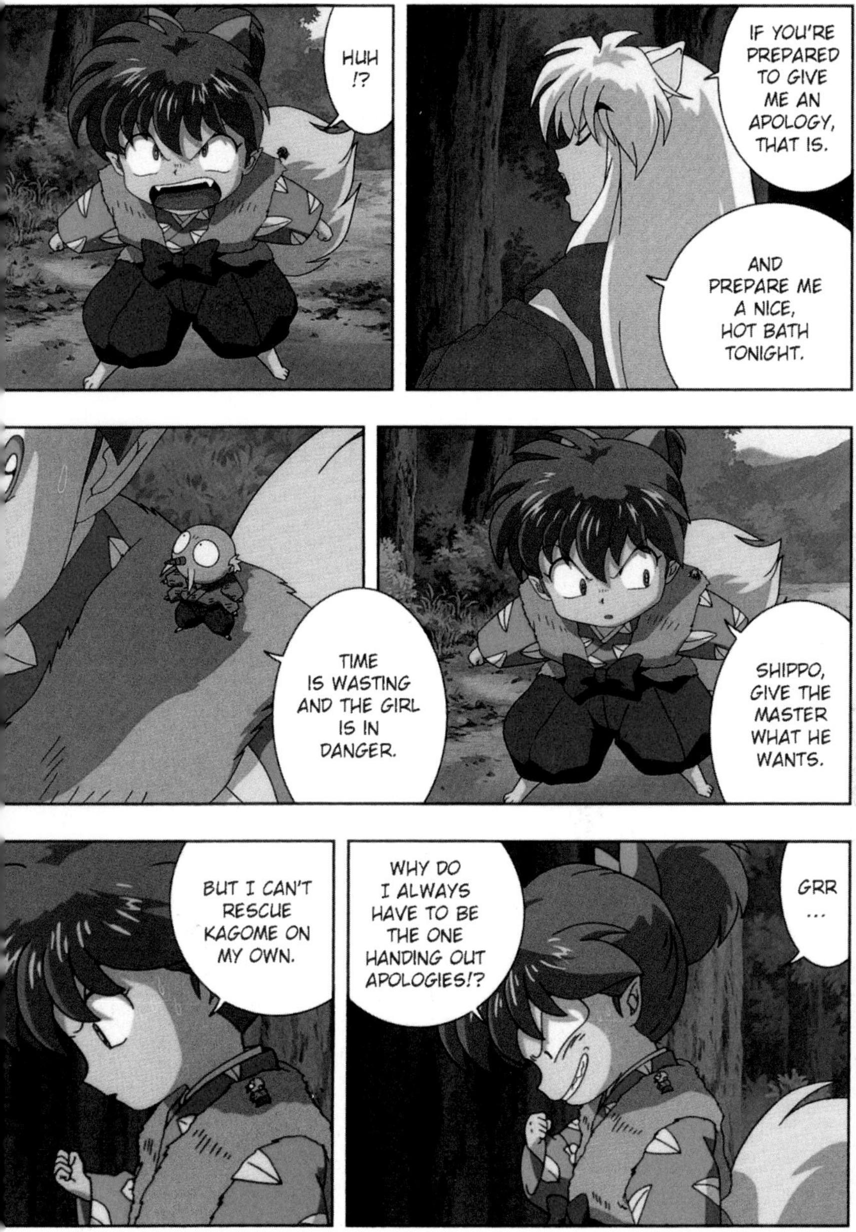
IF YOU'RE PREPARED TO GIVE ME AN APOLOGY, THAT IS.
AND PREPARE ME A NICE, HOT BATH TONIGHT.
HUH !?
SHIPPO, GIVE THE MASTER WHAT HE WANTS.
TIME IS WASTING AND THE GIRL IS IN DANGER.
GRR ...
WHY DO I ALWAYS HAVE TO BE THE ONE HANDING OUT APOLOGIES!?
BUT I CAN'T RESCUE KAGOME ON MY OWN.

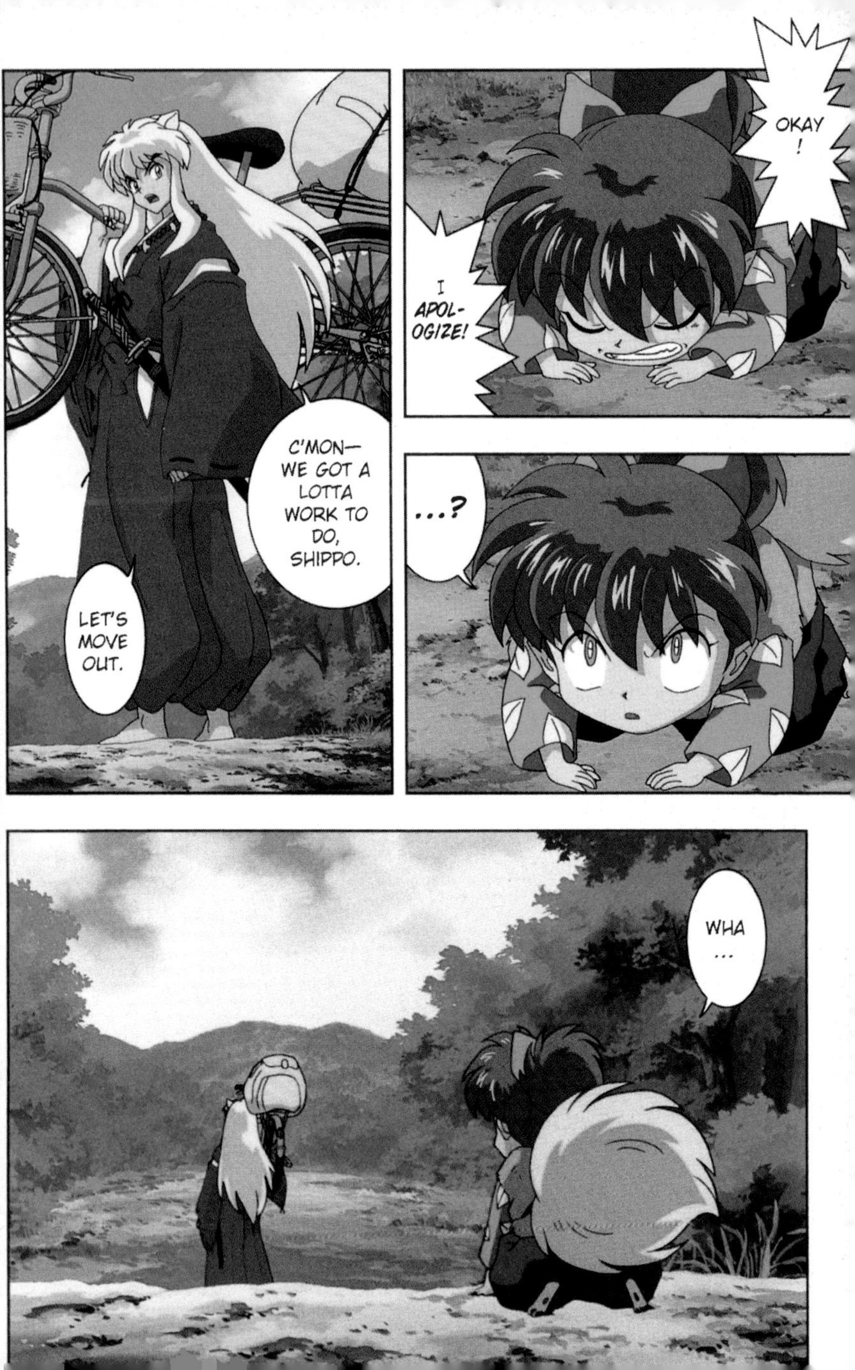
OKAY!
I APOLOGIZE!
...?
C'MON— WE GOT A LOTTA WORK TO DO, SHIPPO.
LET'S MOVE OUT.
WHA ...

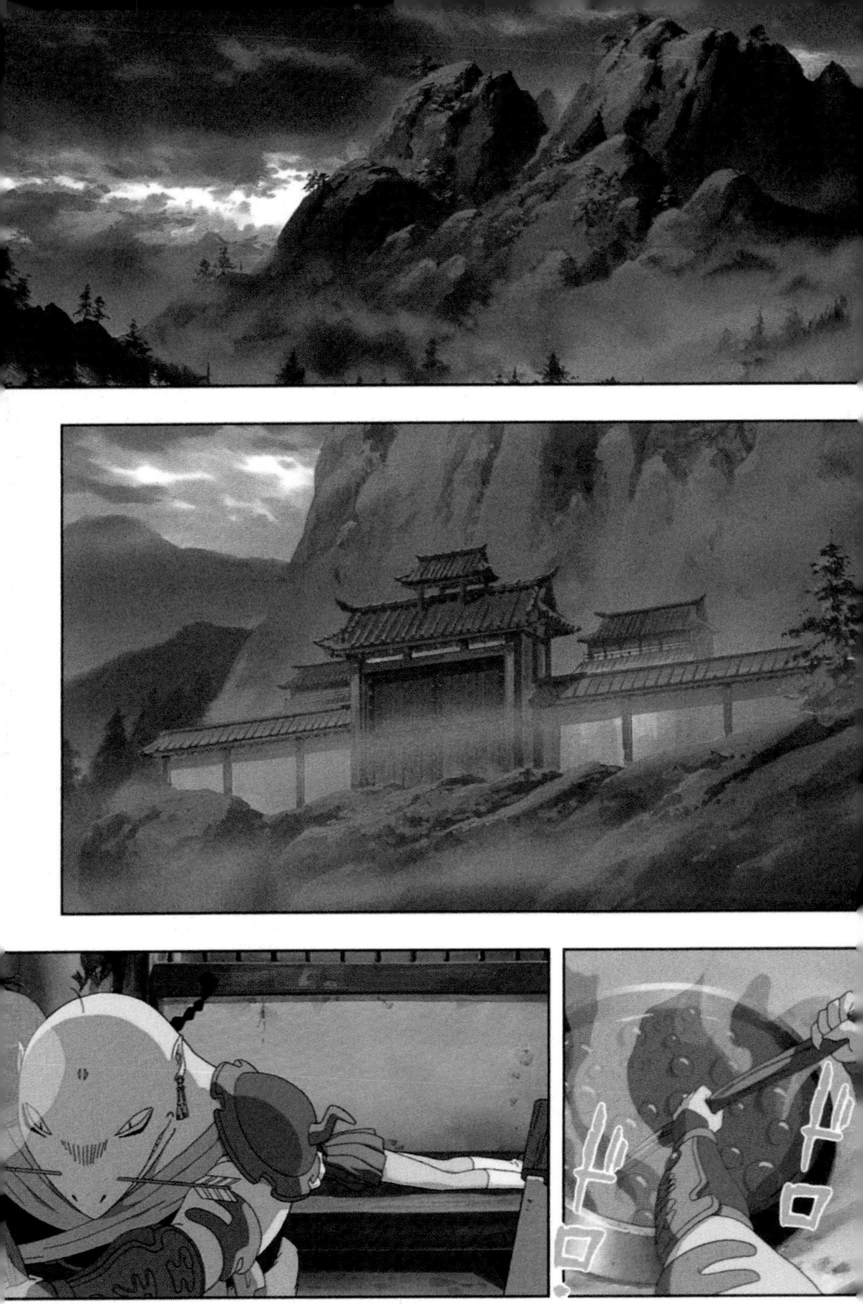

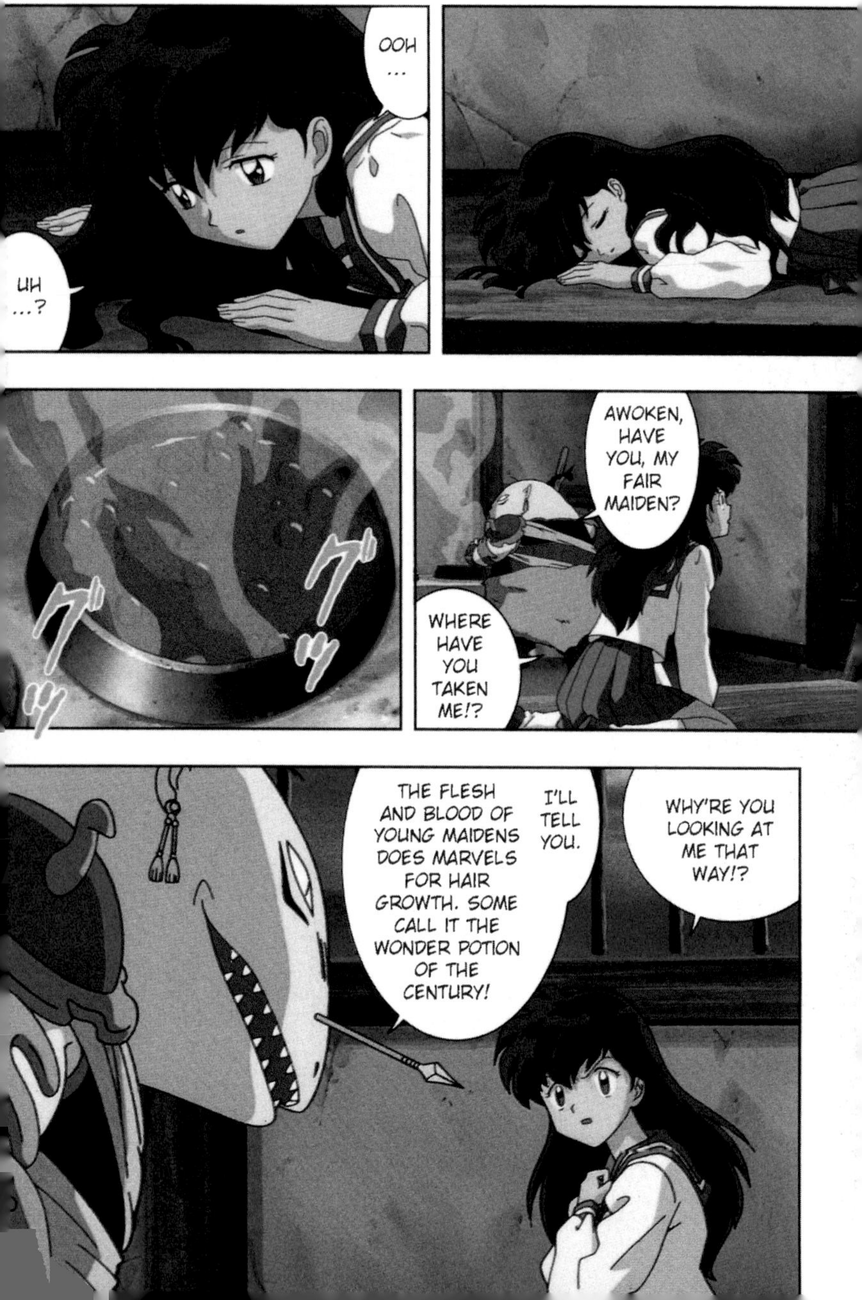
OOH ...
UH ...?
AWOKEN, HAVE YOU, MY FAIR MAIDEN?
WHERE HAVE YOU TAKEN ME!?
グッ
グッ
WHY'RE YOU LOOKING AT ME THAT WAY!?
I'LL TELL YOU.
THE FLESH AND BLOOD OF YOUNG MAIDENS DOES MARVELS FOR HAIR GROWTH. SOME CALL IT THE WONDER POTION OF THE CENTURY!

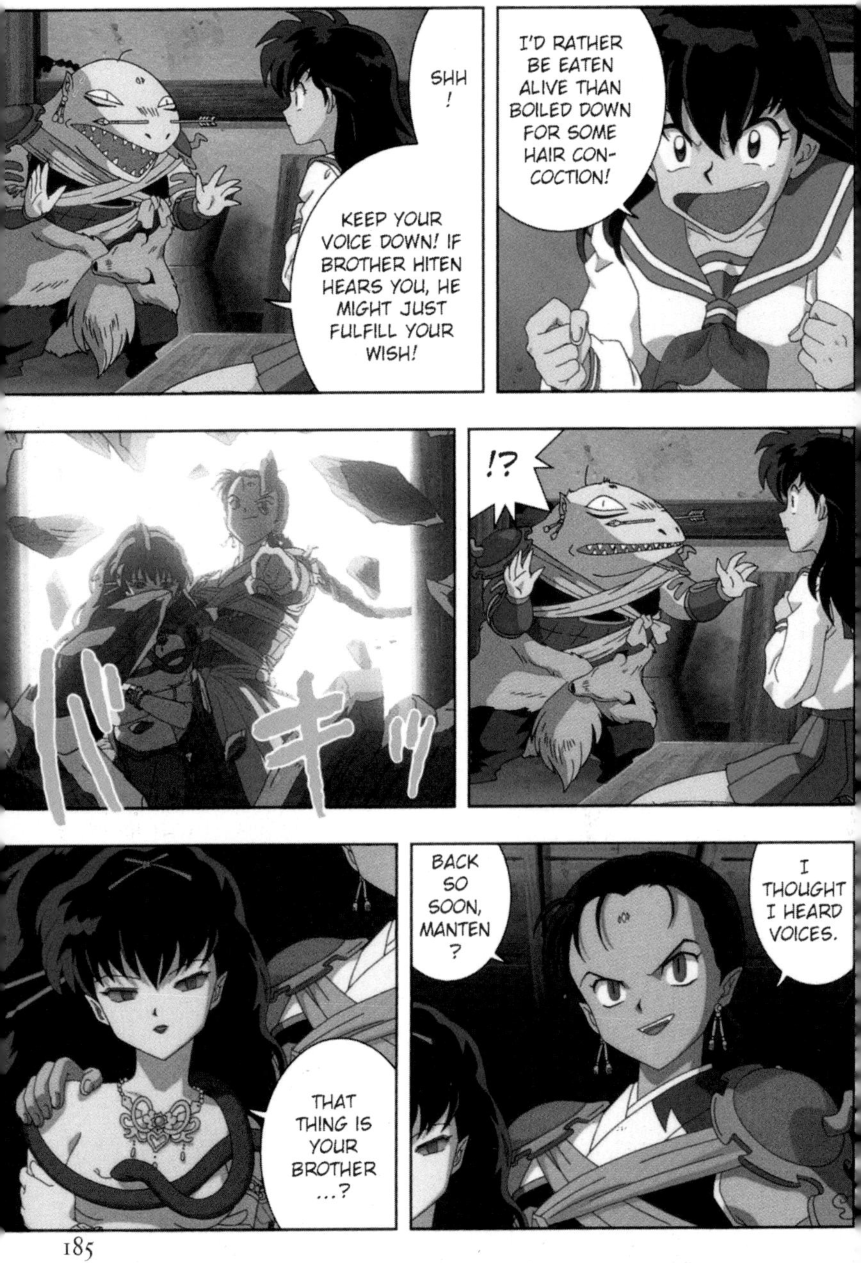
I'D RATHER BE EATEN ALIVE THAN BOILED DOWN FOR SOME HAIR CONCOCTION!
SHH!
KEEP YOUR VOICE DOWN! IF BROTHER HITEN HEARS YOU, HE MIGHT JUST FULFILL YOUR WISH!
!?
I THOUGHT I HEARD VOICES.
BACK SO SOON, MANTEN?
THAT THING IS YOUR BROTHER ...?

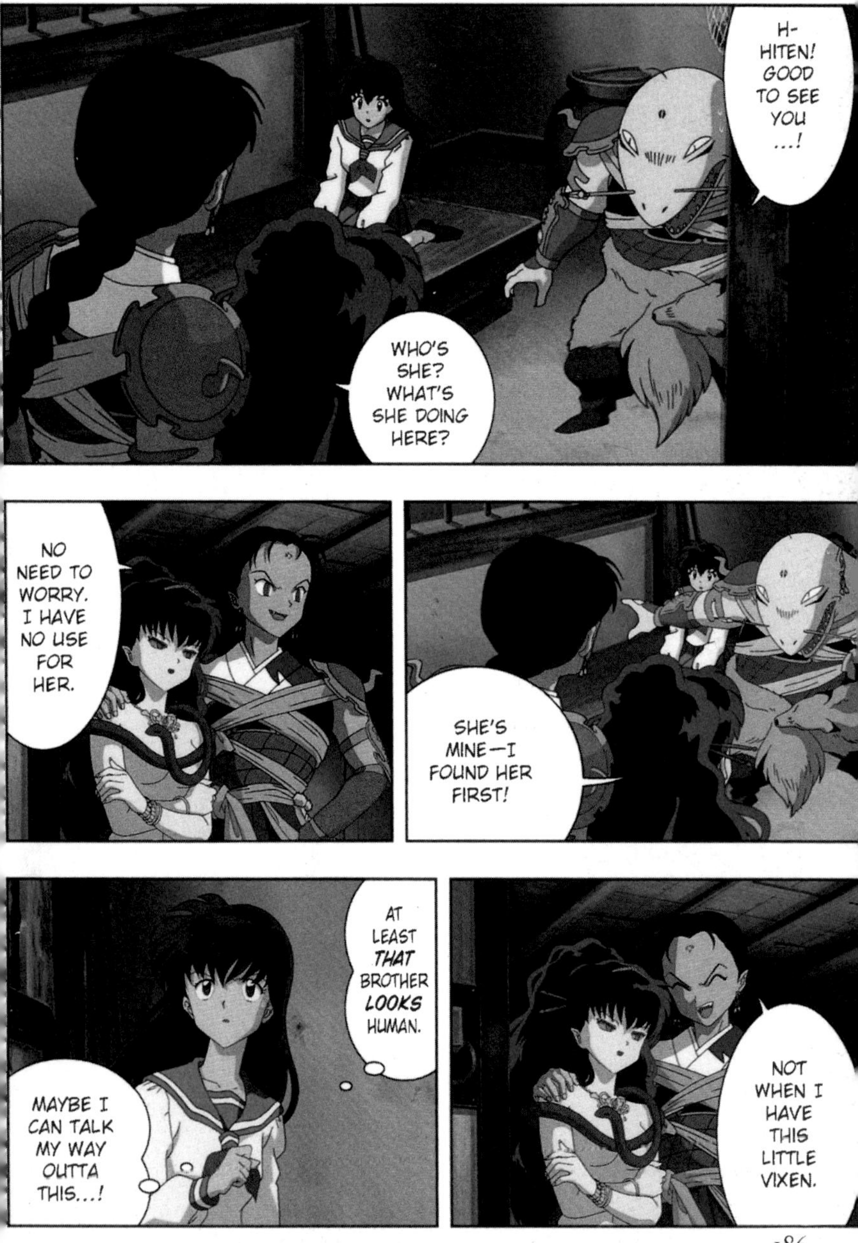
H- HITEN! GOOD TO SEE YOU ...!
WHO'S SHE? WHAT'S SHE DOING HERE?
SHE'S MINE—I FOUND HER FIRST!
NO NEED TO WORRY. I HAVE NO USE FOR HER.
NOT WHEN I HAVE THIS LITTLE VIXEN.
AT LEAST *THAT* BROTHER *LOOKS* HUMAN.
MAYBE I CAN TALK MY WAY OUTTA THIS...!

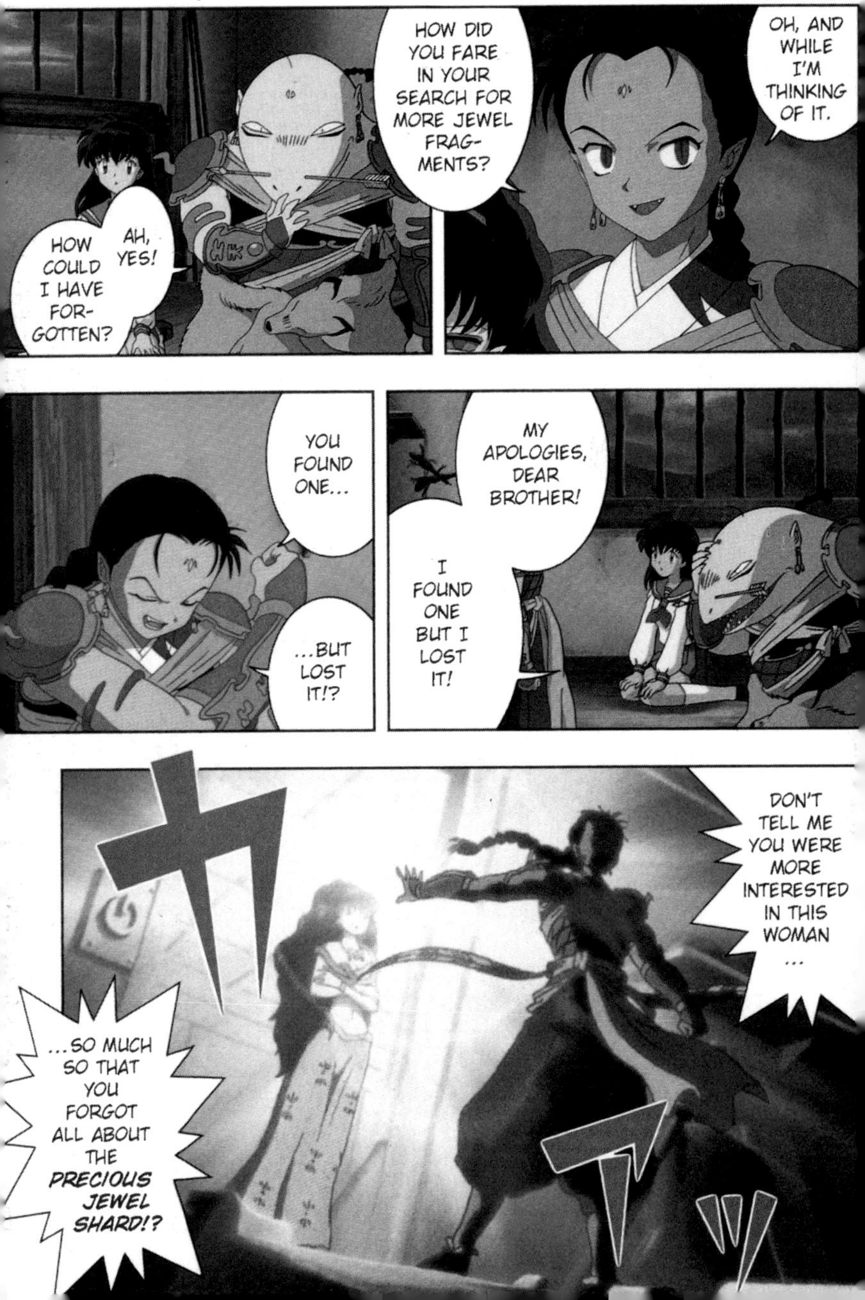
OH, AND WHILE I'M THINKING OF IT.
HOW DID YOU FARE IN YOUR SEARCH FOR MORE JEWEL FRAG- MENTS?
AH, YES!
HOW COULD I HAVE FOR- GOTTEN?
MY APOLOGIES, DEAR BROTHER!
I FOUND ONE BUT I LOST IT!
YOU FOUND ONE...
...BUT LOST IT!?
DON'T TELL ME YOU WERE MORE INTERESTED IN THIS WOMAN ...
...SO MUCH SO THAT YOU FORGOT ALL ABOUT THE **PRECIOUS JEWEL SHARD!?**

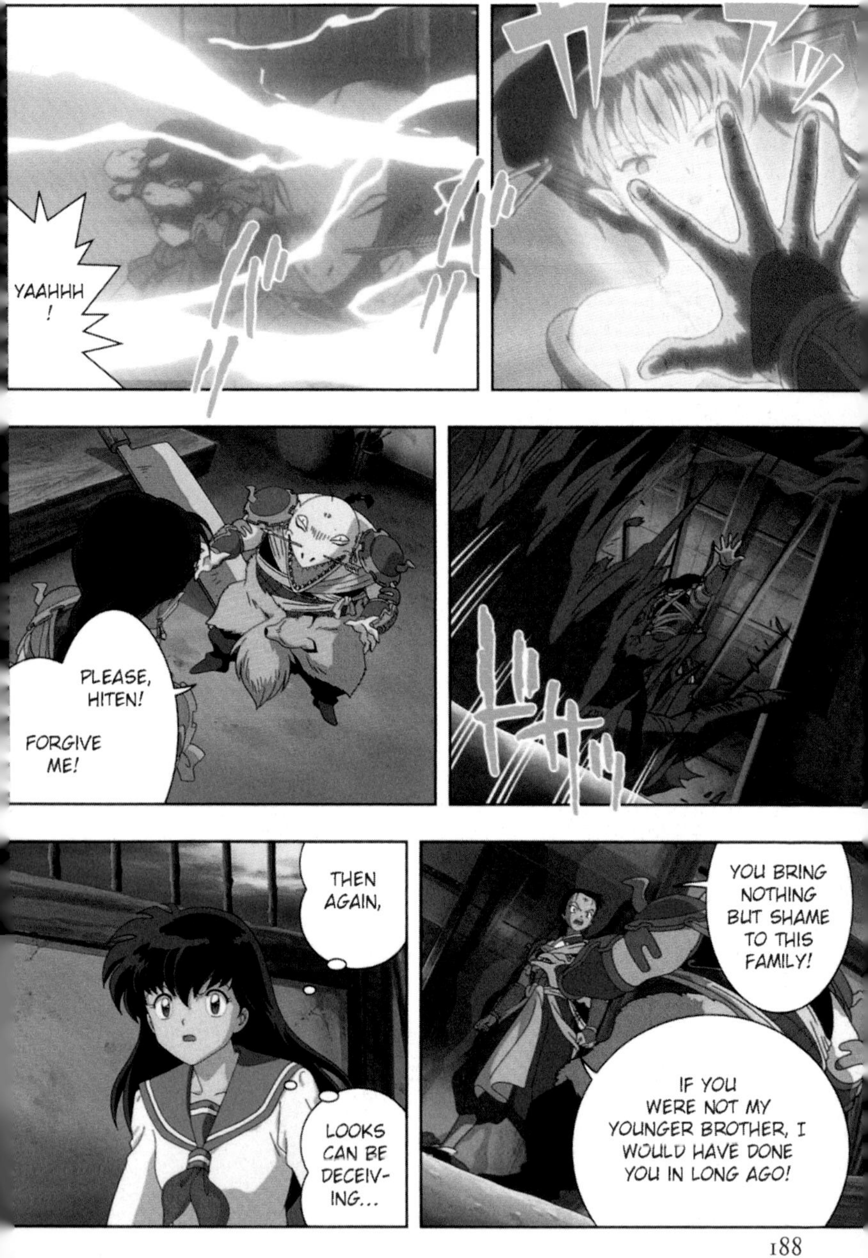
YAAHHH!
PLEASE, HITEN!
FORGIVE ME!
YOU BRING NOTHING BUT SHAME TO THIS FAMILY!
IF YOU WERE NOT MY YOUNGER BROTHER, I WOULD HAVE DONE YOU IN LONG AGO!
THEN AGAIN,
LOOKS CAN BE DECEIV-ING...

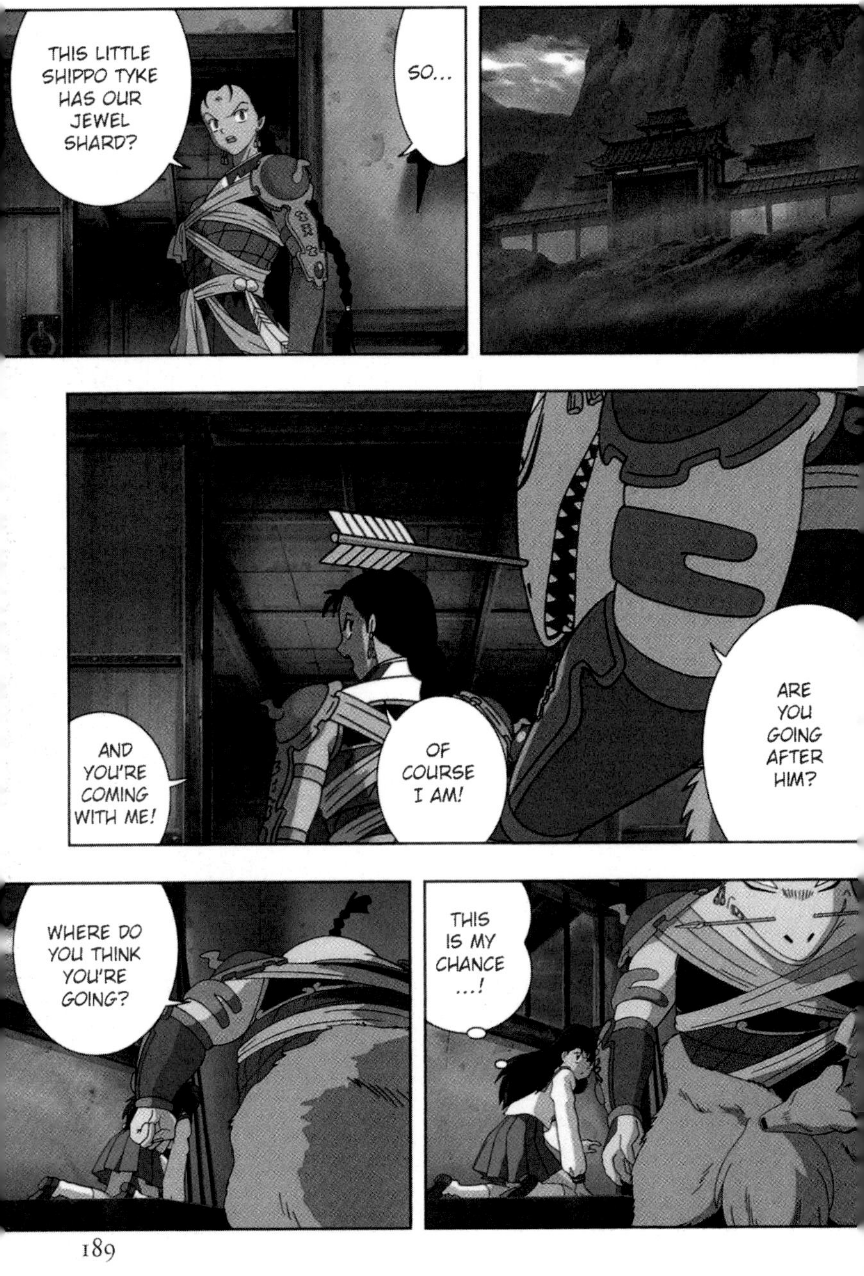
SO...
THIS LITTLE SHIPPO TYKE HAS OUR JEWEL SHARD?
ARE YOU GOING AFTER HIM?
OF COURSE I AM!
AND YOU'RE COMING WITH ME!
THIS IS MY CHANCE...!
WHERE DO YOU THINK YOU'RE GOING?

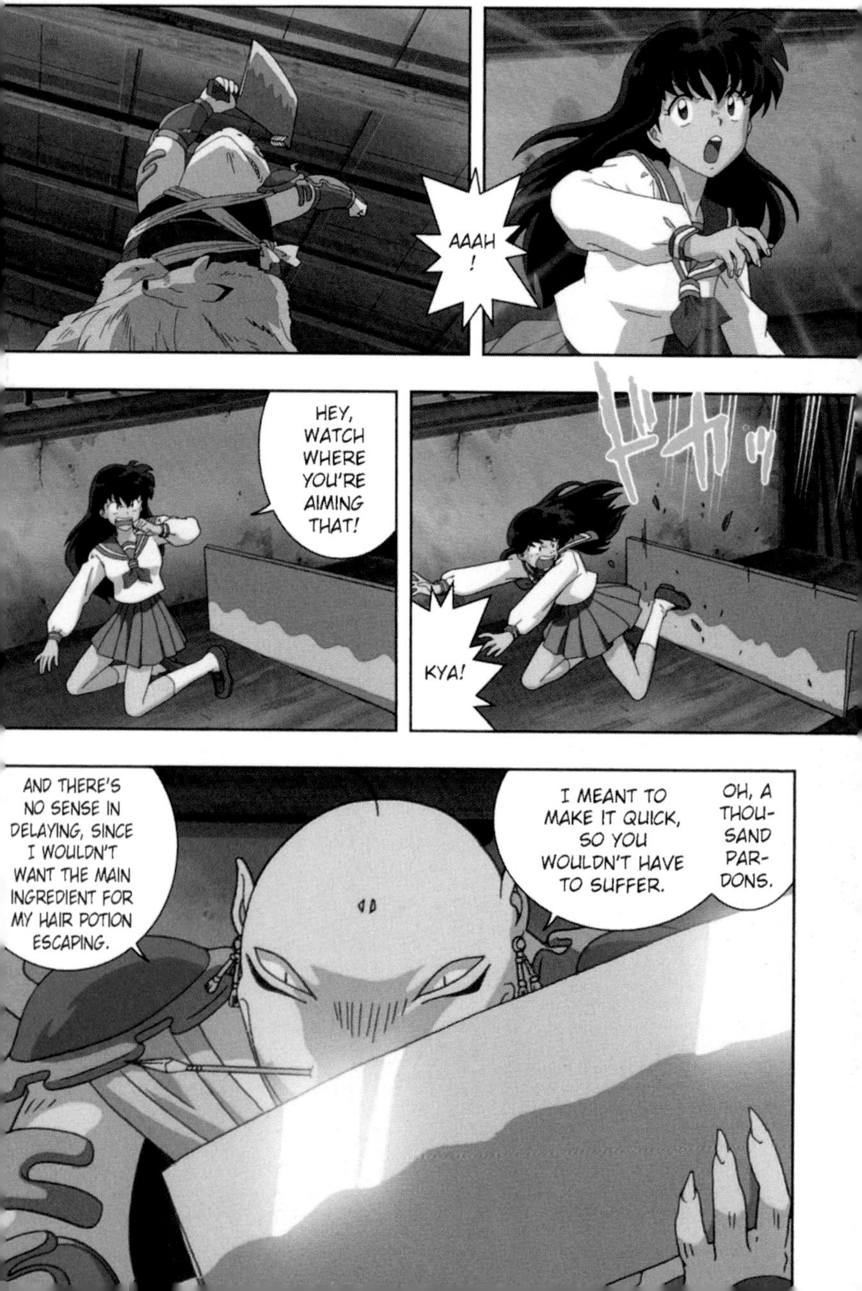
AAAH!
ドカッ
KYA!
HEY, WATCH WHERE YOU'RE AIMING THAT!
OH, A THOUSAND PARDONS.
I MEANT TO MAKE IT QUICK, SO YOU WOULDN'T HAVE TO SUFFER.
AND THERE'S NO SENSE IN DELAYING, SINCE I WOULDN'T WANT THE MAIN INGREDIENT FOR MY HAIR POTION ESCAPING.

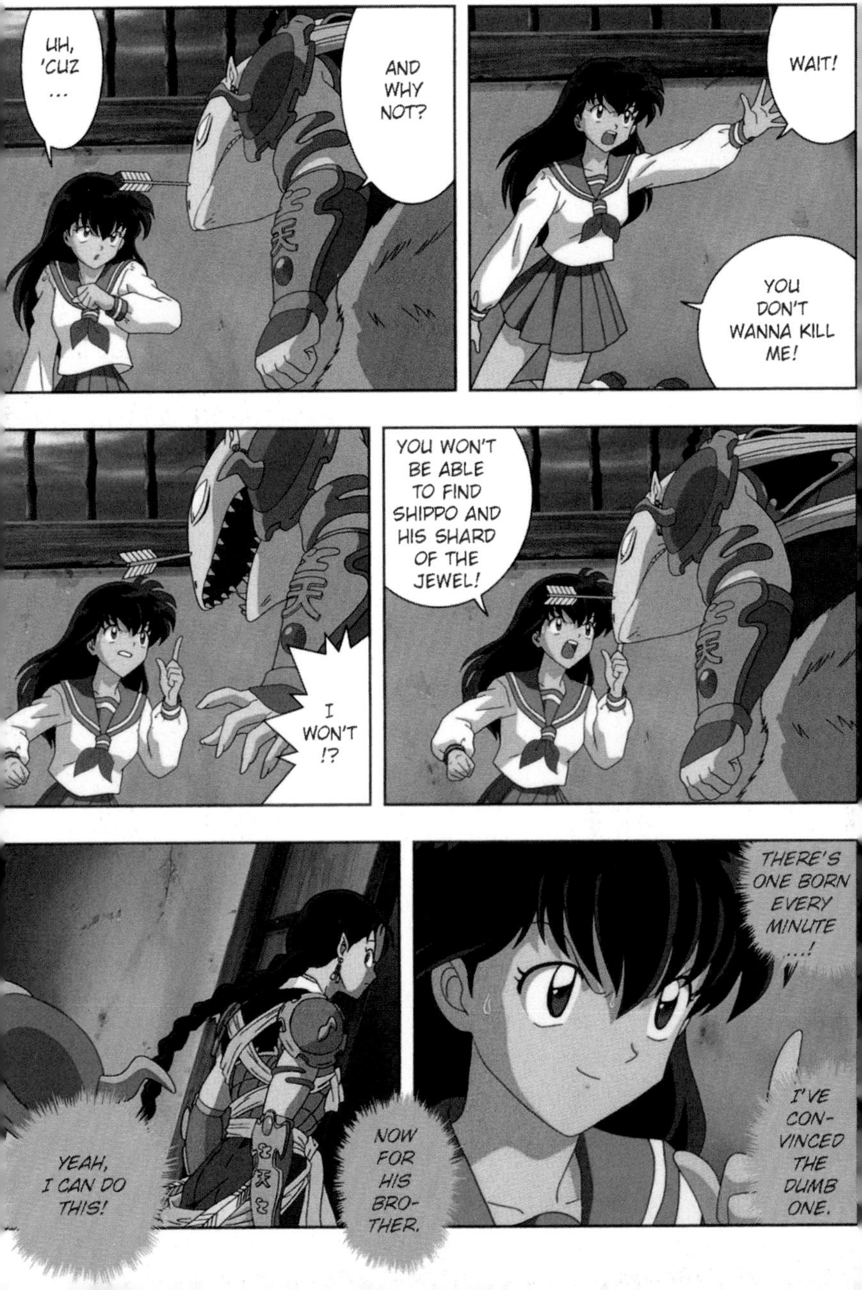
WAIT!
YOU DON'T WANNA KILL ME!
AND WHY NOT?
UH, 'CUZ ...
YOU WON'T BE ABLE TO FIND SHIPPO AND HIS SHARD OF THE JEWEL!
I WON'T !?
THERE'S ONE BORN EVERY MINUTE ...!
I'VE CONVINCED THE DUMB ONE.
NOW FOR HIS BROTHER.
YEAH, I CAN DO THIS!

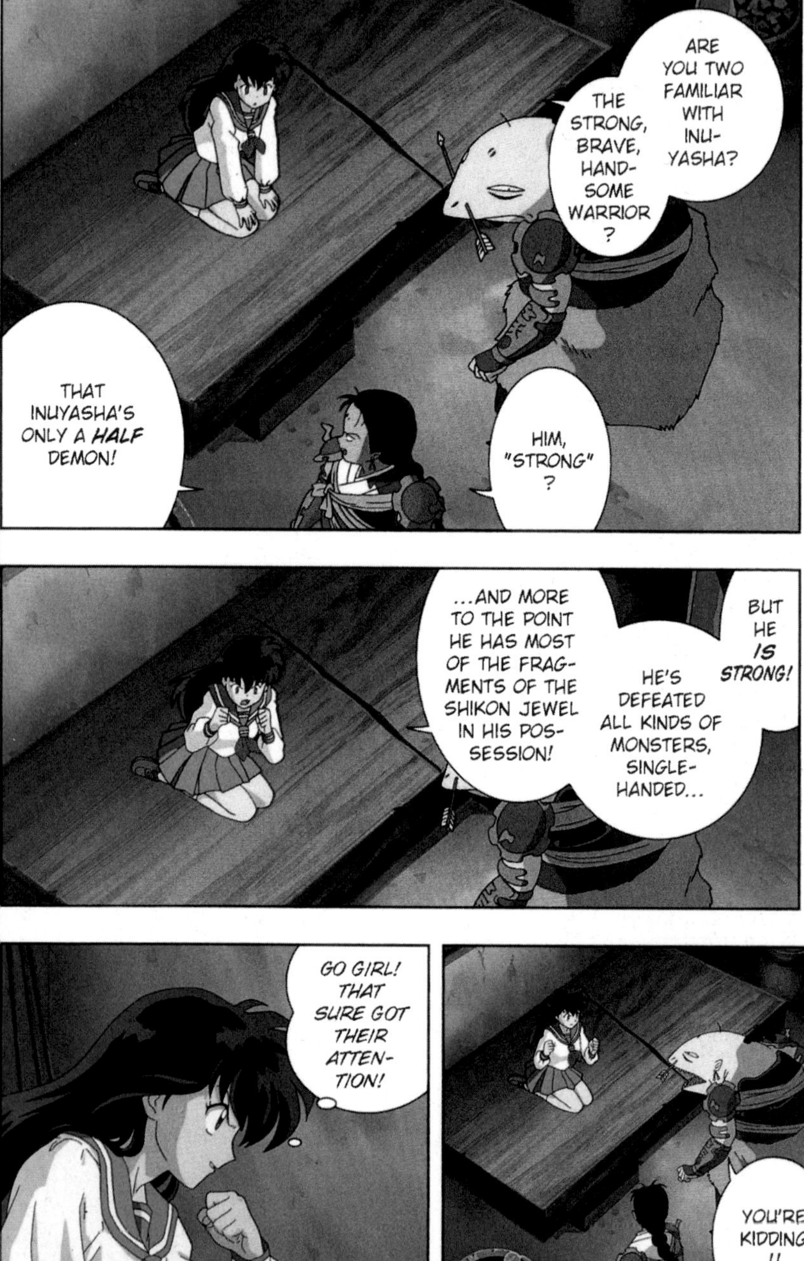
ARE YOU TWO FAMILIAR WITH INU-YASHA?
THE STRONG, BRAVE, HAND-SOME WARRIOR?
HIM, "STRONG"?
THAT INUYASHA'S ONLY A *HALF* DEMON!
BUT HE *IS STRONG!*
HE'S DEFEATED ALL KINDS OF MONSTERS, SINGLE-HANDED...
...AND MORE TO THE POINT HE HAS MOST OF THE FRAG-MENTS OF THE SHIKON JEWEL IN HIS POS-SESSION!
YOU'RE KIDDING!!
GO GIRL! THAT SURE GOT THEIR ATTEN-TION!

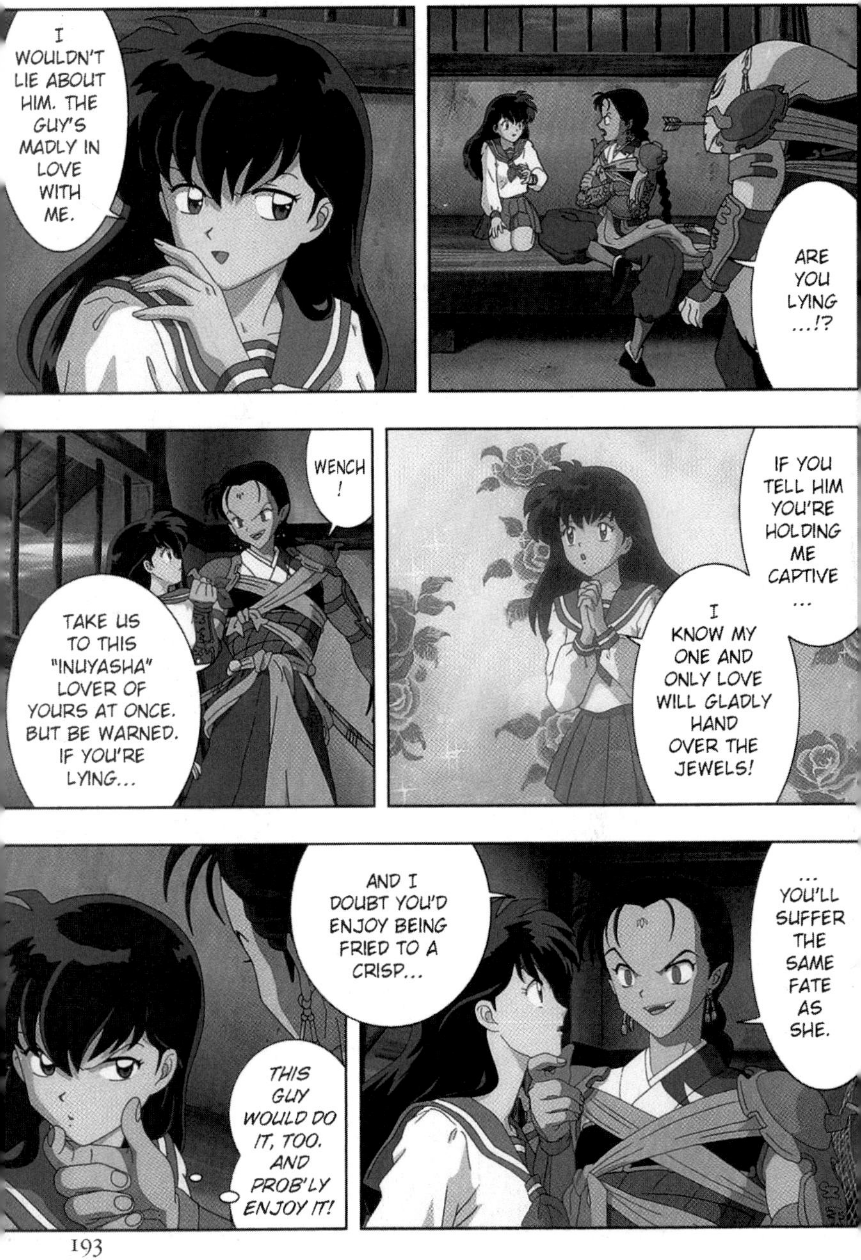
ARE YOU LYING ...!?
I WOULDN'T LIE ABOUT HIM. THE GUY'S MADLY IN LOVE WITH ME.
IF YOU TELL HIM YOU'RE HOLDING ME CAPTIVE ...
I KNOW MY ONE AND ONLY LOVE WILL GLADLY HAND OVER THE JEWELS!
WENCH!
TAKE US TO THIS "INUYASHA" LOVER OF YOURS AT ONCE. BUT BE WARNED. IF YOU'RE LYING...
... YOU'LL SUFFER THE SAME FATE AS SHE.
AND I DOUBT YOU'D ENJOY BEING FRIED TO A CRISP...
THIS GUY WOULD DO IT, TOO. AND PROB'LY ENJOY IT!

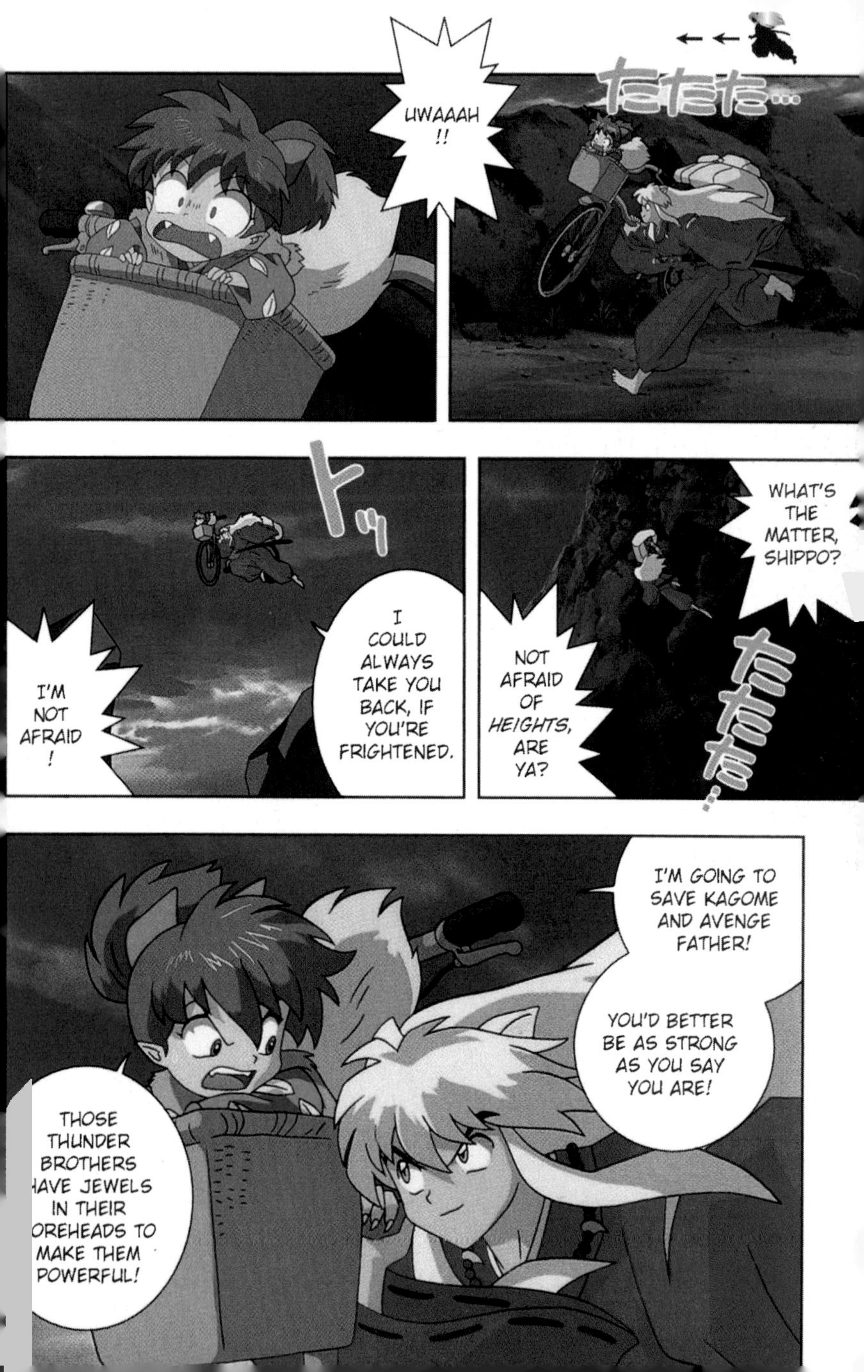
たたた…
UWAAAH!!
WHAT'S THE MATTER, SHIPPO?
NOT AFRAID OF HEIGHTS, ARE YA?
たたた…
ドッ
I COULD ALWAYS TAKE YOU BACK, IF YOU'RE FRIGHTENED.
I'M NOT AFRAID!
I'M GOING TO SAVE KAGOME AND AVENGE FATHER!
YOU'D BETTER BE AS STRONG AS YOU SAY YOU ARE!
THOSE THUNDER BROTHERS HAVE JEWELS IN THEIR OREHEADS TO MAKE THEM POWERFUL!

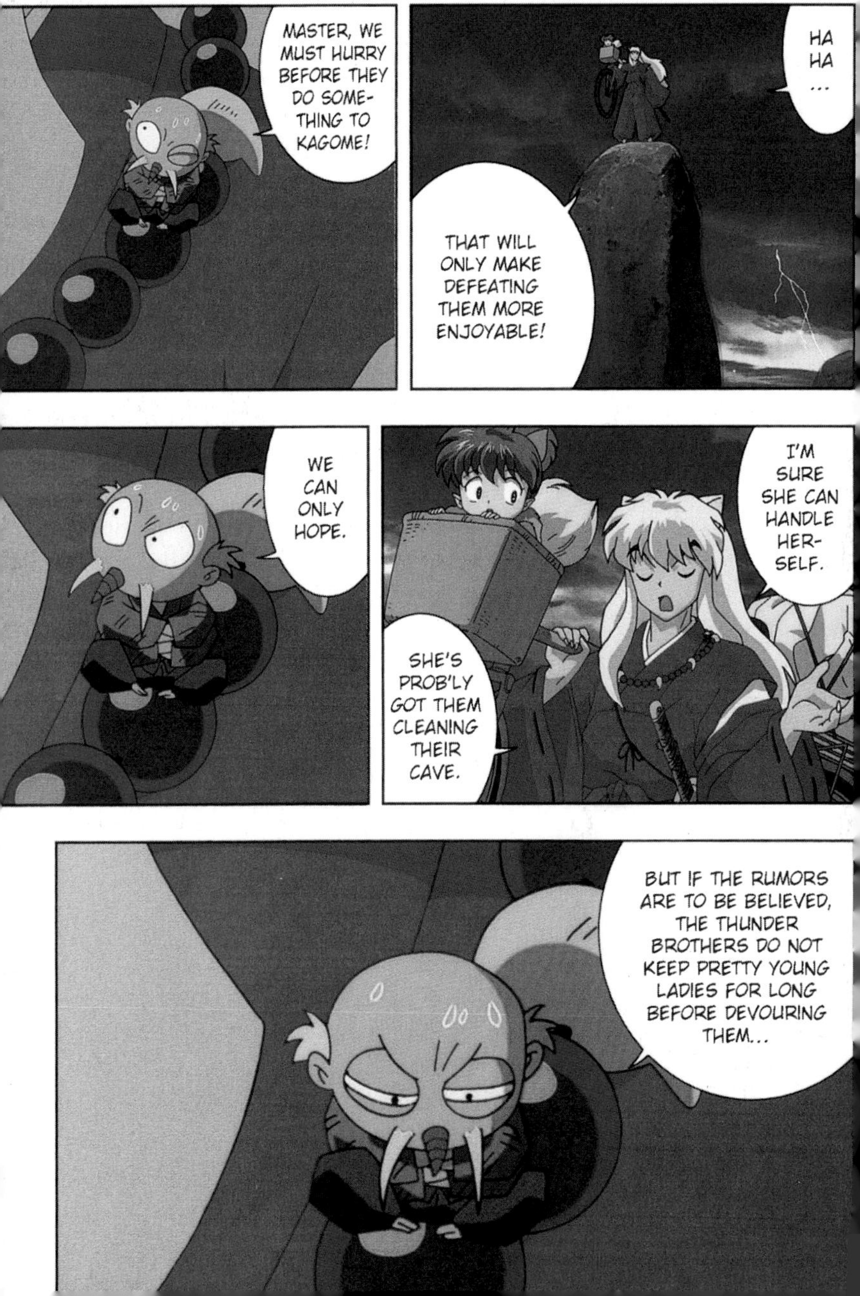
MASTER, WE MUST HURRY BEFORE THEY DO SOME-THING TO KAGOME!
HA HA...
THAT WILL ONLY MAKE DEFEATING THEM MORE ENJOYABLE!
WE CAN ONLY HOPE.
I'M SURE SHE CAN HANDLE HER-SELF.
SHE'S PROB'LY GOT THEM CLEANING THEIR CAVE.
BUT IF THE RUMORS ARE TO BE BELIEVED, THE THUNDER BROTHERS DO NOT KEEP PRETTY YOUNG LADIES FOR LONG BEFORE DEVOURING THEM...

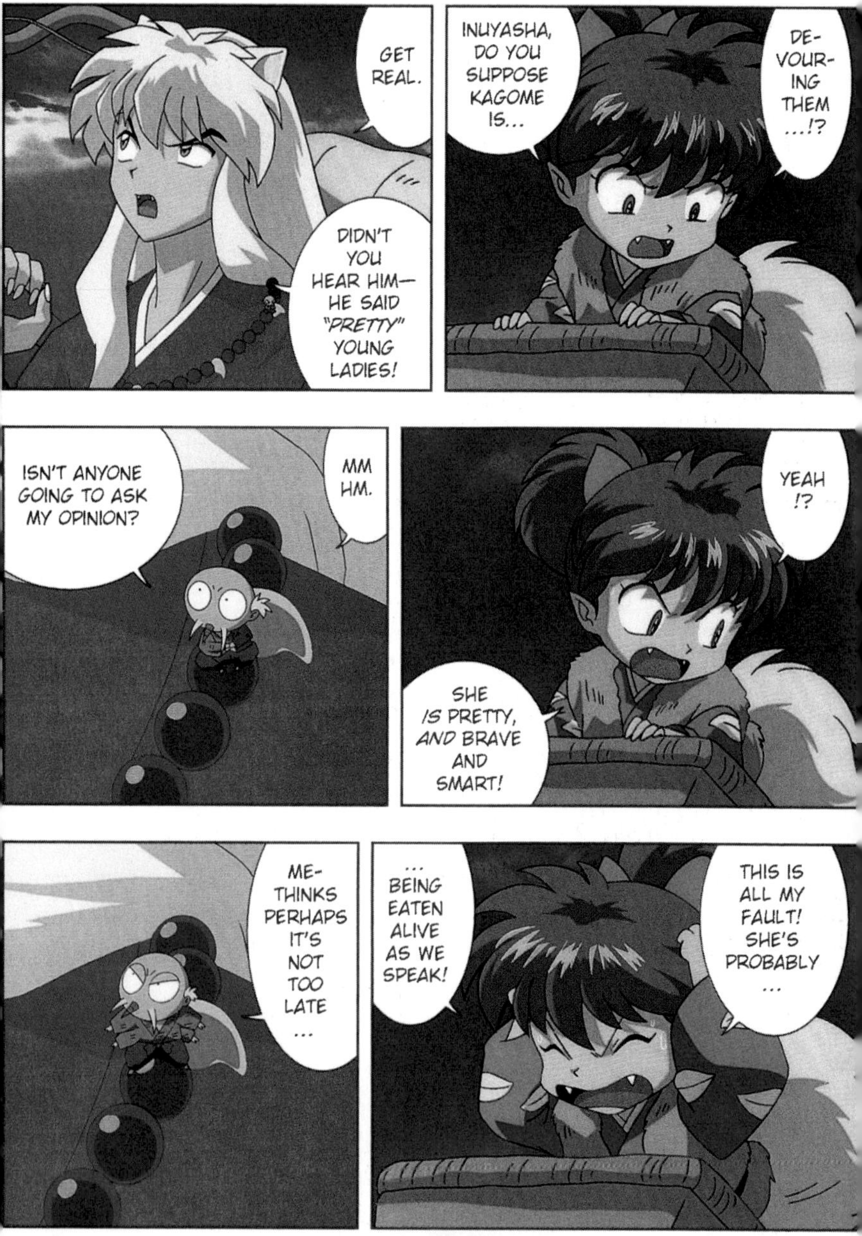
DE-VOURING THEM ...!?
INUYASHA, DO YOU SUPPOSE KAGOME IS...
GET REAL.
DIDN'T YOU HEAR HIM— HE SAID "PRETTY" YOUNG LADIES!
YEAH !?
SHE IS PRETTY, AND BRAVE AND SMART!
MM HM.
ISN'T ANYONE GOING TO ASK MY OPINION?
THIS IS ALL MY FAULT! SHE'S PROBABLY ...
... BEING EATEN ALIVE AS WE SPEAK!
ME-THINKS PERHAPS IT'S NOT TOO LATE ...

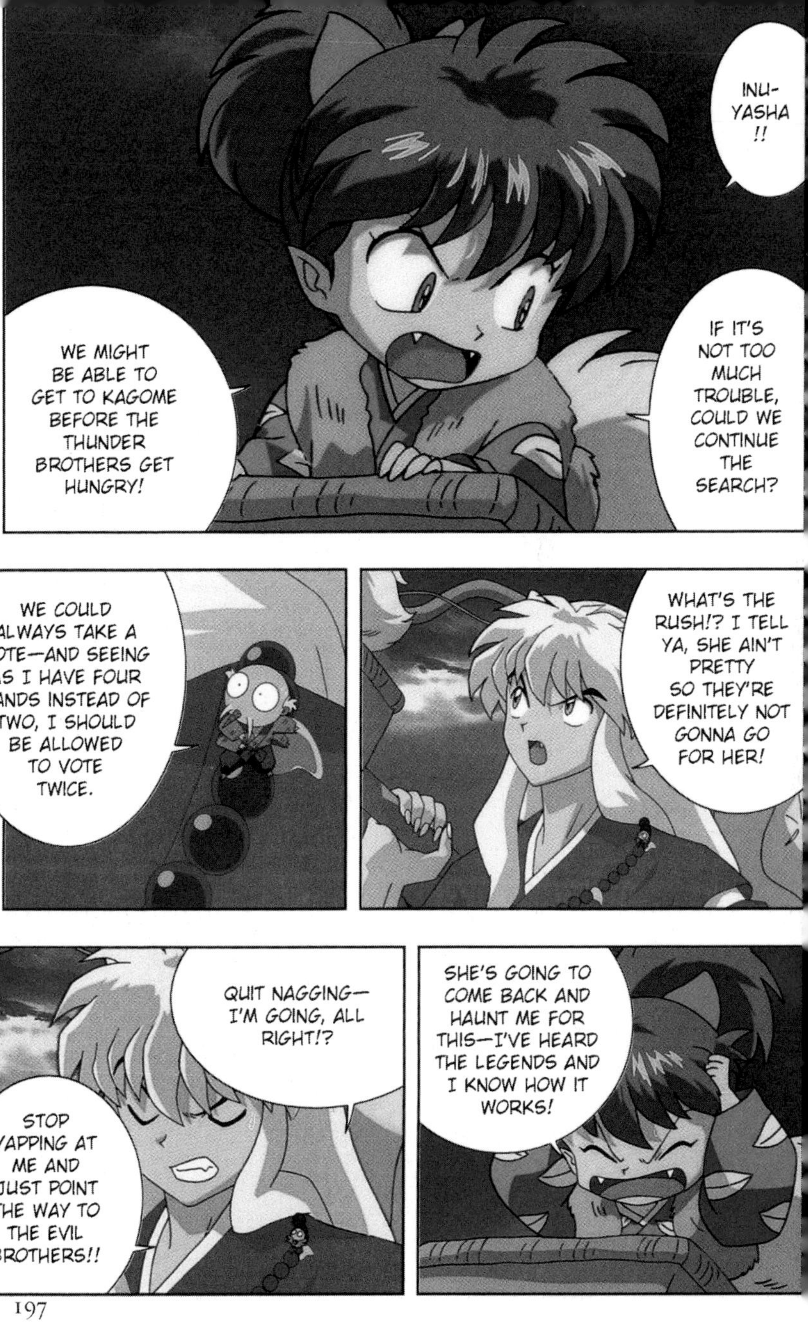
INU-YASHA!!
IF IT'S NOT TOO MUCH TROUBLE, COULD WE CONTINUE THE SEARCH?
WE MIGHT BE ABLE TO GET TO KAGOME BEFORE THE THUNDER BROTHERS GET HUNGRY!
WHAT'S THE RUSH!? I TELL YA, SHE AIN'T PRETTY SO THEY'RE DEFINITELY NOT GONNA GO FOR HER!
WE COULD ALWAYS TAKE A VOTE—AND SEEING AS I HAVE FOUR HANDS INSTEAD OF TWO, I SHOULD BE ALLOWED TO VOTE TWICE.
SHE'S GOING TO COME BACK AND HAUNT ME FOR THIS—I'VE HEARD THE LEGENDS AND I KNOW HOW IT WORKS!
QUIT NAGGING—I'M GOING, ALL RIGHT!?
STOP YAPPING AT ME AND JUST POINT THE WAY TO THE EVIL BROTHERS!!

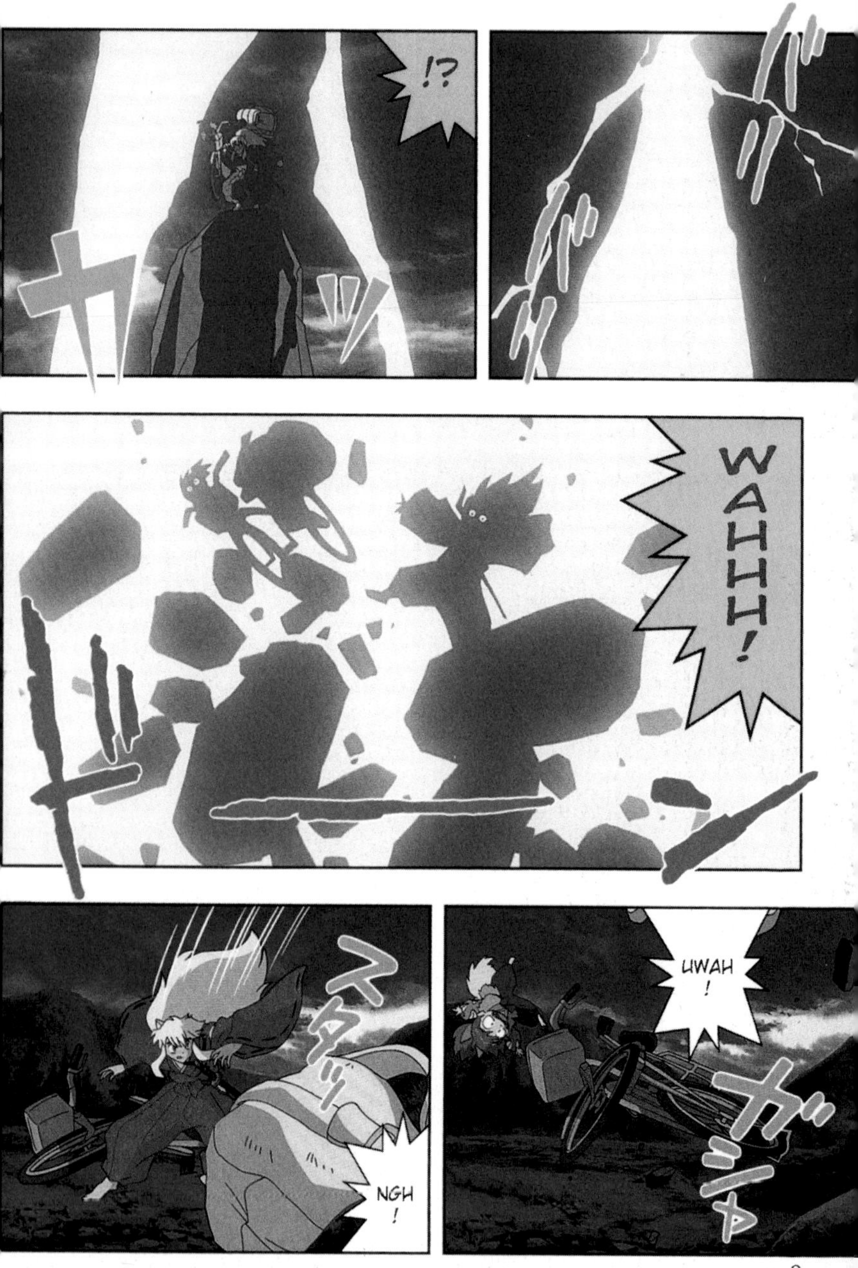
!?
カッ
WAHHH!
UWAH!
ガシャ
スタッ
NGH!

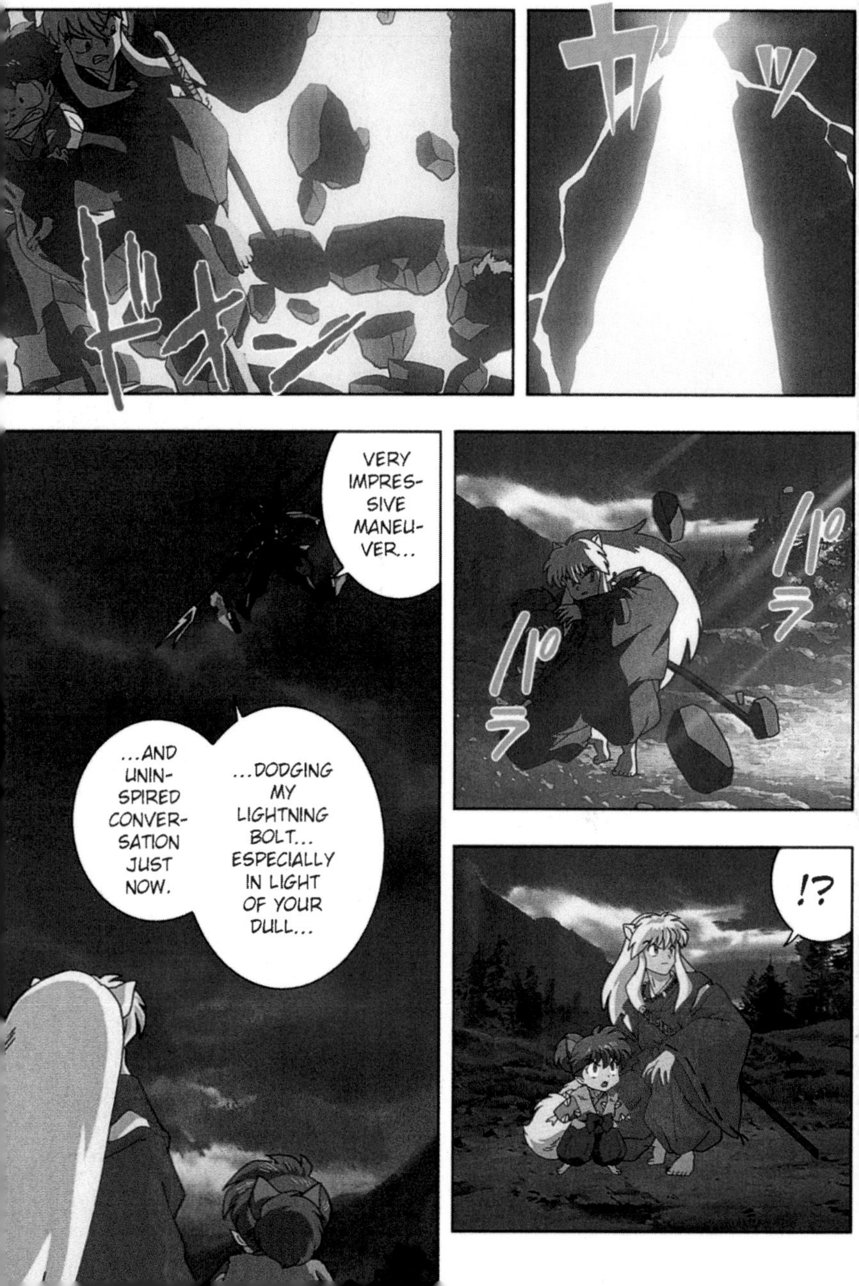

カッ
ドオーン
パラパラ
!?
VERY IMPRESSIVE MANEUVER...
...DODGING MY LIGHTNING BOLT... ESPECIALLY IN LIGHT OF YOUR DULL...
...AND UNINSPIRED CONVERSATION JUST NOW.

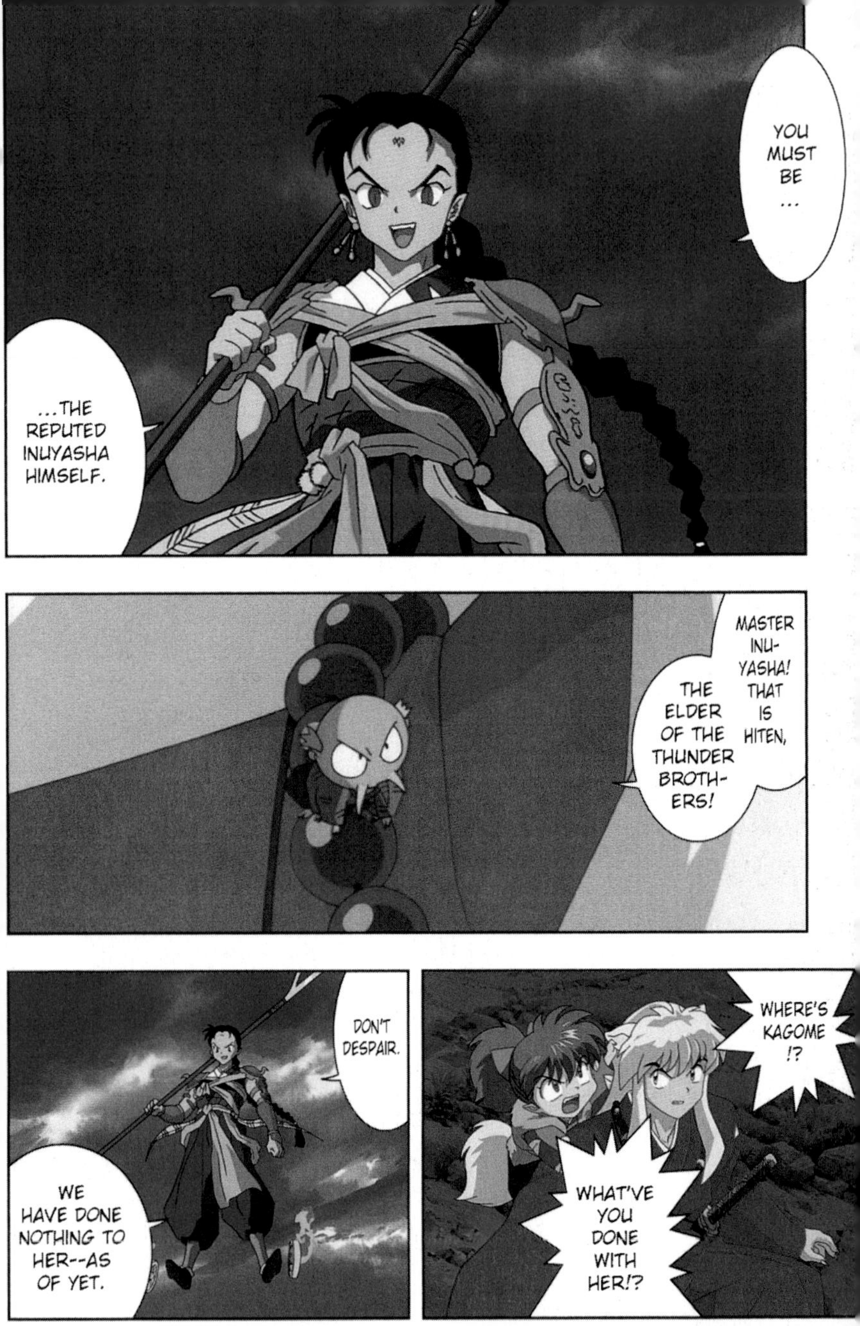
YOU MUST BE ...
...THE REPUTED INUYASHA HIMSELF.
MASTER INU-YASHA! THAT IS HITEN,
THE ELDER OF THE THUNDER BROTHERS!
WHERE'S KAGOME!?
WHAT'VE YOU DONE WITH HER!?
DON'T DESPAIR.
WE HAVE DONE NOTHING TO HER--AS OF YET.

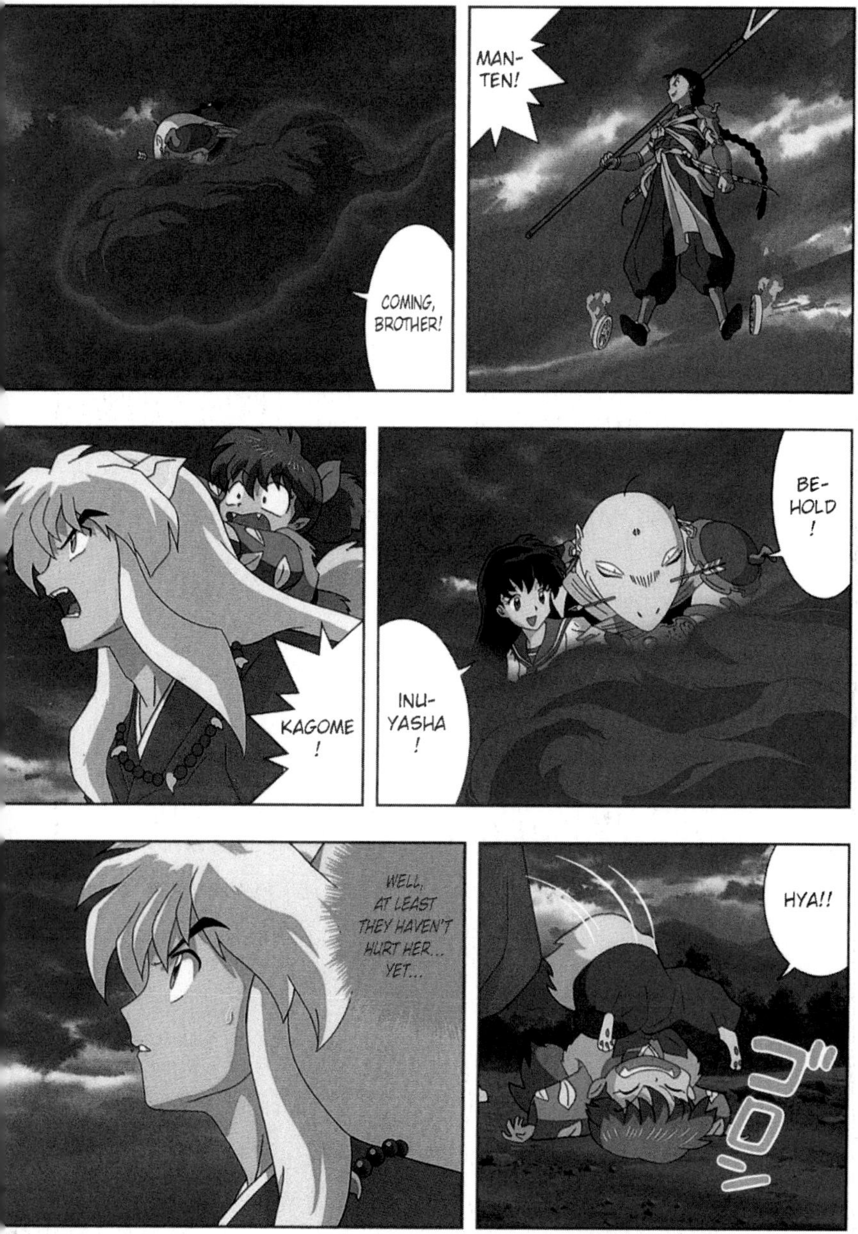
MAN-TEN!
COMING, BROTHER!
BE-HOLD!
INU-YASHA!
KAGOME!
HYA!!
ゴロン
WELL, AT LEAST THEY HAVEN'T HURT HER... YET...

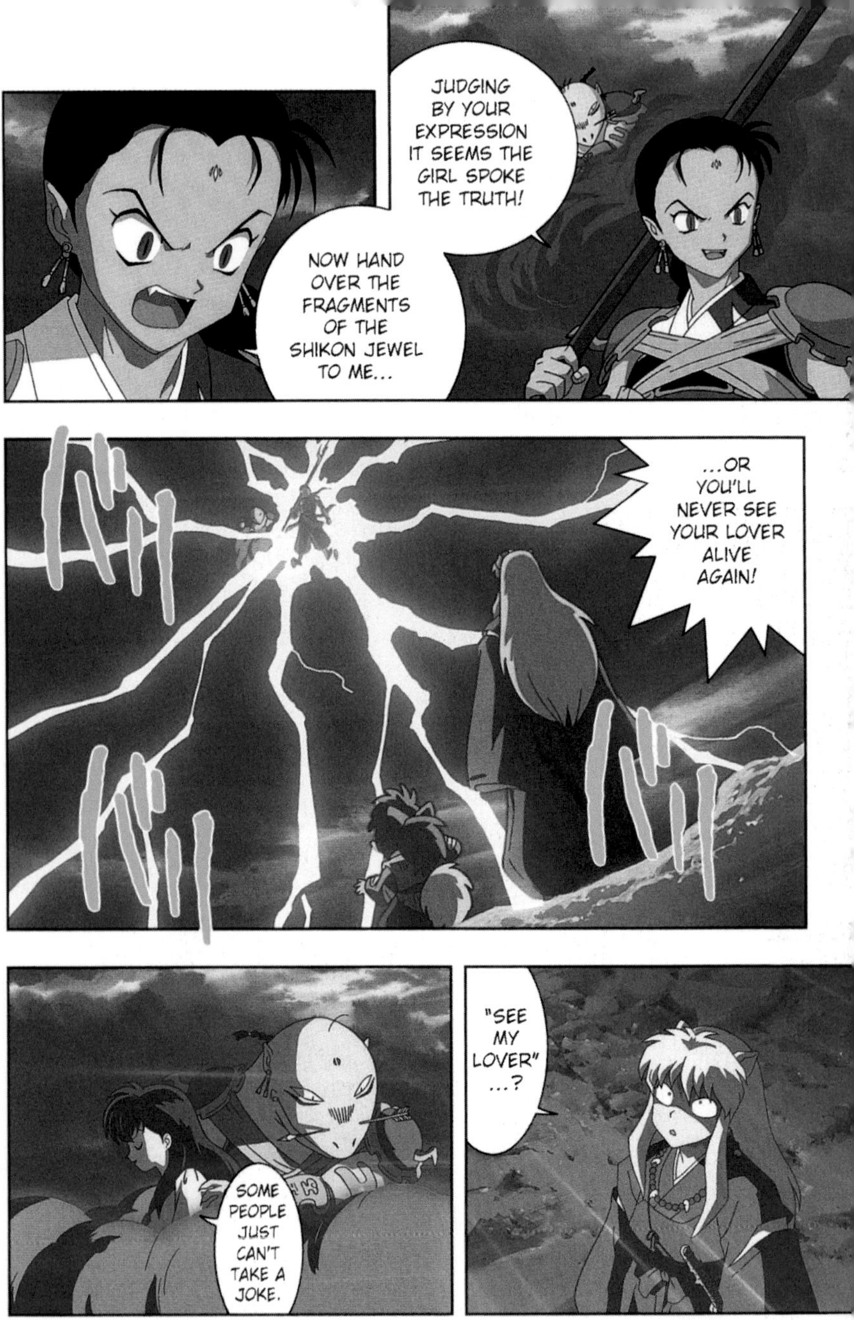
JUDGING BY YOUR EXPRESSION IT SEEMS THE GIRL SPOKE THE TRUTH!
NOW HAND OVER THE FRAGMENTS OF THE SHIKON JEWEL TO ME...
...OR YOU'LL NEVER SEE YOUR LOVER ALIVE AGAIN!
"SEE MY LOVER" ...?
SOME PEOPLE JUST CAN'T TAKE A JOKE.

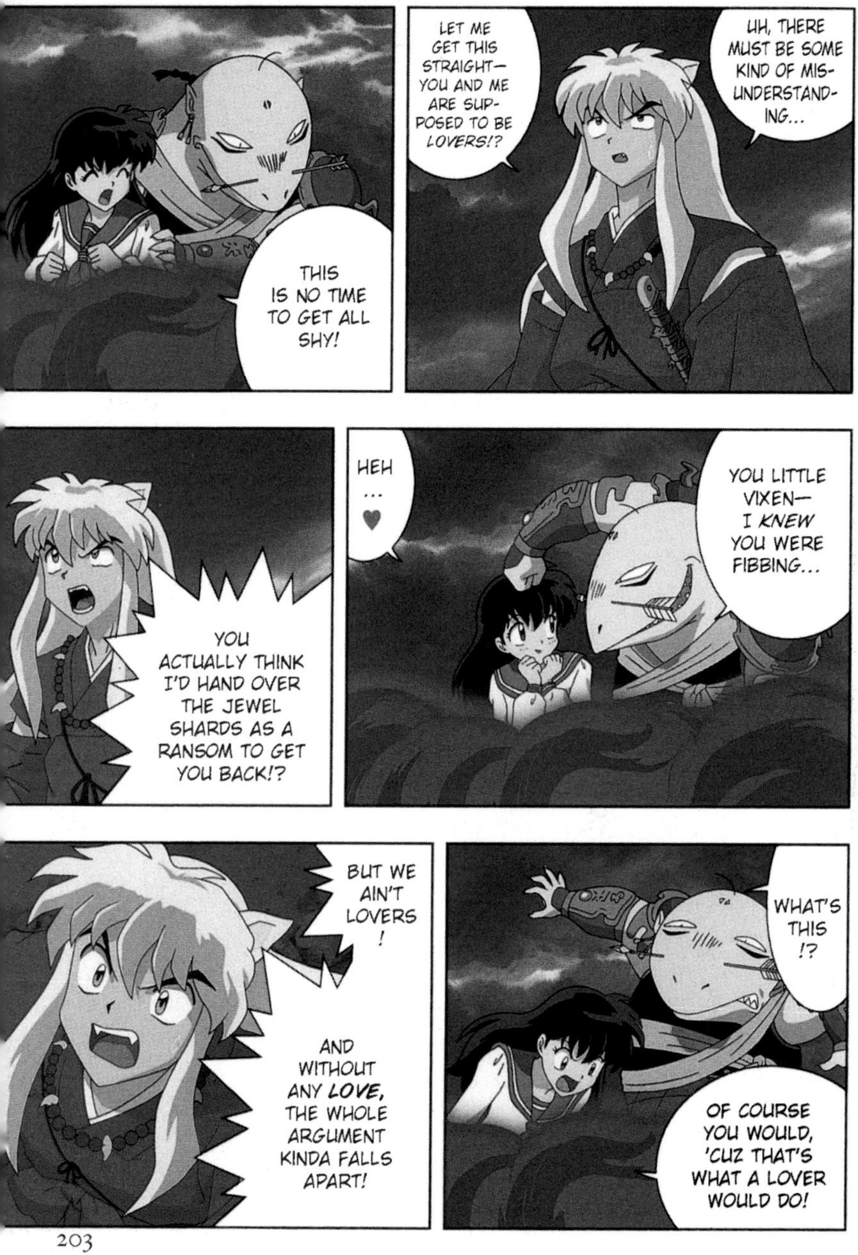

UH, THERE MUST BE SOME KIND OF MIS-UNDERSTANDING...
LET ME GET THIS STRAIGHT— YOU AND ME ARE SUPPOSED TO BE *LOVERS!?*
THIS IS NO TIME TO GET ALL SHY!
YOU LITTLE VIXEN— I *KNEW* YOU WERE FIBBING...
HEH ... ♥
YOU ACTUALLY THINK I'D HAND OVER THE JEWEL SHARDS AS A RANSOM TO GET YOU BACK!?
WHAT'S THIS !?
OF COURSE YOU WOULD, 'CUZ THAT'S WHAT A LOVER WOULD DO!
BUT WE AIN'T LOVERS !
AND WITHOUT ANY ***LOVE,*** THE WHOLE ARGUMENT KINDA FALLS APART!

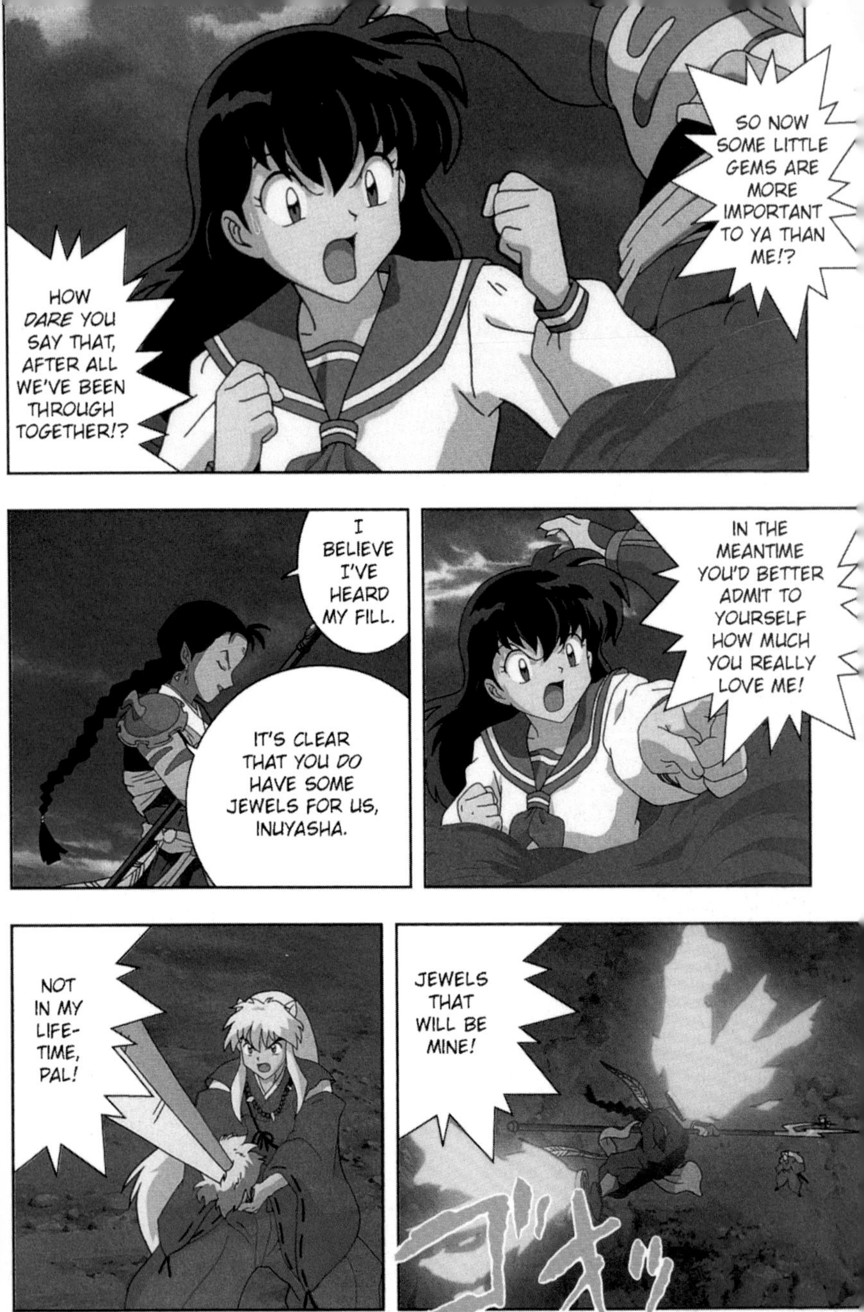
SO NOW SOME LITTLE GEMS ARE MORE IMPORTANT TO YA THAN ME!?
HOW *DARE* YOU SAY THAT, AFTER ALL WE'VE BEEN THROUGH TOGETHER!?
IN THE MEANTIME YOU'D BETTER ADMIT TO YOURSELF HOW MUCH YOU REALLY LOVE ME!
I BELIEVE I'VE HEARD MY FILL.
IT'S CLEAR THAT YOU *DO* HAVE SOME JEWELS FOR US, INUYASHA.
JEWELS THAT WILL BE MINE!
ゴキッ
NOT IN MY LIFE-TIME, PAL!

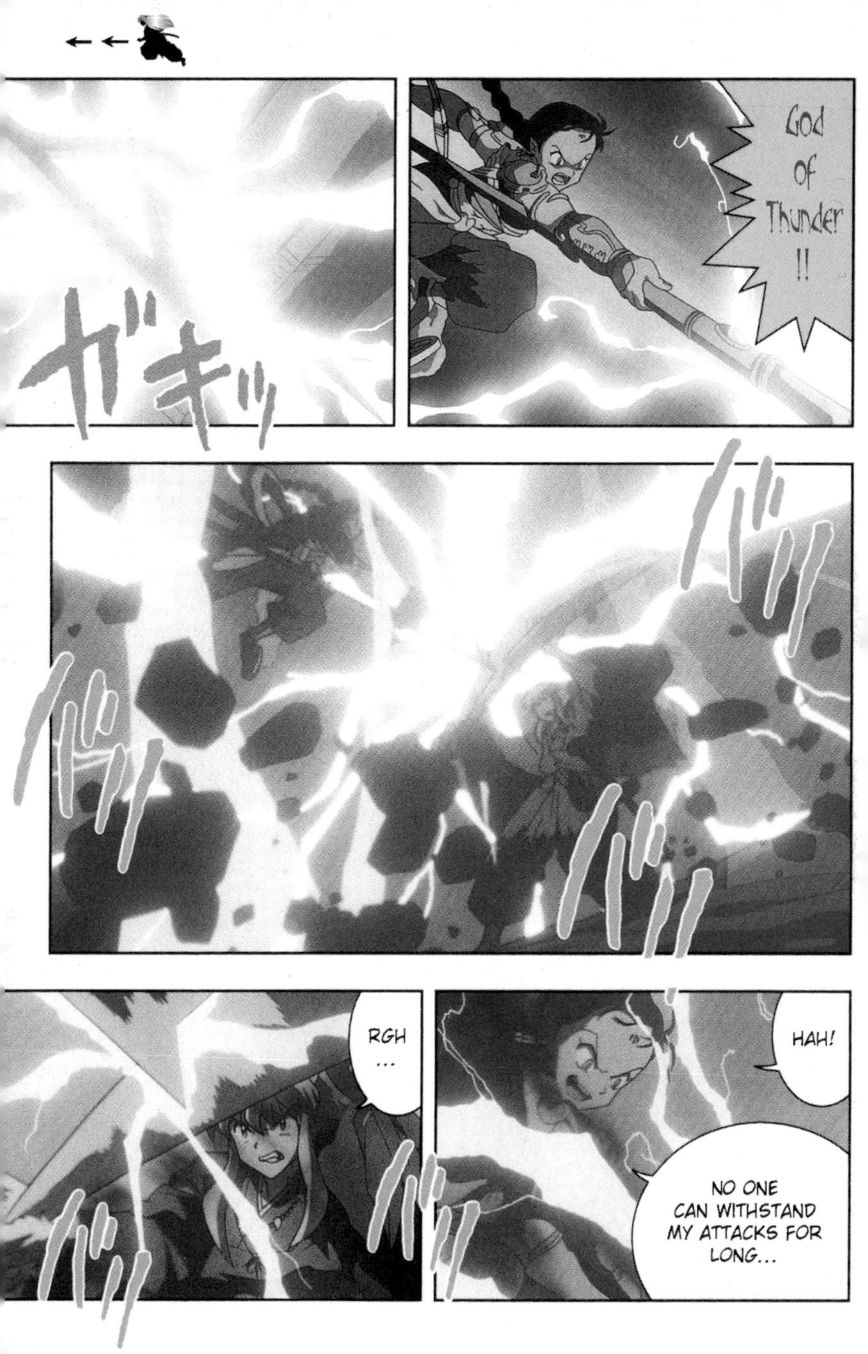
God of Thunder!!
ガキッ
HAH!
NO ONE CAN WITHSTAND MY ATTACKS FOR LONG...
RGH ...

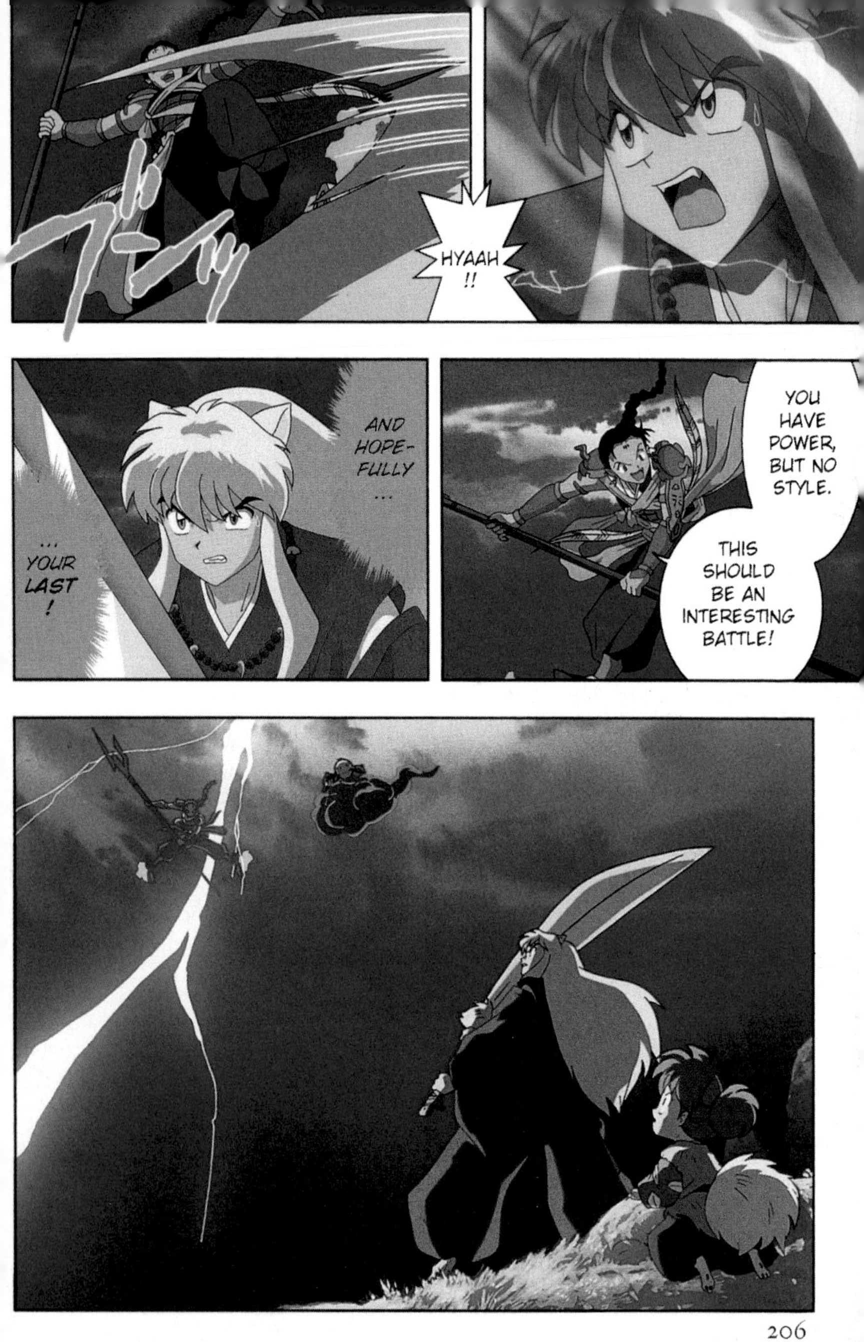
HYAAH !!
YOU HAVE POWER, BUT NO STYLE.
THIS SHOULD BE AN INTERESTING BATTLE!
AND HOPE-FULLY ...
... YOUR LAST !

Glossary of Sound Effects

Each entry includes: the location, indicated by page number and panel number (so 3.1 means page 3, panel number 1); the phonetic romanization of the original Japanese; and our English "translation"—we offer as close an English equivalent as we can.

19.5	FX:Zoro zoro... (people moving away)
22.3	FX:Ta ta ta... (running)
22.4	FX:Gin (smack!)
23.1	FX:Su (Sesshomaru levitates)
23.3	FX:Da (spring)
23.4	FX:Gin (smack)
23.6	FX:Toh (Sesshomaru lands)
	FX:Za (Inuyasha lands)
24.1	FX:Boro (Sesshomaru's armor crumbling)
26.4	FX:Ka (Sesshomaru getting angry)
26.5	FX:Goh (Sesshomaru's magic)
27.2/3	FX:Zu zu zu... (Sesshomaru's muzzle elongating)
27.4	FX:Dohhn (transformation)
29.4	FX:Da (spring up)
30.3	FX:Gin (strike that fails)
30.4	FX:Goh (Sesshomaru flying)
30.6	FX:Do--n (Sesshomaru swats with a paw)
31.1	FX:Suta (Inuyasha jumps down)
31.4	FX:Dara... (poison goo sound)
31.5	FX:Shu shu (Hss hss as the bones dissolve)
32.2	FX:Pyon (hop)
32.4	FX:Pyu—n (Myoga fleeing)
33.2	FX:Shu shu... (more icky poison dripping)
34.2	FX:Zan (big paw smashes down)

Episode 7:
"Showdown! Inuyasha vs. Sesshomaru"

7.2	FX:Ba (swoosh)
7.3	FX:Za (Inuyasha leaping)
7.4	FX:Su (Sesshomaru appears)
8.1	FX:Za (Inuyasha stepping on skulls)
13.2	FX:Ba (Sesshomaru's magic)
13.3	FX:Ba ba ba ba (more magic)
14.1/2	FX:Doro doro doro... (dripping slime)
14.4	FX:Da (Inuyasha pushing off)
15.1	FX:Su (whoosh)
15.2	FX:Zuun... (strike)
15.3	FX:Shurururu...(swirl)
15.4	FX:Gui (Sesshomaru's whip tightens)
16.1	FX:Goh (whip crack)
16.2	FX:Zuza (Inuyasha slides across skulls)
16.3	FX:Dohn (Inuyasha smacks against wall)
16.5	FX:Goh (whip crack)
17.1	FX:Pishi (whip swishes by Inu)
17.2	FX:Dohn (Inuyasha slams against stone wall)
17.3	FX:Zun... (Inuyasha hitting floor)
17.5	FX:Po---n (ball being kicked)
17.6/7	FX:Po----n... (ball being kicked)
18.1/2	FX:Po----n (ball bouncing)
18.4	FX:Poi (ball thrown)
18.5	FX:Po------n (ball flying over bridge)
18.6	FX:Ta ta ta... (Inuyasha going to get ball)
19.4	FX:Zoro zoro... (people moving off)

54.1 FX:Ka (poof)
54.2 FX:Shururururu... (Sesshomaru shrinks down to a pearl)
54.5 FX:Shururururu... (pearl falls farther away)

55.4 FX:Pita (Preparatory squish)

56.5 FX:Kira kira (sparkle, sparkle. Inuyasha is all twinkly-eyed here, because for a brief and shining moment, he thinks that Myoga believed in him all along)

57.4 FX:Puchi (Inuyasha squishing Myoga)
57.5 FX:Hara... (Myoga zipping off)

58.1 FX:Zu zu zu (swirling of portal/vortex)
58.2 FX:Suto (touch down)
58.3/4 FX:Shuuuu... (hole shrinking)
58.6 FX:Shururururu... (pearl spinning down toward Inuyasha)

62.3 FX:Dokun (pulse)
62.4 FX:Dokun (pulse)
62.5 FX:Zubah (sword swipe)

64.5 FX:Toh (touch down)

67.3 FX:Suta suta (Kagome walks off bridge)
67.4 FX:Pita (Kagome purses her lips)
67.5 FX:Dobon (splash)

Episode 8:
"The Toad Who Would Be Prince"

70.1 FX:Bachya bachya (swimming sounds)

71.3 FX:Pyon (hop)
71.4 FX:Za (quick movement--zip)

72.1 FX:Za za za (someone zipping around)
72.2 FX:Za (zip)
72.3 FX:Za (Inuyasha zips off)
72.5 FX:Za za za (Inuyasha zips through trees)

74.1 FX:Pi----... (whistling for monkey)
74.2 FX:Pi----... (whistling for monkey)

36.3 FX:Ta (jump)
36.4 FX:Goh (Inuyasha jumps)
36.5 FX:Suta (Inuyasha lands)

37.1 FX:Guwah (Sesshomaru's loud growl)
37.2 FX:Gah (Sesshomaru chomps down on Inuyasha)
37.4 FX:Za (Sesshomaru lands in poison)

38.3 FX:Doga (Inuyasha sticks sword in eye)
38.5 FX:Za (Sesshomaru falls)

39.1 FX:Dohn (Sesshomaru lands)
39.3 FX:Goh (Inuyasha jumps)
39.5 FX:Suta (Inuyasha touches down)

40.2/3 FX:Gohhhhhh... (lion's quiet roar)

41.4 FX:Sa (Myoga zipping off into bush)
41.5 FX:Pyu--- (Myoga running off)

42.1 FX:Za (Sesshomaru lands)
42.2 FX:Ta (Inuyasha lands)
42.4 FX:Gin gin (sword swing)
42.5 FX:Zun (big paw lands)

43.1 FX:Za (whoosh)

44.1 FX:Pero (lick)

46.3 FX:Ta (Inuyasha touches down)

47.4 FX:Dokun (sound of blade beginning to pulse)

48.1 FX:Dokun dokun (more pulsing)
48.2 FX:Dokun dokun (pulsing)
48.4 FX:Kan (smack!)

49.3 FX:Za (sound of Sesshomaru leaping)

50.2 FX:Da (Inuyasha jumps)
50.3 FX:Zubah (slash)
50.3 FX:Zuun... (Sesshomaru falls to ground)

53.3 FX:Zubah (sword swipe)

74.3 FX:Zaza (zip, zip)
74.4 FX:Pyon (hop)

75.1 FX:Goso... (rummaging in bag)

76.1 FX:Ga ga (muncha cruncha)
bag:Poteto chippusu (potato chips)

78.1 FX:Chu----- (slurrrp)
78.2 FX:Pashi (slap)
78.3 FX:Hira hira (smile with eyes shut)

79.3 FX:Niko... (smile)

80.3 FX:Sara sara (pen scratching)

82.4 FX:Dosa (sound of falling)

86.3 FX:Karan (bowl dropping)
86.4 FX:Baki (toad boy steps on the bowl and breaks it)

89.3 FX:Da (jump)
89.4 FX:Buo (flies through air)
89.5 FX:Ta (touch down)

92.4 FX:Ban (abruptly sliding open door)

93.3 FX:Guo----h (snoring)

94.2 FX:Chuuuu... (slurrrrp)
94.3 FX:Pashi (slap)
94.4 FX:Harari (Myoga drifting to floor)

96.2 FX:Gusu (delicate sniff/sob)
96.4 FX:Peta peta (froggy footsteps)
96.5 FX:Peta (froggy footsteps)

99.1 FX:Peta peta (more froggy footsteps)
99.4 FX:Peta peta... (even more froggy steps)
99.5 FX:Za (Inuyasha flies in front of Toad Demon)
99.6 FX:Da (dash)

100.1 FX:Ba (tongue sound)
100.2 FX:Zan (zot!)
100.4 FX:Zuba (forceful bandage removal)
100.6 FX:Toh (Inuyasha lands)

101.4 FX:Fura... (fainting)

103.1 FX:Guhaah (breathing out toxic gas)
103.4 FX:Doh (Inuyasha smacks into ground)

104.4 FX:Chari (drawing sword)
104.6 FX:Bi (tongue shoots out)

105.1 FX:Doh (tongue splat)
105.2 FX:Doh (Nobunaga collapses)
105.5 FX:Dokah (Toad demon leaps)

106.1 FX:Peta peta (footstep)

107.4 FX:Da (dash)
107.5 FX:Ta ta ta... (running)

108.5 FX:Baki (Inuyasha smashes through)

111.5 FX:Bun (smack with sword)

112.1 FX:Dohn (slice)

113.1 FX:Zuru... (squishy egg-sac escape sound)
113.2 FX:Zuru... (escape from egg-sac)
113.3 FX:Shuuuuu... (slurrrrp)
113.4/5 FX:Suu... (wound disappearing)

114.4 FX:Zuru (slime escape)

115.3 FX:Gyu (squeeze)
115.5 FX:Gan (whack)

116.1 FX:Chari (Nobunaga draws sword)

121.1 FX:Bachin (sword being sheathed)

122.1 FX:Doshu (the tongue piercing shoulder)
122.2 FX:Dosa (more tongue)

124.1 FX:Peta... (froggy step)
124.4 FX:Dokah (strike)

126.1 FX:Ta ta ta... (running)
126.2 FX:Ta ta ta... (more running)

127.3 FX:Ta (running)

128.1 FX:Dosa (Tsuyu falls)
128.5 FX:Pyon pyon (hop, hop)

129.2 FX:Byun (tongue shooting out)
129.4 FX:Doh (falling, hitting ground)

130.2 FX:Da (running)

132.1 FX:Dosa (Inuyasha smacks into ground)
132.3 FX:Gohhh… (major flames)

133.1 FX:Gohhh… (still more flames)
133.2 FX:Shuuuu… (toad elongates)
133.3 FX:Zuru… (toad swells)

134.1 FX:Zuba (slice)
134.3 FX:Pohh... (Jewel pops out)
134.4 FX:Pashi (Inuyasha swipes the shard out of the air)
134.5 FX:Chya (Inuyasha tucks away the shard)

135.4 FX:Shuu shuu… (fssss - smoking/steaming)

137.1 FX:Zudeh (pratfall sound)

139.5 FX:Niko (small smile)

140.5 FX:Hiku hiku... (twitch, twitch)

Episode 9:
"Shippo and the Thunder Brothers"

142.1 FX:Pi pi pi... (alarm ringing)
142.2 FX:Pi (alarm shut off)
142.3 FX:Zuru zuru… (slurrrp slurrrp)

145.1 FX:Zuru zuru… (slurrrp slurrrp)
145.5 FX:Zu zu zu (magic swirl noise)

146.3 FX:Shuuu… (something appearing in the sky)
146.4 FX:Pon (beach-ball blowing-up sound)

147.3 FX:Goh (Inuyasha's hand reaching out)
147.4 FX:Pan (Inuyasha smacks balloon)
147.5 FX:Shurururu (balloon deflates and sails off)
147.6 FX:Pohh… (something appears in the sky)

148.1 FX:Pon (Shippo emerges)
148.2 FX:Zudeh (Shippo lands on head)

150.1 FX:Gei (statue pulling Inuyasha down)
150.2 FX:Zun (throb)
150.4 FX:Bara bara (Shippo tosses stuff hither and yon)

151.1 FX:Shuuuu… (Shippo disappears)
151.2 FX:Pon (pop)
151.3 FX:Toteh toteh (Shippo trying to tip-toe off)
151.4 FX:Toteh toteh (tip-toe, tip-toe)
151.5 FX:Gu… (Inuyasha making a fist)

152.1 FX:Shu shu (spray, spray)

154.1 FX:Kaah (noise foreshadowing the Thunder Brothers' entrance)
154.5 FX:Fu… (wind blowing clouds over moon)

155.2 FX:Gorogorogoro… (thunder roll)
155.3 FX:Kah (Thunder Brothers appear)

156.2 FX:Bari bari (lightning crack)
156.3 FX:Dohn (big flash)
156.4/5 FX:Gohhhhhh… (flames)

157.2 FX:Bun (throws thunderbolt)
157.3 FX:Doh (blade strikes earth)
157.4 FX:Pari pari (crackle, crackle)
157.5 FX:Dohn (flash/explosion)

158.3 FX:Kaah (Manten begins to unleash his power)
158.4 FX:Go— (flames from Manten's mouth)

161.4 FX:Ki (Kagome braking on bicycle)

163.3 FX:Gan (whack)
163.5 FX:Gan gan (whack, whack)

164.3 FX:Dokah (heavy Jizo statue landing on Inu's

hands)

164.4 FX:Peta (pasting on spell scroll)

165.5 FX:Dohn (Shippo bumps his head into Kagome's)

166.1 FX:Goh (releases ball of magic)
166.2 FX:Toh (touches down)
166.5 FX:Ta (running)

167.3 FX:Gasa (grass rustling)
167.4 FX:Ta ta ta (running fox footsteps)
167.5 FX:Za (Manten appears through grass)

169.2 FX:Ta (Shippo jumping)
169.3 FX:Baki (smack/slap)
169.4 FX:Za (lands in grass)
169.5 FX:Koron (tumbling to ground)

170.2 FX:Gohhhh… (small flames)
170.4 FX:Suya (arrow piercing nose)

171.3 FX:Da (Shippo takes off running)

172.2 FX:Shun (arrow flies)
172.3 FX:Gohh (arrow zooms towards Manten's head)
172.4 FX:Ka (arrow flies through Manten's hair)
172.5 FX:Pita… (Manten grimaces)

173.1 FX:Harari... (Manten's hair falls out)
173.4 FX:Da (running)
173.6 FX:Bari bari bari (small lightning crackles from Manten's mouth)

174.1 FX:Dohn (fireball sound)
174.2 FX:Gohhhh (fire)
174.3 FX:Dosa (Shippo falls)

176.3 FX:Gohh (flying sound)

178.3 FX:Beri (Shippo removes spell scroll)
178.4 FX:Pon (pop)
178.6 FX:Dokah (smack)

179.4 FX:Koron (sound of fall)

183.3 FX:Doro doro (sound of stirred goo)

184.4 FX:Gu gu (bloop bloop)

185.4 FX:Baki (Hiten bursts in)

187.5 FX:Kaa (Hiten getting angry)

188.1 FX:Kaa (Hiten's magic)
188.2 FX:Bari bari (crackle crackle)
188.3 FX:Dosa (push/impact)

190.2 FX:Dokah (cleaver slams)

194.1 FX:Ta ta ta… (running)
194.3 FX:Ta ta ta… (running)
194.4 FX:Toh (jump)

198.1 FX:Bari bari (lightning strike)
198.2 FX:Ka (lightning hits nearby)
198.3 FX:Doh---n (rock shatters)
198.4 FX:Kasha (bicycle clatters)
198.5 FX:Suta (Inuyasha lands)

199.1 FX:Ka (lightning strikes)
199.2 FX:Dohn (rock shatters)
199.3 FX:Para para (rocks fall)

201.5 FX:Goron (falling to ground)

202.3 FX:Bari bari bari (lightning crackles)

204.4 FX:Gohh (flames)

205.2 FX:Gaki (lightning strike)
205.3 FX:Bari bari bari (lightning crackles)
205.4/5 FX:Bari bari (crackle)

206.2 FX:Bun (strike)

COMPLETE OUR SURVEY AND LET US KNOW WHAT YOU THINK!

☐ Please check here if you DO NOT wish to receive information or future offers from VIZ

Name: _____

Address: _____

City: _____ State: _____ Zip: _____

E-mail: _____

☐ Male ☐ Female **Date of Birth** (mm/dd/yyyy): ___ / ___ / ___ (Under 13? Parental consent required)

What race/ethnicity do you consider yourself? (please check one)

☐ Asian/Pacific Islander   ☐ Black/African American   ☐ Hispanic/Latino

☐ Native American/Alaskan Native ☐ White/Caucasian   ☐ Other: _____

What VIZ product did you purchase? (check all that apply and indicate title purchased)

☐ DVD/VHS _____

☐ Graphic Novel _____

☐ Magazines _____

☐ Merchandise _____

Reason for purchase: (check all that apply)

☐ Special offer   ☐ Favorite title   ☐ Gift

☐ Recommendation   ☐ Other _____

Where did you make your purchase? (please check one)

☐ Comic store   ☐ Bookstore   ☐ Mass/Grocery Store

☐ Newsstand   ☐ Video/Video Game Store ☐ Other: _____

☐ Online (site: _____)

What other VIZ properties have you purchased/own? _____

_____

How many anime and/or manga titles have you purchased in the last year? How many were VIZ titles? (please check one from each column)

ANIME	MANGA	VIZ
☐ None	☐ None	☐ None
☐ 1-4	☐ 1-4	☐ 1-4
☐ 5-10	☐ 5-10	☐ 5-10
☐ 11+	☐ 11+	☐ 11+

I find the pricing of VIZ products to be: (please check one)

☐ Cheap   ☐ Reasonable   ☐ Expensive

What genre of manga and anime would you like to see from VIZ? (please check two)

☐ Adventure   ☐ Comic Strip   ☐ Science Fiction   ☐ Fighting
☐ Horror   ☐ Romance   ☐ Fantasy   ☐ Sports

What do you think of VIZ's new look?

☐ Love It   ☐ It's OK   ☐ Hate It   ☐ Didn't Notice   ☐ No Opinion

Which do you prefer? (please check one)

☐ Reading right-to-left

☐ Reading left-to-right

Which do you prefer? (please check one)

☐ Sound effects in English

☐ Sound effects in Japanese with English captions

☐ Sound effects in Japanese only with a glossary at the back

THANK YOU! Please send the completed form to:

NJW Research
42 Catharine St.
Poughkeepsie, NY 12601

All information provided will be used for internal purposes only. We promise not to sell or otherwise divulge your information.